transitions

Dickens to Hardy
1837–1884

The Novel, the Past and Cultural
Memory in the Nineteenth Century

Julian Wolfreys

palgrave
macmillan

First published 2007 by
PALGRAVE MACMILLAN
Houndmills, Basingstoke, Hampshire RG21 6XS and
175 Fifth Avenue, New York, N.Y. 10010
Companies and representatives throughout the world

PALGRAVE MACMILLAN is the global academic imprint of the Palgrave Macmillan division of St. Martin's Press, LLC and of Palgrave Macmillan Ltd. Macmillan® is a registered trademark in the United States, United Kingdom and other countries. Palgrave is a registered trademark in the European Union and other countries.

ISBN-13: 978-0-333-69622-4   hardback
ISBN-10: 0-333-69622-0   hardback
ISBN-13: 978-0-333-69623-1   paperback
ISBN-10: 0-333-69623-9   paperback

This book is printed on paper suitable for recycling and made from fully managed and sustained forest sources. Logging, pulping and manufacturing processes are expected to conform to the environmental regulations of the country of origin.

A catalogue record for this book is available from the British Library.

A catalog record for this book is available from the Library of Congress.

10   9   8   7   6   5   4   3   2   1
16   15   14   13   12   11   10   09   08   07

Printed and bound in China

Contents

General Editor's Preface

Transitions: *transition–*, n. of action. 1. A passing or passage from one condition, action or (rarely) place, to another. 2. Passage in thought, speech, or writing, from one subject to another. 3. **a.** The passing from one note to another. **b.** The passing from one key to another, modulation. 4. The passage from an earlier to a later stage of development or formation . . . change from an earlier style to a later; a style of intermediate or mixed character . . . the historical passage of language from one well-defined stage to another.

The aim of *transitions* is to explore passages and movements in language, literature and culture from Chaucer to the present day. The series also seeks to examine the ways in which the very idea of transition affects the reader's sense of period so as to address anew questions of literary history and periodization. The writers in this series unfold the cultural and historical mediations of literature during what are commonly recognized as crucial moments in the development of English literature, addressing as the OED puts it, the 'historical passage of language from one well-defined stage to another'.

Recognizing the need to contextualize literary study, the authors offer close readings of canonical and now marginalized or overlooked literary texts from all genres, bringing to this study the rigour of historical knowledge and the sophistication of theoretically informed evaluations of writers and movements from the last 700 years. At the same time as each writer, whether Chaucer or Shakespeare, Milton or Pope, Byron, Dickens, George Eliot, Virginia Woolf or Salman Rushdie, is shown to produce his or her texts within a discernible historical, cultural, ideological and philosophical milieu, the text is read from the vantage point of recent theoretical interests and concerns. The purpose in bringing theoretical knowledge to the reading of a wide range of works is to demonstrate how the literature is always open to transition, whether in the instant of its production or in succeeding moments of its critical reception.

The series desires to enable the reader to transform her/his own

reading and writing transactions by comprehending past develop-
ments. Each book in the second tranche of the series offers a peda-
gogical guide to the poetics and politics of particular eras, as well as to
the subsequent critical comprehension of periods and periodization.
As well as transforming the cultural and literary past by interpreting
its transition from the perspective of the critical and theoretical
present, each study enacts transitional readings of a number of literary texts, all of which are themselves conceivable as having effected
transition at the moments of their first appearance. The reading
offered in these books seek, through close critical reading, historical
contextualization and theoretical engagement, to demonstrate certain
possibilities in reading to the student reader.

It is hoped that the student will find this series liberating because
the series seeks to move beyond rigid definitions of period. What is
important is the sense of passage, of motion. Rather than providing a
definitive model of literature's past, *transitions* aims to place you in an
active dialogue with the writing and culture of other eras, so as to
comprehend not only how the present reads the past, but how the
past can read the present.

Julian Wolfreys

Abbreviations

The following editions are used throughout *Dickens to Hardy, 1837–1884*. Where I have referred on occasion to more than one edition, both are given, citations of editorial material given by editor's name, followed by abbreviation. In every case where two editions are given, it is the first in the following list to which I refer, or which I cite.

AB George Eliot. *Adam Bede*. Ed. and Intro. Stephen Gill. Harmondsworth: Penguin, 1986.

C Elizabeth Gaskell. *Cranford/Cousin Phillis*. Ed. Peter Keating. London: Penguin, 1988.
Elizabeth Gaskell. *Cranford*. Ed. Elizabeth Porges Watson. Intro. and notes Charlotte Mitchell. Oxford: Oxford University Press, 1998.

CP Thomas Hardy. *The Complete Poems*. Ed. James Gibson. Basingstoke: Palgrave Macmillan, 2001.

DD George Eliot. *Daniel Deronda*. Ed. and Intro. Barbara Hardy. London: Penguin, 1986.

DR Thomas Hardy. *Desperate Remedies*. Ed. and Intro. Mary Rimmer. London: Penguin, 1998.

EGE George Eliot. *Essays of George Eliot*. Ed. Thomas Pinney. New York: Columbia University Press, 1963.

FMC Thomas Hardy. *Far from the Madding Crowd*. Ed. and Intro. Rosemarie Morgan and Shannon Russell. London: Penguin, 2000.

L Thomas Hardy. *A Laodicean*. Ed. and Intro. John Schad. London: Penguin, 1997.

LGE Elizabeth Gaskell. 'The Last Generation in England'. In *Cranford*. Ed. Watson. 161–8.

LTH Florence Emily Hardy. *The Life of Thomas Hardy*. London: Macmillan, 1962.

LWTH Florence Emily Hardy. *The Life and Work of Thomas Hardy*. Ed. Michael Millgate. London: Macmillan, 1985.

M   Wilkie Collins. *The Moonstone*. Ed. Sandra Kemp. London: Penguin, 1998.

         Wilkie Collins. *The Moonstone*. Ed. Steve Farmer. Peterborough, Ontario: Broadview Press, 1999.

MC   Thomas Hardy. *The Mayor of Casterbridge*. Ed. Keith Wilson. London: Penguin, 1997.

         Thomas Hardy. *The Mayor of Casterbridge*. Ed. Norman Page. Peterborough, Ontario: Broadview Press, 1997.

MSPL   George Eliot. *Middlemarch: A Study of Provincial Life*. Ed. and Intro. Rosemary Ashton. London: Penguin, 2003.

         George Eliot. *Middlemarch: A Study of Provincial Life*. Ed. and Intro. Gregory Maertz. Peterborough, Ontario: Broadview Press, 2004.

PBE   Thomas Hardy. *A Pair of Blue Eyes*. Ed. and Intro. Pamela Dalziel. London: Penguin, 1998.

PP   Charles Dickens. *The Posthumous Papers of the Pickwick Club*. Ed. and Intro. Mark Wormald. London: Penguin, 1999.

RN   Thomas Hardy. *The Return of the Native*. Ed. Tony Slade. Intro. Penny Boumelha. London: Penguin, 1999.

TD'U   Thomas Hardy. *Tess of the D'Urbervilles*. Ed. Tim Dolin. Intro. Margaret R. Higonnet. London: Penguin, 1998.

TM   Thomas Hardy. *The Trumpet-Major*. Ed. and Intro. Linda M. Shires. London: Penguin, 1997.

TT   Thomas Hardy. *Two on a Tower*. Ed. and Intro. Sally Shuttleworth. London: Penguin, 1999.

UGT   Thomas Hardy. *Under the Greenwood Tree*. Ed. and Intro. Tim Dolin. London: Penguin, 1998.

W   Thomas Hardy. *The Woodlanders*. Ed. and Intro. Patricia Ingham. London: Penguin, 1998.

WH   Emily Brontë. *Wuthering Heights*. Ed. Ian Jack. Intro. Patsy Stoneman. Oxford: Oxford University Press, 1998.

         Emily Brontë. *Wuthering Heights*. Ed. and Intro. Pauline Nestor. Preface Lucasta Miller. London: Penguin, 2003.

Introduction: *Hesitating, Perhaps*

Centuries are the children of one mighty family, but there is no family-likeness between them. We ourselves are standing on the threshold of a new era, and we are already hastening to make as wide a space, mark as vast a difference as possible, between our own age and its predecessor.

Letitia Elizabeth Landon, *On the Ancient and Modern Influence of Poetry* (1832)

The first of the leading peculiarities of the present age is that it is an age of transition. Mankind have outgrown old institutions and old doctrines, and have not yet acquired new ones.

John Stuart Mill, 'The Spirit of the Age' (1832)

Fundamentally, form is unlikeness . . . every difference is form.

George Eliot, 'Notes on Form in Art' (1868)

. . . the essence of an epoch of expansion is a movement of ideas.

Matthew Arnold, *Culture and Anarchy* (1869)

I

Sir Walter Scott was dead, to begin with.

Dickens to Hardy is organized around close and contextual readings of a small number of broadly canonical early to mid-Victorian novels. The focus of these readings is on their middle-class protagonists, audiences and authors in order to construct a case about the ways in which middle-class history in the nineteenth century is the locus and site of struggle for emerging discourses of identity and modernity – and, indeed, of modern identities themselves. All the selected texts are in some mediated sense 'historical' fictions in that significant elements of their plots take place noticeably prior to their moments of production and publication. I exploit this detail strategically, in order to make a case for the contradictory and double nature of the Victorians' sense of themselves. They perceive themselves, on the one hand, as undeniably modern and up to date while, on the other hand, they apprehend themselves as inflected and infected by the incursion of the past(s) – the presence of the past as well as its 'pastness' are woven together into a complex web of influences, to borrow a central metaphor from *Middlemarch*.

The readings of individual texts offer combinations of different approaches, as is dictated by the singularity of each text. What will be encountered throughout is a close textual scrutiny aligned to important contextual information. For example, I consider repeatedly and in passing the inventions that affect people's perceptions of events, from telescopy and microscopy to the steam train. At the same time, I also interlace into the close readings perceptions of the mediations in self-representation brought about by major pieces of legislation such as the Corn Laws and the various Reform Acts. In this way, the readings open from the singular texts and my responses to those singularities, in order to mediate and modify the critical understanding of these texts, hopefully in what will be, for the reader, striking ways. In this procedure, where history and culture are taken not as monolithic 'contexts' but vast matrices at once textual and material, I pursue close readings in order to test the ideological rhetoric of broadly realist writing. In this, the contextual discussions demonstrate the effects of current affairs and technological advances on that rhetoric.

A major motif, interest, and let us call it a *focus* also running through the chapters is the question of visual perception – ways of seeing oneself and others, from the narcissistic self-absorption of a Rosamond Vincy to the obsession with the lives of others that leads to altruism in Dorothea Brooke and to gossip in Mrs Cadwallader. Placing a text like *Middlemarch* in the contexts of the broadly picaresque *Pickwick Papers* and the largely static *Cranford* demonstrates, appropriately, a broadly evolutionary history to narrative fiction, with each subsequent generation, having seen the actions of the previous generation, adapting the models to be found in earlier texts in order to survive in the literary market-place of the present. Thomas Hardy, arriving at the end of the book and of the period, is then shown to mark a break with the traditions of the mainstream of Victorian fiction – a break seen in his use of certain tropes common earlier in the period, and his testing of those tropes to destruction. In Hardy, the past retains its presence, as with earlier Victorian fiction, but its presence is not reassuring: the past erupts into the present not as a nostalgic yearning, but as a reminder of violence.

II

One might wonder why, in a volume addressing Victorian literature, I choose to focus on so few works and at such length. Each text is a singularity, and must be read as such. In drawing out similarities between texts for the purpose of broad historical argument, I do great violence with respect to the singularity of that text. Furthermore, in its singularity, no text arrives without the signs of its histories, its cultures, its ideologies; and these must be attended to as faithfully as possible, risking a reading that treats of their idiomatic relation to one another in a given network. A further point to be made, however, is that there is no one-to-one correlation, and neither is the cultural relationship of text and context static. A text will bear the signs of being overdetermined by many other historical and cultural moments because language is a thoroughly historical, material medium, its signs, devices, and processes shot through at any given moment by the oscillations of its entire history. Furthermore, one can of course argue that what novels share is an adherence to and the expression of narrative. But then it has to be said that what goes for the idea of the novel also stands true for the notion of narrative. Like the novel, narrative (and for that matter 'the Victorians') cannot by example be commented on in general. Whether one speaks of 'narrative' or 'novel' one can only respond to, speak of, the experience of a singularity and, possibly, a singular experience of reading. As George Eliot remarks in one of my epigraphs, 'form is unlikeness . . . every difference is form' (Eliot 1990, 232). If *Dickens to Hardy* is guided by any single principle, it is a principle that asserts difference before the selfsame. Hence, the respect owed to singularity.

Despite this, in addressing just five texts over a fifty-year period, and restricting those texts to novels by canonical writers, *Dickens to Hardy, 1837–1884* still commits acts of violence on its subject. Undeniably, and perhaps, to some readers, outrageously, it excludes many other writers, both canonical and minor, who might reasonably be considered as equally important to our understanding of what we *conventionally* call 'Victorian literature'. If anything, the choice of authors appears solidly canonical, perhaps alarmingly conservative, old-fashioned, anachronistic. What is taking place here, it might be asked? Where is Eliza Linn Linton, Ellen Wood, or, come to think of it, Mary Elizabeth Braddon? Why are there not chapters on the Sensation novel, or the New Woman? Why no chapters on science, industry and technology, on empire, or religion, for that matter? Why no consideration of Darwin, Carlyle, Ruskin, Swinburne, or any other writer of the nineteenth century (not to mention Matthew Arnold) from the cast of thousands published in the period in question, many, if not all, of whom are now regularly taught? Why is the reader not invited to consider the importance of the Neo-Gothic or Pre-Raphaelite? Where are the social reformers, commentators, and documentarists – Chadwick or Mayhew, or the Besants, for example? And why is there not a chapter given over to the discourse of history, as popular as it was during the nineteenth century, whether one pauses to reflect on the novels of Sir Walter Scott, Thomas Carlyle's history of the French revolution, so influential on Dickens in the writing of *A Tale of Two Cities*, Macaulay's history of England, or Gibbons's *Decline and Fall of the Roman Empire*?

Given such, not unreasonable, demands, an obligation appears to have placed itself upon me in this introduction therefore to explain, without seeking to justify, if not the choices I have made, then the reasons why I have chosen as I have and, at least by implication, the omissions also. It should be noted that I say 'without seeking to justify' for good reason. As I shall make plain, there can be no justification, whether initially or ultimately, in terms of either inclusions or exclusions, especially when drawing only the fewest number of threads from such a small list of publications, themselves taken from a century the literary output of which is, in sheer numbers alone, quite overwhelming. Arguably, any reasonably competent scholar of the nineteenth century could draw up a list of readings, each of which would have as much, if not more, to recommend it as my own. Even an anthology as broad in choice (more than sixty poets) and huge in length (nearly 1,500 pages) as the fairly recent, wonderful and yet daunting *Broadview Anthology of Victorian Poetry and Poetic Theory*, admirably and expertly edited by Thomas J. Collins and Vivienne J. Rundle, cannot account for or accommodate in full 'Victorian poetry', as the editors themselves admit (Collins and Rundle 1999, v). I will not presume to claim therefore any authoritative status for my selections, and neither will I have the temerity to suggest that this volume amounts to a truly representative overview of Victorian literature, so-called, even though it appears to play with the very idea of such an identity. If *Dickens to Hardy, 1837–1884* from its title alone appears to be a survey of an era about which, even at the beginning of the twenty-first century, we believe we know something, then there can be no doubt that from what I have said so far, the one truth of which you can be reasonably certain is that you cannot judge a book from its cover.

The concern and caution that I have already sought to indicate should be understood as having to do with the very act of reading itself; in this, I would draw your attention to the fact that along with circumspection comes the necessity of self-awareness and self-reflection that accompanies all good reading. This is not some 'postmodern' or 'poststructuralist' gesture. Contrary to such a supposition, the reflective pause or hesitation in which I am engaging is a gambit recognized by particular authors in the nineteenth century, and called by J. Hillis Miller 'self-reading' as a facet of the ethics of reading (Miller 1987, 81).

Self-reading is more than simply self-representation, although it may, on an initial glance, bear similarities. Self-reading is, it might be said, the process of an opening from within self-representation, in which an other reading begins, an other reading and a reading of the other: in short, an act of reading in excess of the reflection situated in self-representation. While self-representation may be critical or, at least, a critique of social and historical self, such a critical stance can still be generated from the same ideological or philosophical positions as the identity being held up for critique, and hence produce or illuminate blind spots that are, themselves, the signs of a particular text's historicity. Thus, the language of criticism and the object of the critique circulate within the same economy of identity. Self-reading interrupts and moves beyond the merely critical; at least, in principle, this is what it should do.

Such self-reading is at work in many, if not all, texts throughout the nineteenth century, albeit, and on each occasion, in highly singular fashion. A title such as Trollope's *The Way We Live Now* makes this abundantly clear. You might believe that you and the people with whom you live know how you live, collectively or as individuals within that community or society; and that, moreover, in having first-hand experience, the very last thing you need to do is to consider the way you live. Yet Trollope's title states that it is going to show us *the way we live now*, as if the habit of living had called a halt to thinking, self-awareness, self-reflection concerning identity. That such a title arrives indicates, I believe, that the task of opening to ourselves *the way we live now* is ethically compulsory, an obligation.

Of course, we cannot make the same claim for every nineteenth-century text considered in this volume because – and to insist on this point again – every literary work is singular, even if many, if not all, share a degree of self-reflexivity. However, while every self-reflexive text *is* singular if this ethical self-awareness shares anything from text to text, then what comes to be shared and transmitted is a demand to call into question the very structures of present cultural identity in the nineteenth century. It is a matter of making visible that which is unthought, and which is historically and culturally other. And in the gesture of self-reading, such an opening must come within, and as a mediation of any comfortable assumption concerning the stability or permanence of identity. Singular acts of self-reading take place from an ethics of reading that refuses to 'take as read' any supposition that identity or meaning is firmly in place, permanent and unassailable. If *Dickens to Hardy, 1837–1884* is to be a book therefore about the identities we name 'Victorians', 'Victorian literature', or 'Victorian culture' in any faithful way – assuming for the briefest of moments that we imagine we know what any of these terms mean – then it has to strive to be a book that respects the ethics of self-reading that operates in a number of texts published in the nineteenth century and, in doing so, be faithful, as far as this is possible, in its own acts of reading to the interrogative opening that self-reading announces.

Every act of reading involves a risk and a responsibility, therefore. Fundamental to the responsibility owed to the other, in this case the literary text and the pasts of those texts (the pasts in which they are produced and the pasts to which they bear witness), I have to take the risk of *inventing* something. I use *invention* here in its less well-known sense, meaning to find that which is already there rather than producing something new, while remaining faithful to that other. On the one hand, therefore, at the risk of repeating myself I am committed to respecting the singularity and alterity of each text. On the other, I have to acknowledge in some fashion the historical moment of textual production, without retreating from either the historicity or the materiality of the texts. I have to risk an invention of reading that addresses Victorian literature and culture, so-called, all the while remaining alert to the impossibility of assigning such umbrella terms. I must do this, recognizing all the while the implacable inexhaustibility of every work of literature.

This is not simply some impossibly vague problem. It pertains to every detail of reading, its details, its minutiae, as well as to any general statement that one may make concerning an author, a particular work, a body of publications, the publications of a single year or decade, or indeed those produced in any given century or what we have conventionally assumed to be periods, eras, epochs. For example, if one is to take merely the difficulties, not to say the impossibilities, attendant on periodization, the quandary is not resolved institutionally by speaking of, or teaching, the 'long nineteenth century' as opposed to either 'Victorian literature' or the conventionally understood nineteenth century, even if the extension of the period might be one possible step in a (not *the*) right direction. The questions with which we still find ourselves faced are: when does a period or era begin? When does it end? I have chosen dates as parameters for this book – and have had to, according to the requirements of the series. But those choices, though they might be explained, are still arbitrary nonetheless and ultimately unjustifiable.

III

Despite the fact that scholars now commonly acknowledge that the notion of historical periodicity is, at best, open to question, 1837 is at least a convenient sign, the signature of an instituting fiction if you will. As with any date or other inaugural gambit, it offers what George Eliot called the 'make-believe of a beginning' (Eliot 1986, 35), a starting point or departure. Let us consider therefore the problem of locating the beginning of a period. The inaugural date marked in the title of the present volume, 1837, is the year in which Victoria is crowned and Charles Dickens publishes in one-volume form his first novel, *The Posthumous Papers of the Pickwick Club*. Of course, being the year in which Victoria ascends to the throne, 1837 appears to allow for a more sure-footed location of a beginning, for all its being arbitrary, than the coincidental appearance of what is now considered to be a major novelist's first work. But, while one may apparently with some confidence indicate a beginning of sorts, such a gesture is no less knotty for all that. Does a period in fact begin with the crowning of the monarch for whom the era will come, belatedly, to be named? I remark that this is only apparently obvious and at the same time problematic because it has to be pointed out that naming a part of the nineteenth century Victorian is itself an act of reading on the part of the so-called Victorians themselves, or some of them at least. It is the imposition of identity and meaning, a delimitation of all the various, heterogeneous elements, events, beliefs, practices, publications, productions and so on.

Endings are equally troublesome. In 1884, the date with which I choose to conclude *Dickens to Hardy, 1837–1884*, Queen Victoria still has another seventeen years to live, dying in 1901, two years after the publication of what is now regarded as one of the key texts of

modernism, Joseph Conrad's *Heart of Darkness* (1899). The author
with whom I have decided to end, Thomas Hardy, will live even
longer, not dying until 1928. Yet, were you to spend some time
constructing a narrative of endings from the chronology at the end of
the present volume, 1884 might seem a not unreasonable eschatological moment. In this year, the Fabian Society is founded, *The Oxford
English Dictionary* begins publication, the Prime Meridian at
Greenwich is established, and the third Reform Act is passed, extending the franchise further. Through these decisive cultural moments,
the significance of which echo throughout the twentieth century,
dating serves to affix provisionally something amounting to a trace or
mark arriving and announcing so much more than its bare visibility,
that 'so much more' being irreducible to the merely historical.

As you can see, affixing dates is, if not an entirely capricious
matter, then one that is certainly concerned with manipulating and
directing the reader in particular ways, along certain paths, towards
more or less visible ends. It all depends on the stories you want to tell.
The dates and proper names that appear as the title of this volume
make this especially clear. What is equally apparent is the fact that the
very idea of a period or era is as unjustifiable as the assignment of a
beginning or an end. Indeed, as I remark above, I have not done away
with such a structure, nor is it entirely possible to do so. Instead, what
I have chosen to do is to trace and so *invent* narratives of
'Victorianism', offering countersignatures to different and differing
nineteenth-century identities, resonant with one another and yet
neither commensurate with each other nor reducible to either a total-
izing or homogeneous or organic whole, to which any one identity
can be pinned. And these countersignatures are affixed repeatedly to
the nineteenth-century perception of the past apropos a self-read
sense of modernity.

Understanding these issues, we can remark that the historical event
leaves its traces in texts. Nevertheless, those texts, in their translation
of what we are calling history, do not simply translate, leaving everything of the historical reality intact. Such a thing is impossible. Such
traces, such marks, come to inform not only the composition of a text
but also subsequent readings and writings. Thus, something exceeds
the historical moment or context, doing so in an immaterial way
which arriving at another moment nonetheless can have, in my reading, a material effect that I cannot control, and which, furthermore, I
cannot explain. The temporal space between the writing of, say,
Middlemarch or *The Moonstone* and the various times of my reading of

them is porous. The trace travels across it, though never itself remaining intact. Thus 'history' is, at best, itself a porous concept; the past transmits, and continues to transmit, signals that *parasitize*, which inhabit in a strange manner, and which therefore, also, haunt – not only the texts of another moment, but also every word I use, every phrase I write or speak. What I call 'my language' is no more my own, any more than one can speak, say, of the language of Dickens or Eliot. Language is a swarm of phantoms, the signs of many times other than our own. Thus, if I receive the strangeness of the text from another moment in time, if it arrives in an unforeseen manner, despite institutions and conventions, and, having done so, causes me to invent a countersignature, this is because of a certain intensity.

Traces, inscriptions, encryptions enact a kind of historical border crossing. They cross many kinds of borders in attempting to communicate between 1832 and 1872, or 1884 and 2006. What we might say crosses over, what arrives from a past which is always a foreign country, are the signs of a memory discourse. The memory is not ours, of course, but the text remains, nonetheless, as we read and receive it, the manifestation of some ghostly arrival. This arrival is also a return, for what returns to us is a memory, are memories which have never been ours, and if we receive it at all it is because the text refuses to remain buried historically. Certain texts do not and cannot be made to fit easily into 'history'. In their singularity literary texts are always of and yet other than their times. If they have a chance of being received in other times, such works remain other, for they are also other to the time of reception and revenance. The texts I have chosen, despite their canonical status (or, to suggest a reading it is impossible to pursue), are available to our readings as other to their times. Despite our best efforts to decode them, they remain other, and thus disturb.

Part I

Cultural Memory

1 'The old story . . . with a difference': *The Posthumous Papers of the Pickwick Club*

'What strange things these are you tell us of, Sir', said Mr Pickwick, minutely scanning the old man's countenance, by the aid of his glasses.

Samuel Pickwick

Signs of the past

In addressing Charles Dickens's first novel, *The Posthumous Papers of the Pickwick Club* (1836–37), what, it might be asked, is this book *about*? What does it think it is doing, and around what focal points will it circle?

One answer might run as follows: the visible, visuality, visibility, vision, visions, visualization, invisibility, view, prospect, observation, perception, sight, insight, hindsight, foresight, introspection, retrospection, eyes, reflection, appearance, spectacle, spectacles, optics, magnification, apparitions, phantasms, microscopes, telescopes, focal point, dream, looking, gazing, glancing, mental picture, hallucination.

One of the most visible details of *The Posthumous Papers of the Pickwick Club* is just this: the insistent, iterable, recurrence of motifs, figures, and terms having to do with visuality, vision, observation (in the multiple sense of sight, intellectual consideration, and critical commentary), the visible, and visible effects. There is sight. There is seeing, there being around 600 conjugations of the verb and of course the act it names in the novel. Eyes are everywhere; people are observed observing, and reflecting on their observations, while others observe the appearance of eyes; there are spectacles (of two kinds, those that are worn and those that take place as public events). Appearance itself has a noticeable frequency. Though scarce, references to optics are to be found, as is one to magnification. Apparitions have their moments, though they only appear indirectly, being the ghosts belonging to tales told by various characters. We witness visions, and there are the occasional appearances of devices such as telescopes and microscopes (literally or metaphorically) for aiding vision and for making visible that which is too far away to be seen with the naked eye. Even Mr Pickwick's name is illuminating, in this regard, naming a device for trimming or straightening a wick on an oil lamp. Mr Pickwick provides us with visions of culture and society, illuminating to the reader the historical specificity of a recent, but rapidly disappearing past. All such figures are presented, apprehended or intimated to draw attention to *how* one perceives and the ways in which one fails to see how one does not necessarily see correctly.

Another question forms itself. I see it coming into focus.

Why?

In order to consider the relationship between the present and the past, and to open to the good reader's view a perspective on history and memory, and with that the question of how one views such topics, we must look at 'history' and 'memory' and their significance in the constitution of the modern subject in the nineteenth century, as that subject is constituted in turn by a possible sense of national identity and by their (at least apropos *Pickwick*) historical situation in the middle classes.

This in turn leads us to other questions.

How does one see oneself in understanding one's difference from one's parents? And how may this vision maintain the traces of the past without being overwritten by them or without erasing them entirely? What are the proper perspectives for the reiteration of particular visions of English national identity, seen in historical perspective?

Answers to such interrogations are, in part, what *Pickwick* may be read as bringing into the light, through a double process of focalization that simultaneously looks to the past and at that which is to come. In this way, the reader is 'enabled to find and recognize himself [*sic*] in the actions of the fictitious individual' (Costa Lima 1988, 135); and also to perceive his difference in the imaginary vision of the fictional individual's failure to see him- or herself in the proper light, and thus to be a *figure* of fun, the manifestation of a tropological cultural structure. The structure of vision is one which therefore offers the chance of producing for the reader a *self-reading* (Miller 1987, 81). *Pickwick* is a success in the early nineteenth century for a number of reasons not immediately obvious. It signals to its readers through parodic imaginary visions of a recent past a constellation of cultural identities available to memory, and which, arguably, were in danger of being forgotten in the desire to mark as great a distance from that past as rapidly as possible. At the same time though, this distance allows a mode of self-reading. *Pickwick* announces the moment in passing as informed by a crisis of representation, even as it affords its readers a glimpse of the difference of their being from that of their predecessors, and so their becoming-different. One is afforded an apprehension of one's identity through reading the recently receded traces of past identities as outmoded. Boz, *Pickwick's* narrator and 'editor', announces occasionally that he cannot possibly comment on or interpret events. Thus the reader is left to decipher similarity or difference from the events transcribed, and the characters therein.

My title – *the old story . . . with a difference* – is a line taken from the novel. It comments on just these translation effects of *The Posthumous Papers of the Pickwick Club.* On the one hand, one particular aspect of translation in one language is its power to render the past, *with a difference.* This takes place particularly throughout *The Pickwick Papers* through the generation of images and scenes concerned with sight, looking, the response to visions, and other phenomenal manifestations, as well as the subjective and historical, rather than scientific, experience of being witness to, and so interpreting, what is seen. On the other hand, there is that interest in narrative transmissibility, and the concern with the ways in which marks, signs, and traces of the past (*the old story*) come to be transmitted through their iterability (*with a difference*), in order that the reader might have the chance to see the past through the interpretive lens by which the materiality of history is transformed into the materiality of the letter.

What comes to be seen is that *Pickwick* intervenes in, ruptures, and remakes the narrative presentation of historically mediated identity through the projection of successive vignettes and stereotypes. The facets of identity and the modes of its becoming thus envisioned involve the English middle classes, a particular sense or manifestation of Englishness, and, with that, the identity we now refer to with hindsight as 'Victorian'. As if it were some strange kaleidoscopic optical device, *Pickwick* may be said to illuminate through sharp and often satirical juxtaposition a few of the ways in which those heterogeneous middle classes we call the Victorians saw themselves, and how they believed they saw themselves becoming different in distinction from previous generations through their experience of events and occasions still haunted by the traces and structures of earlier cultural practices and beliefs.

As a projection of English cultural identities in the early part of the nineteenth century then, *Pickwick* is not merely or solely a mirror or simple representation of its times. Rather, if the reader comes to *see* him- or herself, partially or at all, it is as through a glass darkly, to echo Carlyle's own distortion of *Corinthians* (1991, 84). Dickens's text offers a moment of such partially occluded self-reading, in this case of particular bourgeoning middle-class English identities in the first third of the nineteenth century. It is this which arguably makes *Pickwick* phenomenally successful and, in the modes of its representations, thoroughly *modern*. The singularity of *Pickwick*'s modernity is that it re-marks its historical moment and experience through an archival coming into being. Through often satirical or parodic gestures and visions of cultural self-reading, *Pickwick* moves beyond the merely critical, unveiling otherwise 'invisible' cultural and ideological habit and convention. Through its emphasis on vision, the visible, and the visual, allied to its invitations to its reader to consider *how we see*, *The Posthumous Papers* offers the good reader a simultaneously timely and untimely anachronistic and haunting reminder of the importance of a certain vigilance having to do with memory, bearing witness, and the signs of the past.

Times of appearance

'Admirers of *Pickwick Papers*', John Bowen tells us, 'have often seen it as a beginning like no other . . . an inaugurative creative act' (2000, 49). What though, if anything, was *inventive* about *Pickwick*? *The Posthumous Papers of the Pickwick Club containing a faithful record of the perambulations, perils, travels, adventures and Sporting Transactions of the corresponding members. Edited by 'Boz'* (to restore its full title) was written and published in serial form (in monthly instalments) between 1836 and 1837, when Dickens was 24. Though it was to become Dickens's first novel, it was not his first book, this being *Sketches by Boz*, a collection of loosely associated 'scenes' of contemporary London life. In addition, Charles Dickens had already published (and continued to write throughout the rest of his career) reviews, essays, reports, and other journalistic sketches.

From its inception in March 1836, when advertisements were placed by publishers Chapman & Hall announcing the serial publication, *Pickwick* was an 'experiment' (*PP* xi), as the editor of the Penguin edition, Mark Wormald, remarks. The experiment lay in the publishers' *invention* of an apparently 'new' periodical. *Pickwick* was though not a new periodical. It was not a magazine or journal in which was included either the serialization of old established novels or diluted commentaries on recent scientific advances. It merely had the appearance of being such a publication. It 'masquerad[ed] as a serious periodical' (*PP* xii) in an era of 'miscellanies, accessible collections', when 'weekly and monthly magazines and papers took few risks' (*PP* xi). In producing *The Pickwick Papers*, Dickens employed his editorial persona, 'Boz'. In doing so, he drew on 'the traditional novelist's device of constructing a fictional editor' by which Dickens 'align[ed] himself with the likes of Walter Scott' and others (Grossman 1997, 180). Additionally however, Dickens also 'construct[ed] his own beginning as a novelist' through the fiction of a 'verbose editor who [was] at once a parody of Dickens and yet Dickens the parodist' (Grossman 1997, 180).

Moreover, through the mimicry of authorial tradition an ironic *self-reading* is constructed through the fiction or device of the 'editor' Boz. Hence, the borrowed literary convention serves also as the sign of a distancing, self-aware parody. This is also figured through the title. The alliteration of the full title was an aural and graphic reminder of other publications, designed to call to mind the image of the familiar and comforting. Yet in its echoes of that familiarity it also drew attention to the mechanisms by which comfort was generated. *Pickwick* was a simulacrum of the 'real thing', anticipating, wagering on a readership eager to respond not to novelty but a publication bearing all the signs of familiarity and tradition. As Mark Wormald asks, 'how better to signal your own proper distance from a world whose passing you half regretted than by laughing at someone's slightly ridiculous heartiness?' (*PP* xi).

As is well-known, this *faux* periodical was originally intended as a vehicle for the popular caricaturist Robert Seymour (1800–36), who specialized in sporting scenes. Seymour himself had proposed to the publishers a series of illustrations of Cockney sporting life at the end of 1835.[1] However, almost from the beginning of publication Dickens argued with Chapman & Hall that the story, not the illustrations, should provide the principal focus. Following the second serial part Seymour had a nervous breakdown, dying shortly thereafter, having provided illustrations for the first five chapters only, leaving the fate and adventures of the Pickwick Club in Dickens's hands.[2] Following Seymour's death, Dickens swiftly inaugurated a number of changes to format, doing away with Seymour's original idea of the adventures of a sporting club (one of the familiar forms of periodical entertainment), and producing a monthly publication that went from a length of 24 pages with four illustrations to 32 pages with two illustrations.

Serial publication of fiction was not a new phenomenon in the 1830s, of course. Literary magazines conventionally serialized fiction. Novels such as Sir Walter Scott's *Waverly*, which had already been published in volume form, were serialized with much success. *Pickwick* was, however, a significant publication in that it presented the world with a wholly new story, one not seen previously in volume form, and thus was untried, untested. At first contemporary reviewers were fully taken in by the periodical as the genuine item (Chittick 1984, 328–35). *Pickwick* was reviewed not as a novel but as a maga- zine, reviewers accepting as real the fictive Boz as compiler of disparate sources. With its initially 'wandering and almost plotless form', which 'revel[led] in a fluid and fragmentary life, acknowledg- ing only the temporary unity of vignettes' (Grossman 1997, 173, 175), *Pickwick* began, and was accepted as, an oddity, 'a periodical, with only one article' (Chittick 1984, 335). *Pickwick*, then, 'usher[ed] in a new era in the serialization of novels. With *Pickwick*, for the first time a serial begins drawing on the material that an author is producing month by month . . . *Pickwick* itself is news' (Grossman 1997, 171).

A hypothesis therefore: such novelty may itself have had an effect on the identity of the novel. For *Pickwick* demonstrates – indeed performs – the internal, narrative transformation of the novel in its foregrounding of hybridity, fragmentation, and the intimation that 'the novel, as Dickens improvised it, may follow the principle of a miscellany' (Chittick 1984, 335). Thus the *modern* novelty of a 'novel' genre, the novel-in-ruins as it were; in this is the visible symptom and expression of literary modernity in the nineteenth century. In inter- vening in the market in this manner, Dickens marks the practice of fiction writing in a particularly striking way, one which is not simply a moment of transformation but also one which knowingly departs from convention. Similarly, the reception of fiction was also trans- formed, and not merely for the reading public. Serialization led to more rapid and widespread reviewing than had been customary for novels appearing in volume form. Dickens and his publishers turned the conventions and the institutions of serial publication on their heads, doing so not with a markedly 'new' type of tale, but writing a tale greatly indebted to earlier forms of narrative (*the old stories*). Novelty and modernity have to do precisely with the out of date.

Viewing Dickens's novel in such a manner allows the reader to perceive *Pickwick*'s particular moment of appearance as the admittedly accidental manifestation of a range of cultural, ideological, and aesthetic forces. It might even be argued that the publication of an entirely new story in a recognized and established mode of production, one which bears all the signs – however satirized or parodied – of earlier narrative forms, marks and may be viewed as 'the entry of memory into the public sphere' through the specific act of making visible for a mass market a range of 'phenomena of identification' (Ricoeur 2004, 129) simultaneously commensurate with and dislocated from earlier manifestations of Englishness.

To reiterate then: Dickens's inaugural novel, in both its narrative forms and the forms of its appearance on the literary scene, is informed simultaneously by tradition *and* innovation. The 'novelty' of this production announces itself internally through the narrative's estranging pastiche of the old. In this a gap is opened to our gaze between old and new, then and now; which breach is readable as the articulation of a cultural consciousness mediating the moment of its coming into being. *Pickwick* is simultaneously *institutive* and *conservative* (Derrida 1996a, 7). It is, in effect, a cultural *roman à clef*, staging a moment of being-English. It offers a number of countersignatures to all the impressions left on it, and to which it responds, by those earlier fictional forms and material publications. The countersignatures in turn inaugurate and authorize a double economics – of forgetting *and* anamnesis. In this, they affirm themselves through their difference as 'signatures of the age' (Benjamin 2002a, 139). An archiving of the literary (as we shall see), *Pickwick* is also, in effect, a 'capitalization on [cultural] memory' (Derrida 1996a, 12) in an epoch when English middle-class identity is striving to mark its distance from earlier manifestations of that memory. Moreover, *Pickwick*'s narrative, aesthetic capitalization serves to make its mode of publishing a 'capitalization' also, whereby 'art comes into contact with the commodity; the commodity comes into contact with art' (Benjamin 2002b, 143) in a manner that is noticeably different from earlier modes of literary–commercial enterprise.

Temporal and visual modalities

Harry Stone has commented of *Pickwick*'s election scenes that they are, 'among many things, rethought and reworked versions of the four satiric scenes in [William Hogarth's] *The Election*' (1755–58: Stone 1994, 50–1). The Dickensian process of textual anamnesis in which memory of other texts arrives, but in a partially remembered, partially translated form, puts to work the traces of cultural and social memories so as to give it relevance and meaning for the modern reader. This is the necessary work of translation; the visions that appear on the page bear the indelible signs of both past times *and* the cultural moment of envisioning as re-visioning. This process is marked therefore by an intertextual and formal difference that is also the articulation of the text's historicity. Hogarth is, though, not the only artist who leaves his trace in *The Pickwick Papers*. Sterne, Smollett, Sheridan, Cervantes – these and others were Dickens's sources. The comparison between Cervantes and Dickens in particular is a long-standing one, amongst the first to remark this being Washington Irving in a letter to Dickens in 1841, with subsequent remarks made notably by Edgar Johnson and W. H. Auden (see McMaster 1983, 595).[3] Reading *Pickwick*'s indebtedness to his literary precursors, Alexander Welsh also comments on the Pickwick–Quixote resemblance, observing that Mr Pickwick would have been immediately recognizable to many of the serial's readers as a nineteenth-century Don Quixote, with Sam Weller his Sancho Panza (Welsh 1967–68, 19–20). However, this resonance, while significant as the sign of Dickens's personal literary inheritance, can also be read for its difference, thereby causing to become visible the traces of ideological inflection and the material conditions by which the temporal moment comes to be traced.

Class relations are revealed in the comparison between Mr Pickwick and Sam. As N. N. Feltes has argued in his materialist analysis of *Pickwick* as commodity-text, the 'significance of the relationship between Mr. Pickwick and Sam lies . . . in its representation of an aspect of early Victorian England's *way of seeing itself*' (Feltes 1986, 15–16; emphasis added). Further, 'the implied parallel between Mr. Pickwick and Don Quixote . . . *together with* the difference in class and historical period, interpellate that specifically bourgeois Victorian sense of self' (Feltes 1986, 16; emphasis in original). The acknowledgement of intertextual reference allows for a kind of anamorphic reading. We are given a sidelong glimpse at how some readers of Dickens could be understood to be self-readers, gleaning a sense of identity in the early nineteenth century. Indeed, we apprehend how *Pickwick* is understandable as an act of self-reading involving the play of historical, ideological, and cultural differences between the Spain of Quixote and the England of Pickwick. Such play in *Pickwick* produces an image of early-nineteenth-century class relations in the novel, which, while haunted by its literary antecedent, *works* precisely because it offers a representation that is traced by, as it mediates, its own historicity.

With this in mind, let us come back to Boz, to the ways in which his figure functions in the novel. The assumption of an editorial function on the part of the author is one Dickens knowingly borrows from the past, as we have stated. The idea of the fictive editor is borrowed from literary tradition, from those authors with whom Dickens is familiar, such as Scott or Smollett, Defoe or Richardson.[4] Thus *Pickwick* is haunted by a particular mode of narrative production taken from the tradition of English fiction. In being employed by Dickens in the 1830s though, the function of the editor no longer has the same historical or cultural significance it once had. There is as great a difference between 'Boz' and the 'editor-function' of Richardson's *Clarissa* as there is between Mr Pickwick and Don Quixote, or Sam and Sancho Panza. It might be asked, not unreasonably: what makes difference possible, and in what ways does difference inform the specificity of any literary text? *Pickwick* (like any work of literature) is not merely the production of its author but also a publication taking place 'within a determinate subensemble of emerging industrial capitalism, the production of written texts' (Feltes 1986, 3). The editor-function or effect, in this case named 'Boz', is merely the prosopopoeic figure for such a historically determined *subensemble* of culturally and ideologically determined practices. And it is through that which the editor *chooses* to let the reader see of his characters' limited changes of apprehension – unlike the 'inalterable permanence of characters' of the eighteenth-century novel (Miller 1958, 27) – that we come to perceive the historical difference in representation.

Such difference is announced in *Pickwick* itself, through the gap in perspective between Mr Pickwick and Boz, or, to put this another way, between 1827–28, when the events of the novel take place, and 1836–37, when the novel is written and published. While we see that Mr Pickwick is not exactly unalterably permanent in his perspectives on the world, he at least 'does not expect what he sees will involve or change himself' (Miller 1958, 7), and this is a matter of being caught unawares by historical change. In this, Mr Pickwick is presented as if he were 'a kind of camera eye' (Miller 1958, 7). There is a naivety, not to say reflective myopia, in Pickwick's belief in the scientific truth of empirical observation that is historically grounded. Unlike Boz, who always lets the reader in on another perspective, Samuel Pickwick is unaware that there is an inescapable transformative dimension to sight and vision. Take, for example, Pickwick's response at Jingle's being paid off in return for giving up Miss Wardle (Chapter 10):

> If any dispassionate spectator could have beheld the countenance of the illustrious man, whose name forms the leading feature of the title of this work . . . he would have been almost induced to wonder that the indignant fire which flashed from his eyes, did not melt the glasses of his spectacles.
> (*PP* 141–2)

Boz knowingly calls upon the reader's powers of visualization in a manner that invites the reader to step into the narrative, to step back in time metaphorically and so witness both the appearance of Mr Pickwick and his gaze. What the scene gives us is double: on the one hand, it suspends narrative motion in favour of the time of visualization and the gaze; on the other hand, in being triggered from the position of an impossibility – the dispassionate spectator – the glance is seen to issue not from any subject as such, only the hypothesis of one. Thus, the glance in its differentiated network gives itself to acknowledge that there is always the other's view. Boz's imaginative hypothesis draws attention to this through his own, otherwise invisible, mediation of the scene, doing so in order to direct our view to an eccentric place within the representation. While Mr Pickwick does not expect to be changed, Boz does see that what is seen *does* transform the viewing subject emotionally (whether Pickwick in his anger or the reader through laughter), and in such a way that the only appropriate, if comic, means of representing this is through the focus being directed to the act of looking; or, more precisely, one gaze looking at another, and at yet another.

For the reader must *see* the dispassionate *spectator*. This hypothetical figure is in fact not there at all. A phantasm of sorts produced by Boz so as to direct the gaze, this spectral figure is looking at something which also does not exist as such: the metaphorical, and therefore not literally visible, appearance of fire. This displaced and volatile sign of indignation, produced in the mind's eye as an approximate doubling of Pickwick's particularly intense stare, and which the editor imagines has the force to melt glass, ironically appears only to draw attention to the act of looking. The problem for Pickwick is that he 'reads literally and so loses *sight* . . . of the essential indeterminability' (Marlow 1985, 946; emphasis added), produced by that difference which opens perspective from within itself. Boz does not, however, and so there is a doubling of perspective between the editor and his subject, as well as a historical difference.

It is important that we recognize the significance of that simultaneous proximity and distance that is marked by the decade between the novel's imaginary events and the editorial transcription of the posthumous papers. Located in the years 1827–28, *The Pickwick Papers* situates its adventures over the course of some eighteen months. *Pickwick* is precise about its starting date, 12 May 1827 (*PP* 15). Such an act of dating foregrounds itself, and draws our attention to itself in its visible and graphic precision. If we look closely we perceive that 'Boz' is a curious kind of witness, not of the events he transcribes, but of the traces of those historical instances, and through these to other ghostly spectators, whose only signs of witness are those documents signed by various hands. James Marlow has observed how Boz is at a remove from events, how the act of writing is foregrounded (1985, 939). The self-advertising 'editor of these papers' (*PP*15) refers to 'the secretary, to whose notes we are indebted' (*PP* 16); and again Marlow: 'every episode supposedly bears the traces of at least two mediators' (1985, 939). There is no possibility of unmediated vision, then, when one is referring to the past. This affirmation of material difference announces *Pickwick*'s modernity, and, with that, the departure from its recent past *in the very condition of its modes of historical perception and inscription*.

As should be clear, temporal doubling of the kinds I am describing effects a disturbance in any supposedly stable present moment (once again), and also the means of representation of such an event and any experience of that. The tropes of vision, sight, and visibility introduce motion, overflowing static and reductive notions of past or present as temporally discrete moments. Such a doubling process is markedly cultural, social, and material, not to say historical. If, as Raymond Williams has it on the occlusion of feeling, experience, and subjectivity in certain Marxist critical discourses, it is 'the reduction of the social to fixed forms that remains the basic error' (Williams 1977, 129), then doubling, division, and flow overcome such fixation and such error. The motion of replication/division/iteration informs and reveals *how* the reader is invited or directed to see in any crucial moment within 'the flux of historical process' (Goodman 2004, 3). As *Pickwick* brings to light, the modes of perception by which an act of 'historicization' takes place in nineteenth-century textuality are far from Cyclopean. They have to do frequently with *how* we see, and so see ourselves, in seeing others, in 'that immanent, collective perception of any moment as a seething mix of unsettled moments' (Goodman 2004, 3) as are commonly found in *The Pickwick Papers*.

Such a seething mix may best be termed a *figurative economy*, which in *Pickwick* is informed by 'impulse, excess, and misdirection' (Bowen 2000, 79). Dickens's economy is one in which the 'interest in radical

social change' shared with its 'Romantic precursors' is figured
'through the use of what are essentially pastoral [and comic] conventions' (Bowen 2000, 77). In assuming such an economy Dickens
invites his readers to *feel* as well as to *see*. He therefore structures the
possibility of perception and vision through an anachronistic modality. Like Wordsworth, Dickens understands history, the past, and
indeed contemporary social conditions that produce the 'life of the
People' (as George Eliot has it in 'The Natural History of German Life:
Riehl'; 1990, 271) as examples of 'evacuated ontology', so that collectively they inform *Pickwick* with an 'absence that is the very possibility of the "here and now"' (Liu 1989, 39). Furthermore, 'sentiment is
Dickens's *forte*, and he uses it to manage history as effectively as Eliot
uses speculative philosophy ... melodrama provides Dickens with a
mode that is "historical" in its insistence on a past that is lost but not
forgotten' (Crosby 1991, 70). Dickens wagers everything on the past
not being forgotten through the structuring forces of sentiment and
melodrama and what those forces carry with them from one moment
to another.

Sentiment and melodrama are then significant, alternative historical modes of representation. Dickens's historicizing 'system', his
'fictional economy', is one determined by 'loss and gain, of absence
and presence'. In creating a world close enough to be remembered by
its readers, a world present apparently only a decade before, and yet
vanishing from sight as 'the ever receding ground of the present'
(Crosby 1991, 96), *Pickwick* projects the very possibility of nineteenth-
century middle-class national identity as a condition of loss, absence,
and undecidability. It does so in two principal ways: first, through its
close attention to matters of vision and sight, and the often comic
consequences that arise as a result of the unreliability of interpretation stemming from empirical evidence; and second, through its
relentless proliferation and circulation of texts (letters, found tales
and manuscripts), various forms of communication, and the multiplication of embedded stories within the principal narrative. Dickens,
like Scott before him, responds to a 'demand for an approach to the
past that would interest a middle-class public by treating aspects of
experience with which they could empathize ... in a manner that
would engage their imaginations and their sympathies, thus allowing
them, as it were, to experience the past anew' (Rigney 2001, 71)
through that solicitation of the subject by the force of sentiment.

When Kevis Goodman remarks of New Historicism's readings of
Romantic literature that 'the significance of some kind of "feeling" ...

as a mode of historical manifestation is an underexplored or undeveloped *insight*' (2004, 4; emphasis added), she offers a comment appropriate to the reading of Dickens. Dickens knows that, more than merely mawkish feeling, sentiment can be a powerful, conservative tool. Sentiment is not simply an emotional distortion, even though too much of it can cause this. Sentiment is a figure of affect denoting a 'corona of forces and effects extending inward and outward from the body' (Goodman 2004, 145, n. 12), which is most directly perceived in *Pickwick* through the structural relay of vision (recall Mr Pickwick's intensity of gaze imagined as metaphorical flames, to which our gaze is directed by Boz via the hypothetical dispassionate spectator). It should be remembered, of course, that sentiment can cloud our vision. It can make us misty-eyed. What we think we see swims before us, and thus it is all the more necessary that we find a means of focusing that is clear-sighted. However, we must not forget that sentiment does not always signify the misrepresentation of an excessively emotional perspective, thought, or view; indeed, as we shall see through the example of Rachel Wardle's view of Tracy Tupman, sentiment is available, in *The Pickwick Papers* at least, to a cynical and satirical consideration, which distances the reader from the event and so produces an estranged relation to the historical.

Not taken too far though, sentiment, the *OED* tells us, is an awareness gained from vague sensation, a mental feeling. It is the feeling or meaning intended by a particular passage in literature, or it is a wish or view expressed as an epigraph. When not taken to extremes, sentiment gives another name to the structural play of perception and conscious experience. Put another way, sentiment figures simultaneously the inescapability of perspectival perception and the risk of a certain misapprehension arising from the very same situated consciousness. Sentiment thus doubles itself in a contradictory, not to say paradoxical, or even perhaps an aporetic fashion. Inseparable from itself into two distinct conceptual formations, the notion of sentiment oscillates undecidably. How do we decide whether sentiment offers the proper perspective or an overly coloured view? As we shall see further on, sentiment distorts the vision of Miss Wardle, but admits the past to be conjured at particular seasonal moments. There are at least two ways to look at sentiment, and the very idea of sentiment is inextricably caught up in the question of how one sees, as well as the processes of translation that are always intimately entwined in the act of looking. *Pickwick* gives this to be seen. How we see, how we read, marks us historically and ideologically, for 'there is no natural seeing and therefore there cannot be a direct and unmediated contact with reality' (Williams 1981, 167).

Phantasms of experience, or the mechanism of the fictive gaze

At the beginning of Chapter 25, we witness the following scene, in which an idea is bodied forth:

> ... the mob, who, indignant at being excluded, and *anxious to see* what followed, relieved their feelings by kicking at the gate and ringing the bell, for an hour or two afterwards. In this amusement they all took part by turns, except three or four fortunate individuals, who having discovered a grating in the gate which commanded *a view of nothing*, were *staring* through it, with the same indefatigable perseverance with which people will flatten their noses against the front windows of a chemist's shop, when a drunken man, who has been run over by a dog-cart in the street, is undergoing a *surgical inspection* in the back-parlour. (*PP* 328; emphases added)

As David Trotter has observed so perspicaciously, 'the microscopic inspection . . . seems to require as its complement a macroscopic inspection, which . . . produces nothing at all' (Trotter 1996, 215). Yet another double scene: of looking *and* looking at nothing; of nothing to see, *and* the analogy that structures the passage between one moment of collective observation and another. Or perhaps we might suggest that the latter observation on the collective gaze projects the phantasmic, analogical image of the former. Such duplication and reduplication stages four distinct locations from which the look is directed, each involving an observing narrator and observed crowd.

And yet the supplementary scene is not *of* the order of narrative events. The nearly silent shift to present tense – people will flatten their noses against the front windows of a chemist's shop – introduces the 'hypothesis of a perspective' (Williams 1983, 161). If not exactly fruitless, the act of looking, in response to the paucity or absence of any referent, turns back on itself. However, the very idea that motivates the act unveils itself as far from pointless. It is that which is *in* the vision, which we come to perceive. In the face of seeing nothing empirically, we come to see 'the invisible *of* this world . . . its own and interior possibility' (Merleau-Ponty 1968, 151), which is of course the rule that motivates all fiction. My argument is that Dickens's text announces its historical moment, as well as its distancing itself from the past, through opening the mechanism of the fictive gaze to our inspection through the play between what the reading contract between author and reader assumes as there, and what is 'there' but not there as an interiorized phantasm of the narrative event. Let us look closely at the structure of the scene, its order and its content.

The observers, observing nothing and yet intent on 'staring', are themselves transformed into the 'something' at which to be looked. They become the vision and the source of a commentary on the collective gaze. Their act of looking makes them worthy of extended, hypothetical observation. Through the refraction of the relay that structures focalization, the reader is illuminated about the comic nature of the collective gaze through editorial reflection, in which the invisible scene – those people with their flattened noses – and its own microscopic double – the surgical inspection and the image of the imagined man undergoing such inspection – appears as the doubled, phantasmic other of its visible counterpart, that anxious mob. Another vision is suggested in this moment, a strange uncanny projection. The violent anterior scene of a drunken man being run over by a dog-cart hovers for the reader as yet one more imagined a priori event. There is a disordering temporality within and *as* the very possibility of this structure. Any distinctions between that which is internal and that which is external to the narrative are erased by the multiplying lines of sight even as the distinction between the empirical, albeit mediated vision and its phantasmic counterpart crumbles. To state the order of form as straightforwardly as possible: structurally, response to the empirical scene is followed, in the face of nothing, by the magnification of the primary scene's idea, itself given projected form; the supplement takes on a greater force than the prior moment as, in being *invented* from within the inaugural instant, it passes from the invisible to the visible. The dimension of vision is opened from within itself, the idea of vision assuming a more coercive currency than any mere representation of some supposed empirical referent.

That anxiety to see that informs the mob's persistent view of nothing arises as the perhaps disquieting manifestation of some collective scopophilic desire. It might be said that the editorial intervention in the moment and its reflection leading to the ghostly arrival of that abyssally structured analogy with its temporal regression invites the reader to see him- or herself. For reading is precisely just this 'looking-at-nothing' in the desire to conjure a vision. In Dickens's structural and visual hyperbole we perceive that the author 'adds . . . a register that turns the story itself into an object of representation' (Grossman 1997, 188); and, we would add, a narrative about, on the one hand, the re-presentation of representation while, on the other hand, a representation of re-presentation. We find ourselves involved in a world of endlessly shifting perspectives, in which frequently Mr Pickwick, setting out as a *spectator*, one armed with spectacles and telescope for the aid of bringing detail nearer and into focus, repeatedly 'becomes himself a spectacle' (Miller 1958, 16).

Boz's revelation of the shared structures of perception and the visual as that which opens to our gaze the non-synonymous structures of feeling accords a mobility to narrative that refuses to acquiesce to any fixity of representation. Furthermore, it makes possible the presentation of a *'perspective* which is [otherwise] not socially or politically available' (Williams 1983, 161). In this it renders *Pickwick's* vision as other to its times and irreducible, either to any simple or simply determined past or to any simply assigned ideological location or frame. Having entered the 'strange domain' of vision's ideality, 'one does not *see* how there could be any question of leaving it' (Merleau-Ponty 1968, 152; emphasis added). *Pickwick's* vision acknowledges this everywhere. In doing so, it makes visible 'a force [Dickens] knows not to be in the existing balance of forces that was there [in the 1830s] to be observed' (Williams 1983, 161); and so *invents* 'a crucial variable in the question of realist fiction' (161).

Some form of commerce in the fictional economy operating under the name of Boz takes place between the very idea of narrative qua representation of a history and the material act of writing as envisioning. This is not peculiar to Boz. It takes place as a result of all writing. But it is the singular aspect of Boz's mode of production, relating the visionary with vision, the past–invisible with the present–apparition that interests us here. The immaterial is given a quasi-material support, expressed specifically through the foregrounding of the medium of the editorial process and, less directly, though nonetheless forcefully, through the attention given to repeated devices. There occurs an 'invisible transpiercing', by which the reader witnesses 'a world sometimes more visible than the real world' (Marion 2004, 11). Something takes place in Dickens's writing between the verbal and the visual, the unseen and the seen. Strictly speaking, however, this 'something' is nothing as such, either material or 'real'. It is as if, in the very mark on the page there is a disturbance in the field of vision, which disruption, though invisible, is always already under way. It is as if these non-synonymous figures relating to vision are haunted by, or disclose themselves as, examples of phantom syllepsis or zeugma waiting expectantly to be completed.

Now Dickens employs zeugma on a number of occasions in *Pickwick* with telling comic effect (*PP* 69, 353, 369, 482, 662, 720). Zeugma or syllepsis relies on the confusion between the literal and figurative in their structures. Consider the following examples: 'all the girls were in tears and white muslin' (*PP* 369); 'he threw off his green spectacles and his gravity' (*PP* 662). The tropological immanence of such destabilizing rhetorical movement is at work in the language of vision, though its function is more than merely comic. As the examples I have considered make clear, the hypothetical spectator can appear so as to present to view that which is otherwise not there, the metaphorical, as a figure for what is, the gaze. As with all such doubling figures we do not know quite how *or* where to look, as it were. The noticeable incidence of such figures and their tropic dimension is all the more intriguing because the frequency of their appearance seems to bear no direct relationship to the narrative, other than to draw our attention to acts of seeing and, often, their precarious conditions. Beyond zeugma, however, the attention to what is literally or figuratively visible draws our interest.

In Chapter 2, following the meeting with Jingle, Mr Pickwick, consulting his watch, remarks 'let me see'. Clearly, the remark refers to both the act of looking at the timepiece and reflective consideration. Though not an instance of zeugma strictly speaking, there is in Mr Pickwick's words the ghost of the effect at work in this otherwise commonplace phrase. On another occasion the zeugmatic structure is split between two subjects. In response to Jingle's tales of poetry-writing and dog-keeping, Mr Snodgrass and Mr Winkle remark in turn 'I should like to see his poem' and 'I should like to see that dog' (*PP* 29). In Chapter 8, there occurs a curious instance when Mr Tupman and Joe consider one another at length (*PP* 110). The passage is peppered with figures of vision. Mr Tupman 'looked around', in response to Joe's 'large circular eyes', which were 'staring'. That the eyes and not the fat boy are staring is somewhat unnerving, uncanny perhaps, but explainable partially because Joe apparently suffers from some form of narcolepsy. Mr Tupman, in return, 'gazed at the fat boy', and, reciprocally, 'the fat boy stared at him'. Once more, Mr Tupman 'observed' Joe. A potentially infinite relay of gazes is established, leading to no definite information, meaning, or knowledge; for Mr Tupman convinces himself that 'he either did not know, or did not understand, anything that had been going forward'. Sight, seeing, and visible appearance are intimately connected to the impossibility of certain interpretation. What we do see is that the attempted economy of editorial process, in its efforts to be faithful to the scene, gives way before the abyss of the gaze. The motion of vision overflows representation's mimetic containment.

Figures of the visible and visual are gathered then in order to impress on the reader the necessity of looking carefully, even if they are not to be governed in or by acts of reading, writing or editing. Reading has the power to bring back the past, whether we call that memory or history, in the form of a vision. It translates the visible marks on the page into visions for the mind's eye, visions that come to occupy our imaginations. As Susan Horton has noted, 'in the Dickens world, this kind of play with visuality is not unusual . . . Dickens' narration regularly turns readers into watchers of characters watching one another watching, often watching one another's reflections' (1995, 1–2). This very odd, not to say uncanny, structure is also used to comment on processes of thought. For example, one frequently says 'I see', meaning 'I understand'. There is a motion, if not a slippage, at work therefore in the language of vision as well as in vision itself in *Pickwick*. That words such as 'spectacle/s', observation, and sight operate in *The Pickwick Papers* in a doubling manner, whether directly or implicitly, indicates an instability in language to which I have just referred and recalls by analogy the motions of figures such as zeugma, syllepsis, or catachresis.

It is as if the verbal signs signifying vision are not internally coherent. They appear to threaten to unloose themselves from within. In solution, as it were, phrases allude more or less indirectly through the process of flux and transport to a fraught relationship between seeing and reading, and by analogy between the empirical, historical event and the inscribed record. There are many such moments. 'The Bagman's Story' begins with a conditional clause involving the possibility of observation that seems to invoke preternaturally the opening of a novel by Thomas Hardy – 'One winter's evening, about five o'clock, just as it began to grow dusk, a man in a gig *might have been seen* urging his tired horse along the road, which leads across Marlborough Downs, in the direction of Bristol' (*PP* 185; emphasis added). What follows, though, is anything but Hardyesque. This being a *Pickwick* narrator, he self-reflexively draws attention to the moment of the view within the narrative structure:

I say he might have been seen, and I have no doubt he would have been, if anybody but a blind man had happened to pass that way; but the weather was so bad, and the night so cold and wet, that nothing was out but the water . . .

In the gesture of presenting to his audience's hypothetical view the limited visibility due to the time of day and the atmospheric conditions, the narrator recalls the Boz of the *Sketches* who makes the paradoxical claim that 'the streets of London, to be beheld in the very height of their glory, should be seen on a dark, dull, murky winter's night' (Dickens 1994, 55). This comparison aside, though, in its inauguration through the vision – in both senses – of a phantom subject, 'The Bagman's Story' operates through another of those hypotheses of perspectives that remind us that there is someone intervening between events and ourselves.

On another occasion in Chapter 14 (*PP* 266–7), Sam Weller's father appears for the first time in the novel and to the reader through a series of repeated looks, stares, gazes, and observations directed towards Sam and Mr Pickwick. In the course of two paragraphs, the first of which begins with an apparently straightforward 'description' of a room in an inn, our attention is drawn to a 'stout man' who has also 'attracted Mr Pickwick's attention'. We thus have our attention directed in two different locations, the second of which involves our seeing Mr Pickwick looking at Tony Weller; from this moment of doubling and division, we are treated to a virtual semaphore: 'looked', 'another look', 'look', 'stare', 'see', 'Mr Weller's observation', 'he saw Mr Pickwick's eyes every now and then turning towards him', and 'he began to gaze'.

The Posthumous Papers of the Pickwick Club is peppered with such illustrative cases. Not only are there stares, looks, gazes, observations, and 'meaningful' looks marked (*PP* 312), there is also that proliferation of eyes mentioned. Sam 'eyes' Job, while Job's eyes fill with tears, and he applies a pink handkerchief to his eyes (*PP* 311, 312). Tom, the protagonist of 'The Bagman's Story', is noted for 'marking . . . little evidences with the eye of an experienced traveller' (*PP* 187). This eye wanders, however, on the occasion of Tom becoming sentimental (*PP* 188). He comments, also, on a 'smartly dressed girl' as having a 'bright eye' (*PP* 187). The 'principal figure in Mr Winkle's visions' is 'a young lady with black eyes' (*PP* 368). Mr Pickwick's lawyer, Mr Perker, suggests the strategy of throwing dust in the judge's eyes (*PP* 410), which, however obviously metaphorical, nevertheless conflates comprehension with vision. There are to be observed 'horn spectacles' (*PP* 594), a 'gold eye glass' (*PP* 473), 'green spectacles' (*PP* 508), and yet more spectacles (*PP* 629, 637, 540, 639). Additionally, we see 'brilliant eyes' (*PP* 477). At the ball in the Assembly Rooms in Bath, in another of those social spectacles, certain ladies, including the Dowager Lady Snuphanuph, 'no sooner set eyes upon Mr Pickwick' than 'they exchanged glances' (*PP* 480). Mrs Dowler shrieks as a result of having 'caught sight' of events in the street, while, in the same scene, 'the first object that met the gaze of both' Mr Dowler and Mr Pickwick is Mr Winkle (*PP* 493).

Chapter 41 opens with a quasi-performative gesture. The reader 'sees' initially a scene in which Mr Pickwick opens his eyes. The performative dimension here is that the reader sees nothing until Mr Pickwick's consciousness is announced through his gaze; what appears for him appears after a fashion, though from a different perspective for the reader. In the same chapter, Sam engages in 'a comprehensive gaze'. Mr Smangle attempts the fruitless activity of 'staring' Sam 'out of countenance', which is of no avail of course, because Sam, ever indefatigable, continues 'to look steadily' at Smangle (*PP* 557). Mr Pickwick acknowledges the relationship between seeing, understanding, and interpretation, when he says to Sam, 'I see you comprehend me' (*PP* 570), which idiom is structured by its abyssal play between *see* and *comprehend*. In a more encoded moment, there is 'a perfect alphabet of winks' (*PP* 576).

Vision frequently exceeds empirical data. As a result of this power, the reader can of course glimpse the past that informs the present and, beyond any immediate or recent context, the traces of other past moments. Writing is the very medium that enables such historical and visionary transport, as the 'bundle of soiled and tattered papers, yellow with dust and dropping to pieces from age' (*PP* 546) observed by Mr Pickwick in the Fleet Prison attest in mute witness. Though we cannot read these papers their condition affirms their temporal passage. The visionary force is all the more powerful for the risk it takes in seeing the invisible, and so reading inventively through the inauguration of a fiction the structure of feeling. In being asked to see, we are also asked to feel. Through the mediation of, and meditation on, what *might be seen* a perspective on society *in solution* is opened therefore, which, though otherwise not socially or politically available, is capable of presenting the traces of the past in translated form, if we attend to the possibility of vision. It is this economy of vision and the visionary that informs the Christmas chapter, Chapter 28.

But, concluding this section, we may suggest that it is *as if* in the febrile oscillations that the editor-machine sets in motion, *Pickwick's* vision mediates a broader cultural 'fascination with perceptual aberration' and the obsession in nineteenth-century visual theory across the discourses of aesthetics, psychology, and science with 'vision gone awry' (Smith 1995, 5). That vision goes awry is not in question; that it can be powerfully productive rather than limiting or negative is.

Temporal frames and loops

At the structural centre of *The Posthumous Papers* is Chapter 28 (there are 56 chapters). This is 'A good-humoured Christmas Chapter, containing an account of a Wedding, and some other Sports beside, which although in their way, even as good customs as Marriage itself, are not quite so religiously kept up, in these degenerate times' (*PP* 360–90). That the title draws our attention to customs and degenerate times implies that the old story is very much transformed by temporal difference. A narrative composed of tales, an interpolated story, a song entitled 'A Christmas Carol', and also marked by numerous references to sight, eyes, vision and so on, as well as being peppered with various linguistic disruptions of the kind that this chapter has addressed, Chapter 28 'enacts a work of remembrance, particularly of the dead' (Bowen 2000, 76). The work of writing is revealed once more as a strange and estranging optical machinery, which brings before our eyes many haunting figures and memories otherwise unavailable and invisible.

It is *as if* the chapter, constructed as both a series of narrative frames embedded within one another and as an endless temporal loop of images, aspires to the condition of phantom zoetrope, figuring in itself an impossible and excessive structure replaying over and over an excessive phantasmagoria of tropes and images, in an act of hospitality and remembrance. Each structure, each projection, invites us to *see*. And as a preface to the scenes of celebration, we read the following passage:

> We write these words now, many miles distant from the spot on which, *year after year*, we met on that day, a *merry and joyous circle*. Many of the hearts that throbbed so gaily then, have ceased to beat; many of the *looks* that shone so brightly then, have ceased to glow; the hands we grasped, have grown cold; the *eyes* we sought, have hid their lustre in the grave; yet the old house, the room, the merry voices and smiling *faces*, the jest, the

laugh, the most minute and trivial circumstance connected with those happy meetings, crowd upon our mind at each *recurrence* of the season, *as if* the last assemblage had been but yesterday. (*PP* 359; emphases added)

The initial shift to present tense in the opening clause of the sentence accompanies a reflective acknowledgement of the act of writing. In a constant flux between past and present, 'in which every perception is already memory' (Bergson 1999, 150), we move; 'we' shuttles between loss and gain, absence and the numerous phantom presences which 'crowd upon our mind' with every temporal reiteration. The motion is also caught in the shift from *now* to *then*, in its motion from *looks* to *eyes* to *faces*, and in the circular and temporal movements of the annual cycle and the recurrence of gathering. (One might also catch in the more obscure echoes of *circumstance* the motion of surrounding that encircles and gathers together the fragmented images in a gesture of connection.) The good reader will note the syllepsistic doubling in the first sentence. The temporal recirculation of *year after year* finds itself doubled in the image of the *merry and joyous circle*, which figure exceeds its own image of the gathering of friends to announce the refolding of time past and time future in the constant slippage of the otherwise invisible time present briefly apprehended in that figure *we*. *Our* perception, *our* memory – which is to say not only the memory that might be ours but also the memory *of* ourselves as others – finds itself interwoven into that 'multitude of remembered elements' (Bergson 1999, 150) that the citation performs as well as observes, through the inaugural, self-reflexive affirmation that *we write these words now*. Attention to the present yet ephemeral moment of the graphic mark as trace admits even that 'our consciousness of the present is already memory' (Bergson 1999, 151).

The passage thus proceeds as the inscription of visionary memory and writing as both the bearer and structure of anamnesis, and through which, though 'we' remember now, 'we' are projected back to the memory of 'our presence' in that company. It is not only *as if* the scenes had occurred, but also *as if* we were part of the 'assemblage' – which in effect *we* become, in being written into the phantasy scenario that *we* read. There is thus produced an overlaying of supposedly discrete times in the trope and motion of circularity. Through the vision of assemblage a composition of eyes, faces, hands, voices, looks and laughter becomes visible as itself an assemblage of momentary visions. Here an image of multiple moments comes into focus through its unfixed temporal motion. Writing's spectral projection, with its power to produce visions, moves in several directions at once, producing a sight more real than any empirical evidence could suggest. The spirit of the past is maintained here, through the sentiment of awareness and feeling. And this is so because for this brief, ever-present epoch, we 'appear' to ourselves joined in mortal community, where death is what makes imaginable the very idea of community. For this is not only a Christmas past, it is also the spirit of every Christmas to come. In the act of writing *we* the novel comes to confront its own imaginary. At the abyssal heart of the novel, memory, vision, and the materiality of the letter come together in an 'oratorical visualization' (de Bolla 1989, 292).

Such an act of memory, which is also one of mourning, demands that we keep alive an ethical commitment to bearing witness, in excess of any mere historical record, even though such an act threatens to betray what it relays through the force of feeling. Writing relies on the very phantoms that it conjures, in the articulation of the 'mournful imagination' of a writer 'determined to offer hospitality to an array of . . . spectralized subjects'. This suggests in turn in this particular instance a 'politics of the hospitality to the Other . . . Even melancholia is a form of hospitality to a fundamental Otherness' (Ricciardi 2003, 126). The 'phantasmagorical vision of culture' (Ricciardi 2003, 128), given singular expression in the image of the Christmas gathering with its interpolated tales and other heterogeneous elements, attests to the becoming-posthumous of one particular manifestation of national culture and identity. Phantasmic visualization draws attention to both the return of the other and the role of narrative in the present in opening a relay to the future that is the reader.

Thus the editor- and translation-effects of which we have spoken risk witness and betrayal in order to maintain the mediation of a binocular dissimilarity and distortion by which iterable communication has its chance. In this, *The Posthumous Papers* affirms literature's responsibility to bear witness to those traces of the past that are, and remain, 'as inaccessible as [they are] ineluctable' (Derrida 2001, 144). And literature's force as witness is what is borne in literature-in-ruins. Attestation is signalled in that endless motion between the verbal and the visual, in 'imaginal transfiguration', which is 'from the very start fantastic or phantasmic'. Under certain conditions 'all history is at issue here' (Derrida 2001, 151). In privileging the phantasmic, and in exposing the instability of language in its generation of meaning, Boz acknowledges the extent to which history is at issue, and demands that we *feel* responsible, that we *feel* accountable. In this chance, there might come the responsibility of mourning and memory in excess that is arguably *the signature* of Englishness in the nineteenth century.

Historical frequencies

The frequency of the figures of vision and sight and their tropological operation to which we have given our attention is fascinating, if not perplexing. The very frequency remarked through so many graphic instances causing the narrative to stutter might be taken as a curious manifestation of some spectroscopic wavelength. One may propose that the proliferation of the tropes of visuality and vision in Dickens's text is a symptom of broader epistemological and ontological changes in the nineteenth century. A sense of a doubled, and therefore a divided, subjectivity comes to be produced in the early part of the century, specifically in relation to sight and the optical.

For Rosalind Krauss, the effect is one of phenomenological uncanniness, brought about by the dissolution of psychic boundaries caused by technological advances. Optical devices such as the zoetrope put the viewer simultaneously outside and inside the experience of watching. As she describes what amounts to a doubling simultaneity, 'I'm *in* this experience; I'm *watching* this experience' (Krauss 1988, 58). This disturbing duplication of subject position is arguably analogous with that phantasmic experience of the reader, already described. This experience of a troubled subjectivity is echoed elsewhere. As Susan Horton comments in the wake of Jonathan Crary's work on techniques of observation, the Victorians 'were caught between two models of vision: that of the empirical senses, which were proving the eye of the observer unreliable and subjective [and therefore in principle open to the translations and editorial effects of sentiment], and that of the various romanticisms and early modernism, which posited the observer as an active, autonomous producer of his or her own visual experience' (1995, 8).

The historicity of the subject-position as informed by visual experience would appear to be *in solution* in a manner that resonates with the perceptions of optical–subjective phenomena as proposed by Krauss, Horton, and Crary. The effects described above are clearly visible, even though the commanding technology of the visual is not an optical device but the editorial pen. In apprehending the fluidity perceived and mediated by Boz we may, then, catch sight of a far from static condition of subjectivity. At the same time the eye of any given character as observer is notoriously unreliable, the image it produces and relays equally so. Moreover, such is the dissolution of boundaries affected by particular effects in Boz's writing that the reader encounters the disquieting experience of both *watching* and being *in* the experience. If Boz does not situate his characters or readers as caught exactly, he at least places them *in suspension,* and so in a medium within a vignette of the event, in which there is subjective and visual flux – between locations, between perceptions, between sensations or emotions, and occasionally between the present of the event and the memory or image of another temporal moment.

With this in mind, we will consider in the remaining pages of this chapter two scenes, from Chapters 7 and 38. Both mobilize figures of vision in the service of narrative effect. Both echo also with particular encrypted historical resonances, which might, arguably, mark the one set of parameters of Englishness from the seventeenth to the nineteenth centuries. Whereas *Pickwick* has been observed to mediate the vision and historicity of this identity through its intertextual literary allusions thus far, in the two examples to be considered the discourse of science from the 1660s to the early 1800s can be read as swimming in and out of focus.

In Chapter 7, Isabella Wardle's infatuation with Mr Tupman is recorded in optical terms. 'In her eyes', we are told, 'Tracy Tupman was a youth; she viewed his years through a *diminishing glass*' (*PP* 96; emphasis added). The initial metaphor whereby emotional perception is rendered as sight orients the sentence. Moreover, feeling and vision are intimately entwined. In both cases we come to see how 'our physiological apparatus is again and again shown to be defective, inconsistent, prey to illusion, and, in a crucial manner, susceptible to external procedures of manipulation and stimulation that have the essential capacity *to produce experience for the subject*' (Crary 1990, 92). That metaphor beginning the sentence does double service: at the same time it figures the distortion that romantic fascination lends to the gaze as well as offering indirectly – through a kind of rhetorical refraction – a supplementary 'lens' through which the reader is able to 'view' what is invisible, Miss Wardle's 'translation' of Tupman's physical appearance. This 'translation-effect' works to reveal the power to make visible, however cynically or satirically, the ways in which sight is never simply empirical observation. We 'see' Miss Wardle all the more clearly because we gain insight into the way in which she views the beloved. The translation is all the more effective because in neither part of the sentence does the metaphor fall into the weak device of simile. Mr Tupman does not 'appear': he 'is' a youth to Isabella Wardle. The reader is thus directed to look in two places at once. In this opening of the structure of the image, the moments that make up the instantaneity of the gaze are restored, magnified, and so revealed in their hitherto invisible suspension. However, Boz is not content to leave it at this. It is not merely a matter of the unveiling of the work of a phenomenological, interpretative process economically registered in the figure of sight. In the second part of the sentence Miss Wardle's 'sight' is aided artificially. A technological prosthesis is introduced as a medium of viewing between subject and object when it is revealed that 'she viewed his years *through a diminishing glass*'. We see here a performative doubling akin to that which is witnessed in the language describing and observing (twice) the reiterated gaze of Dr Slammer (*PP* 36). The second clause is, effectively, an enlargement of the work of the first part, the sentence thereby moving in its operation from the constative to the performative.

Boz's happy choice of phrase 'diminishing glass' should not be overlooked. It offers the reader a view of a slight though perhaps important cultural and historical trace. The phrase 'diminishing glass' is a now obscure, somewhat poetic, figure for the compound microscope. The phrase was employed by Richard Hooke (1635–1703), who devised the compound microscope, reporting his findings in his *Micrographia* (1665), one of the decisive texts in the emergence of a 'modern and heterogeneous regime of vision' (Crary 1990, 3), which regime extends historically from the seventeenth to the nineteenth centuries. Though it is hardly likely that Dickens was drawing deliberately on the history of scientific inquiry into optics, the self-deceiving example of Isabella Wardle demonstrates that, a century and a half after Hooke, the matter of vision and its amplifications or distortions remains a focal issue in English cultural identity. If Boz receives a somewhat encoded history of technologies of vision, however accidentally, his language also finds itself inscribed by a discourse on the interpretation and misuse of visual phenomena, and thus renders itself as markedly historical.

Boz teaches his readers to distrust the pedagogy of the eye, or at least to be suspicious of any claims to clarity or supposedly unmediated vision. Concomitantly, he educates his reading public to see the defects and distortions if not with a jaundiced eye then certainly more clear-sightedly. For as much as Dickens's first novel is indebted to the forms of the novel in the eighteenth century,[5] it is also the case that there is to be found at work a 'spectatorial model' (Goodman 2004, 40), the genealogy of which is indebted to various discourses belonging to the period of, but not restricted by, the texts of Addison and Steele, Defoe, Fielding, and Richardson, amongst others. *Pickwick's* references to the panoptical array of sight- and vision-related terms partakes unmistakably of and is encoded by the previous century's obsession with the gaze and its accompanying lexicography. The tropology of the eye and its non-synonymous cognates works in conjunction with satire, cynicism, and irony in order to produce a 'discordant affective awareness' (Goodman 2004, 40) on the part of the reader. Such awareness arguably produces an estranging disjunction that is temporal, separating the reader in all his or her modernity in the 1830s from the visible signs of the distant and recent pasts, out of which is produced *Pickwick's* comic capital.

To return to the scene with which we were concerned: via the medium of the novel's 'self-consciousness about sensory mediation' (Goodman 2004, 41), it is as if we are to understand, to imagine in the mind's eye as it were, Miss Wardle placing Tupman under a microscope. Far from 'diminishing' him in her eyes as a close inspection might, the spinster's phantom prosthesis amplifies all those invisible qualities, attributes, and details that are unavailable in the unmediated image of Tracy Tupman. We comprehend that Rachel Wardle does so in order precisely *not* to see him as he is, but to 'translate' him into, we might say, the ghost of Tupman past. The 'diminishing glass' produces a memory of Tupman, one which cannot be Miss Wardle's. Even as this takes place, the forensic inquiry is held up in turn to the 'scientific' questioning and scepticism on the part of the editor of *The Pickwick Papers* in the very process of ironic, destabilizing narration. To reiterate: Miss Wardle's sight and the language in which it is couched reveal how technological prosthesis enables translation *and* visibility. Bringing the invisible to the naked eye it nonetheless foregrounds the unreliability of such processes. In this we see that Dickens raises the problem of the role of the novel in the early Victorian present, where, to paraphrase and extend a statement of Georg Lukács's, 'the problem of the present', and concomitantly the autoperception of one's modernity, is inescapably apprehended as a material and 'historical problem', however indirectly that may come to be *represented* (1972, 157). As the example of Mr Tupman illustrates, there is no such thing as an unmediated vision. We should always be wary of *how* we see; we should look at the mechanisms by which we claim to produce a vision or image.

My next illustration shows this problematic effectively, specifically in terms of scientific discourse and the role of observation. In Chapter 38, we read of 'the scientific gentleman' and his observations. This scene again addresses the history of scientific discourse, empirical evidence, textual record, and the unreliability of narrative accounts of what one believes one has seen (*PP* 529–32). Boz's focus on the 'elderly gentleman of scientific attainments' (*PP* 529) directs our gaze away from the comic assignation between Mr Winkle and Arabella. This shift of attention effectively suspends the narrative movement with its own counter-narrative, but this is not the only suspension. Pausing in the act of writing and 'gazing abstractedly' into the night (*PP* 529), the 'scientific gentleman' is observed by the narrator 'observing' (*PP* 529) a series of apparently inexplicable lights, the 'appearances' of which 'had [n]ever been seen before' (*PP* 530). So the brief story of the scientific gentleman continues, with the words relating to sight and appearance dancing before the reader with as lively a frequency as the 'unparalleled appearances' of the enigmatic lights themselves: 'the scientific gentleman seized his pen again, and committed to paper . . . the date, day, hour, minute, and precise second at which they were visible . . . The mysterious light appeared more brilliantly than before . . . he rang the bell for his servant':

> 'Pruffle', said the scientific gentleman, 'there is something very extraordinary in the air to-night. Did you see that?' said the scientific gentleman, pointing out of the window as the light again became visible. (*PP* 530)

The frequency of Boz's comically irritating repetition of the phrase 'scientific gentleman' – it occurs eleven times in three pages – is itself a highly visible interruption, analogous with those flashing lights. Pruffle's assertion that the lights are probably signs of burglars is met with derision on the part of the 'scientific gentleman', who decides to leave his library (where he had been seated) in order to carry his research into the field; at which point the narrative returns to the misadventures of Mr Winkle.

Finally, the narration does return to its account of the scientific gentleman in the last paragraph of the chapter:

> As to the scientific gentleman, *he demonstrated in a masterly treatise that these wonderful lights were the effect of electricity*, and clearly proved the same by detailing how *a flash of fire danced before his eyes* when he put his head out of the gate, and how he received a shock which stunned him for a full quarter of an hour afterwards; which demonstration delighted all the

Scientific Associations beyond measure, *and caused him to be considered a light of science ever afterwards*. (*PP* 531–2; emphases added)

The obvious references to sight, vision, visibility, and observation aside, the conclusion moves from the conceit of the visible in relation to scientific and philosophical knowledge being lampooned here to a number of matters. These concern the materiality of writing and, implicitly, its inherent untrustworthiness either as a technique for visualization or for bearing witness to either evidence or experience, in the wake of unreliable subjective perception. The entire scene is one of reading and writing in fact. Through Boz's mediation, we witness a private moment of interrupted reflection and analysis on the part of the scientific gentleman who, 'seated in his library', is 'writing a philosophical treatise' and is caught 'in the agonies of composition' (*PP* 529). The narration concludes with the editorial recollection of the eventual production of 'a masterly treatise' (*PP* 531). Through the framing vignettes of the elderly gentleman doubt is raised as to the possible illumination that textuality can provide in the absence of materially verifiable visible objects or phenomena. As the passage illustrates, the interest has to do with textual transmission and, therefore, writing as translation of empirical evidence. The comic effects of showing the scientific observer as being in error shed a distancing, ironic light on the veracity of his own recordings, his written 'scientific' observations. Despite the necessity of recording history so as to remember the past and bear witness to it, or providing a written record as an account of the interpretation of empirical evidence, writing is far from being a reliable process; it is internally fraught. Such 'translation' destabilizes rather than fixes meaning, as the singular example of the lights' undecidability becoming the source of writing for the scientific gentleman, regardless of their true 'material' source, shows.

In this instance, the elderly observer might be seen as an uncanny double of Mr Pickwick. Of course, it is impossible to be certain that the 'scientific gentleman' is just such a double. It is, however, this very undecidability that makes this brief, quite literally 'unparalleled' appearance uncanny. The effect is all the more discernible, and the reading of doubleness somewhat more insistent, due to the anonymity of the 'elderly gentleman of scientific attainments'. While the anonymous gentleman 'delighted all the Scientific Associations beyond measure' (*PP* 532), Mr Pickwick's 'Observations on the Theory of Tittlebats' (which, like the scientific gentleman's publication, is designated a 'treatise' (*PP* 19)) 'agitated the scientific world' (*PP* 16). Also like his doppelgänger, Mr Pickwick is described as an 'elderly gentleman' (*PP* 400). There are several other 'elderly gentlemen' to whom the novel refers, and it is not too great an imaginative feat to consider that behind Mr Pickwick's anonymous double there is projected a world of elderly scientific gentlemen for whom meaning and identity, source and origin, are always undecidable.

From observing lights in motion in the dark, the scientific gentleman comes to 'see' those flashes of fire, the phenomena resulting from having been hit on the head accidentally. There is thus a motion of illumination that travels from empirical to subjective experience, from that which is observable with the naked eye to that which is not. We might also read this as a process of internalization of visualization, the motion of which charts certain historical movements from interest in phenomena in the world to those of the mind across the nineteenth century. That movement of illumination in this scene is of great interest, and warrants what I hope will not be taken as too unnecessary a digression.

While I am not suggesting any direct connection between Dickens and contemporary science, the comic concussion and its illuminating effects offer the reader a brief glimpse into the interests of scientific research in the nineteenth century concerning the physiology of the senses, particularly as that research related to matters of vision, physiological optics, and bioelectromagnetism. The principal researcher in this field was Johannes Müller (1801–58), whose understanding of vision and his 'notion of the observer [was] radically alien from that of the eighteenth century' (Crary 1990, 88). Müller, who had published 'two influential books on vision' (Crary 1990, 89) in 1826, discovered that a shock to the optic nerve 'produces the experience of light' (Crary 1990, 90). An entirely coincidental parallel between Dickens and Müller is to be found in the fact that both apprehend 'fundamentally arbitrary relation[s] between stimulus and sensation', and hence the capacity for the observing subject to '*misperceive*' because the eye 'renders differences equivalent' (Crary 1990, 90), of which we have ample evidence in *The Posthumous Papers of the Pickwick Club*.

However, such coincidence aside, it is not unfruitful to speculate that one possible or likely source, at least, for Dickens's elderly gentleman was Sir Humphry Davy (1778–1829). If not a model exactly for the old man, Davy at least can be read as providing the source for the Dickensian satire on the grounds of scientific research and 'proof'.

Known for his experiments with nitrous oxide, and also those in the field of electrochemistry, Davy experimented with electrical conductivity, as well as lecturing to the Royal Society in London on the subjects of light and heat, and observed that spontaneous electrochemical reactions can be used to generate electrical current, taking the form of light. His fascination with what he called the powers and properties of matter were systematized and published in his major work, *Elements of Chemical Philosophy* (1812). In this book, Davy gave attention to what he called 'etherial' or 'imponderable substances'. Of these he remarks:

> It cannot be doubted that there is matter in motion in space, between the sun and the stars and our globe, though it is a subject of discussion whether successions of particles be emitted from these heavenly bodies, or motions communicated by them, to particles in their vicinity, and transmitted by successive impulses to other particles. *Etherial* matter differs either in its nature, or in its affections by motion; for it produces different effects; for instance, as radiant heat, and as different kinds of light. (Davy 1839, 45–6)

Arguably, Davy's definition of such substances accords with what the elderly gentleman believes he witnesses to be those 'unparalleled appearances'.

As a result of successive misapprehensions, Boz is able to chart a course from the external, empirical world and the unreliability of eyesight to the parody of enlightenment as a result of mistaken insight and mental illumination. From this occurrence, the old man is enabled to write that treatise, the result of which is his own 'translation', by which he becomes transformed into 'a *light* of science ever afterwards' (*PP* 532; emphasis added). From the enigma of empirical evidence to neurological disturbance, and from this to the doubtful illumination of faulty knowledge, whereby further scientific insights are seen – all take place through the fortuitous motions of writing enmeshed within the signs of the visual and visible. This internal, loosening play is not something that gradually comes to take place. Apropos the trope of vision, it is there from the beginning of the scene. It is there in the library as the scientific gentleman looks literally, and in vain, for inspiration to write. He looks repeatedly at the carpet, the wall, the ceiling and out of the window (*PP* 529). *Pickwick's* editor makes the twinned processes of suspension and observation highly visible. Subsequently, the reader comes to see the suspension, a moment in time caught reiterating itself. For we are informed about, and thus invited to visualize, the elderly gentleman who, in attempting to write, is caught in the act, *'ever and anon* moistening his clay and his labours' (*PP* 529; emphasis added). This instance of syllepsis relies on the slipperiness that ensues from the performative operation of the verb, as at the same time the repeated application to alcohol in a 'venerable-looking bottle' (*PP* 529) is sought in order to make the writing 'flow', as it were. That writing cannot be turned on like a faucet is given evidence in the implications of the phrase 'ever and anon'.

That prosopopoeic synecdoche for spectral legions of amateur researchers of independent means of whom we have just been reading, the 'elderly gentleman of scientific attainments', is associated with light and with illumination, then, in a number of ways. What is most illuminating about this anonymous figure's presence is that it coincidentally brings to light one dimension of the historicity of bourgeois male life across the long eighteenth and nineteenth centuries. One telegraphic way of signalling such a history would be to remark the trajectory of identity *from Hooke to Davy*, to which construction Samuel Pickwick provides another example. Mr Pickwick himself publishes treatises. One 'paper' to which we are referred is the already mentioned '*Speculations* on the Source of the Hampstead Ponds, with Some *Observations* on the Theory of Tittlebats' (*PP* 15; emphases added). The title of Mr Pickwick's paper serves as an oblique synecdochic indication of the historical and cultural identity out of which Mr Pickwick emerges and in which historical composite he is situated. Reading anamorphically, the title places Samuel Pickwick, however wryly, ironically or comically, as a material product of cultural history, itself the articulation of a particular national identity. Pickwick's title marks him as being encoded and, perhaps, *riven* by philosophical, scientific, and ideological discourses, developed from the 1660s to the early nineteenth century. Read in this light, we witness Samuel Pickwick being produced as the typical educated 'modern' bourgeois English subject.[6] Dickens's novels 'dramatize . . . the constructedness of bourgeois subjectivity', founded as they are 'on a deep awareness of the instability of class identification and of identity as a process of fissure and projection' (Bodenheimer 2001, 216). And this is nowhere more illuminatingly, though sporadically, attested than in the iterable shadowy play of optical and visual figures, their work and their distortions, as these can be traced to particular discourses.

As the encrypted signs of the novel and science might give us to understand, from Defoe to Scott, or from Hooke to Davy, Pickwick and *Pickwick* are available to our reading as singular constructs of the intellectual life of the post-Civil War English middle classes, from the 1660s to the 1830s. They figure the contest of voices and the contrasting images that these envision, in the invention of one particular manifestation of gendered Englishness. Class, gender, and national identity converge through the editorial focalization of Boz, in however estranged a fashion. One thus senses through such singular comic examples the chance illumination of a discontinuous network or relay. Representation itself is represented in a historical perspective, and we are invited to look at how we see the scene. What do we see? We glimpse through that historical parallax beyond the individual examples a way of life; with that we obtain a view of amateur interests, wherein is to be seen the articulation of one symptomatic appearance of Englishness. With this, and the (indirectly) inferred, analogous connection between Pickwick and his anonymous doppelgänger – both of them 'anachronistic contemporar[ies] of a generation past or to come' (Derrida 2004b, 6; translation mine) – there opens to the imagination's gaze the comic perspective of countless bachelorresearchers, diminishing across a number of generations, communicating and miscommunicating.

To summarize then: it is *as if* Dickens stages an encoded historicized view of the national character of a peculiarly English enlightenment and its modern emergence, dating not from the Cartesian cogito but – to give it provisional moments of inauguration and invention and then conclusion – from the microscopic work of Hooke, arriving at Humphry Davy's electrochemical experiments. Such identity is marked by what Peter Ackroyd has termed a 'novel self-consciousness' (Ackroyd 1993, 13), the signs of which are still readable in *The Pickwick Papers*. The definition, illustrating the legacy of a now anachronistic modernity, 'which has exerted a powerful force since its inception' (Ackroyd 1993, 13), might be said to run as follows: to be English is to get things wrong, often hopelessly and comically so. But it is to get things wrong in just the same way as everyone else, who is just like you – and so to communicate a differentiated heterogeneous identity through analogous forms of miscommunication. In this 'dark glass' one sees oneself reflected and refracted. Thus one becomes convinced that the meaning of one's being is true and correct in a selfreading which is also a misreading, albeit one that is productive.

In *The Posthumous Papers of the Pickwick Club* 'experience . . . emerges as a concept of value' (Ackroyd 1993, 16) – and it is this, amongst other signs, which signifies a certain English modernity stretching from the seventeenth to the nineteenth century. Yet experience in *Pickwick*, despite placing the modern male, bourgeois subject at the centre of knowledge and the world, is always caught up with empirical observation, and in this way invariably leads to chaos. There is neither History as Grand Narrative nor the Transcendental Ego in a Pickwickian universe. Experience leads to misunderstanding, to misdirected communications, communications that are not understood correctly or at all, and to the perpetuation and iteration of a self-conscious act of seeing oneself *that fails to see how one sees*. Through the serious play of language Boz creates this reflection on the distortions of misperception as the articulation and maintenance of the phantasmic survival of a particular dimension of Englishness. Life, in this case that of Samuel Pickwick, as narrative trajectory serves as envisioned synecdoche. Articulating implicitly from within itself a cultural imperative to bear witness, it demands that we read the traces of the other within ourselves despite or perhaps because of miscommunications. In its composition from the traces of the past, life as narrative allows a recognition of similarity and difference, all the while expressing the injunction 'do not forget' (to borrow a significant memorial trace from *Little Dorrit*). That distance effected through the comedy of miscommunication authorizes the reader's memories of the past in a specific form. Cultural memory is positioned inside anecdote, vignette, intertextual allusion, and reference. Thus writing's 'distortion' of vision's already distorted images affords the reader a 'smoke-screen memory that . . . removes that which is too close to give us the illusion of perspective' (Augé 2004, 19). In its comic differentiating mode of projection and re-presentation that gives the illusion of being at a remove from the fictional events of the previous decade, *Pickwick* foregrounds its estranged (because distanced) life-as-narrative through 'remembrance-pictures' (Augé 2004, 21). From the unseen posthumous papers through the semi-visible editorial intervention, writing is always materially there to produce the illusion of perspective. *The Pickwick Papers* thus affects us through the return of involuntary memory of a culture in passing as illuminated through the life of a single character, in this case Samuel Pickwick, as he passes through countless *spectacles* of the cultural life, the cultural being, of the nation.

Vision and knowledge

Pickwick is a virtual catalogue of the passing of particular social behaviours. It presents itself as a phantasmagoria or, perhaps, a zoetrope[7] (lit. 'wheel of life') of passing social spectacle. Like the zoetrope, *Pickwick* is caught up in 'a much larger and denser organization of knowledge and the observing subject' (Crary 1988, 30–1). Stepping down from his chair in the Pickwick Club in the first chapter in order to take part in the 'wheel of life', Samuel Pickwick affords the reader various views of Englishness in spectacular motion. Although there is not the space to discuss these at any length, a brief overview can be offered. We see balls and soirées (*PP* 20–46, 494–505). There are representations of the medical profession, journalism, the arts (*PP* 197–210), non-conformist gatherings (*PP* 429–44), the courts, and the legal profession (*PP* 402–17, 445–67); the reader is taken inside and given a sustained view of the Fleet debtor's prison (*PP* 544–611). We witness political life and the processes of gerrymandering, as represented by Dickens's satire of the Eatanswill by-election (*PP* 165–81). An 'old-fashioned Card Party' (*PP* 80–93) is depicted, as is a duel (*PP* 20–46), cricket matches (*PP* 93–106), hunting (*PP* 93–106, 245–58), weddings and Christmas gatherings (*PP* 360–80). With a little temporal give and take, it is arguable that the scenes could belong to any moment in a seventy- or eighty-year span, from the 1740s (at least) to the 1820s. We come to see, to feel even, an odd untimeliness to the representation of such occasions. However, in presenting to the reader's view such a series of cultural spectacles from the perspective of Mr Pickwick and his friends, Boz allows the reader a 'regained impression' of Englishness and thus a 'return to oneself' (Augé 2004, 68). This regained impression endures through an auto-identification that is staged by the text and is what *Pickwick* makes possible in its opening to a past that is not merely representational but also intertextual. For the indirect allusions to and memories of other texts are also the signs of the revenance of the regained impression that causes *Pickwick* and thus the reader to identify themselves with their pasts, but with the necessity of remarking difference from that past.

The double vision that accompanies the marking of difference offers an important mode of historicization: 'As a novelist Dickens was striving for a historical vision, attempting to ride along with the movement of history, straining *to see* the past more clearly in order *to envision* the future' (Palmer 1997, 94; emphases added). Such vision refuses to distinguish in *Pickwick* between 'major and minor' events and so seeks to communicate the idea that 'nothing that has ever happened should be regarded as lost to history' (Benjamin 1940; 2003, 390). However, this is a communication doomed to fail, like so many communications in *Pickwick*. For while it has been argued that

The Posthumous Papers 'carries a redemptive, almost millenarian message' (Rainsford 1997, 103; see Rosenblum 1986, 47–54), one in which historical discourse is a mode 'always open to change, to evolution, to perfectability' (Palmer 1997, 171), humanity for Boz has not yet been redeemed; this remains to come. Boz may turn his eyes to the past; he may wish to linger. But he is driven irresistibly into the future to which he speaks, seeking to drive his readers in that direction also. Such double sight, the act of looking in two directions at once, is intrinsic to *Pickwick*'s vision.

In focusing throughout this study on the odd, insistent recurrence of figures of sight, vision, visualization, and so on in *Pickwick*, I have situated a series of questions. Though already asked, and in part answered, they should now be restated. Why do these motifs, figures, metaphors and forms of *seeing* occur and recur, and why do they keep coming and going, taking place in that *now* of the novel's publication in the 1830s? What, if anything, have the various figures of the visible to do with the act of narration, and, specifically, narration – and by extension the novel – as it undergoes transformation in the early nineteenth century as a result of external forces affecting modes of literary production? What do the visual and visible, sight and observation have to do with that strange notion of 'history', or with historical event, date, or fact, especially in the very singular example of a text that might best be described as articulating 'historicity without history – historicity without reference to actual occurrences but only exposure of its field' (Fenves 1993, 76)? What is the novel's relationship to both its present and its pasts, to the histories of the culture from which it arrives, and how? Finally, if, as Sam Weller comments at his master's trial, we only have eyes, albeit a pair, how can we 'see' and so bear witness to that which is no longer available to our view, without the aid of some technology?

The answer to this last question is of course that we cannot, nor do we ever, simply see. As *The Pickwick Papers* makes blindingly obvious, there is no sight without the possibility of either interpretative interruption or interference. Any sight claiming unmediated veracity is to be distrusted if only because there is no single perspective, as all the examples of eyes watching other eyes watching others inform us. History, the past, these are no longer available to us in any unmediated form. Understanding this, we understand at least the early Victorians' perception of their moment in relation to their pasts. The problem of vision admits also to 'aberrations' of translation and its uncontrollable effects produced by the anachrony of the trace. As the diminishing glass or compound microscope finds a world in solution, so too does Boz through *Pickwick*'s vision. The vignettes of the embedded narratives demonstrate this economically. As they project themselves into the foreground and the present moment of the narrative, thereby suspending the present and presence through the revenance of the traces of the past, so we witness the event and, simultaneously, we are *in* the experience. Writing, as a form of tele-technology or telecommunication enabling the transition from the invisible to the visible, brings about the transition from empirical absence to virtual, specular, and spectral presence, thereby intervening in historical loss.

Writing thus is forced to operate historically through a very specific kind of fiction, which is caught in the phrase *as if*: as if, for example, we could see or visit, or have returned to us the 1820s; as if Mr Pickwick and his friends were, if not alive, then having the capacity at least of returning briefly as ghostly illuminations through the spirit-medium of the 'editor-effect' or editorial projection machine. As Jacques Derrida has remarked, 'the *as if*, the fiction, the *quasi-*, these are what protect us from the real event of death itself, if such a thing exists' (Derrida 1996b, 217). At the same time, though, the fiction of the *as if* which 'protects' us is double-edged. For it reminds us that we are implicated in that historical movement that anticipates our own becoming-posthumous. The modernity of *The Pickwick Papers*, that modernity we now name Victorian, is signalled in its acknowledgement of the materiality and temporality of being; and if we receive the novel at all, we receive it not simply as a collection of comic misadventures, but also as a heterogeneous collection of *memento mori*. Or, as the title has it, *posthumous papers*.

Notes

1. On the literary and cultural interest in the 'Cockney' as urban phenomenon in the 1820s and 1830s, see Dart (2003, 203–23).
2. Seymour was replaced initially by R. W. Buss, whose work was unsatisfactory as far as Dickens was concerned. Buss was subsequently replaced by Hablot K. Browne, who was, in the guise of 'Phiz' to Dickens's 'Boz', to remain Dickens's principal illustrator for over twenty years.
3. See Marlow (1985, 939), for the comparison of Dickens with Sterne; Jacqueline Simpson offers a sharp comparison between Smollett and Dickens (463); Juliet McMaster comments on the comparison between Pickwick and Don Quixote (1983, 595). Other articles addressing the Pickwick–Quixote

relationship are Gale (1973, 135–56), Potau (1993, 105–10), and Easson (2002, 173–88).

4. To take one example, the title page of Richardson's *Clarissa* (1747–48), proclaims that it is 'published by the editor of PAMELA'.

5. Elizabeth Deeds Ermath remarks on *Pickwick*'s indebtedness to the picaresque tradition (1997, 36), while J. Hillis Miller observes of the novel's 'Victorian picaresque' that it is 'more akin to [Smollett's] *Peregrine Pickle*' and that 'it seems to be purely in the manner of the eighteenth-century novel' (1958, 22). Miller also comments, however, and rightly so, that *Pickwick*, 'so closely linked to eighteenth-century optimism, is really a farewell to the eighteenth century' (1958, 34). In his introduction to the novel, Mark Wormald outlines some of the literary and cultural antecedents on which Dickens draws, while also acknowledging the 'eighteenth-century picaresque fiction Dickens grew up with' (*PP* xiv). For a philosophical contextualization of *Pickwick* in relation to eighteenth-century thought, see William Palmer on the influence of Shaftesbury and Shaftesbury's influence on mid-eighteenth century novelists, particularly Sterne, on the matter of sentiment (1997, 24–31).

6. On the historical constructedness of the male bourgeois subject and, with that, the notion of modernity, see Barker (1984), and de Bolla (1989). More generally, for arguments concerning the modernity of English identity as this is articulated between the late seventeenth century and the early nine-teenth century, see Colley (1992), Ackroyd (1993), Lucas (1990), Price (1999).

7. The zoetrope was invented by William Horner in 1834. The zoetrope allowed several viewers to watch its display simultaneously and, therefore, it admit-ted of multiple perspectives on the same scene. Its cylindrical drum used constant motion to create the illusion of motion. Whether or not Dickens was familiar with the zoetrope, the combination of motion and simultane-ously distinct perspectival locations in the machine's representation of life's 'circular' motions is certainly suggestive as a figure for the numerous circuits and journeys of *Pickwick*, with the narrative procession of spectacles.

2 'Our society': *Cranford*

Historicized sites of reading

Whereas *Pickwick* appears a largely masculine affair, its narrative strands seeming to wander wide, if not across the world (or even the nation) then at least across the South-East of England (with a brief foray to the Midlands), *Cranford's* sphere is obviously more circumscribed. In *The Pickwick Papers* men take tours, observe social behaviour in both individuals and groups, and get involved in local communities. Where women appear in Dickens's first novel, their movements are largely restricted to their immediate cultural and social spheres. In this, they are not that different from the women of Cranford. Despite this difference, though, both novels offer mediated visions of Englishness in transition. Gaskell and Dickens trace the ways in which identity is transformed, or has been changed in a relatively short historical period. Both novels approach the subject of national identity in transition in ostensibly similar ways. They utilize the distancing force of humour and comedy as a means by which to comment on social transformation, though this is where the resemblance ends, the comedy of each delineated in strikingly differentiated, singular ways. Such singularity, and such difference as that which allows us access to the singularity of each text respectively, has to do with the texts' perceptions of the cultural and historical inscriptions of gender in a web of relations concerning the historicity and materiality of English national identity. Yet between one singular vision and another, what comes to be reiterated while maintaining difference is that necessary mediation of social comedy in conjunction with sentiment, in order that the reader of fiction in the first half of the nineteenth century might come not only to see but also to feel his or her identity and historicity.

Published initially in Charles Dickens's *Household Words* between 1851 and 1853 (the same period during which John Ruskin was publishing his monumental *Stones of Venice*), *Cranford* concerns a small stratum of society in an equally small town from which

Gaskell's tale takes its name. Set in a relatively recent past, *Cranford* is not the only work by Gaskell in which the narrative recounted is of an earlier period than the time of its writing. *Wives and Daughters* is set in the 1820s, *Ruth* appears from internal evidence to take place in the same period as *Cranford*, and *Sylvia's Lovers* is, like Thomas Hardy's *The Trumpet Major*, a novel of the Napoleonic Wars. It is perhaps because of its narrow focus that *Cranford* has received relatively little attention from materialist and historicist critics, such as Catherine Gallagher and Raymond Williams. Yet, while Gaskell's industrial novels, *Mary Barton* and *North and South* for example, have garnered detailed critical attention as a result of their historical, social, and documentary quality, *Cranford* is Gaskell's 'most determined experiment in ethnographic narrative' (Knezevic 1998, 406). At the same time, it is also what Hilary Schor calls 'a woman writer's experiment with narrative, [as well as] an extended commentary on the ways women are taught to read cultural signs' (1989, 288). Taken from these perspectives, *Cranford* appears therefore as experimental in its intervention with both form and subject matter.

While the political past or the politics of the past are the subjects on which materialist criticism inevitably focuses, what becomes occluded are those narratives that do not foreground in any immediately direct fashion questions of political struggle, class representation, and so on. If today many readers of *Cranford*, male or female, cannot read the signs in all their complexity, indeed, if readers today cannot even begin to perceive the signs as signs, there is little wonder in this, given the dense web of encrypted historiographic signification that takes place in *Cranford* – and, it has to be added, in Cranford also. For both the novel and the town are sites of reading, and the community that reading both inclusively and exclusively constitutes. Such constitution is not merely social or culturally hierarchical; it is also forcefully historical in its nuances and inflections.

I make this double distinction – *Cranford* and Cranford – in order to take up both the formal and ethnographic concerns signalled in the readings of Schor and Knezevic, and also to attend to one of the more forceful, if occluded, modes of cultural and historical self-identification and determination in the text. It is important that we give attention equally to the narrative patterning or structure and the town for which the text serves as imaginative cultural map, and to the work of reading and narrative within both. How one reads, does not read, or fails to read is significant in *Cranford* and Cranford. For in the town acts of reading take place among a number of its habitants with a rapidity that is more than merely telegraphic; its velocity occurs with something akin to internet transmission, the rate of which is only slowed in being drawn to our attention by the narrator, Mary Smith, her consciousness, perception and acts of reading never being wholly of that system.

Generational sedimentation

As some readers will doubtless be aware, the narrative of the social stratum focuses on the events of everyday life for a group of middle-class women, either spinsters or widowed, and the intricately wrought details of social etiquette, manners, and the network of class-based behaviour and attitudes that inform their identities. Taking place for the most part between the 1830s and 1840s, *Cranford* is most precisely dated by death. Miss Deborah Jenkyns dies in 1843, even though her spirit persists thereafter. Captain Brown was 'killed by them nasty cruel railroads' (*C* 55). Immediately prior to the accident, it was reported that he was 'a-reading some new book' (*C* 55), which the reader already knows is *The Pickwick Papers*. Because of internal evidence in the chapter before the Captain's death, specifically Gaskell's reference to Chapter 36 of *Pickwick*, which Brown reads from the serial part, number 13, to Miss Deborah (*C* 47), we know that his death occurs after the thirteenth instalment and therefore in 1837. Railroads and modern literature collide in a particularly violent if somewhat grimly humorous fashion here, as so many signs of the times.

Gaskell's story thus charts the flows, confluences, and transitions of a passing generation of middle Englanders, mostly women who for the most part are as unaware of the forces of history as they are of people belonging to lower social stations – unaware, that is, until the force of history imposes itself more or less violently on their individual and collective lives. Such impositions range from the effects of maintaining colonial forces overseas, the transformations occasioned by the Napoleonic Wars, memories of the French Revolution, and the changes in situation and fortune brought about by unstable financial systems that affected the nation as a whole, to greater and lesser extents, throughout much of the first forty years of the nineteenth century. At the same time, smaller eddies and currents in the flow of history make themselves felt, as in the continuous interest evinced by the women around whom the tale circulates, concerning changing fashions, court news, and other matters of transitory social moment. These too, Gaskell would have us understand, are the traces of material culture, as significant for some as the greater historical incidents.

The location of the town in *Cranford* and the structural motions across its borders suggest that it is a backwater, a topographical site marked by cultural anachronisms that inform individual and collective identities, and that it is thus out of step with the larger, more modern world. The world of Cranford is one of a succession of contretemps – not only do struggles, unfortunate occurrences or remarks often occur, but also they are figuratively, if not literally, 'contre-temps': against, or not of the (historical) times. Indeed, it might even be argued, to push the point, that Cranford, its understanding of itself and the social and hierarchical relations that structure it, is as a whole caught up in a 'motion out of time'. (Hence the possibility of precise dating through the occurrences of death. The town is punctuated, countersigned if you will, by its very own instances of *memento mori*.) The town and its inhabitants to greater or lesser degrees exist in another sense of contretemps; which is to say, collectively they find themselves in disagreement with and positioned against the temporal motions of history, and the 'becoming-modern' of English culture. Against (*contre*) the times (*temps*) in which they find themselves, they are ill-equipped to understand, much less read, the signs of modernity. Already slipping into the past, Cranford is unaware on the whole that it is doing so and sees fault with modernity, although it does on occasion acknowledge change.

But if Cranford is out of time, if its inhabitants and their way of life are running out of time, their return via Mary Smith's narrative and Elizabeth Gaskell's short novel serves as its own *memento mori* to its Victorian readers: they also are marked historically, materially, by the signs of their culture, the culture that they determine as their own, but by which signs they are in turn produced. Thus it is that through a number of devices to be addressed in this chapter, the reader becomes aware of the historial disjunctions, as the narratorial voice commingles distinctions not only between external and internal worlds, but also between rational representations of the past and sympathetic or sentimental figurations. Additionally, what is seen as out of time, disjointed, discontinuous or disconnected serves in its anachronic narrative return to remind the reader of a 'now in common' that causes an intersection between worlds that is also an intercalation of the anachronic within the modern. For as much as there is signalled disjointing, discontinuity, or what Edmund Husserl might call the 'phenomenology of internal time consciousness' (1964) as mediated through the *then-and-now* of Mary Smith's narration, signals an intersection between the *then* of Cranford and the *now* of *Cranford*, between the moment of historical experience and that of subjective, temporal translation. Indeed, it is in the significant dismantling of the boundaries between the former and the latter, the *then* and the *now* as these are enacted in passing through the efface- ment of distinctions between modes of discourse, that the past is opened via multiple perspectives to the reader's view, without the assumption that there is either one or, indeed, a justifiably proper perspective of the past to be gained.

Peter Keating notes both small and great historical transitions and events, and the different perspectives they encourage, observing the attentive intricacy with which Gaskell weaves them together. Giving dates to the action of the narrative further encourages an apprehen- sion of the complexity. It is clear, for example, that the story of the Miss Jenkynses' parents' courtship and marriage in Chapter 5 takes place in the late eighteenth century, the two sisters growing up during the Napoleonic Wars. As Keating also comments, 'in 1805 Miss Jenkyns was old enough to visit friends in Newcastle' (Keating *C* 17). However, this, as Keating observes, provides 'only the most obvious framework' (*C* 17). For 'with precision and subtlety' Gaskell constructs a 'structure of references and allusions . . . to indicate the nature of social change in the early nineteenth century' that includes details of 'furniture, fashions, eating habits, ways of speaking, and books read', as these are 'filtered through the consciousness' of the narrator (*C* 17). Such a process of filtering is significant in this text, and the world of Cranford would not arrive without Mary Smith's consciousness. Her memory bears in it the chronological, topographical, and cultural marks, the historical and ideological 'spacing [of the vanishing world], with its social conventions and the history of its codes, with its fictions and its simulacra, [and] with its dates' (Derrida 1992, 421). Such transference is also captured in 'so-called proper names'. For, arguably, one of the more subtle signs of historical passage, or rather a lack thereof, is to be read in the spelling of the two sisters' surname, Jenkyns. With its *y* rather than the more common or modern *i* spelling, the very name and hence the identities to which it is appended would appear frozen at an earlier time. It serves as a signa- ture of its age, a simulacrum of a past no longer available.

Mary Smith visits Cranford on a regular basis, staying with the Jenkyns sisters, Deborah and Matilda (Miss Matty). Mary functions for the reader as a medium, in two ways at least. She mediates between the 'Amazonian' world (as she archly describes it) of Cranford and the outer world of the reader. At the same time her role is also temporal, for she mediates between the 'present' of narration (which present is indicated repeatedly if indirectly through temporal and historical allusion or reference) and the past of Cranford, as has been intimated already. That past is both the period of the narrator's visits, and also the implied and occasionally presented pasts of the women who make up Cranford society: the Misses Jenkyns, Miss Pole, Mrs Forrester, Mrs Jamieson, and this last lady's sister-in-law, Lady Glenmire. Mediation in the narrative between past and present results occasionally in tensions, and these are often of a cultural dialectical kind. The unresolved debate between Miss Deborah and Captain Brown (*C* 47–8) concerning the merits or lack thereof to be read comparatively between the works of Dr Johnson and Boz is a striking example of one such contretemps. More than a mere cultural clash, this is a contest between past and present, as Keating notes (*C* 17).

Keating's account is detailed, but I would like to expand a little on this. The Johnson/Boz contest is also undeniably a synecdochic and ontological debate concerning competing discursive constructions of manifestations of Englishness, which serves to acknowledge the historicity of national identity and one's being. Such a moment is not simply amusing, having a comic self-reflexiveness heightened by the location of *Cranford*'s initial publication in Dickens's *Household Words*. Gaskell's little bourgeois battle partakes of both a sense for 'the need to break completely with eighteenth-century literary models' (*C* 18) and, more broadly, a desire to break with the past. That Dickens is appointed the combatant for 'modern' English letters bespeaks a culture war peculiar to Victorian criticism and journalism (*C* 18), having to do with the question of stylistic propriety rooted in the persistent perception of Dickens's writing as, in Carlyle's happy phrase, 'Newspaper Cockney' (*C* 18). This last phrase signals also the implicit class struggle in the debate concerning the respective merits of Johnson and Boz.

To pause over the significance of this one scene for a moment: Hilary Schor gives an extended account of the debate over Johnson and Dickens, which highlights the problem of attending to the past, and how we read it if we read it at all, rather than accounting for it in somewhat presentist terms. An interesting and informative article, Schor's essay is nonetheless not wholly accurate in its somewhat dehistoricized account of Miss Deborah's writing style being based on that of Dr Johnson. Schor remarks that part of what is so absurd about Miss Deborah Jenkyns' writing is *simply* that it is in the wrong place: if she were an archdeacon and writing up charges . . . [her] Johnsonian sentences . . . would not seem inappropriate or pompous. Women have no room for the grand style in their writing . . . Literary daughters are not given the language they need. (Schor 1989, 294; emphasis added)

Although this is true to a degree it is not entirely true. Grounded in a moment of fictionalizing – *if* Miss Jenkyns were an archdeacon, and, therefore, a man – Schor's proposal erases the very real signs of that which is historically appropriate. There is nothing *simple* about the problem with which the reader is presented. Anachrony is much involved in the interrogation of location, as well as its concomitant destabilization. As inescapably accurate as the feminist reading is in a somewhat more general, idealizing or universalizing context,[1] nevertheless Schor situates her own argument within a historicized aporia. It is not only, or perhaps even necessarily, the case that Miss Deborah typifies or symbolizes the lack of a gendered literary voice. Instead, it is also, if not primarily, a matter of cultural anachronism. Johnsonian style is markedly out of time and out of place in the 1830s and 40s. If archdeacons have the time to write in such a style in these decades, journalists and commercial novelists do not. Boz mocks, thereby drawing attention to, one anachronistic style, the mock-epic, in the opening, paragraph-length sentence of *The Posthumous Papers of the Pickwick Club*. Such temporal disjointedness was undeniably recognizable to more literate readers of the 1840s and 1850s, whether male or female. Such style has no place in the present of the narrative, much less the present of the date of publication, and the absurdity arises from that.

That Gaskell can stage the debate at all suggests that, whether she is a 'literary daughter' or not, she has arguably invented a language of her own, however circumscribed or circumspect such a language may have been. (It might be asked: who would want *only* to inherit, in all its patrilinear implications, when one can translate the inheritance into something singular, and thus invent, thereby telling, in Mr Perker's words, 'the old story . . . with a difference'?) Irony, parabasis and apostrophe, in concatenated relation to the weaving of multiple historical and cultural threads, appears to give evidence to this, in all the detailed complexity of *Cranford*. As we shall see, a female narrative voice and mode does indeed emerge, albeit accidentally, in Gaskell's short novel. However, to return to the present argument, what Schor fails precisely to account for is as follows. As Peter Keating puts it:

> the many references to Johnson and modern literature are not . . . simply
> local in their significance, but serve to create a wider framework which can
> encompass both the passage of time and the changing nature of funda-
> mental attitudes and values, and the same is true of other kinds of histor-
> ical and social reference throughout the book. Cranford is a town besieged
> by forces it is incapable of understanding and ultimately of withstanding.
> There is no way in which it can adapt itself to the social transformation
> that will inevitably come. (C 21)

We may disagree with that 'fundamental' of Keating's; we may even
wish to remark – with knowledge of the manner of *Pickwick*'s registration of anachronism, the incapability of Pickwickian comprehension,
and the translation of the discourses and epistemologies of
Englishness in that novel – that the effects of the cultural and historical forces on notions of national identity grounded, caught up with,
and mediated by gender are not to be overlooked. But what is certain
is that any partial reading of historicity, or indeed a reading that
avoids as fully as possible an engagement with the materialist historiography that Gaskell charts, is, if not as culturally myopic as Miss
Deborah, then certainly as wrong-headed as Miss Pole, and so cannot
apprehend the singular translation of gendered identity charted in
Cranford.

Distinctions of class and period

The literary dialectic raises the issue of the encounter between past
and present, unveiling that temporal encounter as being a matter of
class negotiation also. The tension between classes is not restricted to
reading matter though, and nor is the example just considered the
only one in which literature as the arbiter of culture is featured. Class
and station are often at the heart of genteel anxiety in Cranford.
Again, the matter of ideological location-as-identity is doubly overdetermined through being intertwined with the strands of gender and
history. If location, whether in time or by class, is indicative of identity, then location is also dislocation, placement, displacement,
according to the instability that is revealed as being at the core of any
culturally constructed identity. In particular, class becomes an issue
when the future of one of the ladies, Lady Glenmire (the sister-in-law
of Mrs Jamieson), arises. Introduced as initially a temporary visitor to
the town, Lady Glenmire soon takes up residence, eventually to marry
Cranford's doctor, Dr Hoggins. Both the move and, more obviously,

the marriage are possible because of death once again, in this case one outside the narrative, that of Lady Glenmire's husband. (A fine cultural and national distinction is made when it is remarked of the late Lord Glenmire that he was only a 'Scotch Baron'.) This alliance is perceived socially more as a *mésalliance*, and much to the chagrin of the various ladies of the small social circle. In its downwardly social motion (at least as far as Cranford is concerned), such a marriage introduces mobility, however limited, acknowledging briefly and quietly the transition in the nineteenth century from concepts of station to those of class. Such movement draws the reader's attention once more to the interrelation between position, literature, gender, and the disturbing echolalia between past and present. Moreover, in this translation from station to class there is to be discerned also an opening to a future, for Lady Glenmire in any case, which cultural breach is not in thrall to the stasis of station where the present is merely an inflection or idiom of maintaining history's status quo. Class rather than station bespeaks mobility and indeterminacy, at least in principle. So too, does the matter of gender identity.

With the exception of Lady Glenmire's new husband, the doctor (of whom there is more to say), men of the middle and upper-middle classes are largely absent from *Cranford* – and, again, Cranford. This is as a result of either the demands of the world or those of death, again, as we have seen with the unfortunate example of Captain Brown. However, when a crisis occurs, occasioned by the ramifications for Cranford of the outer world's activities, men such as 'Poor Peter' or 'Aga Jenkyns', as Miss Matty's brother is variously known in the family, or the strikingly anonymous businessman, Mary's father Mr Smith, arrive to ease the difficulties or otherwise make possible solutions. And to offer a last comment on the representation of masculinity in the novel, apropos the constant oscillation between present and past: men who arrive or return from the past or are otherwise of it, such as Peter, Captain Brown, or even 'Signor Brunoni' are, to say the least, 'colourful'. Gaskell allows these idiomatic figures a degree of agency, if not freedom, in the articulation of their identities. This may have to do with their having been soldiers, and so removed from domestic English culture. While a degree of motion and latitude is afforded certain men, the gender divide is not so simple, or simply drawn, however.

It is as if particular men such as Peter, the Captain, and the Signor are themselves out of time, their anachrony signalled in their not exactly excessive but, say instead, ex-centric identities. This is true of

no male so much as Mr Holbrook. His ex-centricity places him both
out of time and out of Cranford culture. Furthermore, his 'eccentric-
ity' is very much a matter of refusing to conform to, and thereby
resisting any sign of modernization or adaptation to, the nineteenth
century. Mr Holbrook, a cousin of Miss Pole's and estimated by her at
the time of the narrative to be approximately 70, is first mentioned in
Chapter 3. The title of the chapter – 'A Love Affair of Long Ago' –
announces not only the past and the possibility of a narrative
recounting that past, but also a tension between sentiment and
history, the emotional and the rational. As Mary Smith tells us, he had
once proposed to Miss Matty. Holbrook is pointedly, self-referentially,
anachronistic, and in a particularly English way. As his insistence on
being referred to as a yeoman suggests, he apprehends his identity as
synecdoche for a larger collective historical and organic sense of
Englishness 'rooted' as it were in the soil. The first image of Mr
Holbrook appears not with his appearance in the novel but through a
relay of narratives, and is worth presenting in full:

> It seems that Miss Pole had a cousin, once or twice removed, who had
> offered to Miss Matty long ago. Now this cousin lived four or five miles
> from Cranford on his own estate; but his property was not large enough
> to entitle him to rank higher than a yeoman; or rather, with something of
> the 'pride which apes humility,' he had refused to push himself on, as so
> many of his class had done, into the ranks of the squires. He would not
> allow himself to be called Thomas Holbrook, *Esq.*; he even sent back letters
> with this address, telling the post-mistress at Cranford that his name was
> Mr Thomas Holbrook, yeoman. He rejected all domestic innovations; he
> would have the house door stand open in summer and shut in winter,
> without knocker or bell to summon a servant. The closed fist or the knob
> of a stick did this office for him if he found the door locked. He despised
> every refinement which had not its root deep down in humanity. If people
> were not ill, he saw no necessity for moderating his voice. He spoke the
> dialect of the country in perfection, and constantly used it in conversa-
> tion; although Miss Pole (who gave me these particulars) added, that he
> read aloud more beautifully and with more feeling than any one she had
> ever heard, except the late rector. (*C* 69)

This tale of one of Cranford's 'anachronistic contemporaries' warrants
little further explication. It is worth noting, however, that his image
is connected not only to others of his class, but also to generations of
that class, through relation to the land and by title. Holbrook
consciously eschews the modern, and his resistance to 'fashion' highlights aspects of both behaviour and speech, as if to illustrate that

etiquette and discourse are themselves markedly historical and have histories. When it comes time for dinner at Holbrook's, 'pudding' is served before the meat, which gives Holbrook a reason for criticizing what he calls 'new-fangled ways' and the 'new fashion'. This he adamantly rejects, observing that he does as he did when he was a young man, which was to 'keep strictly to [his] father's rule' (*C* 74). To Holbrook, modernization in table manners and order is topsy-turvydom (*C* 74). As the last sign of old-fashioned table manners, Holbrook uses only two pronged forks, his guests obliged to eat their peas using the flat of their knife blades (*C* 74–5). As in the case of other passages in *Cranford*, what is implied about broader social relations and the cultural determination of identity offers a fascinating glimpse of a complex web of related threads and clues as to the historicity of Englishness.

What is less immediately observable though is that Holbrook's anachronistic identity is related to literature and literary transmission from this first impression. He refuses to receive what he takes to be misdirected letters – in the sense that how his identity is constituted through the address to him as an 'esquire' is misdirection; he thus defines himself through a refusal to be determined as a modern addressee, thereby affirming his identity as one belonging to the past. The 'literary' aspect of Miss Matty's old suitor is further confirmed on Mary Smith's first encounter with him; for she describes him as 'a tall, thin, Don Quixote-looking old man' (*C* 70), an impression that is confirmed later, on a visit to Holbrook's: 'He looked more like my idea of Don Quixote than ever' (*C* 73). Holbrook's 'literary' character is further extended when, on taking Mary for a walk around his grounds, she learns that his 26 cows are named each for a letter of the alphabet. As they walk, Holbrook cites poets, 'from Shakespeare and George Herbert to those of our own day' (*C* 73) 'He did this', Mary Smith reflects, '*as naturally as if he were thinking aloud*' (*C* 73; emphasis added). It is as if Thomas Holbrook is composed by the English literature from the sixteenth to the nineteenth centuries, and that his identity is therefore doubly constituted. On the one hand, his is an identity structured by a historical and cultural relation to the agrarian identity of England. On the other hand, Holbrook is 'written', as it were, projected from and inscribed by an English poetics.

However, within its ideological matrix or collective idioculture *Cranford* ultimately rejects the individualist incursions of particular men. As was the case with the Captain, Mr Holbrook dies shortly after he is introduced into *Cranford*; it is as if exposure to the nineteenth century can prove fatal. This I would argue does not take place from a politics of gender. There is obviously a politics of gender to be read from the narrative that is related to the modes of cultural representation. What I am describing, though, as a resistance to men, or specific men at least, is readable as a result of another mode of rejection, pertaining to what may, perhaps hastily, be termed Romantic individualism, or certainly to any perceived relation between masculinity and leisure, as in cases such as those of Mr Holbrook. As may be seen, men such as Peter, the Captain, Mr Holbrook, and the Signor belong to other times than the 1840s. It is therefore not so much a resistance to masculinity on the part of the genteel female inhabitants of Cranford, as yet another of those signs of the times, that the early Victorian world has no time for men who have time to spare on matters other than business or the world at large, unless there are exigent circumstances such as family distress (the justification for Aga Jenkyns's return). In itself an outmoded, anachronistic ideology, Romantic individualism is only figured by those men who have escaped the web of Victorian culture such as Aga Jenkyns, and it will not quite do for a communal spirit. At the same time, however, Gaskell is not wholly acquiescent to the commercial future of Victorian England as captured in the image of Mr Smith (as I will have occasion to discuss shortly). In between these two poles Cranford is poised, ideologically and historically. Gaskell seeks, in Terry Eagleton's words, to 'resolve a structural conflict between [the] two forms of mid-Victorian ideology' (1978, 111). This perhaps allows us insight into the interpolation of what is clearly a narrative overdetermined by multiple contemporary concerns and anxieties of the 1850s into the two decades prior to this, the 1830s and 40s. Such a struggle does not find its only articulation in *Cranford*. As Eagleton has observed, it marks the trajectory between Gaskell's two industrial novels, *Mary Barton*, published in 1848, and *North and South* (1855).

Cranford is clearly concerned, then, with the exploration of a crisis of representation in all its historical resonances as it takes place at the heart of the social locus in a specific historical moment, with the coronation of a new monarch and the equally novel event of commercial transport and adventures in publishing. Yet, if the arrival of the outside world and, with that, implications concerning the arrival of certain futures (the railway and Dickens are but two tropes of this historical imminence) announce motion or instability as well as corporate transformation, that is not to say such movement will be endless, or is understood by Gaskell in this manner. A different future is coming, and with that a different stasis. While Peter Jenkyns is either 'Poor Peter' or 'Aga Jenkyns', Signor Brunoni is both this name and Samuel Brown; he is doubled further by his stage costume and having a twin brother. Neither Peter nor Signor Brunoni is in business, however. The modernity of business practice, apprehended and represented for the most part indirectly, is shown economically with only the briefest allusions or representations with regard to men and not in the abstract. Certainly modern economics can have no truck with the excess of two names or doubled identities. The representation of *homo economicus* is more or less limited to Mary's father, through which synecdochic figure business is understood to curtail effectively the possibilities of motion and mutability of the more adventurous masculine identities. Mr Smith does not have the luxury of free time, not even to compose a letter in Johnsonian style. Of the one letter that he writes Mary remarks, 'my father's was *just a man's letter*; I mean it was very dull, and gave no information beyond that he was well, that they had had a good deal of rain, that trade was very stagnant, and there were many disagreeable rumours afloat' (*C* 172; emphasis added).

Beginning with that cultural code identifying the gender of the writer through the content of the writing, Mary Smith continues to translate its contents, which come down, in telegraphic fashion that presumably duplicates the writer's own brevity, to the weather, economics, and discourse on business practice, expression for the Victorian businessman being circumscribed by that practice. Today, this coded representation of the modern male sounds like a paradigmatic sketch of the middle-class English man of business, lasting from the 1840s at least until the 1970s, and the *Monty Python's Flying Circus* parody of the merchant banker who cannot recall his name but, in his pinstripe and bowler hat, knows that his identity is that of a merchant banker.

Then, the reader is told that the letter turns to pragmatic concerns to do with Miss Matty's shares. Brevity and erasure of identity are not restricted to the letter. Even Mr Smith's very name is suitably economic and generic, as dull as his letters (but equally as revealing). Much like the twentieth-century Japanese term 'salaryman', the name bespeaks anonymity and, contiguously, the erasure of personality; and with that of course the absence of singularity and the lack of chance for change. In that, once more there appears to be available the sign of a conformity to the restrictions of middle-class business and economics, which yet again the female inhabitants of Cranford are either at odds with, or of which they remain unaware. Again, they figure collectively a culture of contretemps. Lack of awareness may of course have its own temporary benefits. Allowing us to perceive such absence of insight, Gaskell invites us to consider different perspectives, viewpoints that are decidedly other than those of a figure such as Mr Smith, who is perhaps the synecdochic cipher *par excellence* for apprehending the modern world outside Cranford.

But to return to the doctor, and with that the matter of literature. In his own right, Dr Hoggins, a professional man but not 'in trade', serves the function of announcing the shift from station to class, albeit in a relatively small manner, as has been indicated. Through yet another sign of cultural location indirectly signalled, Dr Hoggins's lack of social station is wanting in the eyes of the ladies of Cranford. This 'failure' or 'lack' is recorded through it being remarked that he has not read what is regarded as the appropriate literature to have 'raised' his manners, and thus his acceptability. However, the literature in question – *Lord Chesterfield's Letters* (1774) – is decidedly anachronistic. Note the detailed and delicate ideological filigree work in the following remark of Mary Smith's: 'As a surgeon we were proud of him; but as a man – or rather, I should say, as a gentleman – we could only shake our heads over his name and himself, and wished that he had read Lord Chesterfield's Letters in the days when his manners were susceptible of improvement' (*C* 154). Once more, the reification of ideology as class position is achieved – and mystified – through reference to literary acculturation or its absence. Mary's stumbling correction remarked in the parenthetical interpolation that substitutes the more precise yet encrypted notion of *gentleman* for *man* is bound to the first-person collective pronoun serving as a metonymic figure for Cranford society. That *we* operates both as inclusion and exclusion. What is odd, though not wholly so, is Mary's apparent inclusion of herself into that society. Is it ironic or not? Does Mary approve of Chesterfield's letters? Or is she parodying through imitation received opinion, which in itself echoes with the earlier pronouncements of Miss Deborah in the Boz/Johnson war? We cannot tell. So, the work of figure – like that of the Amazons by which Mary figures the genteel female circle (otherwise 'holders of houses, above a certain rent') of Cranford (*C* 39) – remains undecidable, implying minute adjustments, negotiations not only of inclusion and exclusion but also between inner and outer worlds and sites, and differing temporal locations that are to be read as being woven, as well as weaving and unravelling the entirety of the text.

Dr Hoggins's lack of reading offers a telling if tangential insight apropos the earlier discussion of gender, literature, and historicity. Chesterfield's *Letters*, published in 1774 and a hugely successful best-seller (Brewer 1997, 178),[2] were already being read, and mocked by some of the younger generation at least in 1775, as Lydia Languish reveals (Act I, Scene II) in Richard Brinsley Sheridan's *The Rivals* written and performed in that year. In order to deceive her aunt, Mrs Malaprop, as to her behaviour and obedience, Lydia pretends to be reading the *Letters* on a visit from her relative. Her taste is more for sentimental literature, however, borrowed from a circulating library, and extends to works such as *The Man of Feeling*, *A Sentimental Journey*, *The Innocent Adulterer*, and the novels of Tobias Smollett. On hearing of her aunt's arrival, Lydia tells her servant Lucy to hand her the Chesterfield and to 'fling' *Peregrine Pickle* and *Roderick Random* under the toilet and into the closet respectively. If Chesterfield is already being mocked by some at least only a year after publication, then the somewhat outdated propriety to which Cranford ladies aspire (who would be, if not of the same generation, then only a little younger than Lydia Languish) is of a very provincial, petit-bourgeois nature. (Comparisons between Gaskell and Austen suggest themselves quite forcefully here. One might wish to consider the Misses Jenkyns as near contemporaries of Elinor and Marianne Dashwood.) Comprehending this, and bearing in mind the historical dimension, the issues of class position, social change, anachronism, and the ephemerality of authority come ever more sharply into focus here in all their historicizing complexity.

One of the few men hovering always in the wings of Cranford, Dr Hoggins is therefore considered necessary, albeit a little *déclassé* as a result of his profession, name and lack of perceived culture – and this despite the fact that his sister is a Fitz-Adam and therefore a woman of some family and connection – at least as far as the surname might be taken to signify according to one of the Cranford circle. The very idea of family as used by the ladies of Cranford is itself old-fashioned and out of date, having the conservative and traditional sense of expansiveness suggesting large, landed clans. Yet such perceptions of the doctor as we are given insight into are not to be taken as the law for which they intend themselves, and by the perpetuation of which conservative 'cultural fables' (as Laura Brown calls them: 2001, 1) social order attempts to fix its own image. In this image is an act of self-reading as misreading within Cranford. Gaskell once more draws together the various threads of culture, ideology, perception, manners, and the comparative presentation of past literary standards and the apparently lapsarian present, in order to stitch and at the same time unravel an intricate social image.

To understand Gaskell's engagement in this simultaneous double motion of intertwining and unlacing is to admit not only to a formal condition. It is also to apprehend, in distinction from its subject matter, a *way* of working, a performative effect no less appropriate to the historical, cultural, and temporal moment of literary production. In this operation, the literary mode of production arrives in synecdochic relationship to other modes of production contemporaneous with the publication of *Cranford*. Such modes of production may not be necessarily those of nineteenth-century industry (although an argument could be put forward for an analogical comparison of relation between non-identities, relation without relation); they are, however, those of nineteenth-century culture, and the various discursive, subjective and material articulations of the ideological and social fabric that today we name 'Victorian'. For *Cranford* enacts in its form, often at odds with its content, what Laura Brown describes as 'a broadened and complicated definition of the culture . . . generated collectively . . . over a period of time' (2001, 2). *Pace* Miss Deborah Jenkyns and also the haunting prescriptions of Dr Johnson and Lord Chesterfield, *Cranford* as text emerges as a cultural fable 'fundamentally tied to a specific aspect of material culture, imaginatively shaping, registering or reflecting upon the experience of historical change condensed in that material phenomenon' (Brown 2001, 3). If we recognize this, and with that the gap between Elizabeth Gaskell and Mary Smith along with all that the perception of such a fissure implies, we understand literary engagement as cultural estrangement, and the literary text in its guise of cultural fable as a contemporary 'tool [or perhaps machinery] of demystification'. The fable as agent of demystification is effective to the extent that it cannot be ordered, programmed, or presented according to rational, logical, or hierarchical models (Brown 2001, 3). Rather it relies on the transmission of the fictional trope to make us feel its insights.

Singularity and exemplarity

Singularity and *exemplarity* therefore: where every example, in exemplifying, will necessarily differ from every other, and so affirm its difference, its *singular difference*. While in *The Posthumous Papers of the*

Pickwick Club, Dickens – or Boz, at least – had been at pains to maintain the visibility of the staging mechanisms by which any naturalized perspective on the past might be estranged, in *Cranford* Gaskell occludes the very devices and mechanisms of historical – and historicized – re-presentation by which, seemingly paradoxically, it effects the work of demystification. I hasten to add that this assessment is not to be misunderstood as implying that Gaskell may be read necessarily as producing a narrative that offers the illusion, through teleological retrospect of history and narrative, as a seamless, undifferentiated continuity. Discontinuities and tensions are to be read as we have already intimated, although reading takes place from different places. Like Dickens, as already attested, Gaskell projects a narrative of Englishness in all its historicity from an understanding of the necessary work of memory in response to the heterogeneity of history and society, as well as their traces, rather than through the devices of a merely rational, mimetic, or empirically governed recounting. In this, she marks a space between the mode of her narrative and not only the past but also the past in literature, chiefly through comedy and sentiment, wit and sensibility.

As was remarked in the previous chapter, the details that make up Englishness and representations of the past or English society cannot be classified because they are, in Gaskell's phrase (taken from 'The Last Generation in England'), of a 'heterogeneous nature' (LGE 319). Gaskell's modes of estrangement, defamiliarization and destabilization are thus produced in a distinctly different fashion from Dickens's, although both writers rely on what Timothy Clark has called in his discussion of singularity 'the place of the literary in relation to the nature of the social bond, i.e. . . . . the tensions between the uniqueness of each individual existence and the demands of communal life' (Clark 2005, 125). The grounds of images of national identity are carried, communicated, if at all, through the historical transmission of literature and its translation. In this each text projects a reader capable of receiving such a translation. What distinguishes Boz from Mary Smith as fictive functions is that while the former makes claims repeatedly concerning the undecidability of what he reads, the latter risks interpretation while inviting us to feel as she feels. The difference perhaps comes down to the *tone* of feeling, if I can put it like this. For Boz, feeling historically is a matter of mourning; for Mary Smith it is a question of survival through ephemeral celebration. If the past is always to be parodied in *Pickwick* then that past runs the risk of being rendered the same in every imaginative intervention. If, however, everything that makes up Englishness is truly 'heterogeneous', to recall Gaskell's phrase, then it is not available to governance.

Understanding this about Gaskell leads us to apprehend that she asks the following questions, albeit indirectly, in the writing of *Cranford*. Can we know the past? If so, to what extent is such knowledge possible, and in what ways? All that we have said so far concerning *The Pickwick Papers* should make such questions at least open to continued interrogation. The problem becomes no simpler if one seeks to account for the various texts throughout the nineteenth century, which in one way or another return to the past or allow various pasts to return. That a number of pasts appear and reappear in literature and art, like so many virtual realities, parallel universes, or the revenant effect of uncanny cultural persistence throughout the nineteenth century, points to the idea that the Victorians were themselves haunted by these very questions. As with so many things, John Ruskin sought to have the last word on the subject, thereby revealing what is perhaps symptomatic of a structure of cultural anxiety. Quite unequivocally, somewhat stridently in fact, Ruskin calls for the establishment of a 'proper' mode of reading the past that involves 'putting ourselves always in the author's place, annihilating our own personality, and seeking to enter into his' (Ruskin 1903–1912, 18:75).

Concomitantly, one can read Ruskin's imperative as inverted and traced in Miss Deborah's exhortations to imitate the style of Dr Johnson; where for Ruskin the matter is one of reading and in so doing returning to the past, for Miss Deborah it is a matter of writing, and thus bringing the past back. In either mode there is to be witnessed an abnegation of self, in a strange relation to the literary ghost, which would have control of that other through such mastery. Whether one is speaking of Ruskin or Miss Deborah Jenkyns, the structure of anxiety of which I just spoke would appear to have to do with the fear of one's being haunted, and therefore exorcizing such a possibility by an act of historical colonization that has about it more than a hint of erotic possession. Take the other forcefully, Ruskin seems to be saying. In doing so, give yourself entirely, destroy your own being in the process – as if this justified the desire for and violence of appropriation. If 'retrospective narrative is built on an oscillating arrow of time', as Rosemarie Bodenheimer remarks (2001, 215; in a mixed metaphor the construction of which does not bear close scrutiny), moving between retrospect and prospect, or otherwise tracing the spectral effects of retention and protention as I have argued with the example of *Pickwick*, then Ruskin for one is desirous that this arrow pins its subject, thereby stopping it dead as arrows properly should. That there are still critical acts today which persist in pretending that they can apprehend the object as it supposedly was without the mediation imposed by the passage of time suggests that if we are not the other Victorians as Michel Foucault has it in his now well-known phrase, we are – some of us at least – belated Ruskins.

Not so Elizabeth Gaskell. Or for that matter Charles Dickens, as has been observed (whatever suspicions we may hold concerning Boz). What seems to be emerging from the snapshot coming into focus is a sense of a struggle in the nineteenth century between readers of the past. In this snapshot a tension is perceived: on the one hand, there appears the imperative to assume the other's place and the concomitant assumption that one can know the other from some Ruskinian critical height. On the other hand, there is the more or less passive acceptance that a demand is being imposed on one. The writer understands him- or herself as enjoined to respond to the traces of the past and the other according to their unpredictable and aleatory manifestation, and so to invent a reading of history through the literary, which survives precisely because the literary exceeds historical modes of representation and so translates the random and heterogeneous without the demands of historical ordering. Or, as Gaskell herself expresses this: 'I *must* write them down as they arise in my memory' (LGE 319). Here the imperative, expressed through that *must*, bespeaks Gaskell's sense of the inevitable, and therefore passive, reception of the other (the very thing Ruskin implicitly fears), and with that the necessary ethical response – and responsibility – to those instances of unpredictable revenance.

This may well lead to relating what Gaskell calls 'an improper story' (LGE 321) such as that of the cat swallowing and being made to vomit a lace collar (LGE 321; *C* 125–6); but then the other does not have to conform to the prim propriety by which the cultural critic justifies the selectivity of analytical reconstruction. To borrow Judith Stoddart's apt image, 'as Victorian geologists realized, sifting the sediments of culture can be a bewildering task' (Stoddart 2001, 194). It can also involve one in being open to certain unexpected and, to some, excessive, instances of disconcerting overflow. In Gaskell's trope of pussy vomit the big picture of historical rationalization gives way before a rhetorical and emotional force admitting that, with regard to the past, not only can one never know it absolutely, but neither can there be assumed a 'proper perspective', if only because there is no 'it', no one past to which one can give adequate account. That which we try to contain by the facile notion of history cannot be accounted for; there is no final account, no economy of ordering. Memory, like waves of anti-peristalsis, will come, and can arrive unexpectedly. In the resurgence of memory's traces, what comes up, strictly speaking, is that which is unassimilable to any system, order or economy of representation – and we can only bear witness to it, seeking a response commensurate with the event and our subjective experience of that.

It may appear of course a prurient, not to say perverse interest on my part to persist on the subject of vomit, especially as this is not a word Gaskell employs. That she does not use the word, though, suggests the radicality of the other in relation to 'history' in this particular example. So irrecuperable to any mode of directly sensible or intelligible apprehension, that which is disgusting or improper is unnameable, an excessive trace without and resistant to determination. In a novel concerned with propriety and etiquette, the cultural shifts and intimate interplay of details in class relations, and with allusion made to various historical and political backgrounds including the Napoleonic Wars, English colonial activity in India, Victorian xenophobia, repeated national financial collapses between the 1820s and the 1850s, the Irish famine, and so on, this one narrative interruption is striking.

However, if we pause to consider the thorough intermingling of the historical and the melodramatic (however minor its occurrences), the rational and the sentimental in *Cranford*, without any absolute division between the various modes of representation, we might begin to perceive the following: Gaskell's perception of history, involved as it is in the necessary response to the other in its arrivals and returns through the pulses and oscillations of memory, which, in turn, are invented formally through retrospective narrative, offers at least the possibility of thinking history differently and also thinking the difference in history that makes its narration possible in the first place. Taking place here, I would aver, in this one narrative moment (but not confined to this) is a performative politics, a 'politics [which], although it never occupies the centre of the stage, acts upon this discourse' (Derrida 1998, 263); that politics has to do with how we can invent, and so know, if not the past then the traces of the past in order to maintain their alterity.

Cultural traces, parodic or otherwise

There is no cultural history of vomit as such, much less one of feline spew in particular, or a discourse of retching, bringing up, or regurgitation in English literature as far as I am aware. (Chaucer provides us with one of the earliest examples that I have been able to find.) Yet Gaskell's small, interpolated narrative would constitute an undeniably significant moment in such a history. The narrative of pussy's mishap arises in Chapter 8 of *Cranford*, 'Your Ladyship' (*C* 115–27). Told by Mrs Forrester to Lady Glenmire, the story intervenes in an interweaving of social, cultural, and historical discourses and institutions in an especially complex and fascinating way. The tale operates on these other traces, to which we will come specifically, by the rule of analogy. This rule functions through a structure suggestive of equality of interest without resemblance or relationship between two or more different subjects, objects, or matters of interest. The principles of singularity and exemplarity without hierarchy, order or preference thus motivate and govern the rule. But I will return to these matters shortly.

If we consider the particular cultural traces in Chapter 8, merely signalling them in an adumbrated, telegraphic manner, the following markers are to be observed at work: there is, for example, the question of 'speaking to the Peerage', 'etiquettes of address', and ignorance concerning 'etiquettes of high life' (*C* 115). Concomitant to these concerns are questions concerning family genealogy (*C* 116). Here the narrator's function comes into play; for not being completely of Cranford, she has occasion to ask 'Who is Lady Glenmire?' (*C* 116). While the question would appear to be ontological in orientation, its being asked both assumes and receives in return, the genealogical response: identity is relation, providing of course that one's social station is sufficiently significant, or perceived and apprehended as such. This necessitates a cultural encoding of both parties involved in the conversation, the narrator and Miss Matty in this example, with both a certain 'standing' in the serried striations of early nineteenth-century discourses of station and sufficient knowledge of position culturally and socially in order to be able to frame the matter.

The opening of the chapter therefore stages a complex unfolding of the intricacies of rank within a particular era. At the risk of remaining too long on this matter, in this there is a motion between narrow and broader conceptions of family and national identity, the peerage being an intrinsic component in the cultural and ideological infrastructure of the nation, with subtler gradations having already been played out via the code of title and the proper name. The late Earl of Glenmire, and his relation to Mrs Jamieson, had been announced in passing, apropos the 'elegant economy' practised by Mrs Jamieson's serving only 'wafer bread-and-butter and sponge-biscuits' (*C* 42) in the first chapter. Arguably, the names 'Glenmire' and perhaps 'Jamieson' also would have been recognized as Scottish, rather than English, *glen* being a modernized spelling of the Gaelic for a narrow valley and a common topographical nomenclature in Scotland. 'Jamieson' is also of Scottish and Northern Irish origin, being a patronymic for James. In these matters alone, and in the contexts through which they are announced in the first chapter, there is a distinction being signalled to the reader in the mid-nineteenth century concerning the cultural and political differentiations made between English and Scottish aristocracy, which matters arise in passing in *Cranford*: 'Lady Glenmire is but the widow of a Scotch baron after all!' (*C* 116). Also the Baronet never sat in the House of Lords apparently, this being a result of the reduction by the Act of Union (1707) of the number of Scottish peers granted that 'privilege'. Economies of significance are thus threaded through the narrative that interanimates the relation between the peerage, the inhabitants of Cranford, and the mystified codes of food and euphemism peculiar to middle-class practices in the town.

But this is to delay the tracing of the cultural codes to be read in Chapter 8, and also to defer the discussion of 'poor pussy'. Lady Glenmire's visit to Cranford is announced in Chapter 7 (*C* 114). It is this event that opens the discussion of address, and from that to other matters. We read of the propriety of, and assumed station implied in, visiting only 'county' families (*C* 116). Miss Jenkyns's servant can spy on Lady Glenmire in church without impropriety because she does 'not belong to a sphere of society whose observation could be an implied compliment' (*C* 117). The assumption is that what particular classes do is irrelevant. They only become visible when they ignore codes of social propriety. For example, Mr Mulliner, the shopkeeper, '*would* always ignore the fact of there being a back-door to any house' when delivering purchases (*C* 118). In addition to these social behaviours, there are also other telling cultural signs of relevance for the constitution of historically given, class-based identities. Gaskell includes references to stomachers (*C* 120), the price of sugar (*C* 123), the poetry of Tennyson (*C* 122), the Catholic Emancipation Bill of 1829 (*C* 125), and the details of the tea service (*C* 124). Then there is

Mrs Jamieson's furniture; neither up to date nor relatively recent, it is, like the card games played – ombre and quadrille (*C* 124) – material traces, reminders and remainders, of the eighteenth century (*C* 122).

And there is yet another of the many periodic references to the London newspaper, the *St James's Chronicle*, which, first published in 1760, continued in print until the middle of the nineteenth century, and the reading of which signifies both station and the persistence of the past in the habits of the present (*C* 121). It is important to note in passing that the newspaper was avowedly Protestant and anti-Tractarian. As such, its ideological resistance to the suggestion of doctrinal reform on the part of John Henry Newman, John Keble, Edward Pusey, and others marks indirectly a resistance to modernization, signalling once more a cultural contretemps in both senses of that word. Against the times, its anachronism paradoxically remains forceful in the 1830s and 40s in the wider world, and Gaskell thus signifies again an aspect of cultural identity in Cranford obliquely perceived. What is also to be noted is that the cultural details of the chapter are typical of *Cranford* as a whole. And, it might be added, reasoning inductively and so moving out from the singular details that perform the historical and social locus, that which is both singular and exemplary figures without losing its specificity or peculiarity much of provincial middle England in the first half of the nineteenth century. At the same time, the heterogeneity of cultural signs and the absence of any governing taxonomy or other mode of ordering for the appearance of such traces, save for the occasions of the social gathering itself, intimates both an intricacy in the figuring of society and, with that, an apprehension of the extent to which the trace appears as part of a complex cultural process in the production of being. It is a process, a mode of production that will admit of no separation or ordering that demands our attention.

So we arrive at Mrs Forrester's intimate anecdote, the brevity and seeming insignificance of which almost defies commentary: nuns, parliamentary reform, charity school-girls, the proper care for lace, top boots, recipes for feline emetics – these are the various threads out of which the narrative – and, one is tempted to say, the recollection of the lace – are woven. Multiple cultural histories vie for our attention, as they chance to be gathered, stitched together in a design which obviously has been reported before, and which now returns for the benefit of a new member of Cranford society (*C* 125–6).

We return therefore to the rule of analogy. Analogy is without relation. It takes place because there is no direct or mimetic relation available as such, no family resemblance. Analogy operates on the fictionalizing or fabulatory principle of *what if*: what if X were Y? That which is without representation has no history as such, and yet can still be imagined. This is the work of fiction, and we apprehend that mode of production not through an economy or order but through the excess, the alterity of that figure without propriety, outside of all proper representation – in this singular case, *pussy vomit*. In this one figure, indirectly related through the revenance of a communal narration that assumes friendship, familiarity, intimacy without social nicety, Gaskell focuses the effects of every other trace that functions in the narrative of *Cranford*. The analogical and exemplary trope is, without naturalizing comparison, an instance of catachresis; by which nothing is mirrored or imitated and the effect of fiction is unveiled as one, fundamentally, of deformation rather than imitation.[3] From within realism, at its very limits, Gaskell offers us a baroque narrative by which we become estranged from, and yet intimate with, the object of narration. *Pace* Miss Deborah, Mrs Forrester becomes inadvertently the model for *pure* literary production, for a 'non-exchangeable productivity in terms of sensible objects or signs of sensible objects (money for example)' (Derrida 1998, 271). Conveying, despite herself, that the function of artistic and literary activity 'is essentially *parodic*' (Eagleton 1978, 51), her own fabulous regurgitation admits of 'neither . . . use-value nor . . . exchange value' (Derrida 1998, 271).

While any normative model or theory of production would hold that art, as a mode of labour, transforms its materials into a product (Eagleton 1978, 51), the catachresis of vomit affirms a kind of productivity, or a process at least, without useful or utilitarian product. By way of story-telling Gaskell engages in the dismantling of a supposed but impossible dialectic: lace/vomit. Her own narrative, as finely wrought as any lacework, in being simply the ineluctable and necessary work of memory as she admits in her essay 'The Last Generation in England', exceeds all aesthetics, all ostensible use. If lace is, as Christine Krueger has it in a sharply observant reading of Gaskell's novel *My Lady Ludlow*, 'the symbol of a matriarchy that links these women across generations and social circumstances' (1992, 177), in *Cranford* it retains no such historical or matrilineal function. The story in which it gets put to use, however, does bring together in a particular relation narrative, lacework, interlacing, and the threads that memory brings up and brings back. However violently such a process may be effected, we come to read indirectly that there is, nonetheless, the intermittent and surging maintenance of otherwise discontinuous and interrupted ruins, and hence moments of being recalled. This is the aesthetic experience of literature, in which 'the purpose or end of this purposiveness does not appear to us' (Derrida 1998, 279) – not directly at any rate. Aesthetic experience is turned inside out. It becomes other. In this recognition that Gaskell affords us, it is, as Jacques Derrida suggests, the 'purpose-lessness [*le sans-fin*: literally, the without-end] which leads us back inside ourselves' (1998, 279). The figure of *ourselves*, of *us*, is where I shall conclude.

Who (do we think?) we are

If past and present, rationality and sentiment, may be read as collapsing or threatening to fall into one another, erasing and overflowing in the process ideological, epistemological, or ontological borders whether partially or wholly, then this is signalled nowhere more directly and yet nowhere more obliquely than in the title of what became Gaskell's first chapter, and which I have used as part of the title for the present chapter: '*Our* society' (emphasis added). It is in that first-person plural pronoun that continuity and discontinuity meet, where the self and the other hold commune; where we *feel* the past remaining, touching us, haunting us, and writing who we are through its return in necessary acts of memory. It would seem to function both similarly and dissimilarly to that inclusive and exclusive *we*, by which Dr Hoggins's social standing, or lack thereof, was read – and yet not quite, it has to be said; for there is no comparative measure to be found. There is no volume of literature that has been coopted in order to delimit the determination of *society*.

It must be asked therefore: to which society does that *our* refer? Is there not a play, an oscillation of time's arrow, between the *our* of Cranford and the *our* of the implied readership? And does not that *our* signal the shared though heterogeneous 'nature', to employ Gaskell's word once more, of a particular historically determined, though equally historically riven, Englishness? Unlike the earlier *we*, *our* encompasses in its imagination both social snobbery and elitism *and* comprehensive acknowledgement. It confesses to everything that is *our society*, along with all that enters into the social, without the assumption of entry based on the ideology of the aesthetic. If, as was asserted earlier, there is to be discerned a politics that serves in the staging or translation of the cultural discourses in *Cranford*, then this politics is also a poetics of imagined communal production. As Terry

Eagleton argues, 'transhistorical truths are always culturally specific' (1990, 410). How we read that cultural specificity is never direct, never predictable, but the truth of Eagleton's assertion is borne out by the experience of *Cranford*; nowhere more so is this the case than in its final words. Here we return to the articulation of another *we*, one in which 'society' is now articulated in a shared apprehension of love. 'We all love Miss Matty', writes Mary Smith, in a collective present tense from which no one is excluded in principle, and which present tense leaves the novel open to that which is to come; 'we all love Miss Matty, and I somehow think that *we are all of us* better when she is near *us*' (*C* 218; emphases added).

We returns therefore – but with a difference: it is the same and yet not the same, and that difference is what opens onto what Derrida calls, in distinction to the certainty of a future, *l'avenir*, the to-come. That emphatic idiom – *we are all of us* – draws attention to the trans-lation of the *we* to *all of us*, to an *us* which, reiterated as the last word of the novel, after which there can be no last word, excludes no one in its enfolding perception of the proximity of the other mediated by sensible apprehension. Thus, as we have seen amply demonstrated throughout *Cranford* in all its attention to the narrative lacework of historical, cultural and material detail, 'while our shared material conditions bind us together' historically, as Terry Eagleton avers, they also 'open up the possibilities of friendship and love' (1990, 410). Community as rigid social order is transgressed, its self-policed borders crossed in a shared intimacy, whether of feeling or of narra-tive detail. Admitting no distinction in the social niceties or ideology of station, little acts of confession produce moments of transmission and therefore communal sympathy that can be neither anticipated nor controlled (rather like that feline regurgitation which, once under way, is not to be prevented). As figure without representation and thus an improper quasi-figure of representational and historical abjec-tion or unnameability, the undisclosed, unmentionable vomit, far from being in opposition to the discourse-proper of either historicity or mimesis, is that which always already figures in the productivity of such discourses by which the past comes to be represented in Gaskell's writing, and by which there is the chance of opening towards that which exceeds any present. For the moment at least the social locus is displaced onto, translated by the hope for, a utopian and atemporal alterity. Such a solution may well be 'ideologically insignificant', as Terry Eagleton has occasion to remark, apropos Dorothea Brooke's 'abnegation of ego' (1978, 121), but that insignificance in itself remains to be read – and read particularly, like the intrusion of *The Pickwick Papers* and the railways, as a sign of the times.

Notes

1. The context is not one that Schor appears not to recognize as having placed herself in, given that on the second page of her article she seeks to ground the reading of *Cranford* in a manner that acknowledges literary inheritance *pace* Luce Irigaray's demands for what Schor takes to be a universalized female writing (*écriture feminine*) (1989, 289).

2. While I am not suggesting that Lydia Languish should be taken as a model of all that is right, there is undoubtedly a somewhat modish response to Chesterfield that Sheridan is keen to exploit as a register of the times.

3. I borrow this formulation and the reference to the baroque from Terry Eagleton's assessment of Pierre Macherey (1976, 51).

Part II

Questions of Englishness: Being and Historicity

3 'The English mind': *The Moonstone*

> The fancy of the mass of men is incredibly weak; it can see nothing without a visible symbol.
>
> Walter Bagehot, *The English Constitution*

> Who can tell?
>
> *The Moonstone*

Assuming responsibility

In an essay on the knotty relation between history, narrative and responsibility in Henry James's *The Aspern Papers*, J. Hillis Miller asserts that if there is an 'unbreakable connection' in our minds and in the Western tradition between narrative and history, then responsibility, his third term, complicates inextricably the perceived assumption, since Aristotle, that narrative serves the regime of truth in the recounting of the past (Miller 1997, 193–4). The complication arises because, while we assume that 'historical events occurred as a concatenated sequence that can be retold now as a story of some kind' (Miller 1997, 193), the question of how we tell that story is elided. There is a responsibility in the telling, in the 'doing' of the story of history and the past. With that arrives an ethics, an obligation to enter into a performative language that exceeds the merely constative dimension of any allegedly truthful reporting of the facts as they are received and as they issue an 'imperative demand' for an 'ethical response' in the form of responsible narration seeking to attest, and so bear witness, to the past (Miller 1997, 194). More than this, responsibility resides not simply in the teller but in the reader, who assumes responsibility for reading aright what is being narrated, thereby bearing witness to that which, in principle and in truth, he or she can never be witness to, in that the events and persons are absent, dead, of a past irrecuperable as such. History is always remarked by this difference, and narration only serves to foreground the difference, and with it the unsuturable gap between the temporal experience of reading and the temporal moments about which one reads.

The stakes are raised, narration ups the ante, Miller remarks, when we are confronted with a first-person narrative. This is the case because, in such an instance, a further fictional if phantasmagorical scenario is produced: it is *as if*, in reading this account recounted by some other 'I' that I, 'as reader', implicated in an 'intimate and singular experience, had been made the overhearer of a murmuring internal voice . . . that is going over and over the facts of the case as remembered, trying to put them in order, above all trying to justify itself'. This voice 'speaks in response to a demand for an accounting. Someone, it seems, has said to the storyteller: "Account for yourself"' (Miller 1997, 194). A relay is therefore constructed, or, at the very least, received by me, the reader, as already opened and under way. If I am overhearing this intimate and singular experience, then it is, once more, *as if* I had somehow tuned into a frequency for which I had never been the intended recipient, but where now, once the dial has been turned, I have heard something which demands or requires that I assume a position in that relay. It is *as if* the relay, the transmission, is intended for me. I become the addressee or recipient. A first-person narration imposes itself on me, therefore.

We have already witnessed this strange imposition of one 'I' on another, in *Cranford*. *The Moonstone* and those interpolated tales in *Pickwick* aside, the other texts considered in *Dickens to Hardy* are, apparently, calm, ordered, third-person narrations. I say 'apparently' because you may recall or find in *Pickwick*, *Middlemarch*, or much less frequently in Hardy, the occasional interruption or suspension of third-person narrative, brought about by the intrusion of an apostrophic or parabasic 'I', whether 'Boz' the fictive editor, or the anonymous and imperious, ironic narrator of Eliot's novel. In the case of Gaskell, the arrival or, more precisely, the *return* of the other 'I' in the guise of the narrator is directly *there*, so to speak. Or rather, in two places at once, here, telling the tale, and there in the tale being told. This voice, which puts the reader at 'the narrator's disposition in the position of the conscience, the judge or jury' demands, 'in being addressed to me, personally' that 'I alone must act, must respond. I cannot let anyone else read for me' (Miller 1997, 194). I am therefore placed in a position which that other 'I' has, in narrating, already, implicitly, assumed.

With *The Moonstone*, however, the problem is intensified. I have to act as judge and jury by deciphering the 'truth', and drawing out the threads of that truth of the past, from a series of competing voices and the silences around which they form themselves. Moreover, each of those voices in *The Moonstone* is, itself, judge and jury, responding to the demand of another 'I', that of Franklin Blake, himself yet one more first-person narrator. And, as if it were not enough to be confronted with multiple first-person narratives, all of whom present themselves, and are in turn presented, as both truthful and partial, all-knowing in some respects and limited in vision in others, the difficulty is that the past is only made available through a circulation of narratives around what is not known, what cannot be remembered, what is no longer available from the past. The narration of history thus involves a representation of that which cannot be represented in itself, at its core. Structurally, it is this invisibility and omission which attests eloquently, despite the desire, will, or intention to speak of the past, of historical incidents, that informs all historical representation in *The Moonstone*.

Narrative and historical labyrinths

Published in volume form in 1868 *The Moonstone* moves back and forth across several decades in a number of interwoven strands belonging to the principal narrative of the theft of the precious diamond that gives the novel its name. Already published in serial form from January to August of the same year, *The Moonstone*'s narrative is conveyed entirely through documents produced by the several narrators. As I have already claimed in the introduction to this chapter, the past is nothing other than a series of contesting narrative strands, the validity of any of which stands or falls in the light of the reading and subsequent rereading of any other.

Bringing a little schematic order to matters, though, before we become entangled in this narrative mesh, and also as a means to remind ourselves of the complex structure of Collins's novel before we begin, let us sketch and so recall the structure of *The Moonstone* through an account of its narrators. They are: Gabriel Betteredge, the Verinders' House-Steward, Miss Clack, niece of the Late Sir John Verinder, Mr Bruff, the family solicitor, Franklin Blake, nephew of Lady Verinder, Ezra Jennings, assistant to Dr Candy, and the rose-loving policeman, Sergeant Cuff. Collins assigns the first narrative of the story (distinct from the Prologue) to Gabriel Betteredge in a division of the book called the First Period (*M* 59). It is titled 'The Loss of the Diamond (1848)'. The Second Period, 'The Discovery of the Truth (1848–49)' (*M* 255ff.), is divided into the remaining seven narratives, provided by Miss Clack, the solicitor Bruff, Blake twice, Jennings's journal entries, the report of the Sergeant, and Gabriel Betteredge, with whose narrative the Second Period concludes.

There is, in addition, and already mentioned, an Epilogue and a Prologue. The Epilogue is comprised of three statements, by Sergeant Cuff's assistant (1849), the captain of a ship transporting the three Brahmins who are believed by some to have stolen the Moonstone (1849), and Mr Murthwaite, whose eye-witness account of events in India is conveyed in a letter to Mr Bruff (1850). The Prologue is dated 1799. Extracted (and therefore in some fashion 'edited', however minimally) from hitherto private 'family papers' to which the reader will never have access, it returns for the purposes of recounting the history of the diamond and its possession, first by the Herncastle family, and then by the Verinders. The history of the diamond becomes, for the purposes of the novel, the history of family fortunes, as these in turn become entwined with the larger, national and historical imperial enterprise. At the same time, the act of selection and editorial intervention poses, for *The Moonstone* at least, the question concerning what constitutes relevance. What is significant, necessary in an act of cultural and epistemological exploration of the past?

Such a mass of material and its presentation through divers, often competing narrators as *The Moonstone* presents us with might appear to some – certainly Dickens, as we shall have occasion to see – as unnecessarily complex, requiring a more intrusive editorial hand than it has been given. The editorial role is a tease, a seduction as well as a requirement. It might also be taken to be proof of Blake's assertion that 'There is a curious want of system . . . in the English mind' (*M* 91), a sentiment that echoes one of Walter Bagehot's concluding remarks in *The English Constitution* (published the year before *The Moonstone*), on the perception of what he calls 'national character' as the living embodiment of the English Constitution, which is that 'the Englishman is born illogical and that he has a sort of love of complexity in and for itself' (Bagehot 2001, 190). What goes for the English Constitution and national identity, as they are received, interpreted and understood in the 1860s, goes also for *The Moonstone*. Not every reviewer felt so positively about the novel's construction as did Geraldine Jewsbury in her review from *The Athenaeum* on 25 July 1868. Jewsbury comments on the necessity of a second reading to reveal the 'carefully elaborate workmanship, and the wonderful construction of the story; the admirable manner in which every circumstance and incident is fitted together' (*M* 543). On the same day, however, the anonymous reviewer for the *Spectator* thought the novel had little more than plot to recommend it, and that only 'admirers' of 'double acrostics, or anagrams' would find any merit in *The Moonstone* (*M* 544). For this reviewer Blake is an impossible construction – 'no such human being ever existed' (*M* 545) – and 'has no qualities at all' (*M* 545). Furthermore, 'the plot is little better than the characters' and the reading of the novel amounts to little more than a 'wearisome waste of power' (*M* 547). Another anonymous review published on 17 September 1868 in *Nation* takes a similarly negative view of the novel. It is less like a novel than a child's game (*M* 548) or a 'pantomime', the characters appearing in sequence as so many 'puppets' whom 'Mr Collins ventriloquizes' in order 'to give a sufficient number of misleading sounds . . . and the reader is never deceived into thinking that it is anybody but Mr Collins that is speaking' (*M* 549). Supposing that the figures may appear as marionettes, automata for the articulation of culturally and historically specific perspectives, suggests that we are to treat them less as individuals than as idiocultural facets of a multiform articulation, rendered at a given historical moment. If they produce obscurity as much as clarity, this is only to be expected. Occlusion, fogging, mystification: all are historically and ideologically inescapable conditions of any material instant or epoch. What Collins thus presents to his reader's view is an estranging, not to say alienated, perspective on themselves, seen as if from outside themselves, and captured in a photographic distillation of a culture caught up in crises of self-representation, self-awareness, cultural myopia, and self-reading.

The reviewers who dislike *The Moonstone* seem troubled by the foregrounding of construction. This appears occasioned by the fact that they themselves apprehend their own obtusely given forms in such characters, the ideological place-holders who, as material subjects. come to be demystified in the novel, at least in part through a representation of the limits necessarily imposed in self-representational disingenuity. Additionally, there is a sense of disturbance caused by a confusion of identities (is it a game, a puzzle, a pantomime, or a puppet show?) and the sense that the characters are not only 'unreal' but merely mouthpieces for the projection of Collins's views. If Collins doesn't do the police in different voices, neither does he 'do' anything other than present a particular kind of articulation that resists being apprehended as realist. This in itself might suggest that something else is taking place in the novel, that its revelation of structure and its structural reiteration of its modes of presentation serve a purpose other than one of novelistic verisimilitude or an adherence to narrative realism. When the reviewer of *Harper's New Monthly Magazine*, who compares the author of *The Moonstone* with Defoe and Swift, praises Collins for his skill as a 'story-wright', we have the sense that structure is of far more importance as structure than as a medium which in presenting a window onto a world becomes partially or wholly transparent. Whether 'story-wright' suggests either the performance constructed by a playwright, or a structure such as a ship or wagon constructed by a shipwright or wainwright, there is a sense of a greater significance to the medium or vehicle than to what it contains than the reviewers who dislike *The Moonstone* are prepared to admit.

The limits of reading

Or perhaps the problem may be stated thus: what such reviewers reveal in their responses are the signs of their own native limitations and the inability to read, either the difference of form or differently than is their habit. Their negative aesthetic responses make an aspect of their conventional habits of mind – their middle-class Englishness – available to our view. Such an oblique perspective being perceived here might give us to apprehend the critics' own cultural constructedness. They reveal, and make plain in their language despite themselves, their own historical positioning. For what we may see with a degree of critical parallax is the critical blindness to the reading of narrative forms and ontological constructions other than those that serve to mediate in some encrypted fashion for the critics in question a sense of reflected identity. The reader is thus permitted a glimpse of identity blind to itself, which glimpse is made available through the opening of a gap, an incoherence, in that identity. If this hypothesis is in any way accurate, it does at least admit the truth of Blake's assertion, already cited, that there is a curious want of system in the English mind. That 'curious want' admits both to lack and, from another vantage point, to a mode of structuring through apparent absence that informs identity beyond the individual.

Coming back to this critique then, it is worth sketching a brief reading concerning the remark's own structure and the person who articulates such a position, as a means to gaining access to something larger concerning mid-Victorian identity. That Blake is capable of articulating this 'lack' as it appears in a singular identity, given particular ontological determination as the 'English mind', while being acutely unaware of the aporia that constitutes his own psychic constitution, offers the reader a fascinating glimpse of the simultaneity of blindness *and* insight by which any identity may be formed both epistemologically and historically. That such simultaneity occurs, and is articulated without reflection on its pertinence to the subject who expresses this opinion, is, furthermore, a telling registration, an imprint of the materiality of history on the subject. In seeing in others what he cannot reflect on in himself, Blake inadvertently illuminates for the reader one of Collins's principal ironic patterning devices in the novel as a whole. Both contemporary critics and, as we shall witness presently, characters in *The Moonstone* fall into the meshes, snares and lacunae of the textual web, inasmuch as their own particular modes of being and interpretation are, on the one hand, formed out of the very same configuration, while, on the other, limited by having been mediated culturally, ontologically, and historically as the arrangement's subjects. Nor is Blake wholly removed from the moment and ontology of the culture on which he comments critically, as though he were afforded a critical or epistemological distance from that culture. Although the mode of his acuity of perception and self-reflective occlusion is peculiar to himself, Blake's ability to perceive and yet not see himself is shared by most if not all the narrators. The 'curious want of system' is precisely, if paradoxically – and certainly ironically – its own systematic pulse and regeneration. It 'communicates' itself in those very places where communication breaks down. Opaquely illustrating the materiality of Englishness through those moments when interpretation runs up against the limits of its efficacy and mastery so as to reveal the 'absence', silence, or otherness by which subjectivity is constituted, communication in the novel proceeds by the haphazard and wayward transmission afforded through the failures of communication.

So important is this to the novel's patterning that it is worth illustrating in some detail. Each character reads events according to their own myopic cultural interests, and the extent to which they find themselves included or, more often, excluded from the historical and cultural instant of the narrative. In this they are maintained in isolation from one another, whether partially or totally so. For example, Betteredge judges the world according to the interests of the family and his reading of *Robinson Crusoe*. Moreover, although he recognizes that though he has been asked 'to tell the story of the diamond . . . I have been telling the story of my own self' (*M* 65), it remains 'quite

beyond' him to 'account for' this (*M* 65). I know, says Betteredge in
effect, that the romance of theft and desire, will and revelation, is also
a narrative that unfolds a reading of my identity, but how this
happens is impossible for me to state beyond the mere observation
that this is the case. This confession, as apparently incomprehensible
as it appears to Betteredge, is nonetheless important to how we might
read the novel from a perspective other than that of the diamond's
theft. But to turn back to the matter of the characters' misperceptions
and misreadings: Miss Clack misreads the world and its inhabitants
according to her theological prejudices and her desire to impose interpretations from her readings of tracts onto the world. Mr Bruff analyses everything according to his legal training. And so the novel
proceeds.

Restricting ourselves to verbal utterances rather than written
communications, we read nevertheless the traces of a vast network.
Leaving the Prologue out of the question until later in the chapter, I
will concentrate on the narratives of 1848–49, and the Epilogue.
Three modalities come into play, reiterating their formal devices
across the text, from speaker to speaker. In the first instance to be
illustrated, it is observed that as a result of such discursive and epistemological manifestations of self-re-enforcing segregation, characters
are often observed making statements confessing incomprehension,
or asking questions concerning what is, for them, a semantic, epistemological, or ontological imponderability: 'How it was I don't understand' (*M* 64); 'Neither Mr Franklin . . . nor I . . . had the ghost of an
idea of what Rosanna Spearman's unaccountable behaviour really
meant' (*M* 81); 'What does it mean?' (*M* 93); 'The present question for
us to decide is, whether I am wrongly attaching a meaning to a mere
accident?' (*M* 95); 'In the infernal network of mysteries and uncertainties that now surrounded us . . .' (*M* 151); 'I can't undertake to
explain. I can only state the fact' (*M* 158); ' "Do you understand this?"
she said' (*M* 167); 'What on earth did he mean . . .?' (*M* 173); and so
it continues (*M* 181, 186, 203, 223, 239, 261, 263, 266, 292, 314, 316,
323, 326, 328, 329, 340, 346, 348, 380, 449, 487, 506, 519); or, in the
final words of the novel taken appropriately from a letter,
Murthwaite's to Bruff, 'Who can tell?' (*M* 542).

Then there are those phrases anticipating the novel's final words,
uttered by most of the narrators, which attest to the experience of
undecidability. Several such comments appear in the Prologue, but as
that is to be addressed separately in this chapter I shall concentrate
here on the characters immediately implicated in events at the

Verinder house: ' "The question has two sides," he said. "An Objective side, and a Subjective side. Which are we to take?" ' (*M* 97); 'Whether he was sulky, or whether he was bashful . . . I can't say' (*M* 125); 'Whether she was determined to bring matters to a crisis, or whether she was prompted by some private sign from Mr. Bruff, is more than I can tell' (*M* 321); 'Whether the letter which Rosanna had left . . . did or did not, contain the confession . . . it was impossible to say' (*M* 251); 'it was my good or ill fortune, I hardly know which' (*M* 331); 'Betteredge (probably) translated them into polite English. I speak of this in complete uncertainty' (*M* 370); '. . . my love, or my revenge (I hardly know which)' (*M* 385); 'Who that person might be, I couldn't guess then, and can't guess now' (*M* 396); 'Either her mother told her, or Rachel heard what passed – I can't say which' (*M* 405); 'How long I might have remained lost in the mist of my own metaphysics . . . it is impossible for me to say' (*M* 427); ' "Resisted isn't the word," answered Betteredge. "Wrostled is the word. I wrostled, sir, between the silent orders in my bosom pulling me one way, and the written orders in my pocket-book pushing me the other" ' (*M* 450); 'How the interval of suspense . . . might have affected other men in my position, I cannot pretend to say' (*M* 478); 'Whether the man . . . was, or was not, an accomplice in the crime, it is impossible to say' (*M* 524).

Related to matters of both incomprehensibility and undecidability, there are of course numerous attempts at, or otherwise failures or avoidances of, deciphering, translating, interpreting, and analysing, so as to get at meaning or identity, as well as the assumption occasionally of the impossibility of communicating meaning unequivocally: 'It is one of the rules of my life, never to notice what I don't understand. I steered the middle course . . . In plain English, I stared hard, and said nothing. "Let's extract the inner meaning of this," says Mr. Franklin' (*M* 97); 'I leave it for you to fathom for yourself – if you can' (*M* 108); 'I translate Mrs Yolland out of the Yorkshire language into the English language' (*M* 187); 'Do you mean to tell me, in plain English . . .?' (*M* 196); 'If those words meant anything, and if the manner in which he spoke them meant anything – it came to this' (*M* 239); 'Read it as I read it, and you will set the right value on the Sergeant's . . . sending me the news of the day' (*M* 252); 'You have misunderstood me . . . How can I make a *man* understand . . .' (*M* 299); 'I have exposed myself to worse misconstruction than that' (*M* 323); 'My fervour did not communicate itself' (*M* 328). Once more, this iterable pulse reminding one of the limits and failures of interpretation and communication extends across the text, and lack of space permits anything more than the sketchiest signalling (*M* 362, 360, 369, 370, 371, 387, 394, 396, 406, 413, 418, 427, 439, 468, 475, 476, 500, 516).

Translation – its failure and frustration, its avoidance, the desire for its success, the need for its possibility – is at work everywhere here. Aside from the specificity and the local situation of the particular remarks, something else is in the process of being announced in these culturally encrypted iterations. I call these 'culturally encrypted' because, in their being a shared form of expression, they bespeak a code of address that most if not all the characters have in common; in this commonality, a community of incommunication, miscommunication and communicative discontinuity is announced, however indirectly. The desire for translation or its avoidance may be read suggestively as the historical sign of a culture dimly aware of itself as being somehow historically transfixed, embedded or sedimented, perhaps even in danger of becoming fossilized at mid-century. That translation for the most part falls into ruins is admitted as an impossibility, or else comes about faultily through those appropriations in self-reflective terms as acknowledged above, highlights the retrospectively read acuteness of a cultural and historical difficulty that Collins maps and registers twenty years after the majority of *The Moonstone's* events. Most of Collins's figures, in their repeated demonstration of incomprehension in the face of their experiences of the aporetic and their confession to such incapacitation as these experiences produce, announce themselves as going nowhere. Instead, not only do they recycle their various articulations as so many cryptic signals of a culture in danger of becoming meaningless, they articulate themselves as belonging to a community of irresolution, haunted by a familial and colonial past that has come to determine the very condition of their present moment.

Despite the numerous and repeated failures that strangely mark the text as a successful, and successfully frustrating, mode of delivery, there is a forceful example of transcription and translation that succeeds in particular provisional ways. Arriving from a culturally marginal place, it appears as an act of writing in Ezra Jennings's attempt to close the gaps in the fragmentary narrative account given by Mr Candy in his delirium, Jennings offering, for Franklin Blake and the reader, a 'reproduction', as Blake puts it, of the result produced by Jennings, providing the 'original language and the interpretation of it' (*M* 456).

Ezra Jennings is the only character who makes a distinction

between writing and authority. Writing is not proof of anything for Jennings. It is an experiment, to borrow his own definition, 'tending to put my assertion to the proof' (*M* 443). This experiment involves the transcription of Mr Candy's fragmentary statements, his 'broken words, as they dropped from his lips, on one sheet of paper', while Jennings seeks to fill in the gaps, providing 'links' on another, in order to make an intelligible statement appear, to invent it in other words, thereby allowing for the construction – the double writing of the two sheets of paper – to stand in the place between what was 'actually done in the past' and 'something which Mr Candy contemplated doing in the future' (*M* 443). Jennings's experiment is just this putting to work of writing as the medium between past and future, his explanation foregrounding and so demystifying precisely the present ground of *The Moonstone* and the 'experiment' or invention tried by Blake for the purpose of passing on to the future a coherent narrative as proof and assertion of the past's truth. Jennings's attempt to replace the elisions with words that give significance in the context of historical events surrounding the theft of the Moonstone from Lady Verinder's house on the night of Rachel's birthday party are then reproduced as both documents shortly thereafter (*M* 455–6).

Collins's reproduction of both sheets of paper not only present the process, they perform it as if Jennings were returning to fill in the blanks for both Blake and the reader; which, after a fashion, he is, inasmuch as Collins's reproduction of Blake's reproduction of Jennings's reproduction of Candy's delirious voice institutes and replays the relay of recordings across time, from a moment pre-dating Candy's own experiment on Blake, which eventually brings both Blake and the reader, at different times of course, to where they are situated. First-person narrative thus enacts the past through its traces and in doing so demands a response in order for writing to be transported into a future where meaning is delivered, and in this case invented, as the response and responsibility of the readerly 'I' (Jennings) who also becomes the writer. Thus, Ezra Jennings in doubling Candy doubles not only himself but the role of the reader in general, as a historically situated recipient whose responsibility is to take on the signs of the past and so deliver them to a future, keeping the network of transmission open, and maintaining in that process the possibility of a reading to come.

Jennings's translation works perhaps precisely because it can be undertaken from outside the mainstream of the novel's cultural community. As remarked, such risk succeeds in effecting a change in temporal direction. It moves the novel from the stasis that is inscribed through its persistent recovery of the past and its being haunted by the events of the past. Jennings's translation is more powerful than a merely formal transcription. It risks producing a reading in the very places where there appears to be nothing available to read. It invents the signs that cause the text to function. In this, Jennings's translation does more than simply recycle endless repetitions and mimetically faithful, though moribund, self-reflections of a stagnant culture caught up in a crisis of representation. In this, it produces, *invents* (finds hidden rather than makes something from nothing) a new fiction from the old, and makes possible the beginnings of a temporal movement forwards. While every other reader in *The Moonstone* is a passive self-reader who seeks solely to reflect him- or herself in the larger narrative pattern, thereby affirming his or her location as subject to an impasse that is reflective generally of the cultural crisis and suspension of the 1860s, Jennings, in risking the invention of reading, opens the culture to its own possible advent.

Writing and relay

What does Ezra Jennings's effort at filling in the gaps, the 'missing links in the evidence', as Franklin Blake says (*M* 361) teach him, if not us though? Blake tries to assure the reader that 'In the pages of Ezra Jennings, nothing is concealed, and nothing is forgotten' (*M* 465). Yet, this is testimony after the fact. It can only be an act of faith, trust being placed in writing. It is a second-hand affirmation of the truth committed in full to writing: in short that the voice of the dead is more reliable than that of the living. We learn therefore that writing makes possible that which the chatter of voices does not, cannot or will not. If the voices that circulate are in one sense alive, in another they are, in their consignment to repetition and unthinking self-reflection, doomed to an undead half-life. Writing's surface reveals in its motions the weight to be given in any translation to silences and lacks, as well as to what comes to be articulated. Though admittedly only a speculation based on what is *not* presented in *The Moonstone*, I would aver that it is as a result of reflection on Jennings's act of writing, specifically that act that fills in the spaces in Candy's stuttered semaphore testimony, that Blake, in discussion with Mr Bruff, decides to ask of the various so-called narrators to produce written accounts. The written testimonies afford the reader a textual mesh, the very plane of which is composed equally of omissions and occlusions as it is affirmations and confessions – as has just been shown through the signalling of the iterable patterns of reported speech. Historically, writing is all that remains of the past. It arrives between a past that can no longer be directly represented and a moment of reading yet to arrive. This is Jennings's legacy, in part. Yet, it is not only the reconstruction undertaken by Jennings, the historical process of transcription, translation, and narration. In translation there is a process of decryption and the past surviving, returning as other than it was via the tele-technology of writing that performs the effect of becoming-narrative to be sure. More than this, though, what Jennings provides are his journal entries. With Jennings already dead at the time of Blake's request to produce the collected narratives, his testimony is only available as one more act of writing, one that is dated and given in its latter stages precisely temporal markers. These are both historical registers or imprimatur, and also framing devices for the images that return through the punctuations afforded by the connection between history and the medium of writing.

So to recap: the family papers, Betteredge twice, Miss Clack, Mr Bruff, Franklin Blake, also twice, Jennings, Sergeant Cuff, his assistant, the Captain, and Mr Murthwaite. Although Jennings's account is taken from his journal, none of these 'voices' so-called that vie for our attention, and demand their space, are given directly. All arrive for the reader as acts of writing, statements, journals or letters, and are acknowledged as such by each of the writers in question. Each testamentary document is written at the direct request of Blake, as has been observed, following a consultation, reported by Betteredge in the first chapter of the First Period, between Blake and the lawyer. Betteredge is not present at this, but is told of the meeting by Blake (*M* 59–60). A structure of relay and report, commentary and transcription is established from the very outset. And equally from within the very inaugural gambit, the structure is itself complicated; it reorganizes itself through the necessity of incorporating some other deferred, displaced or doubled relation: Betteredge reports, bears witness therefore, on that to which he has had no direct access. Writing arrives before the voice, disordering the conventional relations and privilege predicated on presence over absence, life over death, and so on. In this, the novel remarks its own historicity as a phenomenon of a profoundly tele-technological age, but an age in which cultural obsessions are shared equally between the occult and the technological. If *The Moonstone* assumes the function of a vast intermittent telegraphic system, in which gaps, delays, breakdowns, and miscommunications assume importance, then that system is also one of mediumistic seance. As Friedrich Kittler suggests, 'a medium is a medium is a medium. As the sentence says, there is no difference between occult and technological media' (Kittler 1992, 229).

While one is tempted to disagree with the absolute assertion that there is no difference in general, with regard to the reading of *The Moonstone* certainly the mediation of the past is at least partially an occult occurrence, given the foregrounding of writing as tele-technological medium. The novel plays on the apparent lack of difference, relying on analogical relay and the simulacrum of formal resemblance in modes of communication; facing for the most part backwards, *The Moonstone* strives to move forward in its gathering of the textual weave, even as that gathering involves itself in a tireless unravelling of the knotty mesh of threads and clews. And it must be acknowledged that reports and narratives are not seamlessly woven together. They remain discontinuous accounts, only conjoined by the punctuation of dates, thereby bearing witness in their presentation to discontinuity, breaks in transmission. And everywhere is the affirmation of the risk that is run in seeking to analyse, to read, translate or interpret, to inscribe or reproduce: 'The one interpretation that I could put on her conduct . . .' (*M* 371); 'the English translation appeared at the End' (*M* 353); 'I put the writing materials before Mr Bruff, and asked him . . . to draw out, and sign, a plain statement of what he had seen' (*M* 499–500)'; 'Mr Godfrey pacified her by taking a sheet of paper, and drawing out the declaration' (*M* 274). Letters are even produced verbatim; in these are to be found yet further references to other acts of writing (*M* 304–5). In the foregoing example, Blake reproduces a letter sent to him by Miss Clack, in which she refers to the 'fifth chapter of her humble narrative' to which are attached 'copious extracts from previous publications'.

Signs and missives, acts of dating and inscription obviously serve historically as signals for beginnings, endings, and moments of perspectival and occasional convergence. Throughout the novel, there are other documents, yet more relayed accounts. There are references to journals that are checked (read) in lieu of the reliability of memory and for apparent factual verification; letters or notes are acknowledged, there being more than one hundred references to the former, with half as many again to acts of writing; there are almost one hundred acknowledgements of pieces of paper littered through the pages, the first of which is in Chapter 1: 'This prefatory narrative', says Blake to Betteredge, 'I have already got by me in the form of an old family paper, which relates the necessary particulars on the authority of an eye-witness' (*M* 60); and there are also wills, chiefly Colonel Herncastle's, another 'source' from which the narrative is propelled, and Julia, Lady Verinder's; and so the text proceeds. Indeed, the very first line of *The Moonstone* comes back from 1799 or shortly thereafter:

> I address these lines – written in India – to my relatives in England. My object is to explain the motive which has induced me to refuse the right hand of friendship to my cousin, John Herncastle . . . I request [my family] to suspend their decision until they have read my narrative. And I declare, on my word of honour, that what I am now about to write is, strictly and literally, the truth. (*M* 52)

If we recall my earlier comments on responsibility, narrative and history, this representation of the absent subject in writing must strike us as the acceptance and impossible affirmation of responsibility in relation to the other and to the past. It arrives from that past – it is precisely dated – demanding to be judged. It situates its readers in a double bind. For, on the one hand, it asks that judgement be suspended. On the other hand, it asserts itself from the outset, as though neither judgement nor suspension should be necessary, if the will or intention of the writer is perceived or apprehended before reading, as if no writing had taken place, but one had unmediated access to the intention, the consciousness, and will of the document's author. Yet the author is, by the time we read it, dead. And so there is only writing. This is all that remains as testament to the past.

In entering *The Moonstone* we enter into a textual world therefore, in which the novel in the late 1860s assumes the function of medium (tele-technological *and* occult) 'that registers not only transmissions from the past but phenomena that are not yet meaningful' (Tiffany 1995, 69). That they are not yet meaningful but have an immanence is presciently attested to in those instances when – at those points when a crisis in the history becomes most insistent – Franklin Blake inserts himself into the narrative to demand of the reader that they return to various chapters in Betteredge's narrative in order to reread. Blake's demands and the crisis of personal history have a greater resonance beyond himself therefore, much like his statement concerning the curious want of system in the English mind. For they attest to that which is being signalled by Collins through the very form of his novel, which is that 'not only the literary artifact and the domain of material culture in general but the very concepts of representation and meaning are in a state of crisis' (Tiffany 1995, 69). The implicit, subterranean 'linkage of revolution [1848] and images of the dead' (Tiffany 1995, 69)[1] from the Siege of Seringapatam and 1799 onwards, to the dead figures of Joanna Spearman, Lady Verinder, Godfrey Ablewhite, Ezra Jennings, and any of those narrators who, being old, may naturally enough have died between 1850 and 1868, announces crisis, I would contend, as the very condition of what it means to be Victorian. If we take the claim seriously that I have advanced elsewhere in the present volume that the English in the nineteenth century see themselves as modern, then crisis is the very condition of modernity.

The characters are to be understood therefore, despite their own isolation from one another, and their own self-interested reflections, as more than mere mouthpieces for their ideologies, bigotries and their station in the hierarchy of class relations, even though they are to be read as such talking heads, as I have already stated. They are also prosopopoeic and spectral manifestations in no small degree. They are called back to life through their acts of writing to bear singular witness to particular historico-material discursive traditions, which in their own hermeneutic enclosure fails to connect with the representatives of other discursive formations, thereby rendering all communication problematic while simultaneously registering the peculiarity of their temporal moment. Here we might say is an image of the 1860s as it is stranded between pasts and future, caught in a condition of historicized immobility. This communal discontinuity thus figures an externalized marking of the gap that informs shared psychic identity, as that space between apprehension and incomprehension, insight and blindness. As a result we witness through the staging of these unsuturable spaces a shared mode of cultural presentation that arguably determines in singular ways much, if not all, of *The Moonstone's* narrative. To this structure there is a further spacing: a distance is maintained between the highly intricate conception that informs Collins's inventive exploration of mid-Victorian culture, as this is revealed through the novel's quasi-forensic presentation of events surrounding the case of the stolen diamond, and the frustrations of misdirection and self-reflection that inform how the various narratives are told.

Historical contingency

Through *The Moonstone* we experience a world of writing, a weave of inscriptions, and a culture of intercommunicating documents, all competing for our attention and credulity. Layer on layer, page within page: as with our own experience of reading the novel, every absent page of writing demands a reader's judicious interpretation. It is as if the novel is saying, here we are in 1868, at a sufficient remove from the beginning of the century and the even more recent events of the 1840s that many of those who once could offer direct eye-witness and bear testimony – such as Ezra Jennings – are no longer here. All that remains of the past is writing which, in its interleaved form, invites us to consider not only *that* we are caught up, implicated in the relay as we consider the evidence, but also – to signal that gap and the tensions that strain at the textile weave – *how* we interpret the evidence. How is it possible for one to witness what is not there as such? How can one know for sure which authority is correct? How can one even appeal to an authority historically when the only 'presence' is that of writing? Writing appears to communicate about its own historical contingency, and thus implicitly (and occasionally explicitly) testifies to the absence of any living witness and so, ultimately, to any factual truth. In the face of this vast communicative machinery, on what are we to rely? How can we reconstruct the past? And, importantly with regard to *The Moonstone*, what do such questions have to do with the 'English mind', supposing for the moment that such a thing exists? As Sandra Kemp avers, 'The most important function of the complex narration of *The Moonstone* is that it involves the reader in a mass of conflicting information and unreliable clues and evidence . . . rational deduction does not account for life's chaos and disorder, its multiplicity of detail' (Kemp *M* xxv). This is, in effect, the one 'truth' of which the reader can be certain. More disturbingly though, the historical frames and the punctuations of dated historical events serve to remind at every turn that the want of system *is* the system, and that this systemic corruption is the only means of historical and cultural communication.

The moment of the novel's appearance in 1868 thus calls for the reader to bear witness to seventy years of English domestic and imperial history, in the absence of any system or reliable witness or authority. In her promotion of Ezra Jennings to the position of model reader, Kemp asserts that 'the past, like truth or meaning in narrative terms, is elusive. It is dependent on memory, on present interpretations of

past events, and on an ever-changing complex of emotions (in particular, the way feeling orders perception)' (Kemp *M* xxvi). While in
agreement with Kemp's trenchant analysis, I would go further by
suggesting that what appears merely elusive is revealed by the novel
as undecidable, when read in terms of the historicity of national identity and the attempted justifications of such an identity – or the
unveiling of the fact that there is no justification – in literary narrative. If 'Strategies of self-definition depend upon a new kind of
remembering or interpretation (both historical and psychological)
unweaving trajectories of time, and seeking to grasp the points where
past, present and future overlap', then *The Moonstone* offers itself as a
text with no consolations recuperable from the past. Distinct from
either the demand that we remember expressed by Dickens in *The
Pickwick Papers*, or the sense that it is the annexed narrative, and not
the main currents of history, which bears the possibility of a community of identity carrying the past into the present as witnessed in
Cranford, Collins's novel in its singular experience of the English
subject in history provides no such demands or comforts.

Responsibility to the past, and for bearing witness to that past,
arrives at every present instant of reading in *The Moonstone*. The want
of system suggests that there can be no ultimate justification for that
history or its narratives – and so the English subject must take responsibility and read him- or herself as both historical subject and subject
to a historicity by which he or she is interpellated, for '*The Moonstone*
is . . . as much about a quest for a self as it is about finding the lost
gem through salvaging the past' (Kemp *M* xxvii). That quest, in 1868,
is for the grounds of Englishness when authority is seen to collapse
into abyssal undecidability, and to be haunted by that very possibility. Collins's English subjects are, and find themselves, historically, 'in
the sea of life enisled' to recall a phrase of Matthew Arnold's (Arnold
1979, 121–3, 127–8, 129–31). In short, they are shipwrecked,
stranded. If *Robinson Crusoe* is Betteredge's text, it is then also that of
every other character, however ironically or however much they may
not be aware of this. It is also worth noting, for the moment at least,
that this retrospectively appointed foundational text of the capitalist,
colonial Englishman (as Marx and many others have observed) is also
the tale of someone whose account of himself as an 'enisled', isolated
being is one of solitary existence, broken communication, and belated
testimony – *and attempted justification*.

In being presented as a series of documents, every character in *The
Moonstone* is, like Crusoe, written and writing themselves, their places

in the histories of the Moonstone and halfway through the nine-teenth century, as, in effect, isolated. If the text is a vast telegraphic communication, conversely no one communicates directly with anyone else. Like Crusoe, the characters of Collins's novel can only write their accounts, presenting their evidence belatedly. And Blake's stories – the one he tells of himself and those that are told about him – are, in particular aspects, most immediately like Crusoe's. For both men express in writing and therefore after the fact their cultural 'solipsism . . . [his] homelessness and his constant (often comic) oscil-lation . . . inner and outer, subjective and objective viewpoints' (Kemp *M* xxvii–xxviii). If in this Blake anticipates modernist protago-nists such as Conrad's Marlow and Kurtz (Meckier 1987, 148), then he also echoes Crusoe's own identity. A history of Englishness, certainly a history of English masculinity, is therefore one of an impossible, unending testimony to being as being-outcast, being-homeless, and being-stranded. It is to the question of homelessness, and the unhomely, to which we now turn.

The unhomely house of Englishness

The Moonstone is the tale of a particular house in two senses: it is the story of family inheritance, of what is passed from generation to generation; it is also the tale of the violation of the English house, of a theft from a young woman's room in the sanctuary of her family home. It would appear then that the imperative of *The Moonstone* is to call to us to return to the scene of the crime which is, at the same time, the family hearth: we are called home by *The Moonstone*, and must enter the house. We must bear in mind the home, and the very idea of home; we are forced to consider the house or home as trope for the nation and national identity (and of course analogically we need to bear in mind the family as synecdoche for both house and nation); additionally, we must reflect on all that haunts the house, making it unhomely.

The Verinder house has no master present in 1848, when the Moonstone comes to the house, is subsequently stolen, and the police are called in to track down the thief. However, something else is also at odds with this house. Something is missing from the English family home, and this structure in 1848 is intrinsic to its formation as we receive it in *The Moonstone*. The absence is precisely that of the prosopopoeic figure of the Law of the house, the home, the nation:

the father. In the mid-century, therefore, there is no paterfamilias, and the crisis of the house takes place directly in relation to this absence. To borrow Dickens's formula from *A Christmas Carol*, Sir John is dead, to begin with, and so is always already absent before the novel gets under way. His absence – or, put differently, the partly material, partly symbolic lack of the master's presence – disorders the equilibrium and order of the house. In Betteredge's words, 'our[s is] . . . a scattered and disunited household' (*M* 246). The disunity is not immediately felt though, nor does it have an impact in any noticeable sense. Rather, it is that the 'structure' of the house is readable as having become vulnerable to threat through the death of the patriarchal figure, and the logics that such a figure may be said to authorize. The house's economic, logical, and lawful forms, when implicitly governed by such a socially symbolic identity, lose a crucial architectonic component or keystone in the death of the father. With regard to the novel's plot, this missing element is unremarkable, strictly speaking. More than that, it is unremarked for the most part, and except in passing. Yet, this lack haunts *The Moonstone*'s cultural logic. It drives the narrative to determine how that absence shall be filled eventually, so that order can be restored to the house, and the English family can be renewed.

Obviously, what appears in the gap between Sir John and his eventual replacement, Franklin Blake, albeit briefly, is the Moonstone itself. I say 'briefly' because that too disappears. However, equally obviously, the Moonstone cannot and does not supply what is absent or lacking. It serves to illustrate what is removed by violence from other 'houses'. As we are told in the Prologue, the diamond, initially housed in the eleventh century in a 'famous [Hindu] temple' (*M* 53), is removed to another sacred site for safe keeping from a Muslim 'conqueror'. Here, the diamond remains until the early eighteenth 'Christian century' (*M* 54), when it is taken violently by the Moguls. The Moonstone then 'passed from one lawless Mohammedan hand to another' until it falls 'into the possession of Tippoo, Sultan of Seringapatam' (*M* 55). It is from the Sultan's palace that the diamond is then violently taken by an English officer, John Herncastle.

Thus, the diamond is both the object of desire and also a symbol of what is most precious in a house, secular or religious. Its presence signals both that which holds the house together and that which, if removed, places the house in crisis. Like the absent father, the diamond therefore illuminates and causes one to reflect on that which is no longer there, albeit that reflection occurs in the most indirect manner. If we come to see at all, it is 'through a glass darkly', as it were, as the absence of the father has much to do with the novel's historical trajectories and the confounding within the novel of efforts at interpreting the past in the attempt to restore order to the present. That which was there once must be there once again. The structure has to be completed. A new master has to be found to replace the old master, in order that in a return to the order and logic of the past there can be a movement towards the future. Without this figure, neither temporal progression nor the site of cultural and national identity, the house, functions. To put this differently, the house no longer has its head. It appears as a dysfunctional and grotesque body, decapitated, as it were.

The Moonstone is a novel about such a house, and about the disorder that occurs historically in such a house. That the disorder or dysfunction is both temporal and historical is more than adequately attested to in the novel, through the explicit range of precise dates that it offers as signatures for events, and as a factual means of staying, however momentarily, the vertiginous anachrony by which the narrative moves in the various voices of its different narrators. *The Moonstone* therefore asks the question: what happens when the house is no longer a house according to conventional habits of order, form, propriety and economy? Collins's novel, for all that it may or may not be a 'detective novel', is certainly a novel concerned with locating the new master, and this it does eventually in the marriage of Rachel Verinder to Franklin Blake. It is a narrative in which successive first-person voices are staged, the performance of each testing the limits of each voice as an appropriate 'master discourse'. Which voice, idiocultually, can come to occupy what is missing? What can provide a suitable supplement and substitute for the Father so as to re-establish the English house? Ultimately, this proves to be Franklin Blake, through his eventual marriage to Rachel Verinder. Though Rachel is heir to the house, its genealogical mistress, she cannot assume the legacy of the house. *The Moonstone* makes it apparent that this is a masculine function, if the past is to be restored, and with it the assumption of order that is read as residing in an English past, not one tainted by the foreign gem.

But Blake is the master who introduces into the house, in the absence of its previous master, the Moonstone, the seductive gem. He is also the one who steals it from that house, in a restaging of events that Collins employs in order to make particular points about history and temporality in relation to the cultural and symbolic identities of the English that are addressed here. There is more to be said about this iterable narrative of theft and disruption. On the first occasion, the theft causes the inhabitants to fly from the house, leaving it haunted by its intrusions, its secretive penetrations, its mysteries; all in fact that haunts the house as the exemplary site of Englishness in the mid-nineteenth century. Throughout the present text, the notion of Englishness is understood as an encoded 'matrix of regulative ideas through which the intuited world is rendered intelligible to the cognizing subject' (Johnston 2005, 79). Such a matrix is not static, of course, its formation, re-formation, reformulation and deformation being subject as much to temporal and epistemological recurrences, translations and interactions, as it is to that which takes place within any more or less specific cultural moment. The Verinder house figures a site for the work of the matrix, while simultaneously doing double service as one possible synecdoche for the nation. We should recall at this juncture that the novel presents its narrative as an encoded parallel structure bearing witness to a structural absence, relatively recently put in place, in the national 'family', that of the monarchy. Though set in the late 1840s for the most part, *The Moonstone*, written in 1868, bears the memory of the death of Albert in 1861 and therefore his 'absence'. His figure thus remains as a recently departed, lingering ghost, whose 'foreignness' had finally been assimilated, justified, accepted into the institutional identities of Victorian Englishness.

Franklin Blake similarly mirrors the 'foreignness', the Germanic immunization of English stock through his education and thought. In this, *The Moonstone* plays on the possibility that there is a 'darkness' or otherness that is not exotic exactly, not extrinsic or foreign, at the heart of the domestic scene. The Moonstone may well be Indian but, like its equally 'exotic' counterpart, the opium that causes Blake to steal the diamond, it is merely the device by which the other side of Englishness, and with that a more domesticated element of the foreign, is unveiled. And so we witness in Collins's novel – without seeing it at first, *for a first time* – a staging of the unhomely disturbance to home caused not by the wholly foreign other, but by the very figures to whom the house might be said or assumed, conventionally, most properly to belong. Belatedly and in a gesture of narrative *Nachträglichkeit* (the apparent sign of belatedness or supplementarity, a recognition after the fact), the heart of darkness is understood to be *of* the house itself. The English patriarch is revealed historically and materially as both absent and necessarily the very usurper of the home. Moreover, the Englishness of the father figure or master is commented on as being already contaminated in his own immediate past by that which is foreign and only partially assimilable.

Undoubtedly, Dickens perceives just this 'contamination' or troubling complication in representation in June 1867. Dickens expressed his opinion that *The Moonstone* was 'a very curious story – wild, yet domestic . . .' in a letter to W. H. Wills. *Wild, yet domestic*, the narrative is at once not completely house-trained and yet is understood to belong to a perceived English identity nevertheless. There is something of a family resemblance. This ambivalent assessment was modified negatively the following year, when, in another letter to Wills, Dickens remarked that the construction of *The Moonstone* was 'wearisome beyond endurance' (26 July 1868). However much most readers will disagree with Dickens in his latter sentiment, the enervation to which he admits is not insignificant. It may well arrive for some readers *despite* their admiration of the novel, inasmuch as information, knowledge, truth and certainty go into a kind of freefall as soon as they are sought or addressed. Exhaustion is thus a result of reading, and it is this correlation between detection and interpretation on the one hand and their frustration on the other. For, in the excessive and strategic 'disorder' of *The Moonstone* (which recalls Bagehot's reflection on Englishness, and which is a structural component of its multiple time frames, historical trajectories, anachrony, and numerous narrators), there is that which effectively serves to prohibit the motion of the principal narrative action, while also being a device intended to occlude narrative detail concerning the detective story per se. What I want to propose therefore is that Collins's novel, like its characters, affirms more than merely the sum of its parts: it is a historical and material manifestation of Englishness in all its heterogeneity in the 1860s as the totality of its past narratives, in its written formations and in its lived relations. A novel in crisis, it is a narrative that articulates crisis as central to Englishness, as its historically inescapable necessity and generative 'nature'.

Additionally, there must be considered the wayward force of opinion and indirection that narrators such as Gabriel Betteredge and Miss Clack assume, which itself disorders any straightforward ordering of events. Such 'disorder' in its condition of idling and loitering is not merely a hindrance to narrative form. Again, it *is* that form, it is the other of form. For it informs as it deforms what we might – and certainly Dickens appears to – desire as the ability of the story to get on with its business. The English, the English character, the English home, the English economy – all of these can only function and maintain themselves if they situate a 'wild, yet domestic crisis', which is constitutive of their ontological frames and productive of their identities and interactions. Dickens fails to apprehend, at least in his second assessment, the integral condition of disruption, crisis and excess to form and identity, within and as that which *just is* the ontology of the novel. However, that prior judgement of the novel's being *both* wild *and* domestic captures in its seeming paradox that which is at the very heart of Collins's vision of Englishness in the nineteenth century, as an identity constructed on the one hand in the local narrative of the jewel and the Herncastle and Verinder families across nearly fifty years, from 1799 to 1848, and more generally, on the other hand, in the story of the cultural constitution and mediation of national identity from *Robinson Crusoe* to *The Moonstone*. What might be suggested then is that the absence of the master and the eventual restoration of that figure as a symbolic structural frame are not simply the signs of a historical and cultural loss and eventual reconstitution of containment apropos the various forces of the house as the place in which the staging of identity happens. Between such perfunctory narrative concessions to order and economic management, the stalling, the idling, the excesses of various kinds, all operate so as to offer a period of freeing the subject's apprehensions and reflections.

At the risk of being thought overly fanciful, it is as if Collins has anticipated in his narratives composed of excess, disorder and anachronic rerouting (everything recirculates and returns, whether materially or phantasmatically, thereby confounding linearity of narrative and history) Jean-Luc Godard's 'nonlinear presentation of history in and of cinema in *Histoire(s) du Cinéma*' (Pisters 2003, 1). As this latter work frees the gaze from the territorialism of conventional historical and narrative representation, allowing for a distance which is, equally, a place on which to reflect upon the cultural and national self in history (however obtusely), so *The Moonstone* detaches and 'makes wild' the domestic scene. Narrative exigency is loosened, however temporarily, from within itself, so that, through the specificity of idiocultural self-reflection on the part of particular narrators, there takes place a 'type of nonpersonal individuation' (Pisters 2003, 2). This might well seem paradoxical initially. How can the individual voices of Miss Clack, Betteredge, Blake, or Ezra Jennings be 'nonpersonal'? I have already indicated in a somewhat adumbrated manner how the voice is merely an idiocultural function, operating as the singular representative of particular ideological beliefs and materially specific discourses pertaining to social and cultural practices and behaviours in the mid-Victorian period. Each 'voice' is a medium, if you will, or a recording technology that reveals, through its own analysis and translation of events filtered through the 'personal' – idiocultural – matrix of attitudes, interests and obsessions, the faceted composition of the mid-Victorian English subject. To continue and enlarge upon the mechanistic or tele-technological metaphor, each 'voice' is thus a performative projection device, a machinery for the re-presentation of particular scenes that are, themselves, metonymic figures situated 'on a plane of immanence where past, present and future coexist and can be ordered [or disordered] in various ways . . . [and so] constantly shape the world and its subjects' (Pisters 2003, 3). Hence, the condition and formation of English identity is unfolded through a series of narratives that only come into being as a result of occluded histories of the past resurfacing, coming to light, and rupturing the surface of the present. Our attention is drawn to those voices, which, without the eruption of the past, would not come to be recorded or subsequently replayed. And what causes them to be replayed is the crisis at the heart of the English home, 'within the memory of men still living', as Macaulay puts it in stating the purpose of his history of England (1986, 51), occasioned by the need to find a father figure to fill the gap left by the death of the previous occupant of that position.

Betteredge as witness and narrator or, history from underneath

On the perceptions of the constitution of Englishness, and the 'topsy-turvy . . . actions and attitudes' (*M* 116) of its historical encryption in the novel, we have to consider Gabriel Betteredge's narrative. Not only does it assume the lion's share of the narration, but Betteredge's parabasic asides to the reader, his interruptions of narrative flow, and his constant recourse to *Robinson Crusoe* serve to inform the reader about the percipient nodal points of English identity, from particular perspectives of course. If Betteredge cannot see what goes on directly in front of either his literal or metaphorical nose, he is, nevertheless, uncannily acute with regard to cataloguing the ideologically governed discourses of Englishness. As with so much of *The Moonstone*, Collins may be read as expecting his readers to look not directly ahead of them, but always to one side. Seeing *how* one sees, and, concomitantly, reading *how* something is said, is often as important as the content, if not more so. If the story of the Moonstone is merely an occasional tale, something which, in providing a visible symbol on which to focus, and so to hang other interests and concerns, Betteredge's mode of narration is far from being accidental in its intellectual divagations and seemingly aleatory reflective meanderings. It is a profoundly significant narrative. Taken as a performative act, it invites us constantly to look at *how* it leads us astray in making us believe that it is always on the verge of 'getting to the point' or that it promises repeatedly to do so. The point is not the point, so to speak, but how that point is a focal location for misdirection and misreading, while 'something else' takes place in a performative fashion. All is sleight of hand, and the pun might be risked that Betteredge has a 'better edge' apropos his analytical perceptions than the more conventional reading of his character can credit him with. In this matter of legerdemain though, *The Moonstone* utilizes crime and its reception as the occasion for cultural reflection, social commentary, and the revelation of the constitution of social, historical and personal subject.

In considering the matter of Englishness in Betteredge's narrative, we may take, for example, the following passage from Chapter 9, in which is the account of Rachel's birthday – and which day of course is that on which the diamond is stolen, 'June twenty-first' (*M* 115). These are Betteredge's first words. They punctuate and sign the beginning of the chapter with an apparently precise factual register. The rest of the sentence, and indeed the opening paragraph that the single sentence makes up, sounds remarkably like a weather forecast: 'the day of the birthday, was cloudy and unsettled at sunrise, but towards noon it cleared up bravely' (*M* 115). What, it may be asked, does this have to do with anything pertinent to the story of the Moonstone, its theft, and all subsequent events? It might even be asked, how can weather be brave or clear up 'bravely'? Pausing a moment though: Betteredge's choice of word is interesting semantically and historically in the context of the present discussion. While the more common modern understanding of the adjective would see it as synonymous with 'fearlessly' or 'valiantly' (two of the definitions given by the *OED*), older uses of the word, meaning 'excellently', 'well', 'capitally', or 'handsomely', more commonly signified by 'bravely' in the sixteenth and seventeenth centuries but being maintained in English into the nineteenth century, are all in play here.

This etymological reflection aside, however, is this sentence not, in truth, an unremarkable statement? The sentence is remarkable precisely for being so unremarkable, so seemingly everyday or commonplace. It does nothing to move the narrative forward. It has nothing to do with the narrative as such, or the theft in particular. It advances, promotes, nothing. It is, however, exactly for those reasons that we should pause, as the sentence itself does in performative fashion through the retelling of this apparently inconsequential observation, before continuing. As in so many other places, the reader is suspended at the moment of inauguration. The beginning does not start. It stalls and idles. Betteredge is 'setting the scene' of course. He is attempting to be the good storyteller. Quite how he remembers what the weather was is something that might give us pause, from which opportunity of reflection we might then conclude, perhaps provisionally and hypothetically, that Betteredge employs the language of the weather forecast as gleaned from newspapers of the 1840s.

Though a small point it is not without interest. Such observation might even be said, albeit in passing and out of a sense of historical irony, to pre-date and thus anticipate John Ruskin's concerns with the storm clouds of the nineteenth century, in a lecture delivered on that subject in the 1880s. The interest comes from the very prosaic nature of the statement, a quality of prose combining with what might be described as a very English interest, the weather. Speaking of the weather is a cliché of Englishness. At the same time, in his effort to be a storyteller, Betteredge can be read as 'fictionalizing' or inventing the history through the prosaic, quotidian utterance that extends beyond his particular interests to those of a culture and shared identities. Moreover, his commentary, though an attempt at starting, betrays his narrative amateurism. Such amateurism is telling in more than one way. For it gives us insight into Collins's composition methods – he pays due attention to the fact that his 'writers' are not professional novelists like himself, and so gives to them the inscription of the seemingly unnoteworthy in an effort to provide for the reader both psychological and writerly verisimilitude. More than this though, this technical gesture is performative in another fashion, for it provides the reader reasonably well versed in English literature with a compositional, historical analogy. In reading how Betteredge fails to proceed, rather than perceiving an aesthetic fault in his 'want of system', we may suggest that Betteredge has learnt how to tell a story from his 'paternal' literary authority. He shares his 'amateurism', his apparent lack of narrative technique, with that quintessential and prototypical bourgeois Englishman, Robinson Crusoe. Like Collins's

construction of Betteredge, Defoe gives to Crusoe an amateur authorial style, one which, not knowing what detail to write and what to
omit or edit in some manner, includes the extraneous, the marginal,
the quotidian, without due regard for narrative significance or otherwise. In short, the Englishness of English narrative is manifested in its
'curious want of system' and this is situated as both historical and
cultural in its positioning of voice. This is moreover to be understood
by Collins as being the first step in an oblique, comic, and not a little
frustrating disquisition in the mouth of Betteredge on the historical
dimension of the masculine English subject as narrator of history,
which is translated from period to period. The 'want of system' is thus
apprehended as both singular, marked by the traces of its cultural and
historical, material contexts, and shared.

It is thus that we come to read that which Franklin Blake fails to
read, that dimension of narrative witness to which he is blind: a
shared cultural identity as inscribed in the mode of representation
between the two men, the shipwrecked Crusoe, and the baffled
Betteredge (whose state of mind, it might well be surmised, is
frequently shipwrecked, foundering as it does on the contradictory
reefs of personality, information and event). Through formal analogy
constituted in the resonance between acts of reading and writing as,
in turn, signs of the constitution of the male English subject as
modern Englishman, Collins remarks the invisible maintenance of
the historicity of that subject in a trajectory between 1719, the publication date of Defoe's novel, and both 1848 (the year of the
Moonstone's theft) and 1868, the year of Collins's publication. The
difference between 1848 and 1868 is perhaps precisely one of unreadability and readability. What is not available to Blake is available to
Collins. This can only be conjecture, of course, but the transhistorical
significance of *Robinson Crusoe* for the constitution of the English
subject has not gone unremarked. In 1919, Virginia Woolf had
commented, in an assessment of *Crusoe* that affirmed the Englishness
of Defoe's work, that it 'resembles one of the anonymous productions
of the race itself rather than the effect of a single mind'[2] (Woolf 1919,
125). To this one might add *The Moonstone*, with the revision that for
Collins, the English mind is to be written not singly, monologically,
but as a discontinuous, fragmented, and heterogeneous collective of
singular contesting experiences and memories, of which Betteredge's
voice is but one facet and example. His belonging to this multiple
articulation arrives as one instance in a constelled structure, subsequently refracted through the twenty years between the events of the

novel and the time of Collins's writing *The Moonstone*. The novel thus figures itself as a literary–historiographical archival sedimentation of the national subject, its projection, its inscription and its effect. The articulation of English national identity in its modernity is thus again understood as having a specifically determinable horizon and history, as well as being one sign amongst others crystallized, we might argue, from out of the discontinuous and coterminous synchronic flows and forces, whether molar or molecular, micro- or macrocosmic.

Thus it is, in this, as in *Robinson Crusoe*, as readers as divergent in their perspectives as James Joyce or Karl Marx have observed of Defoe's protagonist, that Betteredge stands in relation to the reader as the privileged agent and 'family retainer' (to employ a somewhat Victorian euphemism for a servant of some standing). As the notion of a retainer, a form of vessel, might suggest, Betteredge 'contains' the traces of Englishness, its attributes and attitudes, its articulations and blindnesses, which in the conjunction that we come to find them are neither isolated nor individual. Rather they are the instance of a singular articulation and experience of Englishness, of national identity as this comes to be figured, embedded and embodied, materially and historically. Such imprinting or sedimentation is given full articulation in the paragraph that follows immediately on from the opening sentence of Chapter 9.

In the paragraph in question, Betteredge lays out for the reader his method of proceeding on the birthday, with regard to the staff's and his conduct towards Rachel. He begins with a parallelism and analogy, thereby figuring himself in relation to the head of the body politic and the national 'house': 'I follow the plan adopted by the Queen in opening Parliament – namely, the plan of saying much the same thing regularly every year'. He continues:

> Before is delivered, my speech (like the Queen's) is looked for as eagerly as if nothing of the kind had ever been heard before. When it is delivered, and turns out not to be the novelty anticipated, though they grumble a little, they look forward hopefully to something newer next year. An easy people to govern, in the Parliament and in the Kitchen – that's the moral of it. (*M* 115)

Encapsulated here is the work of analogical comparison at many levels: between social microcosm and macrocosm; between servant and master (or in the case of the Queen, mistress, which is ironically appropriate given that the master is dead in the Verinder household);

between family structure and national structure in the regulated enactment of ritual. That Betteredge's speech occurs on Midsummer's Day suggests a minor inversion of ritual and hierarchical order, and this is further figured in the comparison made – perhaps irreverently? Is this even readable? – by Betteredge, between himself and Victoria. The comparison between the servant and the head of the house is further re-enforced in the detail that the Queen, through the offices of Black Rod, must gain permission to address the House of Lords before entering (no monarch having been permitted entry to the House of Commons since 1642, when the Speaker of the House refused to allow Charles I to arrest five members of Parliament). Thus while at the national level, the monarch is made momentarily and constitutionally subservient to the government, reading a speech prepared by governmental committee, Betteredge retains the power over the house for himself. This small moment of subversion allows apprehension of the cultural and historical dimensions of the constitution of the English subject in a telling manner.

In its narration it admits, moreover, of the local 'historical' recycling of events in the house as part of the identity of house, household, and family (in which structures the servants are also located). Anticipating Ezra Jennings's restaging of the events of the birthday night and the jewel theft, which re-enactment cannot take place without the aid of Betteredge in the opening up and running of the house, the discourse on the house admits in turn of the functions and failures of function in that site as inscribed through reiteration, revenance, and what might be termed performative cultural memory. They are thus structurally integral, in their recirculation, to the reconstitution and re-memorialization of identity's truths in the narrative of *The Moonstone*. Arguably, the house, once more, is understood as crucial to the delineation of Englishness, to which identity the diamond and its theft are merely peripheral phenomenon and event. In that circular temporal form, there is also the analogous figure of the historicity of the opening of Parliament and the Speech from the Throne, constitutionally regulated and formalized in 1642, as already observed. Thus the house, which cannot operate without the servant, stands in for the hereditary, rather than the elected House of Parliament, the Lords, and its ritual reiteration of symbolic governmental inauguration. As Betteredge is given to observe, the speech remains more or less the same and this occasions a little, just a little, dissent (very English), and with that 'government' returns to order, and so both nation and house, and of course the subjects constituted as English indirectly through such acts, continue.

Disorientations of perspective and presentation

That only a few observations and asides from Betteredge lead the reader a dance across particular modes of discourse, cultural histories, and the coincidence of historical moments and dates, might be taken as of analytical interest with regard to the rest of the novel. Certainly, given the number of documents with which the reader has to contend, dating and the precision with which historical events, whether real or fictional, whether directly mentioned or indirectly alluded to, are necessary markers in the text. That the text rapidly and repeatedly becomes enmeshed within its own narrative and historical snares as lines cross and recross, even while they displace the certainties of knowledge in an abyssal condition of undecidability, does nothing to alter the fact that dates – and eventually times – serve an important function throughout the novel. Often, dates are all that remain for the reader to navigate by, to refer back to, and by which to reorient him- or herself in the textual and historical labyrinth.

Take the very inauguration of the novel, for example, to which I have already referred and to which it is important that we return. Beginning before it may be said to begin properly, and thereby doubling as well as displacing any assertion of origin or source, *The Moonstone* opens with a prologue. As remarked, the Prologue recounts the 'storming of Seringapatam', the date of which is given as 4 May 1799. In itself a historical event, the looting of Seringapatam by English troops led by Sir David Baird serves Collins as the location from which the narrative of the Moonstone's theft by John Herncastle arises. In telling the story briefly, the Prologue, presented as a collection of extracts taken from 'family papers', moves sketchily back to the origins of the stone's adventures in 'the eleventh century of the Christian era' (*M* 53). The history of the diamond dates back therefore to a period roughly the same as the Norman Conquest of Anglo-Saxon England. However, even as the reader is presented with the adumbrated history of the Yellow Diamond (as the Moonstone is also called), a 'counterfeit' narrative of a 'semi-transparent stone of inferior order of gems' pertaining to superstitions in Ancient Greece and Rome is acknowledged, without apparent purpose (*M* 53). From the outset then, the reader is trapped in conflicting and competing mythical and historical narrative codes, the 'truth' of the diamond, its very identity, opened to uncertainty as the authority that the narrative would seek to establish for itself in the presentation of an accurate history becomes undercut in its very articulation. Seeking to offer a faithful representation of the past and with that how the past may be read in an effort to understand how one arrives at the present, John Herncastle's cousin leads himself into a narrative that confuses rather than clarifies, which seduces through mythological and irrational mystification instead of offering a coherent historical account.

Standing back from this strangely *confused* narrative report, what might be said concerning the *how* and the *why* of the presentation, rather than offering merely a commentary on the presentation of a history? Of what can one speak if pausing to reflect on the location of the transmission of this version of events, which is itself not a beginning but the only place, after the events, from which we can start (and this only because the silent editor of the volume, Franklin Blake, has ordered his material so)? I speak of the narrative as *confused* because in bringing together, in fusing differing narrative strands, the tale appears needlessly to seek to justify or confess its subject through the appeal to prior histories involving conflicts. It appears to want to admit silently to its own limits in its commentary on the struggles between Muslims and Hindus, as well as in its more general narrative of pagan lunar worship as an explanation of perpetual cycles of irrational struggle and what might be called 'cultural *lunacy*', which, in itself, takes on the semblance of the *only* explanation, albeit irrational in nature (necessarily so), of the history of successive civilizations. Form *performs*, the version of events admits of an inescapable, possibly *lunatic perversion*. This comes to recycle through the various sensational adventures, down to the single image of 'John Herncastle, with a torch in one hand, and a dagger dripping with blood in the other . . . like a madman' (*M* 56, 57). The light brings illumination, not only to the palace but across the years from 1799 to the date at which the family papers extracted are inscribed, so that the reader witnesses the violent work of the English abroad. We should pause to reflect on the following: is it not the case that, if we are reading this, Franklin Blake, the absent editorial and authorizing presence, has transgressed the desire of the writer, who 'beg[s] it to be understood that what I write here about my cousin . . . is for the information of the family only' (*M* 57)? This is no small detail. What is to be read here, however, is that all authority comes to be undermined, even as transmission takes place, and that the structure of the novel is always caught up in this deferral of truths and identities, of injunctions and authorities, even as it seeks to acknowledge their claims.

Take, for example, the very opening of the Prologue, its first paragraph. I have already cited and considered this briefly above. I want to return to it once more, however, it being the first document, the primary evidence and 'witness' in the case of the Moonstone. In the present tense, as if the author were in a place where he is not, that is, alive and standing before us as we read, there is the assertion of the desire to explain the past. This desire is announced in order that misunderstanding, misreading, might be undone. The present tense thus arrives in an uncanny and untimely fashion to seek in its inscribed revenance a perpetual and spectral return, in effect, to ask for and authorize a right reading, on the pretext that this has not taken place as yet. At the same time, the author of this desire and these documents strives to assert 'on my word of honour, that what I am now about to write is, strictly and literally, the truth' (*M* 52). Yet, as we have already witnessed, the 'truth', so-called, is confused through the conflation of competing narrative interests and the undecidability that arrives in the author's *authoritative account.*

Moreover, this authority has been called into question before the present writing ever arrives – the family has already misunderstood the reasons for the schism between the author of the 'Prologue' and John Herncastle – and subsequently in Blake's publication of the papers. This must lead us back to that ellipsis. What was omitted from the quotation is a parenthesis on the part of the author, who includes the following clause (I shall re-cite the line, this time in full): 'I beg it to be understood that what I write here about my cousin (unless some necessity should arise for making it public) is for the information of the family only' (*M* 57). The parenthesis appears in the desire and injunction with the force of a judicial clause intent on the possibility of a corrective act of retrospective rereading to occur at some unspecified point in the future of reading that authorizes the transgression of authority – *unless some necessity should arise for making it public.* Blake does of course make the extracts public, along with a great many others, as we know. What the necessity is or might be, however, is never explained, and thus remains encrypted as that which motivates every page of *The Moonstone*. More than this, it might be said that the encrypted necessity is at once nowhere to be seen and yet everywhere, on the surface of the text. It is nothing other than the text in short, and thus is always hidden.

Authority thus authorizes its own undoing, it confesses to the contingency by which authority is established, on the premise that it authorize its own undecidability as either the first or final word. The truth, history, origin, and a final 'true' reading all rely on the fact that there is always at the heart of the very possibility and the desire for such a reading the impossibility of any such true reading or access to any truthful, factual account, to which can be appended any signature as guarantee of a strict or literal truth. That such undecidability haunts the author of this version of events, this auto-occlusive account for the full and economical accounting of which any authority is revealed as unequal – one can only economize on the abyss in a more or less violent and unreasonable fashion, consigning reading of the encryptions as that which remains to come – is acknowledged at the close of the Prologue. Having testified on his word of honour that what he is telling is the truth, strictly and literally (the truth, the whole truth, and nothing but the truth, as the phrase goes), in the penultimate paragraph of the Prologue the author undoes his own authority. If this is not in direct relation to what he has asserted as the truth, it nonetheless should give the reader pause. Despite having told of the events leading up to the discovery of John Herncastle with the bloody dagger, Herncastle's cousin remarks that 'Whether this is true or not, I cannot prevail upon myself to become his accuser' (M 58).

The remark is an odd one in the light of the earlier demand that what is said is to be taken as the strict and literal truth. Such a testimony is itself accusation if it is to be believed. Of making events known to the public, the author remarks, again curiously, that 'I have no evidence but moral evidence to bring forward' (M 58). He continues: 'I have not only no proof that he killed the two men at the door; I cannot even declare that he killed the third man inside – for I cannot say that my own eyes saw the deed committed' (M 58). All that is *seen* is a man with a bloody dagger and a torch. This is the only fact in the case, other than the date of the siege, and the words of John Herncastle as heard prior to the raid. Even the words of the dying Indian uttered at the feet of John Herncastle are the subject for doubt on the part of the author: 'if those words were pronounced to be the ravings of delirium, how could I contradict the assertion from my own knowledge? Let our relatives . . . form their own opinion . . . and decide for themselves' (M 58). Finally, the author of the Prologue extracts remarks that, whatever the truth or otherwise of the diamond's legend, he is 'influenced by a certain superstition of my own . . . It is my conviction or my delusion . . . that crime brings its own fatality' (M 58). Superstition resides not outside in the legend, or in some foreign other, but in the Englishman, in the supposed source of knowledge and authority. The testimony becomes nothing; for in its authoritative account of the facts, it admits that the facts amount to nothing very much at all, only an admission – or a confession – of undecidability.

Thus at the heart of the rebus that is *The Moonstone* is the credibility of the English mind, a mind that admits to its own fallibility, to the possibility of superstition as the other to empirical rationality. And, apropos English identity we read the rhetorical affirmation of undecidability concerning the self and its perceptions in that acknowledgement that *conviction* and *delusion* hold sway equally as those possible elements in the constitution of the English subject in his interpretations. Thus, the Prologue announces in its revelation of the how and why of historical narrative a testimony of its own: that history as the narration of the English subject has no authority on which it can rely, *especially in those instances during which the narrator appeals to authority.*

Narrative countersignatures

The narrative appeal to authority acts as a countersignature within itself, and as its other to its own status as authoritative truth-telling. For, in appealing to a prior authority, the narration confesses, secretly and yet in public, that its own authority is not exactly authoritative. Structurally, something is lacking, missing, absent, within the articulation of the first-person narrator. And what is missing is precisely that sense or delivery of authorizing source or origin, the paternal or patriarchal voice from which narrative can set out, and around which it motivates itself as an implied structural and historical centre. Inasmuch as we apprehend the inescapable necessity of this in Collins's novel, we must return to Gabriel Betteredge and the first chapter of the first period of the story proper.

In Chapter 1 of the First Period, the story of the loss of the diamond, dated 1848 in the title line, Gabriel Betteredge's account presents the reader with a curious opening gesture. The steward of the Verinder's Yorkshire house 'starts' with a double gesture: of parabasis and reading. 'In the first part of *Robinson Crusoe*, at page one hundred and twenty-nine, you will find it thus written' (*M* 59). Betteredge's commentary appears to imitate scholarship, and appeals, not a little, it must be felt, and in addition, to the discourse of the sermon. A sense of mockery, perhaps parody, insinuates itself into this, the first line of the opening chapter. In a novel arguably readable as a pastiche, if not of literary styles or genres, then certainly of cultural discourses as the inscriptions of historically and materially determined praxes, one begins with deferral of the narrative and the undercutting of authority through the pastiche of authority that the first sentence embodies, if not enacts. Such a device is not merely formal. It is also profoundly historical, however invisibly the pastiche work may take place. For it is important that we do not forget that *The Moonstone*, a novel in which the majority of its apparently principal events take place in 1848, is in fact written and published twenty years after that date. Collins solicits the reader's attention to the historicity of discourses, even as he produces a text the purpose of which is to allow the Victorian subject to read him- or herself as the interpellated and overdetermined subject of those discourses that are the subject of pastiche.

In its appropriation or co-optation of cultural discourses, *The Moonstone* offers a pastiche of pastiches. It puts together a discontinuous patchwork of imitative first-person narratives. Each of these are verbal 'gestures' signifying ideological and epistemological structures into which particular English subjects of the 1840s–1860s are inserted, and into which, being interpolated by such discourses, they situate and so constitute themselves. This is the case whether one considers Miss Clack's fundamentalist, dissenting Christianity, the law as embodied in Mr Bruff, Mr Murthwaite's articulation of colonial ethnography, the cosmopolitanism and education of Franklin Blake, Ezra Jennings's scientific and philosophical discourses, or the more complexly encoded discourse of Englishness as signalled through the text of *Robinson Crusoe* as interpreted by Gabriel Betteredge. *The Moonstone* weaves together, even as it unravels the occluded interrelations of such seemingly disparate and heterogeneous matters, a textual articulation in which every narrator is shown as a *pasticheur*, consciously or otherwise. Thus, the novel offers the reader a glimpse into cultural and historical subjectivity as constituted implicitly counter to the very idea of authority or the identification of a single author's hand. What we might fail to read in the twenty-first century is the extent to which we are being made 'equal players with the characters', as Sarah Waters has it in her introduction to Mary Elizabeth Braddon's *The Trail of the Serpent* (Waters 2003, xxi). Certainly some readers – though by no means all, as Dickens's perplexed annoyance reveals – in the 1860s would have understood this, Geraldine Jewsbury amongst them. What some of us, and a number of nineteenth-century readers, perceive as merely comical or irritating 'tics' of personality, clichés of characterization, are historically embedded glyphs, which serve to either exclude or admit entry into the culture from which the novel emerges, and which it in turn mediates. As Waters continues in a remark as applicable to the reading of Wilkie Collins as it is to Mary Braddon, 'we must learn, with [the characters of the novel], the slipperiness of signs; we must ponder the proper management of those semipermeable social membranes through which we experience the lives of others and risk the under- or over-exposure of ourselves'. *The Moonstone* is perhaps the novel par excellence of the nineteenth century to attempt to decipher, or at least show, how one manages the semipermeable social membranes by which we are constituted as historical subjects.

Such management, economy, and order are at stake in the very appearance of *Robinson Crusoe* and the citation of that text in the opening paragraph of the first chapter. It introduces a first-person narrative – Betteredge's – that sets itself up in response to a prior first-person narrative. In responding, it takes responsibility for its response, identifying its historically located position in a relay of English voices. It affirms responsibility for its act of reading as being far from value free but being, in effect, at the heart of historically, culturally, and materially determined Englishness. Responsibility can only take place in the absence of the other, the father. And one must assume the role *in loco parentis*, as paterfamilias. This is the historical crisis that the novel stages as the condition and grounds of nineteenth-century ontology and modernity in relation to its pasts, to the past as family history, as colonial history, and as the historicity of English national identity. Whether we are to approve or be critical of the arrival of such a gesture as inaugural, to accept it as an authorizing or authoritative text, or find it ideologically problematic in the historical construction of the English subject is rendered undecidable from the outset. Undecidability and the cultural *Sehnsucht* that is the hallmark of Collins's pastiched Englishness reveal themselves in the authority that reference to and citation of the quotation would confer on belatedness and the concomitant admission that one cannot know if one's decision is right until after a decision has been made.

It is as if *The Moonstone* is precisely the documented archive of the *Sehnsucht* (yearning, craving, nostalgia, or desire) of the English subject in the mid-nineteenth century. Seen in this light, the novel is received, and readable, as a multifaceted cultural phenomenon. In reflecting and refracting the various 'sides', if you will, of a fractured and heterogeneous subjectivity in the period of the 1840s through to the 1860s, the novel confesses repeatedly to a historical loss, and therefore an irrefragable absence *as and at* the core of that sense of modern Englishness. Such a core must retrospectively be read; that is the imperative, the mission of the English, but ultimately any justification of such a project is impossible through teleological retrospect, as that very retrospect repeatedly makes plain at every turn in the documents that make up the case and adventure of *The Moonstone*. Collins thus enacts through the novel the endless work of constructing a historically valid and authorized national identity. It is worth observing of this strange beginning (which anticipates everything in the novel, every aspect of its telling, its form as serial sequence of first-person narratives that assume responsibility) that it questions inauguration in its performative beginning. It thus authorizes only the impossibility of giving authority and therefore justification to such an act. Writing must arrive *and* so return, folding back on itself, and illuminating the beginning as haunted by a prior document, a prior first-person narrative, to which it is indebted and must respond. All writing is a form of return, of revenance. In order to be read, it has to have already departed from the event, the datable or historical instance that is the moment of inscription in order to be transmitted and readable. Written in 1719, detached from its author, *Robinson Crusoe* arrives and returns at least twice on the first page of the chapter – in 1850 (of which more in a moment) and 1868; and of course subsequently at every moment that every reader opens *The Moonstone*. Writing thus speaks on the 'folly' of beginning in the moment that beginning promises to get under way. Moreover, it arrives as a form of encrypted knowledge, the implication of which concerns its own arrival. Far from being simply a commentary, the remark of Crusoe's re-marks Betteredge's writing, authorizing it, even as Betteredge de-authorizes that authority by reading it according to events that take place outside of any possible intention on the part of Defoe. That to which Crusoe confesses in the quotation has to do with the impossibility of a timely interpretation, analysis or reading of experience, event or any series or sequence of events understood retrospectively as 'history' or the past.

The question of a particular untimeliness or belatedness (Crusoe only sees after the event, and so 'sees' 'too late' (*M* 59)) is only available to being understood *after* one is under way in interpretation, whether the question concerns reading a text or apprehending the world. In this, the apparent prescience for the Verinder steward of Defoe's novel is, in effect, a reminder of the anachrony that informs any act of reading, whether of a text of the past, or indeed, of one's own memory. That the text precedes event suggests an inversion of order. Or, to see this differently: a disorder of a temporal nature is announced from the place of a beginning that is neither the source nor the origin either of the narrative or of events. Instead, it is itself announced as the narrative of events taking place two years after the events of the novel and occurring in between the Prologue and Chapter 2, which begins by questioning the proper place from which to start. To reiterate the point, Betteredge's opening gambit under-mines therefore the very idea that one can begin from, or is justified in, situating an undeniably authoritative inauguration or genesis. The authority of the origin falls into ruins even as we seem to set off, the first narrator acknowledging that he is only 'first' in response to a demand made on him. That Betteredge attempts to date events, albeit in parenthesis, announces all the more stridently the futility of locat-ing a fixed point from which to depart. The date given – 21 May 1850 – is already preceded by 20 May, the day on which the passage from page 129 of *Robinson Crusoe* is read. Betteredge's response to Mr Blake is further complicated inasmuch as while Betteredge acknowledges the interpretative belatedness that marks the idea of a beginning, whether the encounter that spurs the response is with another person or with a text, Blake is not himself the sole 'author' of the request.

This comes about as a result of conversation between Blake – who at the time of this first chapter is already the 'new' master of the house, although Betteredge omits to mention this, referring to him as 'my lady's nephew' – and Mr Bruff, the family lawyer. Betteredge's acknowledgement of Blake's relation to the now deceased Lady Verinder has a couple of consequences. On the one hand, it displaces Franklin Blake from his position as master of the house, thereby elid-ing his authority. For Betteredge, and therefore the reader, Blake is not the new master, the replacement father figure. On the other hand, though written two years after the events surrounding the diamond's theft, the remark brings back, in its phantasmic reconfiguration of relation, the dead Mistress, as if she were still alive. Betteredge's apparent inability to keep temporal sequence in mind undermines his own dating of the passage. More than this, however, it also admits to a 'drift' (a word Betteredge will use concerning communication, intention and meaning) of its own, a temporal drift effected in writ-ing that disrupts writing as an accurate and reliable means of repre-sentation of the past. However, coming back to Blake's own tale, of his previous conversation with Bruff, the result of this discussion is the conclusion that the whole of the story should be committed to writing, 'in the interests of truth' (*M* 60). This notion of *truth* has already motivated writing, of narrative in the service of a true accounting of history, as we have seen in the Prologue.

Yet, as we can already tell, writing does nothing to secure or guarantee the truth, whatever truth might be taken to be. Blake's insistence on 'a record of the facts' (*M* 60) is important, for, as he argues, its principal purpose is to preserve the 'memories of innocent people' for 'those who come after us' (*M* 60). Writing thus becomes an imperative, externalized mode of memory, an archive and repository for transmitting truthfully the events of the past to the readers of the future. In Blake's justification, writing takes the place of the present. As a result, in being the communication between past and future, writing erases the solidity of authoritative presence, which, ironically, that writing is desired to convey. Betteredge's reflections tacitly acknowledge the undercutting of authority. First, he admits that he did not at the time perceive Blake's 'drift'. Following further amplification, Betteredge writes, 'I failed to see what I myself had to do with it' (*M* 60). Whether this is merely Betteredge's reflection of what takes place or whether this is a remark made to Franklin Blake is not clear. In the possibility that it could be read as either or indeed both we read the impossibility that writing can record the facts unequivocally, that it can convey without ambiguity the story in a truthful manner, resistant to questioning. Indeed, Betteredge's 'failure', his inability to perceive, is a sign that even in the presence of Blake, communication is flawed, open to miscommunication.

Framing and erasing

While the Prologue and Epilogue appear to frame the story, there are elements in both which exceed and so erase at least partially the work of such framing devices. Within this structure another formal framing occurs, Gabriel Betteredge providing the opening and closing narratives within *The Moonstone* 'proper'. He 'close[s] the story up' (*M* 535), much as he is responsible for closing – and opening – the Verinder house on behalf of its inhabitants. This structure is specifically played out as the analogy between narrative and house, and Betteredge's function in both, when he is given instructions by Ezra Jennings and Franklin Blake to open the house in order to stage, as nearly as may be possible, a repetition of events from the previous year. This second moment not only replays events but also the narrative itself, up to a point, with the important aspect being that in not being the same there is a movement onwards in the narrative that has been held in abeyance up to this point – with that comes also a movement into the future for various characters, so that they are no longer held in narrative suspension. Nothing, the novel tells us, can go forward without repetition. The future cannot begin to arrive, regime change cannot occur, without the re-staging of crisis so as to displace perceived threat and set up in its place the new head of the house. Crisis is both real and symbolic, therefore, and must be perceived in its double function. If one needs a father figure, then even a steward or stand-in is better than none at all. Culturally, all the energies of the English, their institutions and familial structures tend towards this end in the novel.

At the same time, the re-staging of the night of the theft speaks structurally to the frames within frames and the movement across the borders of such frames as implied in the structural anaphora of iterable phrases, idioms and so on, not only within one narrative but from one narrator to another. The motion of iterability is double. While we as readers and characters return to various places, and while each narrative is an iterable variation, playing on a displaced repetition of previously narrated events, however indirect or implied, there is also the sense in which events return as the traces of themselves in the various narratives. This motion of return is figured perhaps most strongly in Franklin Blake's narrative, the third narrative of *The Moonstone*.

Blake begins the 'third narrative' by dating its first sentence: 'In the spring of the year eighteen hundred and forty-nine I was wandering in the East' (*M* 357). The date, once more, marks a beginning as a memory of a prior moment, and so turns back in recalling, while returning and disturbing the present instant of inauguration with the trace of memory to which writing responds. The past always haunts the present in *The Moonstone*. Blake's narrative 'begins' also through the receipt of letters calling him to change his plans and return to England. One letter, sent by Mr Bruff, informs Franklin Blake 'that my father was dead, and that I was heir to his great fortune. The wealth . . . brought its responsibilities' (*M* 357). Writing, relay, transmission, the death of the father, responsibility and response: all inculcate the English subject here, overdetermining the meaning of his being. The past in all its traces and manifestations has a 'terrible influence' on the subject's 'present position and future prospects', as Blake remarks. It paves the way, as he puts it, 'for the slow and toilsome journey from the darkness to the light' (*M* 400). Following his return to

England – this is his second return, remember: Blake is always *returning* to England – he inquires into the case of the missing diamond, and comes to the conclusion that 'there are missing links in the evidence, as *I* left it' (*M* 361). That emphasis indicates the assumption in first-person narrative of responsibility, and that responsibility turns Blake towards Betteredge. With the aid of Betteredge amongst others, Blake begins 'picking up the fragments of evidence which Sergeant Cuff . . . left behind him' (*M* 366), and so assumes responsibility in the wake of another, now absent authority, the figure of the Law, whose own Englishness is marked in its singularity through the love of roses. There then occurs the reading of Rosanna Spearman's letter (*M* 371–2), the text of another dead person as authoritative imprimatur in the absence of the living witness, which directs Blake to the Shivering Sand, as recollection admits that 'all these strange results of the abortive inquiry . . . [which] were clearly present to me again' (*M* 373). First-person narrative is marked in its forward movement by the unequivocal traces of the past, whether manifested in written form or in the apparitional resonance of memories. Forward temporal motion can only be motivated by what is absent, deferred, translated and translatable, hence particular references to meaning, interpretation, and emphasis placed in forms of writing (*M* 368–72).

The climax of this physical and mental action is that Blake is forced to focus on a paint stain on the discovered garment buried in the box in the Shivering Sand, and, utilizing the stain as a means of taking a 'leap from present to past', put memory to work, so that, despite his absence, the words of Sergeant Cuff are issued like some phantom injunction to action. The words 'travelled over my memory, repeating themselves again and again with a wearisome, mechanical reiteration' (*M* 376). The text thus assumes a mnemotechnic function through the transport of its traces, as the novel attempts to recover the truth through covering ground previously traversed, both in the imagination and materially. And this of course leads to the estranging presentation to Franklin Blake of the incontrovertible evidence of his own name stitched into his nightgown, providing the evidence of himself as an other, as the thief of the diamond. As Blake puts it, 'I had discovered Myself as the Thief' (*M* 377).

Blake supplements the doubling effects of reading in foregrounding the role of memory and in contesting memory – specifically the memory of the reader, which is to say nothing less than the reader's authority (self-assumed) as a good or reliable reader – with documentary evidence, by suggesting that one turn back to earlier parts of the narrative: 'A glance back at the sixteenth and seventeenth chapters of Betteredge's Narrative [*M* 194–209] will show that there really was a reason for my thus sparing myself' (*M* 399). The reader is enjoined to turn back in the book and so to move to a place of departure from which the reader has already departed. Blake defers his own authority to that of another, and in doing so admits that the master is not the master of the servant but dependent on the authority of the subservient household figure. In this admission of dependence, social order is inverted and so Blake's authority in the English house usurps and undermines itself. Such potentially subversive reliance is all the more marked, if we recall the significance to Blake and the reader, not only of Betteredge's narrative but also the letter, the confession of Rosanna Spearman, reproduced *in toto* (*M* 392–8), and also the posthumous papers of Ezra Jennings. The authority and centrality of Englishness is structured by its need to seek support from its marginal and subservient cultural others.

Furthermore, if we consider Blake's injunction to the reader to turn back to previous pages, we apprehend a distrust implicit in Blake's inescapable reliance on writing, echoing that assertion in the Prologue that the truth is being presented or can be presented. We also may read a distrust on the part of the Englishman to consign the judgement of the present in its posterity to the future reader. In referring the reader back to Betteredge's chapters (M 399 (*M* 194–209); *M* 405 (*M* 104–15); *M* 453 (*M* 121–33)), we witness Franklin Blake seeking to shore up his identity with the ruins of the past, as the basis of the future, but also distrusting the act of reading beyond his control, beyond his presence. This desire for mastery of meaning and the future is of course impossible. Indeed, by citing or alluding in his own present first-person narrative to the chapters of other first-person narrators, and in reproducing documents while remarking on occasions that memory fails or that he cannot interpret, Blake undoes any authority he may desire to situate in his person. Nor will the reader be much help in turning back to other chapters. Such returns can never produce the same reading every time, however, because one returns to particular chapters and narrative moments with a different perspective, different information, and so on. Therefore one reads the chapters differently, and so the time of reading as a dislocation of anachrony – before and after knowledge but never as the revelation as such – becomes implicated in the structure of the story as its very condition, in *The Moonstone*'s investigation into the role of hermeneutics in the constitution of a precisely historicized English subjectivity.

The doublings, repetitions or reiterations, and the processes of displacement enacted throughout the narrative of *The Moonstone* are both structural, that is to say, spatial, and historical/temporal. In such a manner is it possible that we witness how narrative, in taking responsibility for history, enacts the conditions by which 'the past and present rose side by side' (*M* 409). Such a structure, one which is further amplified by the 'silent' distance between 1868 and 1848, has, itself, a double, simultaneous function. It affirms cultural distance and invites us also to read that distance, those distances, while also installing the signs that reading is impossible, it can never come to a close. One particular aspect of inheritance unveiled through cultural distance – an aspect of inheritance that might also be read as a return of the repressed in a particular manifestation of the national cultural psyche – is the novel's indebtedness to the Gothic. One subtle inheritance and transformation of Gothic is to be read in Collins's use of the 'formal device of multiple narrators' (Schmitt 1997, 8), silently and graphically doubled itself in the implicit yet overt display of the documentation of those narrators. 'In the service of legalistic realism' the formal multiplication of *The Moonstone* 'replicates Gothic doubling and perspectivism' (Schmitt 1997, 8). If there is to be read a difference engendered by and signifying such relation between historically marked and determinate manifestations of the novel, it is in this: ultimately, while the Gothic novel in its first appearances desires and strives for the illusion, if not the representation of narrative and therefore epistemological closure, *The Moonstone* always implies an abyssal undecidability, the very prospect of which is only thinly veiled in the pretence of narrative resolution, as this is proffered in the narrative return of Gabriel Betteredge. Betteredge takes up the narrative, taking it to its conclusion 'proper', thereby seeming to close the case of the Moonstone much as he closes up the house following Ezra Jennings's experiment (another narrative and structural duplication and displacement, wherein the occluded event has its iterated staging). But the house, though closed, remains haunted. Betteredge can no more keep the English house safe than can his master Franklin Blake authorize the correct reading. For there arrives, beyond the closure of the end, that fatally disruptive, disturbing supplement of the Epilogue, comprising not one but, somewhat exhorbitantly and comically, three documents as witnesses to conclusion's impossibility. And the very last of these, from the explorer Murthwaite, concludes with a defiant rejection of any pretence to authority, mastery or meaning. It ends with an admission of history's cyclical revenance and iterability, drawing itself to an end that is no conclusion in remarking how history, the temporal motions of past into present and on into future, effectively erases in its repetitions and its iterable, yet singular events any linear progression:[3]

> So the years pass, and repeat each other; so the same events revolve in the cycles of time. What will be the next adventures of the Moonstone? who can tell! (*M* 542)

Notes

1. The revolutions in Europe beginning in 1848 in France and continuing in Europe for the next four years arise out of calls for suffrage and concerns with national identity. While some readers may feel my admittedly tenuous connection between the date of Collins's novel and the European events as being something of a stretch, I have no wish to make extended claims for the synchronicity, beyond a perhaps deeply encrypted symbolic resonance. Hypothetically one may risk suggesting that Collins places his novel at this historical juncture, writing *The Moonstone* very shortly after the second Reform Act of 1867, so as to intimate a complex sense of crisis in the English in relation to European events of twenty years before.
2. Woolf is not alone in observing the Englishness of *Robinson Crusoe*; in their own ways, so too have James Joyce and Karl Marx, as I go on to comment in the body of the essay.
3. While I cite the Broadview edition of the novel, I have followed the punctuation used in both Penguin editions of the novel, edited respectively by J. I. M. Stewart (1966) and Sandra Kemp (1998), which give the final punctuation mark as an exclamation rather than a question mark, as is given in the Broadview, and which would be the more obviously conventional diacritical mark following a question.

4 'Minutely and Multitudinously Scratched in All Directions': *Middlemarch*

Now we are quite grown up, and can put away childish things.

Walter Bagehot (1867)

No formulas for thinking will save us mortals from mistake in our imperfect apprehension of the matter to be thought about. And since the unemotional intellect may carry us into a mathematical dreamland where nothing is but what is not, perhaps an emotional intellect may have absorbed into its passionate vision of possibilities some truth of what will be . . . the artist seizes combinations which science explains and justifies.

George Eliot, *Daniel Deronda* (1876)

Signals

Signals, whether they travel across forty years or almost a hundred and fifty years, can get scrambled. The connection can become frayed, if not broken. Messages, mailed at one moment and intended for more or less immediate delivery, can, if delayed or misplaced when sent on, fail to arrive, or otherwise become degraded, subject to translations and ciphers for which they could not have been prepared. Everything depends on maintaining the network. And yet, the web of tissues, filaments and connections is not only always subject to interruptions, it is always in the process of being restructured, upgraded, redesigned, with different modes of delivery, different languages, protocols and so forth. The question is one of the transferability between operating systems. It concerns how *what* becomes transmitted to *whom*. If the media are encrypted in languages and according to protocols to which we no longer have access, how do we gain access? To what extent, Eliot might be read as wondering in *Middlemarch*, is the recent past as much a Rosetta Stone as some more distant relic, composed of sigla, glyphs, and hieratic signs, numerous

traces, events, and singularities that, once comprehensible at a seemingly intuitive level, now appear illegible, or at the very least in
danger of being lost in translation?

The matter, on the one hand, is one of representation, the representation of ourselves and re-presentation of our others, our ances-
tors, previous generations, those others who still call to us, in us,
defining our identity. To what extent do we constitute, actively or
passively, the others in our acts of representation? And in doing so, in
such representations does the other, do the others, return, despite
ourselves? In the representation is there that ghostly revenance by
which the other makes itself known however *appresentatively*, and by
which we come to represent ourselves as if, in receiving the tattoo of
signals we come to be tattooed, imprinted? However undecidable the
problem remains, the matter is one, undoubtedly, of a coming to
consciousness in a given present moment through our acts of representing the past and thereby structuring our cultural memory of that
past and ourselves, each mediating the other. 'The great question'
therefore, writes Jacques Derrida, is 'that of the value of representation, of its truth or its adequacy to what it represents' (2005, 310).
However one begins to answer that question, one must address *the*
demand put to consciousness for bearing witness to history and the
past, for it is the question of the representation of any number of
epochs in the discontinuous yet interwoven relation between them. It
concerns what takes place, what is transmitted, received, and what
remains to be read between, let us say, the epoch of the 1820s, the
1870s, and 'this epoch' in which we situate ourselves as 'ourselves', as
a self-reflexive and historical consciousness today, from where we
read the past, several pasts. It is a matter of representation within the
representation of 'this epoch', from where we read Eliot reading the
previous generation, those who did not yet know they were opening
themselves to a future, a modernity to be called in retrospect
'Victorian'.

The problem of representation then is one of relation without relation to consciousness in *Middlemarch*. Consciousness in *Middlemarch*
involves a mediation between self-consciousness and consciousness *of*
and for others. Consciousness, as self-consciousness, can become a
kind of reflective and narcissistic, distorting egoism in characters such
as Bulstrode, Rosamond, Fred, and Casaubon. However, consciousness, historically attuned, can cause characters and by extension
narratives to 'take ... responsibility for creating ... alternative
worlds' (Tucker 1991, 788). Eliot thus negotiates through form and

content the historical dilemma of consciousness's creativity, its inventiveness and openness to the other, inventiveness being the means by which 'another's consciousness' might be apprehended, felt, thereby presenting a connective transference of signals in what seems like 'the almost magical possibility of the transfer of one consciousness into another . . . Characters who are alive in the moment to what they hear are most vulnerable to or most powerfully able to meet the consciousness of another' (Young 2003, 227).

Taking this further, in a different direction, the 'trope of the web' in Eliot anticipates or, let us say, receives from the future the traversal of the internet. The web is thus 'intrinsic to [the reading of] history', and also a history of reading and representation, figuring both the 'forces of industrialization' by which a net is produced and the 'weaving, textile production itself' as the trope or motif of form and productivity – and therefore representation – 'radically altered [in Eliot's time] by the industrial revolution' (Givner 2002, 232). That the web remains a potent figure of productivity and transmission, and that one can perceive a connecting skein of fibres between distinct historical instances of consciousness through the transmission and translatability of the 'web' (from hand loom to internet, via factory production) announces in itself Eliot's own prescient sense of a radical break with older modes of representation. It figures the significant and irreversible epistemological and ideological transformations of consciousness historically in response to commercial and cultural modes of production. Representation, as Eliot realizes, is always, simultaneously, representation of some event or experience, and the representation of a consciousness, in a 'prosopopoeic flow of one character into another, from microscopic characters to telescopic ones, from dead characters to living ones' (Givner 2002, 239).

Regarding the novel and its interwoven strands, interrogation moves therefore between the 'what' and the 'who' repeatedly. *What* do we mean when we speak of the past, of history, of identity, and how do we represent or bear witness to these as they reflect us, as they reflect ourselves to ourselves. And *who* do we define ourselves as, *who* do we believe or read ourselves to be in relation to the *whatness* of larger structures of identity? In what ways does the past remain with us, and how can it be read with a view to gaining access and insight into who we are? *What* or *who* defined as an alterity from the past and in any present epoch touches on personal *ipseity* or selfhood connecting us in the articulation, the self-reading of a *who*, which is itself woven into an attestation and representation of historical community and ontology. The convolute of interlaced problems refigured as the constellation ipseity–ontology–memory–history that produces the textile weave of *Middlemarch* requires an approach that disrupts from the outset habitual or conventional modes of thought and representation. This frequently assumes the form of lateral relation identified by Sally Shuttleworth, who observes how strands between narratives and characters are taken up laterally, 'from a larger social issue to its effects upon the thoughts and reflections of a single life', and, it must be said, vice versa (1986, 148). The lateral structure is defined by Eliot in a commentary on 'form' as 'the relation of multiplex interdependent parts to a whole which is itself the most varied and therefore the fullest relation to other wholes' (*EGE* 433). And so on . . .

As a result of this lateralism or multiplex, a form which in opening its own space to its others inevitably introduces into the representation of 'community' an alterity or heterogeneity which is as temporal as it is spatial, Eliot produces effects and repercussions that are 'incalculably diffusive'. Here is the extract in more detail, from which this phrase is taken. It concerns Dorothea, and arrives in the final paragraph of *Middlemarch*'s 'Finale', to intimate an opening beyond formal closure: 'Her *finely touched spirit* had still its *fine issues*, though they were *not widely visible* . . . *the effect of her being* on those around her was incalculably diffusive' (*MSPL* 838). There is disruption within representation here, attesting to unreadable, intimate and yet perhaps historical forces – *perhaps* because incalculable before arrival, reception, before the historicity of afterthought and the untimely act of reading by which one might know that an effect has been produced. Through this, Eliot speculates on and enacts a (self) conscious mediation on the historicity and temporalization of ipseity. At the end of *Middlemarch*, Eliot sends out the spectral touch, along invisible elements, vibrating threads. The sending here is double. For, on the one hand, it is the dissemination from the year in which the novel concludes. On the other, it is the sending on, from 1872. The historicity of this post is rendered anachronistic. Untimely in that it is sent twice, its passage duplicated and divided, the signal of history's largely invisible resonances remains to arrive, and so, for Eliot at least, remains to be received and read.

The reader can never 'know' Dorothea directly. 'Dorothea' remains a trace, a multiplex, to use Eliot's word, of already incalculably diffuse traces, an indirect and phantasmatic presentation or, let us say, staging, no direct representation at all, as that figure 'finely touched spirit' in being 'issued' touches almost invisibly as the effect of the other, the trace of being, might cause one to respond. What Eliot describes in the 'Dorothea' effect, as the work of sending on, is an 'internal "touch" without any visible corporeal surface' (Derrida 2005, 178), and so with that the '*possibility* [the merest chance of this, no more] of appresentative empathy, of indirect or analogical access' as the '*essential* possibility . . . finding itself grounded in an intuitive . . . co-immediacy' by which the reader is touched by the ' "guiding thread" of analysis', coming to feel him- or herself, therefore, 'already . . . *constitutively* haunted, by some hetero-affection' (Derrida 2005, 179) that is ineradicably, inescapably, the trace of being's historicity. And what goes for the hope that resides on Eliot's part in the singularity of the trace given as the name 'Dorothea' goes also for the constitutional haunting effects of every historical sign gathered in *Middlemarch*.

Contested reception

In her essay 'Notes on Form in Art' (1868), Eliot remarks, 'it is often good to consider an old subject *as if* nothing had yet been said about it; to suspend one's attention even to revered authorities and simply ask *what in the present state of our knowledge are the facts that can with any congruity be tied together and labelled by a given abstraction*' (*EGE* 432; emphases added). Note how Eliot ties together epistemology (*state of knowledge*), consciousness in its temporal givenness (*our present state*), relation (*congruity, tied together*), and ontologization (*labelled by a given abstraction*). All are knotted together in the seemingly disingenuous fiction of turning to the familiar or the past – as might be implied in that phrase 'an old subject' – as if it were new, without the layers of interpretation, and to do so not merely for the sake of analysis but in order to begin the translation of that subject so as to meditate and open to inquiry a reading of the collective, though heterogeneous condition of selfhood in the present. *Who* we are is opened through the turn to *what* we believe we know about some form about which we already think we are conscious, and which we tell ourselves we believe we have mastered.

As with most of the novels discussed in *Dickens to Hardy*, *Middlemarch* has endured a contested reception amongst critics in the second half of the twentieth century over the question concerning the extent to which it is 'properly' historical. This contest, and with it the accompanying critiques of Eliot, takes place precisely to the extent that the fully temporal and historicized inquiry into ipseity and ontology is missed, to the extent that in the attention to the content of the realist novel there is occluded the processes by which representation comes to be formed at a given epoch. The question has often been one of whether *Middlemarch* aestheticizes history relying on an overly ornate figural complexity and ambiguity rendering the signs of its historicality unreadable, while also inquiring whether it seeks to convey the force of its ethical convictions through stressing the significance of sympathy and even sympathetic sentimentality, thereby occluding history. In this context, the history of *Middlemarch*'s reception has assumed the quality of a 'head-on collision between literary and historical character', criticism having 'long been divided by divergent interpretive tracks, one which runs along the lines of a . . . march of history, and the other which follows the perhaps slower lines of figurative reading' (Givner 2002, 224). The division in readings illustrates an aporia and, with that, a failure to read the historical differently that Eliot's novel anticipates. To the extent that *Middlemarch* is a historical novel tracing historicity without 'history', without, that is to say, the direct or mimetic representation of History's 'raw facts' or 'big events', it envisions the historical apocalyptically and apophatically. Speaking and unveiling only ever indirectly, and knowing this to be its one possibility of presenting a past that can never be present, *Middlemarch* situates and presents not only a dilemma in historicized representation at a given historical moment. It addresses itself to that dilemma or crisis as the experience of an aporia in memory as the nineteenth century moves forward rapidly and the pre-Victorian, pre-industrial past is on the point of being lost from living memory. *Middlemarch* overcomes the experience or presentment of the aporetic in an act of remembering as phantasmic, singular presentation, thereby serving as the locus of cultural memory in constructing an imaginary consciousness.

That consciousness, memory of a collective, yet heterogeneous, self-differentiating self, writes its selves through a number of perspectives as a nexus of (a)material traces. The consciousness is thus double, informed, on the one hand, by the traces of the moment in which it is inscribing itself in the form of a narrating narrator, and, on the other, staging itself as its other, as a narrated narrator at the time of the events to which it bears witness. 'History' or, more precisely, differentiated cultural memory of a given but otherwise unrepresentable and irrecuperable past, which cannot be staged in any monolithic manner, is presented and enacted. It is witnessed nearly simultaneously as (1) being in transition, and therefore not fully conscious of the events taking place around it but by which it is being shaped and serves to determine, while also (2) being in suspension, the 'suspension' of an observable medium, in which there are the various elements, organisms, or interactions and events brought into focus by the analytic consciousness and the optical 'tools' by which that consciousness gives visible form to the invisible past.

Yet, there has been that failure in the transmission of the historicized consciousness which has resulted in the misreading of the novel. Terry Eagleton, for example, has argued that *Middlemarch* maintains what he calls '"real" historical forces' such as cholera, the first Reform Act and the railways, on the 'margins' of the novel (1976, 126). More than this, Eagleton avers, Eliot's ethical position and her employment of the web metaphor as dominant structuring figure in the novel (1976, 119–20) effectively dehistoricizes and depoliticizes the novel. (How in the same essay Eagleton can speak on the one hand of the web as dehistoricizing while on the other discussing the 'ideological matrix' of Eliot's text is not a little baffling (1976, 111).) To be fair, Eagleton is clearly uneasy in the argument he makes, inasmuch as he suspends 'real' as if recognizing the problem that he cannot make go away or maintain in a binary dialectic: that the idea of the 'real' is not monolithic and not so easily determinable or separable from the 'textual', the 'literary', or 'figural' as he might desire. To propose one 'real', a homogeneous reality or material world, is to maintain a certainty or to attempt to keep in place untenable boundaries between word and world, or between interior and exterior. It is also to assume that one knows exactly where those borders can be discerned. Eliot's concern with that which permeates the boundaries of external experience and inner registration, so that consciousness in the novel is always consciousness of one's historicity and material being, effectively dismantles the binarism on which the materialist critic relies. The 'nature of consciousness' (Young 2003, 224) in Eliot is never an abstract matter. As Kay Young remarks of consciousness in *Middlemarch*, the novel, 'in its representation of a community in the middle – the middle class of a mid-nineteenth-century English province – shifts the ground of the investigation . . . [of the earlier novels named for characters] from "what do *I* know?" to "what do I know of *you*?"' (Young 2003, 224). Statements such as Eagleton's do not recognize that such an epistemological quandary inevitably must entail a grounded, historicized mode of inquiry. Eagleton's remark puts into operation an ontology of the 'properly real', while hiding in its gesture the fact that ontologization requires a mode of epistemological and conceptual, that is to say *figural*, work at the levels of discourse and thought. It is also to ignore that the figural is, itself, historical, or at least the re-marking of historicity's marks, signs and traces.

Such critical oversight is also at work in Daniel Cottom's *Social Figures: George Eliot, Social History, and Literary Representation*. This highly detailed and sophisticated materialist monograph on Eliot's writing argues that it amounts to a 'cancellation of history', which erasure takes place, allegedly, because history is 'treated [by Eliot] as an effect of discourse' (Cottom 1987, 25). Unlike Eagleton's commentary, Cottom's analysis at least seeks a means by which the figural and social can be linked. And this he does in designating the historical moment of the mid-Victorian era as one involving a project of liberal intellectual overdetermination of the social by the figural. Yet, he also reintroduces the separation of the real and the literal into a stable binarism in making the assertion that there takes place a 'process of constructing metaphor through the repression of social reference' (Cottom 1987, 9). In its rush to keep as wide a gap as possible in the binary divide that is installed by the materialist critic, such a violent reading completely overlooks or ignores that in Eliot's writing there is 'the strategic choice of signifiers . . . [that are not nor] cannot be entirely independent of [or indeed separable from] . . . historical readings' (Derrida 1981, 75). Eliot of course apprehends this, remarking this condition and the necessity for a properly historical reading in a number of places, but most precisely in those locations, at those junctures and as a result of those experiences and events, where the nature of consciousness comes to be foregrounded as a mediation of being and the historical.

This is clearly signalled in *Adam Bede*. At the beginning of Chapter 17, Eliot remarks both the passage between empirical observation and experience and the passage to interpretation, and the necessity of bearing witness to the materiality of being in its historical contexts, and so representing 'nature and fact' in order to 'give a faithful account of men and things *as they have mirrored themselves in my mind*' (*AB* 221; emphasis added). That figure of the mirror recurs throughout *Middlemarch*, indicating a concern with both representation and its limits, and also the inescapable realization on Eliot's part that the experience of the real is only ever available as the phantasmatic translation, and is thus always already figural, tropological. This in no way denies history or keeps it at the borders. Far from it, for there is the sense to be read here that in the penetration of its traces, and with that the writing on and of the self by those traces and their indelible hetero-affectiveness, history, the real, the social or whichever monolithic and logocentric term you choose by which materiality and historicity are idealized, refuse to be kept at bay, at the subject's arm's length. Eliot acknowledges as much through her manner of 'complicating' the figure of the mirror and, with it, any simple or naive perception of the role of literature as a simple, faithful mimetic mirror held up to 'nature'. For, she continues, 'The mirror is doubtless defective; the outlines will sometimes be disturbed; the reflection faint or confused; but I feel as much bound to tell you, as precisely as I can, what that reflection is, as if I were in the witness-box narrating my experience on oath' (*AB* 221). The subject's attestation is already a translation, a mediation, and concomitantly the transformed conveyance of that already transmitted to the subject.

It never appears to occur then, to either Eagleton or Cottom, that what they read as the occlusion of history is itself markedly the sign, the constellated gathering of the signs, of historicity's work. It seems as if there is no recognition that there is a struggle to produce a language commensurate in its rhetorical force with those effects produced 'in the real', as it were. Nor do they read the possibility that there takes place the opening of an ironic gap through a discourse that simultaneously mirrors or duplicates, and so distorts or deforms, the subject of its analysis. Thus, when Cottom quite rightly asserts that 'it is in the nature of the middle classes to identify their interests with those of everyone in society' in a process of ideological mystification (1987, 25), he gives no sign of registering that Eliot's identification of middle-class interests might not be part, or in support, of the same project. Eliot's almost exclusive focus on the middle classes in *Middlemarch* at a given historical moment, a focus drawn from a different historical perspective, operates on the formation of the middle classes as cultural and ideological event in order to open fissures in a particularly middle-class mode of representation, on the figural resources of which it borrows tirelessly and parasitically.

Writing forty years on, of historically distant, but culturally proximate middle classes coming into being with a nascent, fragmentary collective and striated consciousness of their own dawning modernity, Eliot produces her narrative as a pastiche or ironic countersignature therefore. This in turn serves as a material intervention in the ideologies of middle-class English modernity across four decades of the nineteenth century. It makes visible the complex processes by which middle-class identification proceeds at a historically specific moment – the years immediately before the first Reform Act of 1832 – in order to open to the middle-class reader after the second Reform Act of 1867 the possibility of a historicized self-reading. This work requires an engaged burrowing or *under-labouring* of linguistic networks as these are marked culturally and historically. Yet, as Givner argues of Eagleton's exemplary historicist critique and that of other critics such as Cottom, there has been typically amongst materialist critics 'a resistance to the notion that figures and tropes might operate as historical and political forces' (Givner 2002, 225). Such resistance is blind to the very properly Victorian sense of history and of being's historicity that is articulated throughout *Middlemarch*. As we shall see, the reading that assumes on Eliot's part a separation of history and literature, the 'real' and the figural, is misguided at best, wilfully ahistoricist at worst, because it is unable in its cultural egocentrism to make visible that which Henry Staten describes as 'the density of historical specification in the novel', which is not itself a 'symptomatic reflection of a "historical impasse," but . . . an intricate analysis of the way in which this impasse is articulated' (Staten 2000, 992) in both the 1820s and the 1870s. Eliot's language effects a kind of double vision, establishing an oscillation between two distinct historical moments. In doing so, the tropological work of *Middlemarch* enacts the historicity of Englishness as it is informed and transformed in approximately forty tumultuous years.

Scratches

Here is a particularly illustrative, not to say illuminating and well-known aside from *Middlemarch*:

> An eminent philosopher among my friends, who can dignify even your ugly furniture by lifting it into the serene light of science, has shown me this pregnant little fact. Your pier-glass or extensive surface of polished steel made to be rubbed by a housemaid, will be minutely and multitudinously scratched in all directions, but place now a lighted candle as a centre of illumination, and lo! The scratches will seem to arrange themselves in a fine series of concentric circles round that little sun. It is demonstrable that the scratches are going everywhere impartially, and it is only your candle which produces the flatting illusion of a concentric arrangement, its light falling with an exclusive optical selection. These things are a parable. The scratches are events, and the candle is the egoism of any person now absent – of Miss Vincy, for example. (*MSPL* 264)

This long passage is one of the more frequently cited extracts from *Middlemarch*. It is markedly intrusive in its self-reflexiveness. More than that, it speaks quite insistently on the subject of 'the irreducible figurative or metaphorical nature of all language' (Miller 1975, 127). Such irreducibility installs a web or weave that, though resistant to the final demands of a stable reading, nonetheless traces and is traced by a marked materiality or historicity, as well as offering a sharp interpretative perspectival insight on the equally irreducible figurative nature of such historicity. Taken from the third volume of *Middlemarch*, it opens Chapter 27 with a direct address to the reader. Turning away momentarily from direct narrative commentary on the inhabitants of Middlemarch and their provincial lives in the West Midlands of England at the end of the 1820s (1829), shortly after the revision of the Corn Laws in 1828 and after the Catholic Emancipation Bill was passed (April 1829), and just a couple of years before the first Reform Act, this particular narrative offers us a hypothetical scene that differs apparently from the tale of *Middlemarch*. Eliot makes this clear in identifying the story as a parable.

More than that, however, between these events and the Second Reform Act, Eliot sets up an aural reflection, as it were, across the decades, engendering a double echo that at least some of Eliot's readers would have registered. Though addressing figuratively the figurative condition of language and thereby reflecting its own work, the narrative is not about itself solely. It does not close itself onto itself in some hermeneutic entrapment, but consigns itself to a historical afterlife, in addressing itself to those unspecified *yous* and also us through the indirect mode of narration. In short, it provides a distorted reflection, the very distortion of which is intended to illuminate in two directions. On the one hand, the purpose of the parable is to shed light on how narrative proceeds, how one might read obliquely in the light of a seemingly realist and mimetic narrative mode. Events, figures, history: none of these are to be taken at face value, or as simple mirrored reflections. Something – let us call this the chance concatenation of scratches – intervenes as a medium for positioned perception and perspective. One should pay attention to the way in which the images are produced, and to the value of representation in the transmission of knowledge, learning to read the modality of projection. On the other hand, the illumination is intended to be that of the reader, to whom the apophatic discourse is directed in a disruption of mimesis and apparently straightforward representation, for the presentation or staging of that which is deliberately artificial, and foregrounded as such.

Through its mode of address, the inaugural moment of the chapter aspires to the rhetorical condition of an apostrophe. An apostrophe is, of course, a diacritical mark indicative of an elision. It signals either possession or omission. It is a written, inscribed mark that silently but graphically directs one's reading, supporting interpretation or translation without drawing attention to its own function. However, apostrophe is also a rhetorical mode of address that turns away from its subject to address a *you*, the reader, a reader, several readers at different times and locations, but most importantly a reader who can only be remarked in his or her absence, whether because imagined, dead, or not yet having arrived. While, through that 'accent of elision', the apostrophe's work appears to be to stress an abridgement or a connection and, with that, the closing up of a space that the apostrophe attempts to stitch closed, it remarks simultaneously the impossibility of such closure. The apostrophe marks the text with an irreducible spacing. Far from being simply a commentary, in its apostrophic eruption *and* disruption it is a performative speech act of sorts. It is performative in that it remarks the operation of writing and so draws attention to the very function that in the narration of events in the history of Middlemarch it would otherwise efface. It enacts a differential opening informed by a displacement that is the result of writing. This is writing's inescapable condition, of course. It is always at a remove and in the process of its inscription remarks or betrays its own being-spaced, spacing itself from any immediacy or presence.

The apostrophe in this form announces, in that spacing or displacement, a temporal condition also, its deferral from its imagined or implied addressees. In effect it remarks, performs, its historicity, its material moment. It turns to speak or write to those *yous* who own 'ugly furniture'. *You* are identified in the passage as owning a pierglass. 'You' is the person instructed to place a candle so as to reveal the scratches. Yours is the candle. Each and every one of those *yous* is thus deferred, until you arrive as that consciousness for whom the apostrophic and phantasmatic scenario is destined and dispatched, but whom it has yet to reach. This displacement or spacing, which is also marked, and remarks itself in its temporal deferral, is therefore impossible to close as we have already observed. And it is, again, an opening between locations that are impossible to situate absolutely, without the relational and relative mediation of the apostrophic break and hinge.

That spacing is a sign of inscription's historicity, even as the apostrophe, turning away from its subjects, remarks itself as being
stranded from the 'history' of *Middlemarch* and the temporal suspension of the Middlemarchers, always enacting their historically specific
experiences over and over again. Those inhabitants are so many
'scratches' perceived from historical distance. They leave traces, *they
are in effect traces* recorded as after-effects, like so many motions in all
directions coming together only to form for a moment an apparently
concentric form, in a narrative writing doubled and displaced, a narrative writing that is at once a narration taking place in the 1870s and,
at the same time, a narration of events located almost half a century
prior to the event of writing. Writing as the apostrophic instance
announces a historical 'writing', the inscription of events on the
surface that one names history, which it both is and is not. *As if* one
were leaving or copying perceived marks or scratches from one surface
to another, writing thus remarks its historicity as if on a still malleable
clay tablet, on which one or more of the *yous* to whom the apostrophe appears to be addressed might have a perspective.

It is *as if* the blank page were the pier-glass or steel surface, which
becomes etched in time, minutely and multitudinously scratched in
all directions. Amongst the topics or 'scratches' that appear in – and
as – this extract (both surface and its content are directly or indirectly
revealed; by the light cast, on the one hand from the apostrophic
turn and, on the other, by a subject whose shadowy presence casts a
light), we may note: philosophy, science, optics, perspective,
servants, domestic economy, class, the universe, illumination, parable (and therefore narrative), representation, prestidigitation, projection, anamorphosis, psychology. It might be said that these
'scratches' gather as an attenuated and distorted concentration of the
concerns of the novelist. To put this in another light, the passage and
its marks offer a performative and highly elliptical concentration of
the novel as historical and cultural recording machine, a *mnemotechnic* that, like the pier-glass, is worked on to produce particular effects,
otherwise invisible perspectival and optical interferences in the
communication.

Thus, we understand, or are meant to understand, our positioned
position, our relation to the past, to cultural memory, and so our own
historicity and inscription as beings in a cultural–historical trajectory.
This is what we are given to perceive by the illumination afforded by
the apostrophe that, in turning away from narrative, sheds its light
on both how narrative functions and where we stand in relation to

interpretation – unless of course we misunderstand our role, seeing and misreading ourselves in an egoistically non-reflective manner. To read oneself in all the interwoven condition of one's being is to be aware, as Will Ladislaw remarks, that '[art] is an old language . . . I suppose if I could pick my enjoyment to pieces I should find it made up of many different threads. There is something in daubing a little one's self, and having an idea of the process' (*MSPL* 206–7). Ladislaw's self-reading affirms the complex historicity of one's being. It is a reading that decentres the self, and in this is a historicization of being in a profoundly textual manner not available to everyone. Perceiving ourselves to be central to a universe existing only for and circling around us, we fail in our historicized self-reading, and are remarked as so many Rosamond Vincys. For, like her brother Fred, Rosamond fails to read and so make connections or observe their threads. She never comes to know 'another soul' because, as is the case with her brother, she has a consciousness 'chiefly made up of [her] own wishes' (*MSPL* 119).

It is perhaps worth mentioning that a 'pier-glass', arguably another mark that remarks the surface as cultural sign, is a large mirror, usually placed between two windows or over a fireplace. Like the page on which writing leaves its signs, consigning, punctuating its moment, the mirror is the support and medium of reflected or mediated representation. The analogy between the page on which there is writing, and the mirror on which there are scratches is not fortuitous. Eliot's suggestion appears to be that there is no presentation, no representation or perspective, which is not distorted, and which cannot be altered by assuming a different position. All presentation or representation, whether narrative or visual, is already a perspective, a selection, which itself is translated by the perspective of the subject, the perspective taken by the subject on the perspective afforded by the medium of its subject. No unmediated or undistorted historical view is available to us, nor can there be. One cannot have access to the past without the help of those signs that also, in their opening a view to the past, serve to distort both what is seen and how it is observed.

Literature is both 'historical', a material production that at given moments has different histories and inscribes itself differently in its different times, and also the structure or support-medium that allows for the material inscription of the signs of historicity and identity in various semantic, philosophical, and ontological ways. In occluding its own operations, at least in principle in its 'classic realist' modes, literature makes possible a 'historicity without history – historicity

without direct references to actual occurrences but only direct exposure of its field' (Fynsk 1996, 223). There are of course *more or less*
direct references in *Middlemarch*. But that *more or less* is itself arguably
the direct exposure rather than documentary reference. Occurrences
take place that open apostrophically an indirect view on 'History',
that is to say, a no longer available or accessible singular experience of
the years 1829–32 and all those instances or events before, and leading up to, those dates. The signs of this 'historicity without history'
are captured in those minute and multitudinous scratches in all directions, revealed by George Eliot in *Middlemarch* through the perspective of what is otherwise invisible on the surface of a table which
comes to be revealed by chance in the light of the candle. Here you
will note, if you have not already done so, that there is an insistence
on refraction, reflection and mediation. There is a question of the visible, what comes to appear, and how one comes to look at what was
previously unavailable to vision. To reiterate the point, and so
proceed, we are, the novel tells us, acted on, as much as we act. We
are positioned by a perspective on perspective governed not by a
subject but through the chance agency of illumination and location,
from out of which the hidden traces emerge, causing one to reflect.
This is the complex work of historicity in any reading or writing of the
past and, concomitantly, a self-reading of one's own historicity, one's
modernity. One becomes the subject of histories, subject, in being
Victorian or being English, to their demands to be read and remembered through having one's location or positionality revealed to one,
according to some arrival, some event or agency of the other, the past,
and the signs of the past's alterity understood not as a past, but as a
writing or structure. That which is experienced as singular, therefore,
is necessarily other.

Furthermore, the figure of a perspective – taking a position, and
therefore risking an invention of perception – affirms its singular positionality, but affirms that there are always other 'multitudinous'
traces and therefore 'directions' which await their arrival and so
remain to be read. Eliot 'invents' perception for the grounded subject,
whose materiality and temporal specificity of being is articulated here.
By *invention*, I intend to signal a double writing. For Eliot 'creates' an
apparently novel perspective concerning how one sees what has
remained invisible. But in affirming the invisible presence of those
traces, she *finds* that which is at work but which had not yet come to
view. In this gesture of illumination and revelation, she invents (in
the less obvious sense of the word, meaning to find what was already

there) a perspective on perspective, which is informed silently, invisibly by the past, much as who one is, what one takes oneself to be, is *found* to be, is *founded on* or invented by the traces of the other.

In Eliot's image the subject of history, having had revealed to her the network of traces awaiting deciphering, is generated as being subject *to* history. In the implicit gaze of the narrator's perception, something arrives therefore, and though revealed *as if* for the first time, it reveals itself as already in place, having taken place, though previously unavailable to any scientific, philosophical or other interpretative measurement. The historical moment, the material conditions and epistemological discourses that compose that moment, make available what had been invisible, not known to exist. Furthermore, that which arrives is addressed to a *you*: a you and a you, in the moment of a reading, and also an impossible number of yous-to-come, who, through the 'conventions and resources of historical truth-telling . . . give space for the possibility of a meta- or supplementary witnessing' (Clark 2005, 156). Like Mrs Forester's cat vomit or Samuel Pickwick's tittlebats, the scratches may be deemed to be irrelevant, of course, but to dismiss them would be to risk the occlusion of history's others that literature archives in its historicity without history.

Literature's inventiveness thus admits to its 'right to say anything in any way' (Clark 2005, 156), so as to articulate and invent history and the material conditions of being otherwise, to make possible a perception which the 'properly historical' regards as improper, beyond the limits of its purpose. It is this which, following the crises of representation apropos history and cultural memory in *The Moonstone*, and in anticipation of Thomas Hardy's culture and network of archival traces as the mesh of identity's modernity, that *Middlemarch* itself arrives in 1871–72. In this moment, it turns its face decisively in two directions, to the heterogeneous events and experiences of a given past and to the illimitable futures of its readers, as it gathers up the minute and multitudinous scratches of cultural memory and modern identity. In the double writing of the apostrophe, Eliot presents a view of what in retrospect appears an irreversible rupture in the historicity and transformation of English national identity in the years immediately before the first Reform Act. However, given that the apostrophic mode does indicate both opening and connection, it might also be read as apprehending in the 1870s the dimly illuminated perception of another rupture, the signs of which are already arriving, and the full force of which remains to be read.

What of the housemaid though, who, along with the eminent philosopher, is the only identified, if unnamed, individual in the apostrophe? Male and female, theory and practice, master and servant – so much is written in this pairing, concerning class, gender, knowledge, education, and society in and across the nineteenth century. To refocus on the housemaid: there she appears, at work, serving to support an imagined household, belonging to the economy of that house, by maintaining the surfaces in which the master and mistress see themselves reflected – or, rather, distorted given those scratches. Though barely visible herself, yet serving equally important a role in the scenario as the 'eminent philosopher', neither experiment nor parable can take place without her. Indeed, while the philosopher has no experiment without the preparation of materials on the part of the housemaid, neither would the writer have available the events leading to narration without the support that subservient and menial work makes possible. This is, we might say, the economy of history laid bare.

Elizabeth Langland comments, 'the invisibility of servants in *Middlemarch* is startling, most notably in the famous parable of the pier-glass and the candle' (1995, 199). Startling? For whom? Presumably, it would not have been startling to many of those readers in the 1870s, whose own housemaids polished their pier-glasses. To be startled one would have to put oneself at the centre of a cultural universe that could not have imagined such a perception. That aside though, is the sentence not a little inaccurate? For having bemoaned the 'startling' invisibility of servants, in what sense can Langland mean that the housemaid, who is resolutely there, albeit in passing, rubbing away, is invisible? She does not 'disappear' into 'a function', as Langland claims. Of course, the 'presence of a housemaid is assumed in the novel's audience' (Langland 1995, 199), but then isn't this the cultural point? In the gesture of apostrophe, which, arguably, is more startling in its assumption of a faux-confidential, doxical and casual tone – as if it were a bourgeois and domestic aside and not a classical apostrophe – than in its attitude towards the servant, the assumption of domestic labour as employment *is assumed*. Though not one of those 'Great Transmitters' identified by Mordechai in Eliot's last novel, *Daniel Deronda* (*DD* 580), the housemaid, like Gwendolen Harleth in that novel, is 'a medium of transmission' (Crosby 1991, 24). In this, the housemaid, the philosopher, Rosamond, and even Eliot herself – all are media of transmission, scratches on the surface recorded and acting as the substrate of readerly playback.

There is, therefore, no insidious mystification on Eliot's part as Langland argues (1995, 199). In this mode of address, it is as if the apostrophe as rhetorical mode were demystified. The appropriation of apostrophe that speaks of domestic economy, inmixed with the discourse of science, is shown not as timeless and merely a formalist mode of presentation but in its own rhetorically marked reflection 'distorted' by the scratches or signs of its own historicity. The 'tone' of casual anecdote adopted here scratches the form. In doing so, it reveals something on if not beneath the flawless reflective surface. Eliot's pen thus marks up, scratches, a scientific truth in a manner analogous to the servant's inadvertent scratching of the pier-glass. Certainly, we may read the apostrophe as a statement blind to the ideology that allows for and authorizes the assumption that there are servants. But then not only is this novel, *Middlemarch*, about the middling orders, the middle classes, middle England, and the Midlands, it is also a novel concerned with vision, visibility, invisibility, and how one's perspective is altered depending on the source of illumination or how one is positioned. The very name of the provincial town suggests the *middling* condition: *Middlemarch*.

The novel then does the work of that paragraph from Chapter 27, on a much larger but still necessarily circumscribed canvas. It sends itself out, having circled back to its earlier historical moment, in order to illuminate and to gather up the scratches in the light of its transmission, to send them to future bourgeois readers, with the attendant risk that some readers will come to see what those amongst previous generations may have not. Eliot's text seeks to bridge a gap between the 1820s and the 1870s through the assumption of class equivalence, the assumption of a relation and sympathy of perception between the bourgeoisie in the earlier period and the middle classes of the latter moment. At the same time, however, it draws attention to the question of agency in illumination and the otherwise occluded supports by which perspective and representation are made possible. The novel-writer is the servant of the bourgeoisie. She makes their histories appear to them, polishing away to reflect them in their best light, but scratching the surface so as to reveal their impurities, what remains hidden except for the illumination that occurs.

As this passage demonstrates, there is truth in distortion if one knows how to read. Eliot subverts that process of keeping the reflective surface clear. Subversion is to be read in the revelation of perspectival relativism that undermines the desire for or belief in an absolute or universal gaze. A gap in vision is thus introduced commensurate with the apostrophic and temporal gap, and, with that, the small signs of a materialist historiography announce themselves. And in case we miss the point, undermining the truth of mimetic reflection and certain retrospective falsifying views of the past, Eliot then states unequivocally that this is a parable. 'These things are a parable', she states unequivocally in the shortest sentence of the paragraph. It is moreover a parable directed at the idiot reader, who is too obtuse to recognize his or her own cultural myopia or, as Eliot has it, *egoism*. And as if this required driving home, the reader is offered the image of that idiot reader in Rosamond Vincy, for example, who, perhaps not surprisingly is like Mr Casaubon, in that, like him, she 'quivers *thread-like* in small currents of self-preoccupation or at best of an egoistic scrupulosity' (*MSPL* 279; emphasis added).

Threads

If one were to seek a riposte in *Middlemarch* to Langland's misfocused critique, one might attend to Timothy Cooper's words, to which I shall turn eventually. For the moment though, Cooper's is the singular manifestation of a consciousness of historical transition given expression as perplexed suspension in Eliot's narrative. While Eagleton argues that the novel reaches a historical impasse effectively suspending history (1976, 120), this does not sufficiently acknowledge the differing layers of the complex web out of which Eliot constructs her historical narrative. I would contest such a perspective by remarking how suspension is the localized effect on a subject's consciousness in response to effects, modes of production and material practices that, being in transition, are not fully available to comprehension. If there is ambivalence this is part of a structure that makes possible the sense, for the reader in the 1870s, that the previous generation could not have foreseen, much less comprehended in full, the radical social experiment in which they were enmeshed, whether as educated as a Tertius Lydgate, as well travelled as a Will Ladislaw, or as worldly as the banker, Bulstrode. If Langland and Eagleton miss the functions of either the housemaid or Timothy Cooper, or indeed the bifurcated historicization, divided between form and content, between the past of content and the present of narration, a present that passes into a past as it sends itself to a future it can neither be conscious of nor programme, then they fail to attend the very question of the partiality of consciousness, its material embeddedness, and its being enmired in both language and its cultural and social moment.

While Langland concerns herself over the mute housemaid and Eagleton frets at the suspension of history, they fail to read the extent to which this is a historical novel about the cultural myopia and provincialism of a firmly rooted provincial middle-class society, caught in the currents of change they barely register, so obsessed are many of them in their own 'egoistic scrupulosity'. That the housemaid makes only the briefest appearance, that Timothy Cooper steps forward to comment on the advent of modernity towards the close of the novel: these are not simple constative gestures of passing acknowledgement. They position themselves, and remain to be read, as performative gestures on Eliot's part. In no small ironic gesture, her discourse of the middle classes unravels itself in small fraying instances to open a hole in the fabric of pre-Victorian middle-class identity and consciousness. The gap once opened cannot be closed and exposes to a future consciousness that which is not available to the parochial bourgeois perception of the Middlemarchers. In this way, Eliot effectively rents the fabric of cultural history, inviting the modern reader, the recipient of forty years of Victorian modernity, to reflect with hindsight on what comes to appear in the smallest moments of unravelling.

In the light of such a hypothesis, one might consider the narrator's following remark:

> I . . . have so much to do in *unravelling* certain human lots, and seeing how they were *woven* and *interwoven*, that all the light I can command must be concentrated on *this particular web*, and not dispersed over that tempting range of relevancies called the universe. (*MSPL* 141; emphases added)

Other critics have commented extensively on Eliot's use of the web metaphor, and it is not my intention to repeat such commentaries here, even though I have already picked at some of the threads of this discourse. What we should attend to in the present passage is that textile trace running like a material thread, whether we read it immediately here, in the narrator's apologia for the limitations that are self-imposed, or in the example of Rosamond Vincy's and Mr Casaubon's quivering 'thread-like'. The *web* is not a dominant image. It is, however, one emblematic trope of thread-like convolutions and the possible transference of oscillations, setting in motion or to work other vibrations. As we have read in the description of Casaubon, in which I have included Rosamond, a human being quivers 'thread-like'. Sympathetic resonance[1] admits then of either the interconnect-edness between oneself and other beings or the self's auto-solicitude. The danger is either that the 'currents' carried along the threads absorb all one's attention, and so gather one up with that egoistic scrupulosity that admits of no connection to someone other than oneself, or that in being too finely attuned to the echoes that cause the threads to tremble, one finds one's concentration dispersed through the generalization one calls a universal. There must be obtained therefore a focus of current or wavelength. One must concentrate all the light at one's command on a particular web, so bringing to bear one undulating modality on another. This is not, as Eagleton would have it, an expression of the 'suffering abnegation of the ego . . . as the answer to the riddle of history' (1976, 121). It is, on the contrary, an affirmation of the proper limits of an ego or consciousness-in-the-world, the responsibility of which is to be aware of both itself and its duty to bear witness in a particular manner, in response to the vibrations and oscillations, the wavelengths and flows, of a given mesh, matrix, or nexus, culturally, historically, and ideologically generated.

The web, though a structural and spatial figure, is not a stable one. It enacts or maps, as it delineates irregular or rhizomic figurality, and substitutes itself, through the various threads it sends out and by which it is connected, for other figures that are thread-like or web-like, such as textile, lacework, webbing, gauze, and so on. What is impor-tant about the web is that it is constituted of a weave of threads touch-ing and interanimating one another, without necessarily being either wholly animate, organic and 'natural', or wholly machinic or techno-logical itself. The *OED* gives precedence to the web and weaving as human modes of production. Arguably, to risk a digression, as folk songs such as 'Four Loom Weaver' attest, the figure or image of the weave or web is iconic in the violent transformation that occurs during the years of the Napoleonic Wars from hand to factory production. These are, therefore, not only spatial figures but also, profoundly, the traces of material changes to large-scale modes of production, as these are themselves intrinsic to English economics and society. Such figures as there are of *unravelling*, *woven* and *interwoven* bespeak not only human labour then but also historical transition from hand looms (such as that used by Silas Marner) to capitalist modes of production.

As the variants, the substitutions, and the drift from any determi-nation insistent on a natural/produced binary attest, the figure is 'historical', as terms such as weave, textile, mesh, netting, any complex system of interconnected elements, or indeed the internet might acknowledge. Eliot is playing on the instability of the figures in order to signify cultural and historical, as well as epistemological and semantic, transformations, transferrals through figural language of oscillations that are materially and culturally determined. What we receive 'historically', what comes to us as cultural memory is not direct representation but only ever the thread-like tremblings of historical anamnesis in the vibration of its strands. And to draw on one more determination of *web*, invoking Eliot's persistent use of metaphors of optics, vision, visuality, envisioning, imagining, and optical devices such as the microscope, by the 1870s the term *web* is employed to speak of fine filaments that, spun by a spider, are used in optical instruments such as heliometers and micrometers. Recalling then Eagleton's objection to the figure of the web, we see that which problematizes his critique – 'the *web* as image of the social formation', he argues 'is a *derivative* organic image, a mid-point between . . . animal imagery . . . and some more developed theoretical concept of *structure*' (1978, 119). Eagleton's logocentric thinking, grounded as it is in an idealist, dehistoricized, assumption of source and origin and a subsequent transition from natural to artificial, cannot and does not account for the extent to which Eliot's various network of 'interlacing' tropes threaded together from 'relatively autonomous strands' (1976, 119) is the constellated sign of a complex historicity.

Far from 'preserv[ing] the essential unity of the organic model' (Eagleton 1976, 120), Eliot's tropes problematize the very thinking of unity, given that in speaking, for example, of thread, one cannot for certain identify in that trope the organic or mechanically produced, the natural or the artificial. In being a sign of both and yet neither, it remains undecidable, and this undecidability contaminates the entire network along its various intermeshing lines, and through the waves that travel along those threads. Moreover, it has to be admitted that figures of thread, or of weave and web, might equally be self-referential. Eliot may well be read as installing herself into a mythopoetic network as a latter-day Ariadne or Penelope, whose narration and unravelling is cultural, transformed by the historical location from which it is spun. The tropes employed by Eliot resonate thread-like with a history or irreversible mechanization and artificial transformation, not only of modes of production, obviously, but also, and as a result, of literary modes of production, wherein the language of literature is itself mediated and translated by the 'real' historical experiences brought about as a result of that complex web of institutions, practices, and effects to which we give the name the industrial revolution. It does do then to reassert the truth of a statement made by Henry Staten concerning the performative level at which history is *shown* in *Middlemarch* to be operative. History is '*woven* into the text in a scrupulous and critical fashion' (2000, 992; emphasis added). 'Woven' is a keyword here, clearly. It harmonizes with Eliot's own figures of web, textile, weave, and all those other non-synonymous quasi-cognates with which *Middlemarch* is threaded, and from which the reader – today, and in other todays to come – perceives and receives 'a suffusive sense' of one's 'connections with all the rest of our existence' (*MSPL* 165).

More than that, however, it announces obliquely the great historical paradox, to which *Middlemarch* attests. It is the novelistic witness *par excellence* of the condition of being caught up in the passage of an historically, ideologically, and materially ineluctable modernity. If we take the undecidability of the matrix of tropes with which I am concerned in this section of the chapter apropos their origins or their condition as 'natural' or 'artificial', organic or technical, as a curious affirmation of historicization, we see the extent to which *Middlemarch* announces the paradox of being-historical and being conscious of this material condition. David Payne makes specific the nature of the paradox for him. He continues, the paradox is that 'one principal means of obtaining assent to the very modernity responsible for desacralization was to infuse literary culture with a moral authority it had never before been asked to assume'. Eliot's accounting for, and inscription of a 'modernizing ideology' achieves 'secularization by eschatology' (Payne 2005, 123). Eliot's incisive and decisive narrative and historical *après-coup* is only quasi-eschatological though, for as she comments in the inaugural line of her 'Finale' to *Middlemarch*, 'every limit is a beginning as well as an ending' (*MSPL* 832). That is to say, any narrative is caught in a weave of influences, which in leading in different directions simultaneously demand the ethical decision concerning that on which one focuses or which one unravels. If the 'paradox' concerns exactly *how* to assume and articulate moral authority – or let us call this a responsibility for bearing witness to the past, and how one comes to be who one is as the modern English subject, with the commitment to speak in response to the others of that identity – then Eliot's response involves immersing oneself in the labyrinthine complexity of the cultural moment. One does not keep at a distance, commenting at an assumed or constructed temporal remove in order to construct idealist or realist images from which the traces of ideology are effaced. Rather, in order to understand history as informing language and reciprocally interweaving oneself into the fabric of a historicity that has already spun one's own consciousness, one takes up the thread or clew, wherever one finds oneself, and is found, in the labyrinthine structure. Suspended thus inside the complex and irregular spatial coordinates, it is impossible to assume an Olympian metadiscourse.

The narrative is thus woven out from an anachronistic practice analogous with hand weaving. Eliot's role inscribes itself in those apostrophes, instances of parabasis and other arch-reflexive asides to the 'modern' reader, in a still place within the weave. But this is a place that changes constantly, hence the insistence on matters of vision, optics, and perspective. The ground shifts strategically and so do the figural threads. Eliot positions herself as the artisan-producer, whose stillness in observing may be mistaken as non-engagement or suspension. Yet Eliot inscribes, even as she traces the doubleness of what is already a doubled border, internally divided within itself. The secular assertion of moral authority for literature, and with that the demand that literature take responsibility for so many 'fragment[s] of a life' (*MSPL* 832) or lives caught in, defined by, a web of events and experiences as the innumerable threads of that web, is itself inescapably the announcement of literature's singular historicity. This is a work already under way in her fiction, from *Silas Marner* to *Felix Holt* and *Adam Bede*. Each novel announces the artisanal workman, the artificer or technician who embodies the singular experience of bearing witness to history. With *Middlemarch*, Eliot steps up production from those earlier 'individualist' novels, to produce and trace the motions and oscillations amongst a socially heterogeneous group placed in suspension, and caught under the microscope of historical perspective.

Should this image of Eliot the scientist looking at the minutiae of bourgeois culture in the 1820s through the microscopic lens of memory sound like a contradiction (as well as a mixing of metaphors) to my earlier models of either the artisan or the subject in the midst of the labyrinth, that is not necessarily the case. Whether scientist or artisan, the work of either involves close detailed attention to the exclusion of all else. It means focusing closely, following carefully particular motions. The gaze, fixed in place, promises the dissolution of one's sense of self as separate from what one observes, until one sits up, or steps away from the microscrope, the magnifying glass, the

Petri dish or loom. The paradox of moral authority may well be the undecidability of ethical responsibility. That being the case, one cannot assume a single position. One's decision and response cannot be programmed ahead of the encounter with the other, or the singularity of a past event or moment. Therefore, whether it is in the figure of the farm-labourer, the housemaid, the weaver, the eminent philosopher, or indeed the novelist, one must always adopt strategically and provisionally the subject position of being a servant to history, giving attention to the minute details, the otherwise forgotten threads of identity's being, which in unravelling are in danger of being dropped across the decades of the nineteenth century.

Between the various figures whose shadows are to be discerned in the previous paragraph, we appear to gain a passing glimpse of social formation at a certain instance in the nineteenth century. There is a vision, however penumbral, of imagined location. This is the consciousness of cultural memory that Eliot seeks repeatedly to foreground in *Middlemarch*. We see one such instance of envisioning in the following extract, which issues from a reflection on, or consciousness of, the near-invisible threads of sympathetic resonance between like-minded 'emotional intellect[s]', for whoever takes responsibility to watch 'keenly the stealthy convergence of human lots' and the 'preparation of effects from one life on another'. It is, as the quotation immediately below and the following passage make explicit, precisely such an oscillation or *timbre*, less rigid or ostensibly, visibly maintained than the divisions of 'modern' class society that defines the interwoven condition of identity in past historical moments, in provincial society: 'Certainly nothing at present could seem much less important to Lydgate than the turn of Miss Brooke's mind, or to Miss Brooke than the qualities of the woman who had attracted this young surgeon. But any one watching keenly the stealthy convergence of human lots, sees a slow preparation of effects from one life on another' (*MSPL* 95). Shortly after, the following paragraph enlarges on the sentiment and vision just witnessed, providing for the reader one of several key cultural reflections on the past, to which the image of the scientist Lydgate provides access, and for which he acts as the connecting fibre:

> Old provincial society had its share of this subtle movement: had . . . also those less marked vicissitudes which are constantly shifting the boundaries of social intercourse, and begetting new consciousness of interdependence. Some slipped a little downward, some got higher footing:

people denied aspirates, gained wealth, and fastidious gentlemen stood for boroughs; some were caught in political currents, some in ecclesiastical, and perhaps found themselves surprisingly grouped in consequence; while a few personages or families that stood with rocky firmness amid all this fluctuation, were slowly presenting new aspects in spite of solidity, and altering with the double change of self and beholder. Municipal town and rural parish gradually made fresh threads of connection – gradually, as the old stocking gave way to the savings-bank and the worship of the solar guinea became extinct; while squires and baronets, and even lords who had once lived blamelessly afar from the civic mind, gathered the faultiness of closer acquaintanceship. Settlers, too, came from distant counties, some with an alarming novelty of skill, others with an offensive advantage in cunning. In fact, much the same sort of movement and mixture went on in old England as we find in older Herodotus, who also, in telling what had been, thought it well to take a woman's lot for his starting-point. (*MSPL* 95–6)

This one extract is so densely and intricately woven that one hardly knows where to begin in unravelling it. Picking up on our initial thread, however, we should recall that the scene is revealed indirectly, as a result of the initially impercipient vibration of that thread, causing one to attune oneself differently, so that consciousness can focus on what begins to return to it: the memory of old provincial society that resonates sympathetically, as if there were an analogical oscillation between feeling and recalled, phantasmatic vision. This is the *subtle movement*, a double motion or motif, captured in the harmonic of apperception and revelation. The subtle movement reduplicates, multiplies itself across the historical, mnemotechnic weave. For not only is there that motion between Lydgate and Dorothea, there is also the flow *between* the two and the consciousness observing. Additionally, this 'echo' is picked up as consciousness recalls the analogous wavelength, itself an echo in that it returns in its recollected multiplicity, *both from and as* the internal tremors within and across the structure of old provincial society. The staging of society in this imagined past moment therefore moves in the troping of flow, and the fluctuation of tropes, from commentary to performative as the passage takes up the fluctuations.

The perception of the temporal and spatial ebb and flow is remarked elsewhere in the extract. It issues from that colon, *as if* Eliot had opened a conduit through which in both directions from past to future there is a flux or current along invisible filaments that deliver image narrative and, with that, the tenor of the time. 'History' thus apprehended arrives and is woven out of those 'less marked vicissitudes which are *constantly shifting* the boundaries of social *intercourse* and begetting a new *consciousness* of *interdependence*'. Again the reader witnesses the performative dimension of the vision, as the consciousness is engendered through the motion of a presentation marked by the tropes of flux. There is *slippage* and a concomitant upwards social motion attesting to the mobility of class position or station, which, unpredictable before the event of cultural change, result in surprising groupings, themselves the phenomena of particular political or ideological *currents*. Amongst this endless *fluctuation*, a few identities remain in place, but largely the network being traced here is one of endless, multidirectional lines of flight describing equally unstoppable deterritorializations and constellated, strategic or provincial reterritorializations. Out of this, *fresh threads of connection* are woven, and it is only in retrospect that the historian can describe the weave of social, ideological and cultural history. Perception and reception are necessarily belated.

This is the inescapable condition and emergent consciousness of identity and historicity in the 1870s, as one peers back on one's past, personally and in the production of a collective memory. Everything is subject to *movement* and *mixture*. That this is a cyclical and iterable historical and material pattern, affecting in this singular instance of English identity and culture in the late 1820s not only personal and social relations but also the composition of communities through migration and the phenomenology of economic exchange and media, is borne witness to in observation of the analogy between early nineteenth-century practices and transformations and those of another, markedly distinct cultural history recorded in Herodotus. The analogy is, yet again, double. For not only is the narrative structure given to historical representation of the 1820s compared with an earlier model, the classical mode of representation touches on the 'present' mode inscribed in the 1870s. An apparently straightforward symmetry or reciprocity is thereby displaced in a more complex triadic historical form. The classical mode is not merely given as contrast. It is actively installed, intimated anachronistically in the implicitly archaic or pagan image of the 'worship of the solar guinea' as if to suggest the moment in the early nineteenth century as in the process of becoming anachronistic, and thus seen retrospectively as always already 'dated', as it were, from the modern perspective of a late Victorian consciousness.

And of course, the passage is dated. Or, rather – to be more accurate – the date is encrypted as the sedimented historical signature, occluded in its becoming embedded in the alluvial deposits of English culture between the 1820s and the 1870s. The 'solar guinea' referred to by Eliot is a gold coin, which, by the time of *Middlemarch*'s temporal moment, has already passed into history, having been replaced by the sovereign in 1813. This change in forms of coinage as a sign of national economic transformation is given a broader context in the observation that 'the old stocking gave way to the savings-bank'. That generalized image of the old stocking leaves a thread hanging for the attentive reader, to insinuate its way across nearly 500 pages of the novel, and the history of Middlemarch given in the novel, to appear as a particular stocking foot, used by the elderly labourer Timothy Cooper, in which, as representative of the older generation of rural rustics surviving from the eighteenth century, he keeps his coins (*MSPL* 560). Indeed, Cooper's identity is given a more thorough discursive historicization than the observation of this anachronistic practice might suggest. He is 'a type lingering in those times – who had his savings in a stocking-foot . . . and was not to be wrought on by any oratory . . . as if he had not been totally unacquainted with the Age of Reason and the Rights of Man' (*MSPL* 560). As tenuous and fragile as the fibre that is stretched almost from the beginning of the novel to a juncture around two-thirds the way through *Middlemarch* may appear, its fibrillary vestige bears the memory of disappearing practices as much as it serves to connect to those discourses of eighteenth-century humanist enlightenment; by which, in turn, Timothy appears to have been touched, however indistinctly or indirectly; and the touch of which he appears to feel with a greater intensity than many a more supposedly literate reader such as Casaubon, who was 'as genuine a character as any ruminant animal' (*MSPL* 195). Of course, Cooper cannot have read either of Thomas Paine's works, published respectively in 1791 and 1795. But Eliot's fictive possibility – *as if* – admits Timothy Cooper to a shared discourse of English millenarian radicalism, which arguably vanishes to a large extent in the political transformations of the nineteenth century. Anticipating the conclusion of this chapter, we may suggest that it is *as if* Eliot seeks to write the threads of a native radicalism and with that an other Englishness rooted in a rural, largely illiterate community, and misapprehended in the latter years of nineteenth-century historiography as the last, largely unchanged remnants of 'feudal spirit' (*MSPL* 560).

It might strike certain readers that Cooper serves a particular function for Eliot, which is partly disclosed in her commentary. Recall that constellation of figures noted before: the housemaid, the eminent philosopher, Cooper the farm worker, the weaver, and the novelist. Add to this the parson, the banker, or indeed Lydgate himself who provides both the focus and the optical lens through which one gains access to particular microcosms of old provincial society. They are each threaded together in a network of differentiated, heterogeneous and hierarchical interlacings not simply as figures in a landscape, as if *Middlemarch* were either a late eighteenth-century or, perhaps more pointedly, a mid-Victorian landscape painting. Eliot may well have had in mind, albeit ironically, the idealized, nostalgic and wholly fictional mid-century paintings of Edward Charles Williams (1807–81), Henry John Boddington (1811–65), or Albert Goodwin (1845–1932), whose canvases provided for the urban bourgeoisie the perjured idyll of a fantasy rural England. But, that being the case, she nonetheless disrupts, from within and at the edges of the frames from which she narrates the illusory sense perception of such landscapes in their evocation of the timelessness of the English countryside. In her narrative, Eliot introduces from within apparently direct representation a somewhat askance, anamorphic or parallax perspective, through her various characters, the types they figure and, more significantly, the dissonant hetero-affective tenor they introduce. In this manner Eliot thereby sets quivering particular strands in the weave of the image, so that one comes to discern, or has the possibility at least of apprehending, a disturbance in the field of vision.

Looking back, and askew, at a self-discomforting angle, at a prior historical moment, and witnessing as if by refraction a distortion of one's own position mediated back, one gains access to differences of being's historicity, through that insight that Lydgate, Cooper, and even those who remain unnamed are seen to operate not as 'individuals' but as materially given and determined subjects, even though they may well remain as distinct singularities. The work these figures are engaged in, skilled, semi-skilled or unskilled, is not merely 'simple historical "background"' as N. N. Feltes remarks of Eliot's doctor in his critique of F. R. Leavis's misreading governed by 'individualism and empiricism' (1986, 50). The 'characters', if one can refer to Eliot's 'signature-singularities' in this way, are material insertions in the text whose various functions are to operate as 'specific ideological determinations' (Eagleton 1976, 113), operating historically and in structural relation to one another in culturally given determinate ways. In each example, great or small, the name and function operate as limits, which can mark, let us remind ourselves, a beginning as well as an ending. Each figures a prosopopoeic boundary or limit up against which the reader is thrown. Whether that is an end or beginning depends on the reader's reaction, his or her becoming engaged with the trope of character as encrypted site of historical tension. In their interplay and as nodal markers of the cultural and social web of provincial class relations in the 1820s, the sustained or more fleeting appearance of such figures serves to affirm the historicity of the image through the production of small 'ripples' on the surface of the historical retrospective representation. Localized effects, they, and the various inanimate transformations in society observed in the passage above, emphasize 'the importance' of '*interconnections* between the various spheres of experience in society' (Price 1999, 15).

If we are to receive in full the impact of this as Eliot herself appears to comprehend it in her insistence on working on the small and local details, rather than in being content to produce the broader brush-strokes of a novelist such as, say, Thackeray, then it is important to perceive the tropes of *thread*, *weave*, and *web*, not as organic mystifications symptomatic of some perplexed liberal retreat from an ethical narrative fully engaged in the responsibilities of historiography and bearing witness to the past. Rather, we should give attention to the interconnections between the tropes of vision and weave, visuality and web, present consciousness and memory, aesthetics and materiality as the gatherings and transmissions determining the site of the past. We need to do so in order to read *Middlemarch* not as an idealized landscape but instead as one of those 'sites . . . containing some of the supremely important dynamics and events in the history of society' (Price 1999, 16). Eliot's characters are therefore instances of such sites, Dorothea and Lydgate being two acutely privileged 'locations', if we may speak in this fashion, because their historicity is the most problematic, troubled and traced as the presentation of dialogical as well as dialectical tensions. They also offer themselves as the narrative's optical–analytic devices for forensic dissections of the societies and the historical flows in which they find themselves enmeshed and so unstitched in their discursive being. There takes place a narrative autopsy of society made available by the ideological determinations of identity, as this is thrown into material relief according to the tensions that Lydgate, Dorothea, and others embody. And such autopsy, such a staging of phantasmatic 'eyewitness', demands a historicized self-reading or self-seeing as a counter-reading to any nostalgic desire for a late Victorian aesthetic expression of mystifying *Sehnsucht* such as is offered in the landscape paintings to which I have referred.

Eliot puts Lydgate to work in just such a manner in the next extract, in a discourse somewhat ambivalently touched by a romanticized articulation. 'Perhaps', she observes, with just the merest suspicion of ironic distancing, the year of Lydgate's establishment in Middlemarch, 'was a more cheerful time for observers and theorizers'. The seemingly wistful sentimentality is turned against itself as the sentence continues: 'we are apt to think it the finest era of the world when America was beginning to be discovered, when a bold sailor, even if he were wrecked, might alight on a new kingdom' (*MSPL* 147). There is arguably an undecidability about this line. On the one hand, it maintains the affirmation of nostalgia. On the other hand, however, in turning away from the conjecture of speculative historical account, it simultaneously employs another model of such account given visionary form in colonial discovery, weighing this against the swerve towards the feeling of a collective readership and its tendencies in the 'present' of the 1870s: 'we are apt'. The uncertainty of *perhaps* has now been dragged down, shipwrecked itself, and been plunged into the abyss of undecidability accompanying the parabasic swerve through Eliot's shift from a view of the past to a reflection of the present, and, with that, the telescopic view opened onto another past. Whatever the view of the past – and the accuracy or otherwise is of relatively little significance – what counts here is the countersignature of the silent but implicit caveat that seems readable, warning against historical misreading. Having thus framed the problem and directed our attention, Eliot continues, taking up the colonial analogy, in a gesture that threads together the figural language of colonial discourse with a degree of historical specificity hitherto absent: 'and about 1829 the dark territories of Pathology were a fine America for a spirited young adventurer' (*MSPL* 147).

The reader is forced up against time, made to confront the different times that structure any supposedly discrete date, through that discursive matrix that renders the narrative as a reading in several tones, and of diverse resonances within the 'raw' date 1829. The heterogeny of discursive and therefore textile formation engenders its space in and through its performativity, its taking place as an anachronic mode of presentation. Observers and theorizers commingle through the momentary vision of the young doctor with colonial adventurers in the dissonant order of differing temporalities. Eliot, it seems, strives to implicate the reader in the weft and woof, while sensitizing her audience through temporal and analogical play to the role of cultural memory, and to the symptomatic processes of falsifying memory work that give shape to 'the permitting medium of our present experience' (Beer 1989, 17). If we remember briefly those critics who fail to account for the possibility that 'figures and tropes might operate as historical and political forces', we can understand how the critic, who remains resolutely on either side of the 'literary/historical impasse' (Givner 2002, 225), is suspended in a 'present experience' of reading that has itself 'forgotten' the function of language in the transmission of cultural memory. Reading 'takes place always in the present' (Beer 1989, 4). But it does so, as Eliot can teach us, only through an encounter with 'the *difference* of the past' (Beer 1989, 4) that informs the historicization of those signals by which a history is told and received, if at all.

That difference may be recognized in broad terms, for example in the reading of *Middlemarch* as an account of the past through the image of a society woven phylogenetically as it were, that is to say in patterns of relation resulting, themselves, in the differences between the times of evolution or transformation of the constituent elements belonging to that society or historically specific group. Or, the difference of the past – the difference produced by the past as well as that which marks the idea of the past differentially as its own matrix – may be read, if one gives one's attention to the details of difference, in small, seemingly insignificant ways which, in announcing the differences, signal their historical and historicizing alterity. Thus, Eliot seeks to throw the past into relief from the present experience, in writing her narrative as a 'history of lights and shadows' (*MSPL* 194), as we have seen at play in the anamorphic and analogical reflection on Lydgate with its various phantasmagoria like so many fleeting 'magic-lantern pictures' (*MSPL* 194).

She attempts this, furthermore, in order to recover a mode of self-reading, an ethical act of bearing witness to the past involving reflection on the self, in order to inscribe 'a historicity linked essentially to man himself [*sic*]' (Foucault 1989, 369). We see the attempt unfolded across the following consideration of Lydgate, which follows on immediately from the sentence recently cited:

> The more he became interested in special questions of disease . . . the more keenly he felt the need for that fundamental *knowledge* of *structure* which just at *the beginning of the century* had been *illuminated* by the brief and glorious career of Bichat, who . . . like another Alexander, left a realm large enough for many heirs. That great Frenchman first carried out the conception that living bodies . . . must be regarded as consisting of certain *primary webs or tissues*, out of which the various organs – brain, heart, lungs, and

so on – are compacted, as the various accommodations of a house are built up in various proportions of wood, iron, stone, brick, zinc, and the rest, *each material having its peculiar composition and proportions*. No man, *one sees*, can *understand* and estimate *the entire structure or its parts* – what are its frailties and what its repairs, without *knowing* the nature of the materials. And the *conception wrought* out by Bichat, with *his detailed study of the different tissues*, acted necessarily on medical questions as the turning of *gas-light* would act on a dim, *oil-lit* street, *showing new connections and hitherto hidden facts of structure which must be taken into account* in considering the symptoms of maladies and the action of medicaments. But results which depend on *human conscience and intelligence* work slowly, and *now at the end of 1829*, most medical practice was still strutting or shambling along the *old paths*, and there was still scientific work to be done which might have seemed to be a *direct sequence* of Bichat's. This great *seer did not go beyond the consideration* of the tissues as ultimate facts in the living organism, *marking the limit of anatomical analysis*; but it was *open* to another *mind* to say, have not these *structures* some common basis from which they have all started, as your *sarsnet, gauze, net, satin, and velvet from the raw cocoon*? Here would be another *light*, as of *oxy-hydrogen, showing the very grain of things*, and revising all former explanations. Of this *sequence* to Bichat's work, already *vibrating along many currents of the European mind*, Lydgate was enamoured; he longed to demonstrate *the more intimate relations of living structure*, and help to define *men's thought* more accurately after the true order. The work had not yet been done, but only prepared for *those who knew how* to use the preparation. (*MSPL* 147–8; emphases added)

We can pursue a number of threads here, as the multiple emphases introduced above imply, in order to illuminate the way in which historicity is linked to the subject, even as the subject is grounded as always a historicized being, a being or identity constituted in the world. Consciousness is consciousness to itself in its historical conditions and its material becoming. Yet, that consciousness is not self-delimiting. It is not so confined by the 'dark closet' of 'verbal memory' that a connection cannot be made by which consciousness of something other than oneself cannot come into being (*MSPL* 280), thereby making possible 'for years after . . . the cry from soul to soul' (*MSPL* 290). Its boundaries or the place-holders by which it defines itself are admitted to be provisional, structural indices within a structural and temporal nexus, through which are mediated the differing and heterogeneous traces of a world which in turn is read as a similar network of threads into which one is implicated.

Specifically, this model is worked through in the passage above in a series of transitional motions crossing boundaries between world and consciousness. Such motion is itself the perception and reception of the historical instant of one's being aware of one's materiality, one's experience of the world and one's groundedness as a consciousness producing and produced by the world. One's productive-production, woven from the weave of filaments and the currents flowing along such fibres, is simultaneously material and amaterial therefore. Consciousness historically is consciousness of being (a)material for Eliot, a condition subject to fluctuation. On the one hand, this is material, a matter of a historicized mode of production. On the other hand, it is organic. Both organic and constructed, and yet neither: this seeming paradox is not one, in fact. It is instead Eliot's powerful registration of undecidability as the ideological and cultural determination of *who*, *what*, and *where* one is in the world. A nexus is thus inscribed in the passage above, which in translated form is already in place or in several places: for there is the nexus of the extract itself, which signals synecdochally the novel and the town, *Middlemarch* and Middlemarch. However, beyond and within those, there is that 'nexus' of Lydgate's consciousness, which is touched by and responds to signals and oscillations from the beginning of the century and Bichat, and from there, through Lydgate's consciousness, to move across the history of medical science in the nineteenth century (and beyond). However, Lydgate's consciousness is not merely the location of one particular weave. It is also the nexus of interrelations intimated through character, town and novel, of England, of two Englands at least, that of the 1820s and that of the 1870s. The nexus or matrix is also one constituted through the temporal weave of hetero-affective interpellations and overdeterminations criss-crossing narrowly the fifty-year period between the times of the novel, but also extending beyond the boundaries of that period in either direction historically.

Let us turn to the excerpt in some more detail. There is illumination (lighting) and illumination (knowledge). Throwing a light on the past brings something into view, much as, historically, the advent of gas-lighting, replacing the oil lights, shows us what was already there in the street but hitherto hidden to view, and therefore to consciousness. Illumination unveils the world and in doing so brings illumination. The transference traced by Eliot is not simply the passage of time, from an earlier to a later empirical condition. Parallel to this trajectory, as the encoded sign of progress, is the movement from intellectual narrowness to enlightenment, as this is marked in the shift from literal to figural illumination. The motion of scientific observation's development is further reiterated in the reference to oxyhydrogen. The oxyhydrogen flame was discovered in the 1820s to produce 'limelight'. Eliot's reference implies scientific use but the combustible compound was quickly used in stage lighting and in the use of limelight for magic lanterns. Eliot situates her reference historically midway, as it were, between science and illusion, experiment and entertainment, for while Michael Faraday was illustrating the effects of limelight in the mid-1820s, by 1837 limelight was employed to illuminate Covent Garden Theatre. At the same time, the light suggests, once more, the aid to greater, artificial modes of vision, whereby what was not available previously to the naked, 'natural' eye, now becomes revealed – *the very grain of things* – through artifice. In the extract there is to be read therefore the historicization of sight and visuality, making visible, insight, foresight, visionary power, reflection, revelation, and so on. As with our earlier discussion, historicization displaces assumptions of the purely or exclusively natural or organic. As the human intellect intervenes theoretically and practically, imposing and foregrounding consciousness and reflection between the subject and the empirical world, so the phenomenological, interpretative medium is given to view.

That intermediary interest in Eliot, the place of mediation in the passage between subject and world, structure and nature is figured in the interrogative analogy, which reduplicates and redirects the analytical scientific inquiry to one of domestic 'science' or 'economy'. 'Have not', the narrator enquires or demands, thereby forcing reflective consciousness or self-reading onto her audience, 'these structures some common basis from which they have all started, as your sarsnet, gauze, net, satin, and velvet from the raw cocoon?' Eliot sheds a light on contexts that remain invisible, so as to bring illumination, to one's own interests and what 'touches' one, quite literally on the body, most closely. Narration draws attention to the connectedness through the non-equivalent parallelism of analogy and also in the foregrounding, making visible, of a *technics* and with that, a broader context, of production. The silent, invisible intermediary is one of work, of productivity elided in its role as modal, economic substrate. Yet, there is another thread here. For, if Eliot's associations invite the good reader to infer the work of 'weaving' as it moves 'from the domestic space of the drawing room to the industrial arena of the factories, the cotton mills, flax mills, and woollen mills' (Givner 2002, 232), so the passage also works at its threads in order to illuminate itself. In tracing the 'close tangle of commercial and textual transaction' (Givner 2002, 233), the passage and its passages are witnessed producing themselves performatively through their various folds, performing their own self-effacing weave, whereby an artisanal operation is assumed to take place in the production of the novel and its role as both witness to history and producer of the historical perspective and, with that, historicized illumination.

Networks, structures, webs, and forms of relation, such as proportion, hierarchy or, formally, analogy and relation-without-relation, are therefore highlighted here, all of which serve to disrupt, displace, and exceed any organic unity or homogeneity. Lydgate is not only a 'man of science' and the discourse of science is not separable from being interwoven in a web like the history of production, invention, and, of course, narration, as the reference to Alexander suggests. Myth and science are not separable, even though obviously they are not the same, or not of the same order of discourse. Lydgate's consciousness is given a microscopic inspection here, and, in turn, in being placed at a forty- to fifty-year remove from the immediacy of its reflections, is placed as one element in Western intellectual, cultural and political history, from Alexander to a moment in suspense, in preparation for that which remains to come. The threads connecting Lydgate to other particular greater strands are not, however, the only filaments in which he is entangled. The condition of a weave is that it does not run in one direction only. For, as much as the discourse of science is traced as being temporal, diachronic, there are also other traces that entwine synchronically, and which, moreover, are shot through, ensnared within and reciprocally constituting other diachronic skeins. Eliot describes this elsewhere as the 'entanglements of human action' (*MSPL* 442). Again, she names this, apropos the effects and practices of realpolitik, the 'entanglement of things' (*MSPL* 504) given form and agency through the proper name, in this case 'Brooke of Tipton'.[2] The effects of oscillation along the threads touching consciousness define 'what is constituted [as] what is constituting' in a *tekhne*, an industrial/organic weaving of bodies, intellects, discourses, ideologies, experiences, events, histories 'all and everywhere', not as a unity or unification but as and in the signs of an 'irreducible *spacing* . . . valid for space as well as time' (Derrida 2005, 181). This is presented as disabling rather than enabling in the following, and the last excerpt concerning Lydgate's 'placement' within the discontinuous indivisibility of the culture, identity, and spacing gathered in the name 'Middlemarch':

But whichever way Lydgate began to incline, there was something to make him wince; and being a proud man, he was a little exasperated at being obliged to wince. He did not like frustrating his own best purposes by getting on bad terms with Bulstrode; he did not like voting against Farebrother, and helping to deprive him of function and salary; and the question occurred whether the additional forty pounds might not leave the Vicar free from that ignoble care about winning at cards. Moreover, Lydgate did not like the consciousness that in voting for Tyke he should be voting on the side obviously convenient for himself . . . What he really cared for was a *medium* for his work, a *vehicle* for his ideas; and after all, was he not *bound* to prefer the object of getting a good hospital, where he could demonstrate the specific distinctions of fever and test therapeutic results, before anything else connected with this chaplaincy? For the first time Lydgate was feeling *the hampering threadlike pressure of small social conditions, and their frustrating complexity.* (*MSPL* 180; emphases added)

The pull of the threads bends Lydgate in different directions, thereby placing a stress on the very fabric of his identity. The demands on Lydgate illustrate quite economically his own involvement in economic calculation. One should not essentialize this moment, however. Certainly, a limit or compromising complication is reflected through the *medium* of Lydgate's consciousness. But it would be wrong simply to ascribe the nexus (from Latin, 'a binding together') into which Lydgate finds himself caught up (*bound*), and so constrained (*bound*) or destined (*bound*) to act. The binding here is both the web in which Lydgate is caught, and the strands of his consciousness. More than that, it is the social and political fabric, from which Lydgate comes to realize, and so illuminate for the reader, that science is never free. There is no such thing as a pure science, and its practice is thrown into historical relief in the experience, however unpleasant, of a coming to consciousness for Lydgate regarding the hindrances of his quandary. The ties of social order and the expedience of desire define the subject, as subject of *and* to the material exigencies of the always-historical experience of his or her subjectivity.

And that we may read this, Eliot underscores not only Lydgate's relationship to the provincial political/ecclesiastical interests and positions, but also Lydgate's historicized self-reading in his constraint under those *small social conditions, and their frustrating complexity.* Lydgate thus forms, and is visualized in contrast to, opposing demands and requirements. Between the secular interests of a culture involved in the appointment of a spiritual representative (the church here is highlighted through the election by analogy with science) and the (perhaps selfishly realized) demands of scientific research, Lydgate is put under the microscope, dissected, and shown to be caught amongst certain *primary webs or tissues* (*MSPL* 147). The trammels (Fr. *tramail*, Latin *tramaculum*: three-layered mesh or net) of materialism allow for no disinterested reflection. So, Lydgate realizes belatedly, we must always reflect on *what* positions us, on that by which we come to be placed, and which situates us culturally and temporally in an irreducible spacing as *who* we are. By this 'fall' into knowledge, Eliot marks the modern moment of the 1820s, throwing both that epoch and the singular consciousness into *relief*.

Relief

Relief is not a word one would immediately associate with the notion of historicization. It bespeaks a form of representation, and with that an aestheticization also, a detachment in its rendering from the real – apparently. Relief is of course produced as a process of sophisticated 'scratching' or marking. It is, to cite the *OED*, 'the elevation of a projection or design . . . in order to give a solid and natural appearance'. It is also that appearance of detachment given by 'the arrangement and disposition of lines', or the 'vividness, distinctness or prominence due to contrast' or presentation. *Relief* therefore stages or presents rather than represents. It involves and foregrounds active intervention, and with that an invisible intermediary, whether mechanical or human. The suffixes *-lief* or *-lieve* are also suggestive etymologically of *lieu*, signifying place or locus, so that *relief* as an artistic term can have implications of giving place in presentation to something returning as that which is absent, and therefore subject to replacement. The relief serves in representing what is no longer there as such, an event from the past, with the presentation of its supplementary representation, some specifically constructed image giving the appearance of something, someone, some event, *as if* these were there, *as if* the past could be screened through the relief, the medium of narrative history.

Relief thus names a complex mediation between the phantasmagorical and the material, which process takes place only for some viewing or reading subject in a given moment. Eliot makes this phantasmatic/material interchange between subject and history clear at the beginning of Chapter 20, in which 'the past of a whole hemisphere seems moving in funeral procession with strange ancestral images . . .

[composed of a] stupendous fragmentariness' (*MSPL* 192). Relief is not merely implicated in the aesthetic though, nor does it remain on the purely phenomenal plane. Moreover it is not, simply or simply reducible to, a technical procedure. More obscurely, relief signals the remains of something, some residuum, such as the threads of traces of the past; it is that which survives as the visible remnants acting also as so many *souvenirs*, memories of the other, as Dorothea comes to appreciate in her visit to Rome. Legally, it is implicated in deliverance or remedy, and one may suggest that for a particular consciousness such as Dorothea's the relief of the past delivers precisely that epiphanic revelation to the self, which throws one's consciousness into relief and so serves as the possibility of a remedy in terms of the historicity of one's identity.

Thus, it may be argued that, in writing of a specific moment nearly half a century before, Eliot throws both the past, various pasts in fact, and the present into relief. In doing so, she constructs a representation of middle-class Englishness in transition. *Middlemarch* is raised ironically as partially separate from, though in many small ways imperceptibly tied to, its representation of the past. Middlemarch stands out, as it were, against a generalized unfocused backdrop in order to give greater contrast to the realpolitik of the everyday, in those very places where the naive reader might well imagine the absence of ideology or the signs of impact from historical currents. In the same instant of unveiling the past, the present moment is also thrown into relief, every relief having two sides. All narrative thus produces the illusion of reality in the play of shadows and light cast by its historical distance and difference. *Who* we are is revealed by *what* we come to see of ourselves as others, historically. Dorothea's consciousness is historicized in just this manner in her honeymoon encounter with Rome, the 'city of visible history' (*MSPL* 192). I have already alluded to the 'dreamlike strangeness' of this encounter between Dorothea and the eternal city, and shall do so again further on in this section of the chapter. For now though, I want to spend some time with the historicizing implications of *relief* as they concern particular strands of cultural memory, narration, and the passage of the gaze across temporal divides, moving then to consider *relief* as it is employed specifically about Dorothea Brooke/Casaubon.

One of the most well-known and discussed passages in *Middlemarch* is that archly self-referential examination of the role of the novelist as historian, at the beginning of Chapter 15. Taking up the thread of 'relief' in a manner at once self-reflexive and yet quietly self-effacing, Eliot observes:

> A great historian, as he insisted on calling himself, who had the happiness to be dead a hundred and twenty years ago, and so to take his place among the colossi whose huge legs our living pettiness is observed to walk under, glories in his copious remarks and digressions as the least imitable part of his work . . . where he seems to bring his arm-chair to the proscenium and chat with us in all the lusty ease of his fine English. But Fielding lived when the days were longer (for time, like money, is measured by our needs), when summer afternoons were spacious, and the clock ticked slowly in the winter evenings. We belated historians must not linger after his example, and if we did so, it is probable that our chat would be thin and eager, as if delivered from a camp-stool in a parrot house. I at least have so much to do in unravelling certain human lots, and seeing how they were woven and interwoven, that all the light I can command must be concentrated on this particular web, and not dispersed over that tempting range of relevancies called the universe. (*MSPL* 141)

Eliot's evocation – another apostrophe – of Fielding acknowledges both proximity to and distance from the novelist. We are afforded a view of the difference, the unlikeness, of the two, and it is a difference that is produced as a result of the temporal and cultural distinctions. Eliot's acknowledgement of Fielding's self-reading – he insisted on calling himself a historian – makes explicit through connection, the always-implicit relation between history and narration, event and representation. Eliot's encomium is slightly satirical, for in its professed admiration of the author of *Tom Jones* it acknowledges the inescapable fact about cultural memory, which is that one must be dead before one can be thrown properly into relief retrospectively or, conversely, given over to the mystification of historical retrospect. This is of course precisely the point made by Eliot in her preface, her perspective on St Theresa, the 'history of man' and how that 'mysterious mixture' called history 'behaves under the varying experiments of Time' (*MSPL* 3). Temporal distance affords one the big picture, but if one looks more closely or draws out one's historical material more finely, otherwise unobserved detail becomes revealed. At the same time, taking the long view historically inevitably means obscuring what is closer to hand, whether temporally or culturally. Mystification occasioned by temporal spacing causes one to believe that the days were longer, summer afternoons spacious, and clocks ticked more slowly. Against that apparently unalloyed nostalgic retrospect Eliot offers a countersignature, subverting the grand perspective on history and the past and the occluding idealism of the subject by noting in a delightfully improper image novelists and historians of the nineteenth century walking about under Fielding's legs.

The extract works on us in different ways also. In its own apostrophic turning – in two directions, note, back to the eighteenth century and forward to its readers, and of course to us – it plays between the inevitable naturalization of metaphor and the estranging force of the same. In the imagined image of Fielding's conspiratorial asides, the cosy domesticity of the fireside chat is shown to be a simulacrum, a stagey device marked by the artifice of the stage frame, which Fielding's act of parabasis would pretend did not exist. Here is captured the difference of historicity's mark. Fielding has the comfort of pretending no artifice is employed; Eliot cannot. In this doubled reading, alluding to Fielding's own judgement of parabasis as that which is the least 'imitable' in his writing, Eliot's own parabasic gesture marks itself and its other (the parablepsic conjuring of Fielding turning to *us*) in their inescapable historicity and singularity. The illusion of one writer's aside is thrown into relief by that of the other, and both are presented, staged by the relief of historical difference.

Every act, every narration is inescapably idiomatic; marked by its time, it becomes almost immediately untimely. Though singular, one can only acknowledge singularity as the belated reader, in the reception of the residuum by which the transmission both arrives and fails to arrive, by which, in its being iterable, it remarks its own projection. Though translatable, it remains culturally inaccessible as such. What takes place historically therefore, and, concomitantly, in and as one's subsequent perspective on or narrative of material events, this is always – always already – a matter of relief, of positioning so as to create the illusion of projection from the flat surface. It is a matter of producing a relief in order to see, despite the specific historical distortions and displacements caused by modernity's speed (which is related to economic constraints), and the discomfort of a makeshift position (the camp stool, rather than the armchair). The relativism allows, through the relief of contrast and the illumination it brings comparatively, a greater self-awareness concerning the historicity of one's identity, the manner of its formation, and the modes of production and reproduction that come to support one's subjectivity. And this of course is necessary. The past must be thrown into relief, but so must the present moment, if one's act of self-reading can be situated so as to unravel the knotted threads, deciphering their complications, thereby concentrating on the weave or web that illumination afforded by a self-aware historicized consciousness that is thrown into relief through iterable dissimilarity.

Dorothea Brooke undergoes just such a process of coming to see herself, to gain a perspective that is both personal and cultural, phenomenal and historical. Moreover, the perspective and refraction she is afforded over time is a matter of coming to realize herself as thrown into relief by events and experiences. Of Dorothea, we read in *Middlemarch's* opening sentence that 'Miss Brooke had that kind of beauty which seems to be thrown into relief by poor dress' (*MSPL* 7). The word 'relief' is used in relation to Dorothea Brooke at least twice. To be more precise, *relief* is used about Dorothea Brooke, while relief, having a different sense from that pertaining to its first usage, is used with regard to Dorothea Casaubon. The difference between Dorothea Brooke and Dorothea Casaubon is a significant one, the length of the journey between the two having less to do with the marriage that effects the name change (though this too is significant to the journey), than with, on the one hand, a process of coming to consciousness on the part of the character, and, on the other, with the movement from outer to inner, from view to perception, from mimetic and aesthetic vision to a phenomenology of self-perception, self-reading. Or, to put this as a somewhat strong reading: from a lifeless objet d'art *thrown into relief* to a spirit that cannot be given external representation except by that form of analogy known as prosopopoeia, via which the invisible spirit, will or soul takes on the apparitional and singular form of a fictional character. The first use of the word 'relief' is by far the most familiar to readers of Eliot, and comes perhaps from one of the most quoted passages from *Middlemarch*. It appears in the opening line of the first chapter, already cited. The second comes in Chapter 76, in which we read the following: 'The idea of some active good within her reach "haunted her . . . like a passion" [Eliot here cites selectively from Wordsworth's *Tintern Abbey*], and another's need *having once come to her as a distinct image, preoccupied her desire* with the yearning to give relief, and made her own ease tasteless' (*MSPL* 760–1; emphasis added). In this latter example, relief assumes its juridical sense of remedy, that sense itself governed by an ethics of consciousness, a 'consciousness of life beyond self' (*MSPL* 1).

The play between the two ostensible meanings of 'relief' is both interesting and telling in the context of *Middlemarch* as a whole, particularly with regard to the perception of a gradual motion throughout the narrative from the external world of mimetically faithful representations to the internal world of phenomenological self-reflection. Of course, the motion is not simply one of the formula 'from A to B'. Rather, it must be understood how the latter always already inhabits, if not haunts – to use Wordsworth's own term, echoing knowingly through the seemingly artificial device of Eliot's citation – the former. As Eliot has it, 'souls live on in perpetual echoes' (*MSPL* 161; though, it must be remarked, there is a degree of irony in this comment, given that it refers to the otherwise unconscious Rosamond's piano playing). Relief can mean a sense of uniqueness caused by contrast, and this is one obvious sense of the use from the first chapter, with also that semantic sense of an elevation of a shape or figure from a flat surface in sculpture, or otherwise the illusion of elevation in painting on which we have already commented. Eliot, we can suggest, seeks to employ a technique of 'relief' in order to 'elevate' Dorothea from being a mere sign, one more inscription, to some level of artistic reality. There is also that sense of 'relief' as a printing process that uses raised surfaces to apply ink to paper; and this, if my speculation might not be taken as being too fanciful, is intimated in the first chapter, in the same paragraph already quoted, when Eliot 'illustrates' her understanding of relief when it is remarked of 'Miss Brooke' that her 'poor dress', her 'plain garments . . . by the side of provincial fashion gave her the impressiveness of a fine quotation from the Bible – or from one of our elder poets – in a paragraph of to-day's newspaper' (*MSPL* 7). The Bible and newspaper counterpoint one another and are both thrown reciprocally into relief – culturally and historically. The former is both the canonical apogee for certain hegemonic aspects of nineteenth-century Christian culture and the archaic text par excellence. The newspaper, on the other hand, is mass-produced, ultra-modern in contrast to the Bible. Another meaning for 'relief', as our second citation gives us to understand, is the release from anxiety or the power to end or alleviate painful experience that Dorothea seeks to effect for Lydgate. There are at least two other semantic resonances in 'relief' that are implicated here. In her effort to help Lydgate, and in her practical plan of taking up the funding of the hospital relinquished by Bulstrode, Dorothea also seeks to be a relief, assuming the task of the banker. She attempts to do so by providing money, yet another form of relief.

So what, precisely, you might ask, takes place between those two 'reliefs'? How do they 'relieve' one another; what is the distance travelled between the two? How can we address this not only in such a manner that we can speak of the development of character in some mimetically or psychologically faithful manner, but so as to account for the transformation of the narrative, to understand more accurately the ways in which Eliot's narrative translates its own concerns, interests, modes of production and forms of presentation? This 'coming to consciousness' across the novel, is not, it must be stressed, merely that of Dorothea. We read the novel incorrectly if we assume it is. Given my insistence thus far on the embeddedness of the historical material, the various events, dates, acts, and contexts that are referred to, and the historicity of consciousness as a 'becoming-self-aware of one's historicity' as a sign of Victorian identity's modernity, there is sketched just this possibility of a greater 'coming-to-consciousness' of cultural identity for which Dorothea is merely a privileged fictive agent. She is *just this* singular example of the ideological and philosophical work of prosopopoeia, as already suggested. For, to stress and reiterate the crux of the matter: if the novel is embedded within history, and if it mediates history in any meaningful though encrypted sense, then *Middlemarch* is undoubtedly also an articulation of coming-to-consciousness as historical process *and also* the historicity of that coming-to-consciousness. For Dorothea serves as its singular expression, in order to throw into relief that very process of historicization by which she herself is thrown into relief, thereby coming to act at the end of the novel in the manner anticipated at its very beginning. Consciousness has a history, and the history of that consciousness is remarked in the network of traces, events, and experiences that are woven in the shuttling and transmission between the two *reliefs*, the two returns of place, taking place and placement as historicized spacing, even as the oscillations of the shuttle leave its marks, those minute and multitudinous scratches in every direction, on the matrix of consciousness.

This is perhaps why, written in 1871–72, the novel situates itself in the period 1828–32, so as to announce both the history and the historicity of a coming-to-consciousness that is related in this singular case to gender. Dorothea's 'evolutionary' development leaves behind location and temporal moment. Rosamond's does not. To behave like a silly heroine in a silly novel by a silly lady novelist (to recall Eliot's excoriating essay) is to remain entrenched, vain, and self-reflective in a fictive manner, unconscious of transformation – hence the frequent employment, as critics have pointed out, of Darwinian metaphors and related sciences as a discourse informing narrative in *Middlemarch*. The movement from one 'relief' to another 'relief', and all that is signified here, is not merely a movement of language, of systems of signification that are apparently purely formal. The motion, the transport, that Eliot effects is one that, in crossing structural boundaries (from one meaning or identity to another, from one discourse to another), also erases those boundaries and makes a connection between the identities. But we must also remember that the interconnectedness, which is a discontinuous formation, is not only structural but historical also, in that it may be read as charting the 'coming-to-consciousness' of an age and a generation, which one can only plot with the hindsight that a span, an opening of perspective over forty years, allows.

If this all sounds a little abstract, that is not accidental. It is a difficulty of which Eliot is all too aware, as when she comments:

> to have been driven to be more particular would have been like trying to give a history of the lights and shadows, for that new real future which was replacing the imaginary drew its material from the endless minutiae by which her view of Mr. Casaubon and her wifely relation, now that she was married to him, was gradually changing with the secret motion of a watch-hand from what it had been in her maiden dream. (*MSPL* 194)

The languages of illumination, of vision, of materiality and phantasmatic projection vie for our attention here, as do the discourses of temporality and historicity in Eliot's tracing of the nexus of a consciousness coming to take a perspective on itself. As we know, time and history move at different rates according to one's own position; there is no absolute measure, only gradual change. The irreversible transition here – perhaps *the* moment in which one can attest to the shift from *relief* to *relief* – is one in which 'reflection upon oneself . . . does not only take into consideration that which is intended by consciousness' (Levinas 2001, 93–4), in this case Dorothea's desire to be the intellectual servant to Casaubon's simulacrum of the scholarly master. From this moment on, we grasp and gain perspective on an epistemological transition, as inevitable as it is irrefragable for Dorothea's consciousness, which transition effects a constitution 'of consciousness in its world' through a 'manner of thinking concretely' which in itself issues 'an appeal to listen acutely for what is implicit . . . what is allusive in thinking' (Levinas 2001, 94). *Here* is the historicization of consciousness, phenomenological consciousness thrown into relief in its historical and cultural moment in the advent of a phenomenal modernity traced across the more than forty years between narration and what is narrated in *Middlemarch*. And it takes place, it is given place in Dorothea's encounter with, and experience of, 'visible history' in the form of Rome, which she sees as a double vision, at once in her time, and yet not of her time. Thus, Dorothea does not die 'of the roar which lies on the other side of silence' (*MSPL* 194). She receives the signals implicitly, hearing them, listening acutely and becoming the addressee of their message in allusive fashion. In this, she moves beyond the suspension, the stasis of incomprehension in the face of change that is everywhere the sign of Middlemarch's historical impasse, its aporetic experience of that which is to come. And, apparently paradoxically, what gives Dorothea emotional *relief* is that apperception of the future projected, thrown into relief by the past, specifically Rome.

In the interaction between the material reality of the city and the phantasmagorical impression made on Dorothea, via which her moods produce a succession of images 'which succeed each other like the magic-lantern pictures of a doze' (*MSPL* 194), Eliot traces the real effects on selfhood, and the processes of self-reading that the world can impose. While this is not obviously economic history or a face to face with contemporary events such as the coming of the railways, nevertheless, inasmuch as *Middlemarch* is a novel charting the transformation of the middle classes in a given formation at a particular historical juncture, it cannot be denied that being and consciousness are written materially and historically. Eliot is keen to stress the aftereffect on memory in the passage just sited, and so anticipates the Freudian notion of belated registration (*Nachträglichkeit*) on the psyche. Dorothea, we are told, in particular conditions of ennui, 'continued to see the vastness of St Peter's, the huge bronze canopy, the excited intention in the attitudes and garments of the prophets and evangelists in the mosaics . . . and the red drapery . . . spreading itself everywhere like a disease on the retina' (*MSPL* 194). Here, the material effects of the real produce a visual allusiveness, itself analogous with a pathology, empirical vision being recalled – made figural – as the weave of personal afterthought and cultural memory, and recorded in its parasitical persistence in the symptomatic simile.

Stepping back from this vision of Rome's haunting force and its apophatic effect on Dorothea, we should look at the city's first impressions, in concluding this particular section of the chapter. Rome is first approached by an allusion to the recent English past at the beginning of Chapter 19. George the Fourth 'was still reigning', the Duke of Wellington 'was Prime Minister', and 'Mr Vincy was mayor of the old corporation in Middlemarch', when 'Mrs Casaubon' travels to Rome (*MSPL* 188). Eliot deliberately portrays the period as one of greater innocence, but also one of aesthetic error and misinterpretation. Displacing the moment as having passed absolutely, Eliot also indicates how different cultural discourses and practices have both differing velocities and rates of transmission and reception. Romanticism, she remarks, 'had not yet penetrated the times with its leaven . . . it was fermenting still' (*MSPL* 188). Romanticism is thus remarked as a continental phenomenon brewed by 'long-haired German artists at Rome' (*MSPL* 188), the force of which can only be read after it has 'entered into everybody's food' in the 'forty years' passage that this paragraph acknowledges. Reading, identification, and consciousness are all the manifestations of so many *après-coups*, it would seem, as Eliot models the late 1820s as a historical and cultural relief, even as cultural memory is witnessed as active, ongoing, flowing beyond, and serving retrospectively to define provisionally the given era. That *relief-effect* is produced further in the juxtaposition of the real and the fictive, between monarch and prime minister, and mayor and the 'old corporation'.

This is the world Dorothea Brooke leaves as 'Mrs Casaubon', and it is tempting to read this as a temporal and spatial distancing providing a perspective *in relievo* on both place and the past. Although the wedding journey to Rome occurs in 1829, the reference to Middlemarch as the old corporation somewhat vaguely situates Middlemarch between the repeal of the Corporation and Test Acts in 1828, which prohibited Catholics from holding public office, and the Catholic Emancipation Bill of 1829.

[A parenthesis and detour: both the Corporation and Test Acts had been in force since the second half of the seventeenth century. Arguably therefore, one may read 'allusively' in this passing reference of Eliot's a gesture of perspectival relief on the history of English modernity, as being bounded at one point by Acts directly results of the 'new' parliamentary democracy of the Restoration, and at another point by the advent of the first Reform Act in 1832. To pull at the threads of this weave in a slightly different direction, and so as to foreground the narrative of a character's ancestry against this larger textile of inclusion or exclusion as the structure providing the frame of a particular Englishness: Dorothea's family is mapped in Book One of *Middlemarch* as providing the thread of a Protestant lineage dating back to Cromwell: 'the Brooke connections', writes Eliot, 'were unquestionably "good"', the evaluation referring to the gentrified station of

Dorothea's forebears. The genealogy continues, 'and there was even an ancestor discernible as a Puritan gentleman who served under Cromwell, but afterwards conformed' (*MSPL* 7). Dorothea's aesthetic taste for plain clothing is a cultural and ideological affectation, to be sure, a narrow self-consciousness or egoistic scrupulosity, as Eliot calls it. But as the genealogy reveals once unravelled – and as supported in Eliot's references to Protestant shock in the face of Catholic specularity in Rome – the economy in dress is also part of a cultural identity and history, it is a 'well-bred economy' (*MSPL* 7) written historically onto the subject as part of 'modern' English bourgeois identity.]

From a time and world in which Catholicism is misunderstood and misrepresented, Dorothea arrives in an anachronistic Catholic world of Rome, an anachronistic location of 'historical contrast' (*MSPL* 193), with its 'oppressive masquerade of the ages' (*MSPL* 193). This world is anachronistic for Dorothea because it forces on her consciousness the unreal spectacle of 'best galleries . . . glorious churches . . . Ruins and basilicas, palaces and collosi . . . Titanic life gazing and struggling on walls and ceilings' in shocking juxtaposition, being set 'in the midst of a sordid present' (*MSPL* 193).[3] The result is that Rome is unreadable, 'unintelligible'. At the same time, however, its aestheticized and ossified past witnessed in relation to the 'breathing forgetfulness and degradation' of the present jar Dorothea, through the simultaneity of contrast, 'as with an electric shock', which in the force has the power to inscribe her 'memory . . . preparing strange associations which remained through her after-years' (*MSPL* 193). Anticipating the reading of Hardy in the next chapter, and specifically the comments of Tim Armstrong, Eliot impresses on the reader the imprimatur of the trauma of becoming historical, of accession to the consciousness of one's historicity. As the earlier commentary on the advent of Romanticism attests, one cannot become 'the historian of one's own philosophy', as Levinas puts it (2001, 96). Dorothea is witness to what, in her given moment, she cannot fully articulate and so receives the shock as traumatic revelation, which returns as its own ghost to haunt her future. In this Eliot gives us to understand – and so opens up the possibility of a perspectival self-reading thrown into relief by the demand to *listen acutely to what is implicit* – how 'there are memories of a lived experience which is not rigorously intellectual' (Levinas 2001, 96), but the *posting* or *sending* of which may be given to another generation, Eliot's for example, for whom she writes, or our own, to receive and to read, through the relief of historical space and difference.

The middle classes in transition: the loom and the postal system

Such spacings take time. While in Chapter 19 George IV was still alive, by Chapter 37 he is dead (*MSPL* 357). The movement of time puts the past in perspective, projects its events in relief. More than the death of a king is needed though: 'Parliament [was] dissolved, Wellington and Peel generally depreciated and the new King apologetic', all of which raw facts stand in contrast to the shadowy suspension of 'uncertainties in provincial opinion at that time' (*MSPL* 357). Yet more gaps are opened between, within, experiences, events, and memory, as the 'intellectual activities of [particular] characters drive backwards' but, for the novel as a heterogeneous whole, 'the flow of inexorable onward movement is never reversed . . . the book's own activity is that of diversification . . . of sequence and consequence' (Beer 1989, 104). This is encapsulated in the haunting afterlife of personal history as figured in Bulstrode: 'a man's past is not simply a dead history, an outworn preparation of the present: it is not a repented error shaken loose from the life: it is a still quivering part of himself, bringing shudders and bitter flavours and the tinglings of a merited shame' (*MSPL* 615). Given the iterable structure informed by the individual tendency to retrospection and yet the general machinic propulsion into what is to come, as if *Middlemarch* were some struggling angel of history, one has to pause to ask what precisely is between past and future, between that which leaves only traces and that which haunts as the possibility of what remains to come? The obvious, not to say simple, answer is, undoubtedly, the *middle* or the 'moment of transition' (*MSPL* 616), wherever one believes one can situate this. If, to recall Terry Eagleton's comment, the novel appears in its details to be suspended, this is not to notice that suspension is also a vehicle or medium of transport. One is caught up in motions of which one is not fully aware; one is always in the midst of ongoing forces. The farce or tragedy of this is that consciousness of the world only emerges in crisis, as Bulstrode's example shows.

    Chapter 61 of *Middlemarch* presents a distanced framing of Bulstrode's perspective, as his personal history returns with all the vengeful, haunting force of repressed revenance. The chapter begins with Bulstrode's return to Middlemarch, as if the chapter's opening gambit is to structure the inevitable onward motion of Bulstrode's narrative history with a recurrence, a folding back on one's own steps as it were, even as memory is just this recurrent echo of one's previous motions. Bulstrode is thus revealed historically in his consciousness and experiences as having his identity informed through the notion of relation to his past. As Bulstrode moves forward in time and so through the chapter, Eliot produces a sense of increasing psychic excitement or anxiety within the banker, and with that a concomitant acceleration and density of narrative time into the future. This is due in no small measure to the fact that, as the chapter progresses, Bulstrode is ever more 'Mentally surrounded with that past *again* . . . the years had been perpetually spinning [the traces of the past] . . . into intricate thickness, like masses of spider-web, padding the moral sensibility' (*MSPL* 617; emphasis added). As my emphasis should attest, the past never returns for the first time but is always already a reduplication in its convoluted iterations. The non-linear matrix of entanglements becomes, by virtue of the velocity of metaphorical transformation, 'the train of causes' (*MSPL* 617), which 'only wove retrospect and fear into a fantastic present, [where] he felt the scenes of his earlier life' loom large to take 'hold in the consciousness' (*MSPL* 615). History is no longer a dead past, as the example of Bulstrode makes clear. Not quite living, it is nonetheless a vital, undead force.

The banker thus illustrates Eliot's understanding that history 'no longer takes place in time, but rather through time. Time is metaphorically dynamicized into a force of history itself' (Koselleck 2002, 165). The time of Bulstrode, gathering as it does through ineluctable conscious reflection the unstoppable flow of the past's traces, is thus an analogical narrative form for presenting 'not only one's own time, but . . . the beginning of a new epoch' (Koselleck 2002, 165). If the Middlemarchers and their lives appear in suspension, this is because they are caught up in this transformation of time and history, and so are read retrospectively by Eliot's narrator as being simultaneously in the middle of this transition, carried along with it, and also unable to apprehend fully the ramifications of this 'new' time, this novel modality of temporal comprehension apropos the subject's historicization and becoming-historical. As Eliot remarks elsewhere, 'Historical parallels are remarkably efficient . . . whatever has been or may be narrated by me . . . may be considered a parable; so that if any bad habits or ugly consequences are brought into view, the reader may have the *relief* of regarding them as not more than figuratively ungenteel' (*MSPL* 341; emphasis added). And she continues with the caveat: 'as to any provincial history in which the agents are all of high moral rank, that must be of a date long posterior to the first Reform Bill' (*MSPL* 341).

Middlemarch, then, is a world in which consciousness-in-suspension is precisely the sign of a modern historicization coming to pass, an epoch *in* and *of* historicization. It is a world in which, being in the midst of events, not knowing them as events, the past returns to one as phantom images that haunt. There is no transcendence historically, unless that is thrown into relief by the distance afforded by taking a retrospective glance. To be in the midst of experience is to be always in the sphere of the undecidable, where perception of continuity is broken by the endless 'zigzag' of the weaving traces of one's being, caught within the loom of history. Eliot's characters cannot represent history, they can only present it, stage it, indirectly, through their actions and personal lives, from which we are left to read the encrypted traces of the historical. Representation is 'something that happens to presentation from the outside' (Gasché 1999, 252). If 'everything begins by re-presentation' (Gasché 1999, 256), then in presenting themselves in the midst of change, the Middlemarchers – and *Middlemarch* – begin the nineteenth century in gathering up and unravelling the threads of collective cultural memory, of the pasts of Englishness in all its middling expressions.

Middlemarch: middling morality, the middle classes, Middle England. Looking back at the 1820s and early 1830s, one perceives a historical and cultural transformation that was also, effectively, an epistemological break with earlier visions of the English provincial middle classes. It was a break significantly not only in the representation of the middle classes in literature, in political discourse, in ideological constructions of social position and relation to other groups in early nineteenth-century English society. It was, and must be seen retrospectively as, an irreversible, historically symbolic and hegemonic rupture also in the multifarious manifestations of a heterogeneous group of people, understood as belonging to the intricate striations of a 'middle class', in their becoming conscious of their material and historical situatedness, their modernity, and of course their auto-mediatory ontological reflexiveness. Turning back to consider this dawning ontological awareness and, with it, the conscious insight and blinkered limits of becoming-historical while also realizing one's being effected and transformed by the broader historical and political currents beyond the immediacy of quotidian experience, Eliot structures a dynamic and irregular structure for her embodiment of transition and consciousness, as I have sought to illustrate. In this, she puts the temporal motion of the historical – signified through the sense of a *march* – in relation to a spatial ontological perception – as indicated by *middle*. The differences between Eliot's readers in the 1870s and their parents and grandparents, those of the two previous 'generations', are then thrown into relief, and accordingly illuminated in a reciprocal manner. Title and town give us access to a perspective, however anamorphic this view might be. Eliot's decision to name her fictional West Midlands town 'Middlemarch' is, doubtless, powerfully resonant for the good reader, but it resounds beyond its more immediately suggestive intimations. I have already commented on the title and name as being indicative of a singular–plural instance of the spatial and temporal dimensions of being. It is as if *Middlemarch* named a collective, though differentiated and therefore heterogeneous, articulation of being in its materiality and historicity, and in its own sense of national identity, a kind of shared *being*.

That Eliot decides on the figure of the *Middle* indicates her sense expressed in *Daniel Deronda* that no narrative or history ever starts at or locates a true origin or source. One always begins, Eliot reminds us, *in medias res*, in the midst of something, a beginning being a response to something earlier. *One begins where one is by re-presentation.* Where *we* are in the 1870s, for example, is only apprehensible through the retrospective inauguration afforded by literary narrative of a *re-presentation* of the grounds of a historicized image of collective being and identity under the signs of English national identity, middle-class modernity, and Victorianism. To re-present is always to place oneself in the midst of a process, leading to an open future. Any apparent beginning is always the location of this intermediate or mediating location between differentiated spaces or events, whether spatially or temporally. The notion of the *Middle* suggests an average, a mean condition, and implicitly in some uses a desired state. If Eliot is using the term as a historical index for the formation of the English middle classes, she is identifying the 1820s and early 1830s not as the beginning of the Victorian era but as a transitional locus in the history of bourgeois, provincial and parochial Englishness.

The intermediate moment is not evenly balanced. Eliot does not locate a median year evenly poised, but indicates, as I have sought to suggest, a period between the establishment of parliamentary rule in 1688 and the 1870s, which in its imbalance insinuates a narrative of uninterrupted organic unity in the consciousness of Englishness until the arrival of the Victorian era. Though Victoria is not monarch in 1829, of course; George IV will die in the following year, succeeded by William IV, whose reign lasts just seven years. There is thus in the

ontological perception of historical identity in *Middlemarch* a teleological retrospect structured by its narrative. This backwards glance
that closes up, even as it articulates the difference between, past and
present assumes a transitory and transitional modernity. This modernity is locatable in retrospect as being the manifest representation of
a temporal epoch suspended as a condition or identity in its own right
of collective 'being-between', inhabiting a space that it articulates
between earlier and later perceptions of identity. Eliot analyses and
illuminates for us the various symptoms of the entity, much as Tertius
Lydgate might dissect an organism for consideration under a microscope, as English culture moves 'under the varying experiments of
Time' (*MSPL* 3) from one predominantly determined in its stratifica-
tions and hierarchies from the thinking of 'station' in its inflexibility
to the discourse of 'class', with whatever limited mobility might be
inscribed in this notion.

It is worth returning to Lydgate once more. Lydgate envisions
himself advancing science through the microscope rather than just
the scalpel. Arriving in Middlemarch 'at the end of 1829' (*MSPL* 148),
at the age of 27, and therefore only slightly younger than the century
itself, Lydgate is depicted by Eliot as the coming hope of medicine in
its theoretical and practical modes. The lengthy introduction of
Lydgate places him firmly in the midst, historically speaking, of transitions in medical institutions and practices, as we have seen. Eliot's
'introduction' of Lydgate, to the reader in one direction and
Middlemarch in the other, typifies her narrative role as historical
intermediary, as she brings to view otherwise invisible connective
tissues and passages. Lydgate's introduction is a retrospective history
in itself, moving backwards to his own past, and his education, to
open onto broader medico-social praxes. His is a thoroughly historicized introduction, his agency placed in a middle, rather than an
inaugural location, even though he believes his perspective to be new,
original, inventive (in this his vision, necessarily historicized, is a
misperception). Of the era it is remarked that 'the heroic times of
copious bleeding and blistering had not yet departed, still less the
times of thorough-going theory' (*MSPL* 142). Moreover, 'it must be
remembered that this was a dark period' in the history of the profession, quackery being commonplace (*MSPL* 145–6; it is worth observing, albeit in passing, that the 1820s as the era of the quack doctor is
indicated also by Dickens in the figure of Bob Sawyer). Lydgate is no
quack, however, even though the Middlemarchers regard him with
some suspicion. Seeing Middlemarch as only an intermediary location

before moving on to greater things, he counts on the possibilities of research, involving particularly 'diligent application . . . of the microscope, *which research had begun to use again* with new enthusiasm of reliance' (*MSPL* 149; emphasis added).[4] Eliot's appreciation of historical movement is clear from this contextual comment. While the pursuit of research for Lydgate is a novelty, offering by its application an adventitious opening to the realization of his visions of the future, its use in medical research is not new. The past returns, older practices informing the present, as the historical instant is unfolded in folding back on itself. One is always under way, and in the middle of temporal passages.

Of course, as Eliot admits in one of those many apostrophic asides in *Middlemarch*, the microscope is not an absolute device. Its truth is not a given. In a dissection of the motivations of Mrs Cadwallader, Eliot employs the metaphor of the microscope. Observe briefly that this is the only metaphorical usage in the novel, wherein 'microscope' is referred to six times, the five remaining references signifying the instrument. The microscope arrives therefore 'before' Lydgate. This is not necessarily remarkable in itself. Taking a historicizing perspective, however, one might note that the metaphor arrives before the literal object, travelling back from Eliot's pen to the late 1820s, in order to serve, by analogy, the function of the pen. *Everything begins by representation.* That is to say, both microscope and pen, in their presentation of narrative events, make visible what is invisible, and reveal, in showing us a past that we cannot witness as such, what is also hidden from empirical view in another manner: the psychological motivations of social and ritual behaviours.

> Even with a microscope directed on a water-drop we find ourselves making interpretations which turn out to be rather coarse; for whereas under a weak lens you may seem to see a creature exhibiting an active voracity into which other smaller creatures actively play as if they were so many animated tax-pennies, a stronger lens reveals to you certain tiniest hairlets which make vortices for these victims while the swallower waits passively at his receipt of custom. In this way, metaphorically speaking, a strong lens applied to Mrs. Cadwallader's match-making will show a play of minute causes producing what may be called thought and speech vortices to bring her the sort of food she needed. (*MSPL* 59–60)

As I have just commented, Eliot's illustration introduces in its presentation of the hidden sources of motivation behind the cause and effect of the interactions between life forms an important note of caution concerning the material faultiness of vision, when dependent on economic resources. The biological analogy is demonstrated by Eliot to be inseparable from, and structured by, contexts and discourses beyond itself. One is in the midst of structures that mutually inform one another. One discourse is interwoven into, and so touches on, thereby affecting, another. Vision, representation, and by extension historical intervention or interpretation can never be neutral. Despite distance, one's analysis, however seemingly disinterested or Olympian, is always touched by, even as it in turn touches, 'the inextricability of community interests' in *Middlemarch* (Beer 1989, 112). The narrator is never omniscient but is always in the midst of the fray. She is always subject to the means available, according to historical economic conditions, for perceiving and so interpreting events. What holds true here in this narrative dissection of the visionary powers of narrative itself at once places the principle of interpretation in the middle of other forces, movements or marches. In doing so, it causes one to reflect on one's act of reading, given that one is positioned. There is no truly objective, disinterested or purely empirical stance, culturally, ideologically, or historically speaking. One is always in the middle. One intervenes, but one's identity or position historically is itself an intervention.

The historical and cultural stage of the middle classes represented in *Middlemarch* in the form of the Middlemarchers, who themselves come mostly from the 'middling' striations of society in their majority, is structured – put under the time-travelling microscope – by Eliot's narrative at an intermediate location, with regard to position in geopolitical space, in time, and according to various hierarchies of order. Middlemarch is thus effectively the expression of a common, if on occasions fraught, factional, self-differentiating polity, which assumes a commonality in the face of changes outside its immediate boundaries, and which either rejects or assimilates just enough of the foreign, the strange, the new, in order to maintain the functions of its system. In considering the notion of the middle, I have implicitly been pursuing a reading of the novel's title, and what it puts to work. To push the reading of the title further, however, if we take the long view of Eliot's title in the spacing that is opened by the novel between the *now* of the 1870s and the *then* of the 1820s, we might, arguably, recognize at the latter end of the by-now Victorian era, a sense of the 1820s as the first months – *March* – of the spring of that epoch. More than this, it is worth noting that *march*, an Anglo-Norman combination of the French *marche* and Germanic *mearc* or *mark*, signifies a border, boundary or frontier, a region, district, country or, more narrowly, a tract of land. A region bounded by borders or the boundaries marking properties or estates, a *march*, figure of border or limit, is also, somewhat more obscurely, a link or intermediary. It serves to connect as well as divide or mark off, and thus *Middlemarch* remarks simultaneously its own connectedness and separation historically and culturally the distinctions between an earlier generation and the present generation for whom the novel is written. Like the work of the apostrophe or the figure of anastomosis, Eliot's text structures an intermediary mode of connection, a means of transport and communication, as it moves between the two. In this, the weave of the text, in gathering and unravelling its various scratches or traces, places the reader in the middle of events.

While I have said at the beginning of this chapter that the apostrophe addresses the absent reader, the reader to come, the novel as a whole operates apostrophically in two directions, from two locations. On the one hand, it addresses, in bearing witness to, the absent dead of the previous generation exemplified in fictive form of the Middlemarchers. On the other hand, *Middlemarch* is the apostrophic address on the part of the middle Englanders of the provincial town to the English to come – or at least this is Eliot's imaginative mediation, in which the novel serves as the *mark* or *march* of history, the intermediary between our others and ourselves. Bordering on both *then* and *now*, it makes communication possible between two temporally distinct 'lands', as it transports the reader through its phantasmatic narrative weave, while simultaneously transporting the momentarily illuminated figures of our others, our dead generations, causing them to communicate with us. Like the apostrophe, or like the narratorial structure that projects the illusion of an 'omniscient narrator', the novel takes place as and in the *march* between the 1820s and 1870s. Its work is to weave between places, thereby travelling (*marcher*) temporally even as it marks the inevitable and irreversible motion, the *march* of time.

Eliot's understanding of the historicity of being in its discontinuous address is also captured in the *march* of Middle*march*, the term naming a footprint or sign. If all the steps one takes leave footprints, so to speak, then those of previous generations leave in their march into the future a mark on those to come, as so many traits of identity, subjectivity and being historically, culturally, ideologically, and materially given. This metaphorical march or marking, perhaps a little fancifully read on my part, relates indirectly to another sense, referring to intention or thought. A person's *march* is also their will, or desire, the directions towards which their thoughts tend. Once again, though barely recognized on the part of the Middlemarchers and available only with the belatedness of hindsight to Eliot and her readers, it is as if there is a historically determined and collective, though heterogeneous, 'will-to-consciousness' that the lives, practices and discourses of those belonging to Middlemarch in the 1820s engender or embody as the early manifestations of nineteenth-century being in its modernity historically distinct from previous centuries, eras, and generations of English identity.

Does *Middlemarch* then present 'history'? Does it, in any objective sense, show its readers the way we lived then? Does the novel engage in the aestheticization of history? Or does it remark, and so stage even as it traces, both the historicization and the historicality of the aesthetic and phenomenal? Does *Middlemarch* give to aesthetic form, through the illumination of the signs of material culture viewed from a certain perspective at a given subjective moment distinct from the moment observed and remembered, a grounding that traces the connection between the aesthetic and the historical or material condition? Is narrative, the novel, proposed or staged by Eliot as the *apostrophic* or *anastomosic* event? Does the novel make a link across the spacing that it presents as the inescapable and necessarily historicized perspective and position between the past of its objects and the unpredictable modality of the future of the reader, that unpredictable modality called by Jacques Derrida *l'avenir*, the to-come. This spacing that connects without assuming or suggesting congruity or relationship allows the reader-to-come a sense of familiarity but also one of distance. Eliot's aestheticization of 'history', if it is in fact this, does nothing less than open the limits of the historical to the multiple fluxes of its innumerable and excessive imminent narratives. Admitting that a story *must* be told, this is one's responsibility dictated by an ethics of empathy. Choice is made, everything begins by re-representation and the admission of partiality – and so Eliot sidesteps the aporia at the heart of that experience of modernity and the past *in those modes of re-presentation as enframing gestures*.

As the pier-glass analogy tells us, Eliot's writing does not simply mirror society, which mirroring is the standard mimetic function assumed of the 'classic realist text' (Beer 1989, 100). Instead, its distortions throw the historicity of matters, the signs of a world sufficiently recognizable as being like our own, into relief. Such traces of projection elevate the lives of the Middlemarchers as a historically specific community and group of hierarchically ordered and factionally contested individuals ravelled up in the flows of politics, culture, and time, and so provide a support for the presentation of historical difference. At once, we witness in Eliot's technique the structuring of a surface on which history is staged and simultaneously the staged projection from that surface of those events and their agents and subjects as these are raised to our view. The past lives of the inhabitants of the West Midlands of the 1820s are illuminated as so many marks, minutely and multitudinously scratched in all directions. *Middlemarch* is thus an archival recording device, a mnemotechnic that is also a tele-technological postal service.

But if Eliot's narrative machinery serves a postal function, it is also another kind of apparatus, an instrument the technology of which composes the scenes or events. *Middlemarch* is readable as a loom – as if it were produced by Eliot's weaver Silas Marner. In its seemingly leisurely motions (*loom* means to move slowly), it produces the history of light and shadows, transmitted from the past to loom momentarily into view. Through its 'discursive twists and turns', Eliot's writing 'set[s] up turbulences which unsteady [those] reflections' by which the classic realist text is read or presumes to screen its world (Beer 1989, 100). And the 'effect is intensified . . . by the ironic abrasions produced by the double time of the novel. The referential circle between the time of production and the first reading – the 1870s – and the time of enactment, forty years earlier, is never quite a closed system' (Beer 1989, 100). If there is then what Beer calls a 'vacillation between registers' to be observed in Eliot's writing, this condition does not sway 'the reader to believe in its inclusiveness' (Beer 1989, 102). Rather, this motion has to be read as a shuttling, a weaving, which throws the historical difference between the narrative *then* and any number of *nows* into relief, depending on when one is reading. Such a weaving is effected on the narrative loom, that machinery for the transmission of the remainders of the past. Writing effectively stitches together the fraying threads of different moments and locations, while drawing attention to the signs of its own motion. In doing so, it produces a 'looming' effect, that is, to use its figurative sense, it produces 'looms', projections of immaterial things. The novel as narrative history is after all a medium as well as a machine for the production and projection of phantoms. It is the material means by which the immaterial is gathered as the traces of a past unavailable as such.

My metaphors of loom and postal system are chosen with a view to historical and material transitions, regarding modes of connectivity, methods of communication, and tropes of transport. They serve to signal material transformations and the structural manifestation of those transformations encapsulated in technological figures that offer economically and synecdochally to trace an otherwise unrelated connection in the passage of the nineteenth century. The shift from loom to postal system is not in any way one of succession or supplement. The postal 'system' is already figural, irreducible to any one kind of technology, machinery or institutional form. The loom as device, whether worked individually or powered by steam or coal, is materially real, despite the history of its own transformations. The analogy holds good though in its gesture of tracing between literal and metaphorical inasmuch as it offers an analogical mirror of a shift taking place during the early decades of the nineteenth century in the monetary system, 'from metal to paper . . . where the promissory or symbolic character of money has come to the fore' (Beer 1989, 113). It is undoubtedly for this reason, as Beer argues, that Eliot 'sets "paper and gold" alongside the action of the heart and the valves' (Beer 1989, 113) in the analogical mirroring of one circulatory system in another, which trope – circulation – Beer argues dominates *Middlemarch*.

Here is what is at stake in Eliot's 'aestheticization' of history, her making literary from the literal, producing the serviceable figure, trope or metaphor from cultural and social systems. Systems transform: they transform themselves and are translated within themselves as their historical condition, adapting and producing effects as a result in the historical subjects of such metamorphic structures. More than this, systems of presentation and re-presentation, in criss-crossing one another, act as recording technologies, giving place and voice. Amongst such 'systems' of communication, of weaving and transmission, we must also consider the novel, with regard to whatever is singular about the relation between representation and reality or aesthetics and history in the nineteenth century. Eliot's system is translated from within itself, in marking in different directions the temporal space between 1829 and 1872, the purpose and operation of the classic realist text. Admitting to its power to exceed the purely mimetic through its allusive, analogical, and economic operations with regard to the indirect presentation or staging of history and historicization, Eliot puts the novel to work to open history otherwise to our view by presenting the relief of the past through a narrative 'study of provincial life'.

The novel's excessive energy, its ability to say more than it says through attentiveness not only to what its characters say but to how they present themselves, despite their own particular cultural, social, epistemological, and historical limits, is captured trenchantly in the one appearance of Timothy Cooper, the labourer. Cooper offers an interesting observation on 'history' witnessed from underneath. Speaking in dialect and thereby re-presenting himself as unavailable to anything but partial translation, he comments on his own role as witness of and subject of economic, social, and political forces:

> I'n seen lots o' things turn up sin' I war a young un – the war an' the peace, and the canells, an' the oald King George, an' the Regen', an' the new King George, an' the new un as has got a new ne-ame – an' it's been all aloike to the poor mon. What's the canells been t' him? They'n brought him neyther me-at nor be-acon, nor wage to lay by, if he didn't save it wi' clemmin' his own inside. Times ha' got wusser for him sin' I war a young un. An' so it'll be wi' the railroads. They'll on'y leave the poor mon furder behind. (*MSPL* 560)

'Oald King George' is, obviously, 'Old George the Third', or Farmer George as he was known. Timothy's remark acknowledges not only the relatively rapid monarchical changes, but also the Napoleonic Wars and the building of the canals. Domestic and political economy are of no significance to the 'poor mon'. In this view of the past, Cooper predicts more of the same for the future, with the coming of the railways, at least as this concerns the rural poor and the working classes. Whether the 'poor mon' was left 'furder behind' in the intervening years between Cooper's observation and Eliot's recording – or perhaps it is reception – of the remark can only be attested to by Eliot's readers. Cooper represents history, but he represents it from the sidelines, from an obviously marginalized though exploited position, for which there is little or no immediate sign of *relief* in any of the Acts passed during the time of *Middlemarch*. If political representation concerned anything therefore in the 1820s and 1830s, it did not represent 'the rights of individuals to participate in the electoral process' (Wahrman 1995, 226). Furthermore, though not founded on or concerned with 'natural rights', the question of reform in political representation 'was based on a conception of society as consisting of different interests or sectors [amongst the middle and property-owning classes], each of which needed to have a voice in parliament' (Wahrman 1995, 226). Clearly, Cooper does not, nor can he ever, belong to this '*new and rising social constituency*' (Wahrman 1995, 226; emphasis added) to whom Eliot is writing nearly fifty years on, and whose historical identity and collective consciousness were founded 'from 1820 onwards' with the historically conspicuous 'coupling of "middle class" with social change and the coupling of "middle class" with demands for parliamentary representation' (Wahrman 1995, 226–7).

What Timothy obviously 'represents', therefore, is the distortion of representation and the occlusion that representation (aesthetic and political) makes possible in its various historical and political claims for self-representation. Cooper's dialect commentary 'represents' the extent to which 'accommodations between aristocracy and bourgeois meant continuous adaptation' (Ebbatson 2004, 114). Cooper's dialect refuses and resists this adaptation in a small local fashion, fashioning in this an affirmation of otherness. In this gambit, how something is said is strategically as important as what the message contains. Dialect 'performs' aesthetically a refusal in the 'early nineteenth century [to be] humanised and be contained by ruling groups', at least figuratively (Ebbatson 2004, 114). In this, Eliot situates a singular recording that exceeds the individual speaking. For, while 'professional' figures such as Lydgate and Bulstrode signify a moment of individualism amongst the novel's 'determinate ideological effects' (Feltes 1986, 50), revealing the ways in which 'professionalism' amongst the middle classes of the early nineteenth century is 'socially and ideologically constructed' (Feltes 1986, 50), Cooper's remarks indicate both another ideological position and an aporia in the historicity of such constructions.

We need someone to bear witness for Timothy Cooper, therefore, to give voice to the voice of the other, historically, so as to send on and to open a relay of communication beyond the historical specificity. Eliot performs this service, standing between us and Cooper as medium and mediator. Timothy, we are told,

> was a wiry old labourer, of a type lingering in those times – who had his savings in a stocking-foot, lived in a lone cottage, and was not to be wrought on by any oratory, having as little of the feudal spirit, and believing as little, as if he had not been totally unacquainted with the Age of Reason and the Rights of Man . . . [He is, Eliot lets us know in an apostrophic turn, one of those] rustics who are in possession of an undeniable truth which they know through a hard process of feeling, and can let it fall like a giant's club on your neatly carved argument for a social benefit which they do *not* feel. (*MSPL* 560)

For all that servants might not appear in *Middlemarch*, the poor occasionally do, if infrequently. Cooper's statement on historical transformation, though directed to Caleb, sends itself in its encrypted dialect transmission beyond the narrative frame. It arrives, if at all, as partial signals, scratches in the recording, the frayed threads of a weave we cannot reconstitute with any sense of completion. It is as if there is received some apparitional posting speaking to the future reader against Cooper's own obliteration, and through which is transmitted the spirit of Thomas Paine. Across fifty years, and subsequently into the twenty-first century, Cooper's singular confession of bearing witness to 'history' should remain to resonate with us. Eliot demands it should touch us in that apostrophic turn where Cooper's words, in their emotionally felt perspective, can fall on *you*. Cooper's commentary should therefore do more than merely resonate. It should touch us directly, not because it has the unassailable force of historical accuracy – though it does – but rather because it affirms inside itself, in its confessional attestation, 'the possession of an undeniable truth', which is known as Eliot tells us 'through a hard process of feeling'.

The historicized coming-to-consciousness that *Middlemarch* charts is always involved in this recording of 'feeling', as its various characters come to differing levels of historicized awareness, not only of themselves but indirectly of how they come to be who they are, haunted as they are by the signals of the past, hurtling in different directions. In this, *Middlemarch* admits to history what 'external facts', which are 'coarse and materialistic', cannot do (*MSPL* 229). History, Eliot whispers from the other side of silence, is marked by this touching force, of the consciousness of an other – the consciousness for us, on the one hand, that *there*, over there in that other space is an other who speaks, who demands response; and the consciousness, on the other hand, *which is*, we somehow feel, the other's, threading itself through us appresentatively, in an injunction to articulate, to construct and transmit the signs and scratches tracing out an ethics of empathy in a radical historicization of being.

If Eliot's system, and the modes of production pertaining to that system, appear haphazard, subject to surges, misinterpretations, misdirections, and failed deliveries; if, furthermore, they operate with little apparent systematic coherence, other than some seeming 'organic' relationship, this is in itself the inescapable encoding of the 'signs of the times', as it were. There was an 'inherent' stability *and* instability in the historical transformation of social and ideological systems, from a model predominantly governed by 'paternal social relations' to one of 'class-based relations' (Price 1999, 329). The slow, endless adaptation and accommodation in social relations addressed by Roger Ebbatson (above) are themselves both the signs and the operations of the equally slow, irregular and internally disordered process of historical change. The result of this was that Victorian social relations were a curiously, not to say idiosyncratically, singular hybrid of paternalism on the one hand, and class interaction on the other. This 'curious quality of mid-Victorian class relations' (Price 1999, 329) lasts in its internally contesting condition at least fifty years, beginning in the 1820s, in the post-war period, until the 1870s at least, in a struggle to conceive consensus over the grounds of identity formation. Read in this manner, Cooper's words, with their unconscious echoes of Thomas Paine, take on the guise of a valediction to one possible, alternative model for radical democracy, as opposed to the reality of makeshift compromises that become in so many ways the Victorian political and social scene. The early nineteenth century marks a 'significant stage', as Richard Price calls it, in the transfiguration and mutation of English society and English national identity. Cooper is the singular locus, if you will, who opposes cynically, rather than out of any native conservatism, the reshaping of Englishness. After Timothy Cooper, we may read a decisive break from a politics and history of Englishness with an 'essentially eighteenth-century context' (Price 1999, 330). *Middlemarch* can therefore only remind us of what we lose in the struggle for the systematic regulation of class relations and modes of production in its particularization and individualization of broader social forces that serve historically to produce the modern English subject.

Notes

1. On sympathetic vibration in *Middlemarch* as a 'physiological account of empathy' and an 'ethic of empathy', see Young (2003, 233–8, 235). Historically, and in terms of being, the ramifications of such an ethics is clear. While we can never *know* the past directly, a sensitive, attentive reading can, in the face of all scientific faultiness and the limits of scientific knowledge, technologies, and modes of analysis, discern or be touched by the resonance of the past, the vibration of the other.

2. Although I cannot go into this in any great detail here, 'Brooke' names not only the 'entanglement of things' synchronously perceived as political interests, he also names an anachronistic 'web' or weave of discourse, intellect, and epistemology. Frequently given synecdochic form and performative articulation in his hesitating, disseminative speech, which frays repeatedly in many different directions, the 'web' falls frequently into ruin as sentences and commentaries remain incomplete. In every attempt to illuminate a situation

through reference to his reading, he fails to gather up the loose threads of texts belonging not only to his youth, but to a somewhat dilatory and old-fashioned education. It is not that the books to which Brooke refers are out of time, it is that he cannot translate them effectively and so make them productive, putting them to work, in the radically different cultural and historical contexts of the late 1820s. His language is thus performative in that it does not work; its mode of tracing a web of connections is outmoded in the face of more modern modes of production and discourse. The 'modern' problem, as far as Brooke understands it, is that once one 'goes into' something, as he has it, 'it leads to everything' (*MSPL* 16). *Pace* Brooke, who at one time or another in the past has 'gone into' matters, whether the science of Humphrey Davy (*MSPL* 16), public matters or the Luddites (*MSPL* 504), Eliot insistently and repeatedly does go into everything in *Middlemarch*, as the principal means of tracing the historicity of consciousness.

3. As Gregory Maertz tells us in a footnote to Chapter 20 in his edition of *Middlemarch*, 'the viewing of the artistic treasures of the Vatican is connected to the historical events forming the background to *Middlemarch*' (Maertz *MSPL* 184, n. 1). The statues being viewed by Dorothea had been stolen by Napoleon and taken to Paris between 1797 and 1800. The stolen works of art were eventually returned and housed in a new extension of the Pio-Clementine Museum. While for Eliot there is clearly a powerful effect to be registered on Dorothea personally, what neither Eliot nor Dorothea acknowledges directly is the particular historicized possibility of witness, which is touched indirectly, but nonetheless intimately entwined within the broader currents of European political history.

4. The compound microscope, we should remind ourselves, is perfected by Hooke in 1665. As with Dorothea's Protestant lineage, and the Corporation and Test Acts, here is yet one more trace of that enframing of English modernity in the historicized but encrypted presentation of narrative.

Part III

The Next Generation

5 'The modern flower in a medieval flowerpot': The Times and Visions of Thomas Hardy

Our time is racked and torn, haunted by ghosts, and errant in search of lost realities, poor in genuine culture, incoherent among its own chief elements.

John Sterling, *Quarterly Review* (1842)

Half my time (particularly when I write verse) I believe – in the modern use of the word – not only in the things that [Henri] Bergson does, but in spectres, mysterious voices, intuitions, omens, dreams, haunted places, etc., etc.

Thomas Hardy, Letter to Dr Caleb Saleeby (2 February 1915)

Generations

Moving forward, we look back.

While particular texts may be said to be other than their times, 'Thomas Hardy' is anachronistic. In this chapter, therefore, we turn away from close readings of particular novels in order to open to view a broader perspective on one particular writer, Thomas Hardy. In turning to Hardy's texts we move, finally, to what is arguably the second 'generation' of Victorians, the generation after that from which all the principal authors in this study have thus far been drawn. Now, 'generation' is a notoriously fuzzy idea. In an 1878 review of one of Hardy's novels, when the novelist was almost 40, *The Athenaeum* (23 November 1878) referred to Hardy as one of 'the younger generation of story-tellers'. This begs the question: how long is a generation? One answer to this admittedly ridiculous question might be: the average interval between the date of parents' birth and that of their children. The structure of this seemingly precise location places very narrow limits on the concept. It is dictated, additionally, after the fact by retrospective calculation and an economic compromise that allows one to fix a moment within that otherwise impossible and undecidable conceptualization. Thus, and quite by chance, all the principal authors considered in this study can be said, according to the generational logic just proposed, to belong to the same generation.

That generation (if it is indeed 'one', which remains open to question[1]) grew up in the decades before Victoria became Queen. Even the youngest, Wilkie Collins, was thirteen by the time of the coronation. It is the same generation as Charlotte, Emily and Anne Brontë, Arnold, Ruskin, Marx, Trollope, Pugin, and Darwin. However varied the education of those writers belonging to the earlier generation addressed in the previous chapters, they can be said to share broadly a similar culture, similar influences, and similar understanding of what constitutes history and the past. (A short comparative parenthesis: Hardy's generation, it is worth observing in passing, is that of Emmeline Pankhurst and the suffrage movement, Freud, Nietzsche, Gerard Manley Hopkins, Rhoda Broughton, Stevenson and Henry James. Hardy's generation [along with some of the previous generation] witnesses the second and third Reform Acts [1867 and 1884] as do some of the previous generation, and the establishment of the Fabian Society, the Prime Meridian and Greenwich Mean Time [1884], to which events only Wilkie Collins in my 'first' generation can attest.)

To return to my point about shared cultural experience: each of the novelists belonging to that first generation experienced to some degree the debates and effects of the first Reform Act (1832). Arguably, this marked a greater epistemic transformation in its effects on the national psyche and its ability to mark a distance between its then-contemporary generation and their predecessors than the subsequent Acts. The effect in George Eliot's case was that, a generation later, she wrote around it, if not exactly about it, in *Middlemarch*. In the case of most of the novels analysed in the present volume, each situates itself at moments or at a specific time before the 1832 Act. The exception is *The Moonstone*, although this too relates and relies on a 'prehistory' to its mid-Victorian narrative as a necessary supplement to which the narrative present is a collective response and gathering or translation of memories in the form of autobiographically inflected memoirs. 'Who we are' in *The Moonstone* is a collective and decisive inflection, mediation or translation of 'how we have come to be'. Being, understood historically for the Victorians, so-called, is a self-reflexively, interpellated affair. Being 'Victorian', then, is in some manner to acknowledge or write oneself as being called by historicity's others.

Of the previous generation, Hardy would have read some if not all the authors discussed in this volume (he witnessed Dickens lecture in 1863). Key contemporary authors for the previous generation's youth, particularly in the years of William IV's reign (1830–37), who served in the shaping of the 'Victorian' narrative form and interests included Sir Walter Scott (1771–1832), Frederick Marryat (1792–1848), Harriet Martineau (1802–76), Benjamin Disraeli (1804–81), and Sir Edward Bulwer Lytton (1803–73). Even on the most cursory acquaintance with the works of these writers and those of the 'Dickensian' era, the good reader will admit to a cultural and epistemic gulf between the two generations.

The unbridgeable gap between generations is marked powerfully by Thomas Hardy in at least one of his novels, the overtly and conventionally 'historical' *The Trumpet-Major*. Though a domestic and largely parochial romance with some comedic interludes, Hardy's lyrical seventh novel, published in 1880 between *The Return of the Native* and *A Laodicean*, stages its narrative against and in confluence with the undercurrents and effects of the Napoleonic Wars. A novel, the narrative of which is at a double generational remove from the time of its production, *The Trumpet-Major* addresses itself, therefore, to the lives of Hardy's grandparents' generation. Of all Hardy's novels, it is perhaps the most cruelly ironic in its perception of the past's importance, and the ways in which the traces of the past can inform, or become occluded in, the present. For, while the novel foregrounds the romantic experiences and intertwined lives of Anne Garland and her suitors Robert and John Loveday (the former becoming a sailor, the latter becoming the trumpet-major of the title), and the squire's nephew Festus, it calls all generic expectations into question through the intrusion of the historical as both literary mode and material reality. It thus disrupts its own reception for the late Victorian reader by upsetting generic convention, causing the traumatic eruption in the past to return to an act of reading in the 1880s, as a reminder of what will not go away, but which remains to be read as a belated apprehension of a specific determinate of Victorian modernity and identity.

The past is always with us, as are our previous generations. They haunt us forcefully, shaping who we are. Nowhere more so is this announced in *The Trumpet-Major* than in the narrative's ending, in which Hardy is at pains to disrupt fictional closure through the narrative of historical consequences, and, in so doing, opening to the reader the transmission of the experience of historical rupture and violence, through the experience of history's others, people such as Robert, Anne and John, civilians, soldiers and sailors who have no historical voice in conventional, broad historical accounts of war. In the final chapter, John is recalled to his regiment to join 'Sir Arthur Wellesley, [the Duke of Wellington] in the Peninsula' (*TM* 299). Hardy's passing reference in this short chapter to Wellington, and the Peninsular Wars (1808–14), marks the fiction rudely with the intrusion of its historical context. It demonstrates moreover, through the reception of a message, how a life and others around it are subject to random currents, and the network of transmissions by which political history operates.

Additionally, Hardy then goes on to recount how, of 'the seven' who take their leave of Anne on the night mentioned in the final chapter, 'five, *including the trumpet-major*, were dead men within the few following years, and their bones left to moulder in the land of their campaigns' (*TM* 300; emphasis added). The titular protagonist leaves for his death. Hardy reemphasizes the destruction to come in the last paragraph, as, seemingly needlessly, in an excess of repetition, death returns once more for John. His face is seen briefly by candlelight, as he backs across the doorstep into the 'black night; and in another moment he had plunged into the darkness, the ring of his smart step dying away . . . as he . . . went off to blow his trumpet till silenced for ever upon one of the bloody battle-fields of Spain' (*TM* 301).

Interestingly, because perhaps disturbingly, Hardy creates a tension between private and domestic identity – John Loveday, the miller's son – and public, historical function – the trumpet-major. It is as if John arrives finally at the title of this novel. It is as if this were the identity for which he is destined. The title reinforces this sense of historical intrusion and determination, as the fictional figure becomes memorialized, even as that same title, doubling his rank and function, erases or promises to efface John's personal identity. In the impersonality of the title, the reader is called on to recognize the historical anonymity of so many. Additionally, the reader witnesses the departure of the dead. And while the reader is haunted by this recognition, within the dated time frame, it might be said that the dead arrive unexpectedly as the ghosts of their living selves, as ghosts from the future. The trace of history thus arrives as a memento mori, a message dispatched and destined to be read by each and every reader of Hardy's. History is intercepted, one might say, by the subject, who is translated, transformed by this arrival, which is also a revenant inscribing the self through the opening of cultural memory.

One might suggest also that Hardy is remarking a specific transformation of literature in this historically inflected gesture as a sign of literature's 'coming-of-age' in the nineteenth century, as well as being a gathering of the generations of the Victorian era, as a community in death. His narrative stages an irreversible and epochal translation of the responsibilities of narrative witnessing. A sign of fiction's modernity is recorded in Hardy's ceaseless inscription of its ability and responsibility to bear witness to the hetero-affective forces and signs of history, the past, and cultural memory, as these are intimately entangled in the previous generations who are, hypothetically, one's direct forebears. Who we are, Hardy affirms in the staging of national identity as a community-in-death, *is* figured through our belated apperception of those others, of whom we speak as generations. To put this slightly differently, Victorian identity is generated by the traumatic experience of obliteration and transformation that the nation undergoes in various ways over the decades from the 1780s to the 1830s.

Returning though, to the matter of generations, and, specifically, the one preceding Hardy's: Dickens, Gaskell and Eliot's generation came to maturity in the years of the Corn Laws (not repealed until 1846). Concomitantly, they would have been privy to news at least of agitation by the Anti-Corn Law League. Though all were born too late to have had direct knowledge of the Luddite movement, the generation of their parents could have heard of the social movement and its radical acts of industrial sabotage. They, along with their parents and their parents' parents, belonged to the generations affected directly or indirectly by the imposition of successive 'Inclosure Acts', laws by which common grazing rights were denied throughout the country through the enclosure of land previously understood to be common land. Though having a long history, the Inclosure Acts were systematized first in 1801 through the Inclosure Consolidation Act, which gave formal consistency to all previous Acts extending back to the twelfth century and extending well into the nineteenth century. The General Inclosure Act of 1845 made provision for the employment of commissioners, whose powers extended to effecting autonomous enclosure, without recourse to parliamentary permission. The 'first' generation of Victorian writers were, then, the last generation during which and for whom what I would like to refer to as the English diaspora imposed its effects: the transformation from predominantly rural to urban modes of existence, the transition from largely feudal to capitalist economic and social relations, the shift decisively to a distinctively modern bourgeois hegemony.

It may have been noticed that the context I have sketched in the previous paragraph insists on legislation directly affecting the rural and farming communities of England, even though the nineteenth century is commonly thought of as the age of industry, of 'steam' (to use a now somewhat quaint and phantasmagorical metonymy for all too material effects), and of empire. This is deliberate. For what should be reflected upon is that most of the canonical writers on whom I have focused in this volume have little to say about rural life. With the exception of Eliot, the other writers in question are by and large urban, metropolitan authors, along with many other authors of their generation. Briefly, it is as if Romanticism offers the last literary gasp, so to speak, the final act of attestation to the irrevocable transformation of English culture produced by the complex of events known as the industrial revolution. Where the countryside does intrude in many of the 'first' generation of Victorian writers, it is, if not as an afterthought, then certainly as an incidental for the most part. It may well be that the rural and pastoral became phantomized by the historical trauma of the first decades of the nineteenth century, serving only in semi-visible and encrypted ways to motivate literary sensibilities and modes of representation. This in turn serves to mark a distance in acts of self-reading for those early Victorians who saw themselves as modern, distinct from and quite other than the previous generations. Where the rural does appear in the novels of the nineteenth century it is arguably primarily as backdrop, stage- or scene-setting device, a literary *trompe-l'œil* only in the service of character-grounded, psychologically motivated realist story-telling. That is, until Hardy's novels.

Apropos landscape and rural identity, comparisons were made by reviewers of Hardy and George Eliot from the first serial-part publication of *Far From the Madding Crowd*. There is a sense in which Hardy's interest in the landscape of England is not merely a matter of biography but is also an inherited one from the previous literary generation. Irreducible to any crude or reductive interpretation of that interest as an often nostalgic longing, implicitly or explicitly, for the rural and pastoral scenes of a pre-industrial England, works appearing from the 1840s to the 1860s – Carlyle's *Past and Present* (1843), Ruskin's *Unto this Last* (1860), George Eliot's *Felix Holt* (1866), Arnold's *Culture and Anarchy* (1869) – articulate in their concerns about the effects of industrialization the irrevocable change of landscapes 'as arenas in which lives are lived . . . [and] as images of how private and communal life could be conducted' (Davie 1998, 243).

Arguably, Hardy not only extends this tradition, he transforms the cultural staging of the rural significantly, making the articulation of other identities possible. Occasionally, a dissenting English alterity emerges, given representation through its indelible impress on the landscape. It is not to be thought that Hardy simply poses a dialectics of hegemonic modernity and a dissident opposition. Rather that which passes leaves its traces to be read by future generations, and its 'dissent' remains to be read simply in Hardy's textual memory work as the gathering of the signs and voices of some other in danger of occlusion or obliteration. The dissent is, at its most neutral, simply the affirmation that 'I do not belong', 'I no longer belong' in the historical and cultural transformation of social and cultural determinations of identity. Hardy gives early expression to this in *Under the Greenwood Tree*, his second novel, published in 1872, which perception is expressed most directly in the words of Michael Mail, who delivers the opinion that 'times have changed from the times they used to be' (*UGT* 22).

Generally, irreversible generational transformation of parochial culture is indicated as one more inevitable change allied to seasonal cycles in *Under the Greenwood Tree*, the story of which is set at the time of initial composition in the early 1870s as being 'less than a generation ago' (*UGT* 7). As Tim Dolin notes in his edition of the novel, from 1872 to the revised edition of the novel in 1896, Hardy changed the temporal distance between reader and events from less than thirty to more than fifty years (*UGT* 191–2, n. 2). A close affiliation or bond is traced implicitly between the 'natural' and 'cultural' worlds inhabited by the people of Mellstock and, particularly, their choir, the group of musicians most personally affected by a cultural sea change. That affiliation is marked by Hardy in his choice of titles for the volume divisions of the novel: winter, spring, summer, autumn. This chronological progression and cycle is abruptly interrupted, as the novelist reminds us that a mode of presentation structures, mediates, and informs our perception of this seemingly natural world and its 'realist' representation. That Hardy chooses to implicate the natural and cultural conceptually in one another is perhaps itself a sign of the material moment of cultural and historical transformation. The reader is suspended between differing modes of perception, between the assumption of an empirically governed worldview and a perspective that is conscious of itself as interpretative perception.

Specifically, the ineluctable change occasioned in the generational shift is marked by the advent of an organ in the church, with which the vicar, Mr Maybold, wishes to replace the Mellstock choir, who provide the music in church on violins, serpents, clarinets and other instruments. The transformation is both generational, an innovation signalling a change in cultural practice, and technical, the organ signifying changes in ecclesiastical attitudes to liturgical practice in the Church of England, as a sign of modernization at some point in the 1840s, the decade in which the narrative is set. One aspect of this historical upheaval – this is not an overstatement – is that it removes the village from church, so to speak. While, obviously, a congregation will remain, the boundary between church and congregation, institution and parishioners, and therefore between ecclesiastical institutional organization and secular life, is erected, a hierarchy made manifest. The overlapping cycles of natural, cultural and historical change are reinforced further, because the organ is introduced in the second volume, 'Spring'. (It is worth noting that Maybold's name symbolizes the force or vitality of spring, of new beginnings. In his name, however, are two signatures: on the one hand, there is the natural seasonal cycle from given identity by language. On the other hand, there is the countersignature of the energy of cultural, social, and historical transformation.) As Mail's uncannily prescient remark cited before testifies, the past inevitably gives way to the arrival of the future. But the members of the choir feel an injustice in the peremptory manner of Maybold's decision.

Visiting Maybold, the choir request that their services not be dispensed with till the following Christmas (*UGT* 65), the time of year at which the novel began. Tranter Dewy's appeal notes the correspondence between liturgical and seasonal cycles in its teleological anticipation, and thus expresses a perception of temporality and historicity that is cyclical. Additionally, it marks the anticipated departure with a respect for symbolic ritual, in what Dewy calls a 'glorious' fall 'with a bit of a flourish' and a 'respectable end' (*UGT* 66). For the new generation, however, given face in Mr Maybold, modernity has to take place with what amounts to impetuosity, if not urgency: 'there is no reason for longer delay' (*UGT* 65). For Maybold organ music is the 'most proper' medium for the musical translation of spiritual feeling, the implication being of course that the older generation's form of music is less proper, or even improper (*UGT* 66). Propriety for the younger generation has everything to do with form and observation, while for the older generation in the body of the choir, the question is one of emotion, expressed by the tranter as 'feeling' (*UGT* 66, 67). Feeling or sensibility is, moreover, revealed through Dewy's remarks to be communal, while clearly, as Hardy stages the scene between Vicar Maybold and the choir *in toto*, modernity's cultural transformation of practice implicates both mechanization – efficiency and economy – and individualism. This is staged in the novel in spatial terms: for while traditionally the choir plays in the gallery, elevated above the congregation and out of immediate sight (the sense being that music, in being invisible, is more truly spiritual), the organ and therefore the organist are foci of attention, in plain view. It is almost as if, without wishing to be overly paradoxical, there is a secularization of liturgical practice to be read in generational modernization, and its usurpation of the practices of the past on the part of an ecclesiastical institution seeking to escape cultural anachrony. The choir does not argue against generational revolution, it merely wants to observe its passing by its last performance taking place on an ecclesiastically significant day. And so it comes to be agreed between choir and vicar that the change will take place 'about' Michaelmas. 'And then', says Tranter Dewy, 'we make room for the next generation' (*UGT* 69).

The scene is neither sentimental nor nostalgic, though an over-hasty reading might assume so. The choir accepts its fate as a sign of that eschatological inevitability that befalls 'mortal men' (*UGT* 69). This is, then, merely the marking of generational and historical process in its constantly dialectical processes and registrations. Were there only this scene, one might be tempted to read Hardy as expressing a longing for the older ways, so to speak, rather than recognizing that his sense of the historical, of the past, is more neutral. It concerns itself in maintaining the traces of the past, his novels readable as so many instances of archiving and memory work, if not mnemotechnic machines. In effect, his texts exemplify the ways in which 'nineteenth-century fiction is a site of interrogation and dramatisation [of the status and meaning of 'history']' (Reilly 1993, 11). Hardy's generational, temporal and historical explorations ask the question 'where does [history] take place?' (Reilly 1993, 11). One answer is that history takes place in the transformation of literature's modes of representation, from empirically governed to phenomenologically orientated modes of narration, for example. Or another answer might be that Hardy traces the taking place of the historical in the transition from framed image, with its controlled predominantly visual, mimetic representation, to the destabilizations of a mobile text 'so that material reality is displaced as the goal of representation by shadowy and spectral anti-realities' (Reilly 1993, 65). Hardy demonstrates this generational displacement from earlier novelistic modes of production in the contest between framing and openness, closure and motion, occurring throughout his novels, especially in the representation of landscape, and not least in the opening passages of *Under the Greenwood Tree*.

The full title of Hardy's second novel is *Under the Greenwood Tree: A Rural Painting of the Dutch School*. The subtitle situates a particular mode of genre painting and realist representation which is highly formalized in its mimetic verisimilitude, and which relies for its aesthetic force on withdrawing the very means by which it causes the stationary image to appear. At the beginning of Volume 2, Hardy offers the reader the writerly approximation of just such an image: 'The chief members of Mellstock parish choir were standing in a group in front of Mr. Penny's workshop in the lower village. They were all brightly illuminated, and each was backed up by a shadow as long as a steeple, the lowness of the source of light rendering the brims of their hats of no use at all as a protection to the eyes' (*UGT* 53). Tim Dolin highlights this image in its 'painstaking composition' suggestive of 'Dutch and English genre painting'. However, as he continues, 'the dramatic chiaroscuro denotes . . . an intensification and abstraction' that is excessive when compared with English artists, though typical perhaps of 'seventeenth-century Dutch landscape painters' (*UGT* 204, n. 2). Accepting this, it has to be said that the mode of representation is already anachronistic, at odds with the period of the narrative and the time of writing. However, taking this further, it is interesting that Hardy seeks both to intensify and to abstract, as Dolin has it. In this manner, Hardy produces an image or representation, of which the energy, or somewhat spectral 'vitality' if you will, resonates in excess of what is being represented. There is a vibrancy irreducible to representation. Hardy's writing overflows the frame. Recalling the subtitle of the novel, we see how representation contains that which cannot be contained. Hardy pushes at the boundaries of representation, threatening to break the frame in a particularly vivid if not visionary manner, having to do with the articulation of the spirit of Englishness, the ghostly afterlife of rural national identity that lives on in generation after generation, despite efforts at historical eradication, transformation, or containment.

Such phantasmatic vigour is a performative aspect of the writing itself. Writing exceeds representation. Literature overcomes painting, succeeding it as it supplements the hegemonic dominance of the earlier historical form, in a mode of representation responding to its rural scene. Hardy produces such effects from the very start of the novel, in its opening scene. Opening with a response to what cannot be seen, the multiplicity of non-human 'voices' heard in the motion of trees in a wood is acknowledged and adumbrated in their singularity (*UGT* 7). From this inaugural double scene of sound and motion, the calm illusory representation of a 'rural painting of the Dutch school' is ruined, its frames and contexts undone. The rural image is further solicited through the recording of the sound of footsteps in the darkness, the 'spirit' of which, unavailable to any painterly depiction, attests to the anonymous figure's 'nature' (*UGT* 7). To this, Hardy adds the sound of the walker's voice, singing a traditional folksong, 'A Rosebud in June', which, with its reference to midsummer and sheep-shearing, provides an untimely counterpoint to the time of year, 'Christmas-eve', at which it is being sung, and at which its words appear on the page. The song's text (an anonymous textual production) arrives, and the reader is left to imagine the tune, if she or he does not know it, or otherwise to imagine its sound in concert with the 'natural' sounds of the various trees and bushes making their distinct sounds (*UGT* 7). The words' arrival relies on text, on writing, on a mode of *sending*, which cannot be accommodated by painting, and which also cannot be anticipated or guaranteed in their delivery. What the seasonal 'round' of song and date suggests is a cyclical revenance to an anonymous yet memorialized Englishness. Countless generations are implicated here in what marks the scene and moment with its historically iterable condition. This could be 24 December 1848, or it could be 1648. We cannot fix the moment. In a vision of rural timelessness and anachrony, and in the virtual absence of any visible landscape, Hardy transmits a cultural memory to which the always 'still-life' of painting is unable to bear witness.

In the visionary and impressionistic uses of rural England that tap into and draw upon folklore, rural history and prehistory, superstition and the supernatural that are to be found in Hardy, there are to be read anticipations of E. M. Forster's critique of creeping suburbia in *Howards End*. Additionally, and more generally, Hardy's representation and understanding of the English landscape and all that resonates invisibly and across time in that landscape may be found in the novels of D. H. Lawrence, Stanley Spencer's apocalyptic paintings, and the poetry of Ted Hughes. Hardy effectively transforms the language of rural representation, and with that the modes of perception of rural topography as it relates to the past, to cultural memory and to the trace of historicity apropos enduring and recurrent manifestations of rural Englishness. In doing so, he provides for future generations a poetics of an other rural Englishness that always haunts the present of any reader of Hardy. Hardy opens history to its count-less others, he structures 'history' differently, and in so doing stages a series of singular interrogations concerning the very ontology of the historical and inquiry into it, as event and discourse in the final decades of the nineteenth century.

Hardy and the ends of history

By virtue of the generational logic generating the narrative and histor-ical trajectories described, Thomas Hardy (1840–1928) must therefore appear as the 'child' of this previous generation of cultures and authors. Of the previous generation by the time that Hardy's career as a novelist began, Dickens was dead, as was Gaskell before Hardy began to publish, and none of the authors considered in the previous chap-ters survive to be potential readers of Hardy's first published volume of poetry, *Wessex Poems* (1898). His contemporaries experienced and interpreted the world in radically different ways from their predeces-sors. Yet, at the same time, their experience of that difference was haunted by traces of earlier experience, informing their own percep-tions. This may sound paradoxical, but it is the spirit, if not the essence, of late Victorian modernity. As the century progressed so the signs of cultural anachronism intrinsic to a sense of modern identity were being registered in different ways – the early modern influence on the Pre-Raphaelite Brotherhood, the fascination with all things medieval as expressed through the poetry of Tennyson, the Arts and Crafts movement of William Morris, the neo-Gothic architecture of Pugin and his followers, and elsewhere.

Thomas Hardy's novel-writing career spanned a generation itself, the last thirty years, more or less, of the nineteenth century in fact, fourteen novels being published between 1871 and 1895. Although he had been writing poetry since the 1860s at least (his earliest extant poem being 'Domicilium'), Hardy's career as a publishing poet, begun in 1898 as already mentioned, lasted another generation, until the posthumous publication of his final volume, *Winter Words*, in 1928. From 1898 until his death, Hardy published poetry during the first three decades of the twentieth century, editing the Wessex edition of his novels in 1912. In all Hardy wrote and published eight volumes of poetry during his lifetime. It is a salutary point in any sketch of English literary and cultural history to recall that, when Hardy died, many of the now canonical works of modernist literature – *Hugh Selwyn Mauberley* (1920), *The Waste Land* (1922), *Ulysses* (1922), Woolf's *Mrs Dalloway* (1925), *To the Lighthouse* (1927) – had already been published. Of Hardy's fourteen novels, nine were published between 1871 and 1882, Hardy completing no more novels until 1886, with *The Mayor of Casterbridge*. The novels published during the 1870s and early 1880s are: *Desperate Remedies* (1871), *Under the Greenwood Tree* (1872), *A Pair of Blue Eyes* (1873), *Far from the Madding Crowd* (1874), *The Hand of Ethelberta* (1876), *The Return of the Native* (1878), *The Trumpet-Major* (1880), *A Laodicean* (1881), and *Two on a Tower* (1882). All but the first two were published initially in serial form in various magazines. The remaining five novels, published in a nine-year period from 1886 onwards, are *The Mayor of Casterbridge* (1886), *The Woodlanders* (1887), *Tess of the D'Urbervilles* (1891), *The Pursuit of the Well-Beloved* (1892), and *Jude the Obscure* (1895).

His first novel, *The Poor Man and the Lady*, was completed in 1868 though never published. Subsequently, it served in part as the basis for *An Indiscretion in the Life of an Heiress*, published in 1878 in serialized form in *Harper's Weekly*. It was, however, never reprinted in collected editions of Hardy's works during his lifetime (Hardy 1994, 43–113). Hardy's first published novel, *Desperate Remedies*, was a sensational mystery influenced in part by the novels of Wilkie Collins. His last novel, *The Well-Beloved*, had been printed first as a serial, *The Pursuit of the Well-Beloved*, in the *Illustrated London News* (1892), three years before *Jude the Obscure*, but was only published in volume form, much revised, in 1897. Though not in any ostensible fashion concerning itself with the themes or interests of what is conventionally referred to as *fin de siècle* fiction, Hardy's fiction inescapably remarks over three decades the sense of an ending, of passage and passing away, of irreparable transformation, translation and, if this is not to put it too strongly, an apprehension of *becoming-posthumous* intrinsic to the identities of many of his 'Victorian' readers, whether this was felt or not on the part of his audience. To give this another perspective, it is the case that Hardy, in being at variance with the sociological or sensationalist preoccupations of his literary contemporaries in the last twenty years of the nineteenth century, manifests the ability to speak or respond to certain deeper, older currents of Englishness, outside the urban, imperial mainstream. Such flows belong to no one era or epoch, but shape the discontinuous narrative of national identity in numerous ways.

My final chapter therefore concerns Hardy because of what Tim

Armstrong describes as the Victorian subject's 'entry into history, the trauma of *becoming-historical* which is central to nineteenth-century conceptions of the historical' (2000, 2). Such an entry, and the trauma accompanying it, is for me the sign of an irreversible, epochal generational change. The trauma of material being as a becoming-historical has already been illustrated through *The Trumpet-Major* and *Under the Greenwood Tree*, two strikingly different, singular texts. I also choose to end with Hardy because he is arguably the last properly 'historical' novelist of the nineteenth century, while also being the first novelist of a phenomenologically inflected self-conscious apprehension of being's materiality and historicity. His works are central to our perceptions of a world in radical transition, as well as being testimonies to the ghosts of memory, as we have already witnessed in the example of *The Trumpet-Major*. Much *fin de siècle* fiction might be read, arguably, as an escape from what Joyce was to call the 'nightmare' of history. Not so Hardy. And while our other novelists speak, directly or obliquely, to that sense of national identity and subjectivity that is supposedly modern in the nineteenth century, modernity being conceived as the tension between temporally distinct senses of self and other in contradistinction to the historical sense of organic continuity, Hardy, of all writers in the nineteenth century, engages most unflinchingly 'the way in which the self is constituted by and writes itself into history', without any overt signs of the modernity of being (Armstrong 2000, 2). This is not to say his largely phenomenological interpretation of subjectivity and being is not thoroughly modern. It is. Instead, what I wish to stress is that in Hardy's worlds, the modern experience of the self reflexively addressed by Dickens, Eliot, Gaskell, and Collins is marked differently, and not focused on the rupture between present and past, self and other.

This has less to do with a distance from past generations and the assumptions of modernity accompanying those perceived or desired acts of distancing than with an apperception of the subject's irreparably *being-riven, being-haunted*. In this condition, Hardy places his characters wherein, always already displaced from any genuine sense of self (of which the characters of the previous generation of novelists still maintain the illusion or believe it to be locatable) and repeating however differentially the actions of generations and cultures before them, they serve to symbolize the anachronic condition of being at the end of the nineteenth century. While most of Hardy's novels situate their events at a generation's remove, or at least at a distance of a couple of decades, from the time of their writing, yet discordantly and anachronically (as, we might say, signs of the times) their experience is markedly 'modern', self-conscious and not necessarily of the time to which they belong. In this, itself a reiterated and iterable structure with singular variations from novel to novel, Hardy presents a world of simulacra and unstable identities, rendered partly incoherent by the ghosts of the past. Hardy's world is one in which there is only and primarily a confrontation with – to borrow a title of Hardy's – the 'spectre of the real' (Hardy 1994, 184–211). Hence, we are given to read the signs of a 'particular kind of historicity . . . [which] is opened up here, painful and elegiac, even as it is inevitable and progressive' (Armstrong 2000, 4). Such historicity is always out of joint with itself, and thus marks Hardy's writing with the sensuous perception of a 'marginalized modernism' (Armstrong 2000, 8) that is at once, again, anachronistic. Never on time it marks its own temporal finitude, and its passing into a past wherein it will remain only to return as so many traces of itself. Hardy's worlds, the one in which he lives as representative of a particular generation and those about which he writes, are, then, as much haunting as they are haunted.

Critical misprision

To approach the question of what haunts Hardy I propose to explore the relationship between historicity, reading, misreading and the self, which I take to be at the heart of Hardy's writing. The problems of perception and reading one's historically determined subjectivity through acts of reading the signs of past cultural moments that accumulate in the fiction of the self inform all Hardy's texts. In a different manner, this question of what haunts reading and reading as the haunt of the unreadable is also the problematic of generational position. Hardy does not belong to the previous generation, by virtue, obviously, of the accident of when he is born but, more importantly, because of a pronounced epistemological difference between the previous generation's perceptions of being, historicity and representation, and Hardy's own. However, this does not mean that Hardy belongs to his own generation. He, or at the very least his text, is other than those times. The misreading of cultural signs, the traces of the past, and the pulses of cultural memory, therefore inform the critical misreading of Hardy in both his own time, and in subsequent generations. Donald Davidson has remarked that there 'was a real intellectual distance between [the author] . . . and almost three generations of critics' (Davidson 1940, 163). As Davidson continues, 'critics have not so much underrated – or overrated – Hardy as *missed* him' (1940, 163; emphasis added). This has come about, according to the critic, inasmuch as those generations of critics were misled, continuously and repeatedly, 'by the superficial resemblance between [Hardy's] work and the product current in their day'. Yet, 'though Hardy was *in* [his] time, and was affected by its thought and art, he was not really *of* that time' (Davidson 1940, 163).

Beyond those three generations of critics, Hardy continued to be 'missed', as it were, the delivery of his text deferred, gone astray, delivered to the wrong address. Terry Eagleton offers the following as a potted history:

> Not all that long ago, a standard account of Thomas Hardy might have run rather like this: Hardy was a self-educated author who struggled his way up from the ranks of the common people, and wrote gloomily fatalistic novels about an English peasant society whose traditional way of life was being undermined by external urban forces.

He then proceeds: 'Not a word of that account is in fact true, except perhaps for "author", and to inquire why not might lead us to a more accurate understanding of the man and his fiction' (Eagleton 2005, 187). Elsewhere, Eagleton identifies four 'distinct stages' in the development of Hardy criticism on which we have already touched (1985, 127). The first two phases read the novelist as 'anthropologist of Wessex' and, subsequently, 'the melancholic purveyor of late nineteenth-century nihilism' (Eagleton 1985, 127). This particular assessment at least accords Hardy a certain comprehension on the part of the reader with the difficulties Hardy encountered in seeking to transcend what he called 'the analytical stage', which he felt novel-writing had reached by the 1880s (*LWTH* 183). Moving beyond this early assessment of Hardy, Eagleton describes the response to Hardy in the postwar years. Formalist criticism of the 1940s and 1950s reads Hardy's work as 'irreparably violated by ideas'. At the same time, there begins a shift towards 'a more "sociological" reading of Hardy' (Eagleton 1985, 127). This latter phenomenon is not, however, unproblematically positive for Eagleton. For, as he argues, much of such criticism focused on what it took to be a safe vision of a lost rural England appealed to by Hardy in sentimental and mythological terms, while also criticizing Hardy for the oddities of his language and style, a critical tendency persisting into the 1970s (Eagleton 1985, 127–8).

Peter Widdowson also encapsulates the 'problem of Thomas Hardy', alerting us to a selective critical reading of the novels aiming to discern a 'true' Hardy who can be made to belong comfortably in the literary canon, while leaving aside those novels which are read as 'exaggerat[ing]' perceived 'flaws' to be found throughout Hardy's narrative oeuvre. 'Taken together', two of the novels written between 1871 and 1884, *The Hand of Ethelberta* and *A Laodicean*, are the author's 'most execrated' novels (Widdowson 1999, 75). Widdowson continues, observing that 'critics have conventionally descried [faults and flaws] scattered throughout his [Thomas Hardy's] fiction – "improbable" use of chance and coincidence, "flat" and "stagey" characterization, melodrama, and an obtrusively over-elaborate style' in the 'critical fashioning of the "true" Hardy' (1999, 75–6). I do not intend to look at those particular academic criticisms. Widdowson provides an excellent summary of positions in the essay just cited, and gives a much more detailed account elsewhere (1989, ch. 1). Yet, it does seem necessary to orientate any critical engagement with Hardy's text with a consideration of *why* persistent misreading has taken place. That Hardy has been misread, poorly read, not read at all – as Eagleton makes clear – is itself suggestive of the estranging forces of historicity, historicality, and anachronism within and on the form of English literature, so that certain readers remain blind to the codes and signs of their own cultures. That this *is* effected doubtless has to do with the belief that one can, in controlling the reception of the past, exorcise the more wayward phantoms from one's own present identity.

Reception, avoidance and identity

The tension between Hardy and some of his readers was present almost from the delivery of Hardy's first publications. An element of critical negativity can be put down to contemporary cultural mores in the face of Hardy's, at the time, frank exploration of desire and sexual relations. For example, following its publication, *A Laodicean* was criticized in the *World* magazine for what was taken to be the novel's 'carnal suggestiveness' (Anon. 1882, 18). Following editorial consideration of *The Woodlanders* during its serial publication, the final sentence ending Chapter 4, Volume II, was excised on the grounds that it was too sexually explicit. The scene leading up to this moment involves Edred Fitzpiers, the young doctor living near the village of

Little Hintock, and Suke Damson. The night is Midsummer's Eve, and a particular folk ritual concerning the divination of future husbands has taken place, in which Suke and other young women from the village have taken part. Running through the woods, Suke is chased by Fitzpiers. Catching her, he begins to kiss her and 'they sank down on the next hay-cock' (*W* 150). The sentence censored from the serial provides the punctuation to this nocturnal scene: 'It was daybreak before Fitzpiers and Suke Damson re-entered Little Hintock' (*W* 150).

There are many more such examples of moral censorship and opprobrium throughout Hardy's career as a novelist, being a result of both editorial intervention and negative critical reception after publication. Such misreadings of Hardy's works in his lifetime, as injurious as they were to Hardy personally, are commonplace enough. Yet, there was that other aesthetic response to form and language, diction and construction, and the perception that Hardy was straining after originality or effect, thereby allowing his rhetoric to get in the way of telling the story. Contemporary reviews of *The Return of the Native* make just such assertions. An unsigned review in *The Athenaeum* (23 November 1878) compared Hardy with 'a person who has a keen eye for the picturesque without having learnt to draw'. Furthermore, his observation was 'disfigured at times by forced allusions and images'. Eustacia Vye is singled out for critical opprobrium, belonging 'to the class of which Madame Bovary is the type'. This comparison with Flaubert is instructive, and the reviewer for *The Athenaeum* is not alone in (presumably) his cultural xenophobia. Going on to remark that 'English opinion' does not allow for the Bovary 'type' in the English novel, it anticipates a comment on the part of another reviewer, W. E. Henley, in *The Academy* a week later, who summarizes *The Return of the Native* as 'all very cruel, and very mournful, and very French' (having already spoken of Hardy being contaminated by 'Hugoesque . . . insincerity'). A third review, published in *The Saturday Review* (4 January, 1879), also commented on the writers of the younger generation who 'scandalize traditional opinions'. Hardy is typical of this 'scandalous' behaviour in using 'eccentric forms of expression' along with 'similes and metaphors [that] are often strained and far-fetched', while the story 'strikes us as intensely artificial'. 'We are in England all the time', continues the offended reviewer, 'but in a world of which we seem to be absolutely ignorant'.

Criticizing the sexual frankness or openness of a Hardy novel is of course only the most obvious way of signalling an inability to read what is taking place, as well as staging a resistance to and avoidance of reading. It is a sign of being unseated from what one assumes as one's habitual cultural positions. What is telling from the foregoing criticisms of *The Return of the Native* is the native anxiety in the face of identities that trouble Englishness (and English masculinity) in their supposedly assured stability. Sexuality taken too far is foreign, distasteful. The taking place of domestic sexuality is a historical threat that serves to figure the threat of a foreign otherness erupting in one's own national home. If the rural is a site of fecundity, this in the 1870s is submerged within an economy of reproduction subservient to the production of foodstuff. Under the sign of an economic production, all reproduction in excess of such consumerist (or, less commonly, theological) narratives is radically disorientating. A second point, if we take the rural as either largely forgotten, or depoliticized and dehistoricized through nostalgic and utopian idealization, is that sexuality rehistoricizes and repoliticizes the rural. It returns the rural to the present of the urban reader, but in a series of representations that cannot be admitted.

Moreover, sexuality threatens the implicit Englishness of the novel as form and idea. Ideologically, culturally and formally, it figures a return of the repressed, an irrepressible difference. Inasmuch as the reviews feel identity to be threatened, this threat is perceived as not only foreign though. Hardy's very Anglo-Saxon 'heart of darkness' is much closer to home. The very ontology of Englishness is in crisis in these reviews, as already noted. For Hardy is repeatedly criticized for the strangeness of his domestic, yet not-quite-English rural inhabitants. The 'language of his peasants may be Elizabethan', remarks *The Athenaeum*, 'but it can hardly be Victorian'. Having introduced the possibility of linguistic anachronism returning from some past to strike at modern identity, the review then goes on to remark on the artificial pitch of the dialogue: 'These people all speak in a manner suggestive of high cultivation, and some of them intrigue almost like dwellers in Mayfair, while they live on nearly equal terms with the furze-cutting rustics'. Class and location (dwellers in Mayfair and furze-cutting rustics, city and country) are inextricably traced here, in a psychic topography of English selfhood and alterity. Critique of dialogue makes the connection, and, on Hardy's part, the 'confusion' of form and genre, clear between the ontologies of cultural and literary identity, signalling in this manner the site from which it is issued. It is as if Hardy contaminates the novel in the last decades. Equally, it is as if criticism issued from the urban centre of nation and empire, the capital, stages in encrypted form the trauma of Englishness in its secret confession that an older, rural England, having been sacrificed to modernity, to urban-centred capitalist modes of production, can be neither remembered as an other to the modern nor re-imagined as vital, surviving.

Identity is also troubled in the confusion of locations from which language appears to come, and to which it may be assigned, as the implicit metropolitan incomprehension of rural subjectivities seems to suggest. This is echoed in *The Saturday Review*. Commenting on the 'unreal and unlifelike' names of Hardy's characters, the reviewer surmises that 'we doubt whether nine out of ten of them are to be met with in the pages of the London Directory. It is true that they may possibly be local for all we know to the contrary'. *For all we know*. Hardy's rural England is so foreign, so untimely, so other than the world as it is apprehended by metropolitan and urban critics in the 1870s and 1880s, that it baffles comprehension even as it assaults the supposed certainties of self from which location reading takes place. As *The Times* put it of *The Return of the Native* (5 December 1878), 'we are transported . . . we feel rather *abroad* here, and can scarcely get up a satisfactory interest in people whose history and habits are so entirely *foreign* to our own' (emphases added).

The strange energy of Hardy's writing is such that it not only challenges critical mastery, but in addition it masters the critic to a degree that estranges the possibility of reading. More than this though, *The Times*'s commentary encapsulates a sense, as I have been suggesting, that the rural English are perceived as more wholly other, or at least as 'unfamiliar' and 'exotic' as any more obviously 'foreign' culture. It is perhaps this strangeness of an English alterity tinged with anachronistic defamiliarization and, with that, the troubling depth of historical and temporal resonance, lost to the traumatic experience of modernity within Hardy's narratives of the English other, which amounts to an assault on Victorian self-reading from within the domestic space of literature. Alterity is thereby revealed as incommensurate with spacing. It is not that the rural English are simply at a remove geographically and therefore definable according to a set of paradigmatic models capable of incorporating difference within the self-same. Theirs is an otherness that will admit of no recuperation, and which, reciprocally, returns in Hardy's fiction to usurp the calm assurance of self-reading seeking a reflection or inflection of the self. What Hardy's fiction presents us with is, we might venture, both a return of the repressed, a revenant reiteration of the forgotten, and, as the many lost signs of pagan and folkloric alterity and archaic historicity attest, *the return(s) of the native*.

[Another parenthesis, given my allusion to Hardy's title: I think a strong reading of the title in the manner just indicated is justified. For, while on the one hand the title may be read as signifying Clym Yeobright's return – he is after all the 'native' of Egdon Heath who returns in the novel to his home only to find it unhomely, and himself a haunting stranger estranged from the familiar – on the other hand, the strong reading is there to be invented, to be unearthed. In every being, however modern, there are always the anachronistic signs of some other, of something 'native'. If we pursue the etymology of *native*, we find buried beneath the more modern sense of someone belonging to a particular country, the older sense, equivalent to the Anglo-Norman *naïf*, signifying someone born in a state of bondage or serfdom. There is in the trait of this older sense the signification of a mark made on someone, a legal inscription that ties someone to a place. In the strong reading of Hardy's title that I would propose, it is this invisible *trait*, the sign of being bound, that 'returns' to the modern subject, as a revenant call of the other, and with that the demands of one's native historicity as the imprimatur, a countersignature of one's being, however modern one believes oneself to be. There is that which is hetero-affective within being. While on the surface, the 'call' is a conscious one to which Clym responds, and so returns, my strong reading argues for this as an unconscious demand that Hardy reads at work everywhere in cultural identity.]

So disquieting is this confrontation that its effects are displaced in the act of reading onto literary form, or, it is arguable, the very ontology of the literary itself. Criticizing narrative on the grounds of form, the excess of its modes of articulation, and an inability or refusal to perceive that excess, exaggeration, and formal play may just be taking place for reasons beyond the comprehension of the reviewer, hints at a problem not with the identity of the novel but with those broader cultural and historical identities assumed by the critic. And such responses to Hardy only highlight the ways in which misreading, as a means by which to assert one's own authority or identity, occur in the face of encountering such haunting, *felt*, disturbances.

'A disproportioning of realities'

We see how, in the responses they garner, the forms, language, and images of Hardy's narratives demonstrate repeatedly the novelist's 'blunt disregard for formal consistency . . . [and his readiness to] articulate form upon form – to mingle realist narration, classical tragedy, folk-fable, melodrama, "philosophical" discourse, social commentary' (Eagleton 1985, 126). Widdowson also identifies the same 'disregard' apropos Hardy's 'always protean *oeuvre*' (1999, 75). To this must be added a perhaps obvious note: that disregard for formal consistency is available to us as material registration of the text's historicity through its formal openness to heterogeneity and resistance to ontological stabilization, as well as being itself a response to particular historical and cultural conditions. This response is double: on the one hand, it has to do with the history of the novel, and the forms it takes in its development over the previous two centuries. Simultaneously and on the other hand, formal discursive, epistemological and ontological play, that which is read as 'fault', 'failure', or 'disregard', signals an equally material response to broader histories, beyond those of the novel, and, with the mediation of cultural identity, the inheritance of the past, the translation in the present of identity, and a sense of destabilized, perhaps undecidable Englishness in Hardy's historical moment as a novelist.

Hardy's disinterest stems from his rejection of 'realism' as art. Art should 'disproportion' the real in figuring, or rather disfiguring, 'distorting, throwing out of proportion . . . [the representation of] realities, to show more clearly the features that matter in those realities' (*LTH* 229). What is witnessed, empirically observable, takes second place for Hardy to that higher, visionary mode of perception in the mind's eye: 'the seer should watch [one] pattern among general things which his idiosyncrasy moves him to observe . . . the result is no photograph, but purely the product of the writer's own mind' (*LTH* 153). What the mind's eye is capable of decoding from the merely real or material is simultaneously a matter of reception *and* deciphering. Moreover, it is a matter of opening oneself not merely to hidden patterns but also to the otherwise invisible echoes of the past, which vision distorts and disproportions the present of the gaze even as it opens the self to the arrival of some phantasmatic arrival or, more accurately, the trace of a historical other, as we shall see shortly. Hardy's novels speak not so much from a single, identifiable voice as from some form of phantom narrating machine capable of translating into narrative or poetic form site, topography, trace, history, and collective memory.

The interwoven patterning of lives, locations, narrative strands, discursive traces, and other material details of Hardy's writing – whether topographical, architectural or archaeological, spatial or temporal – can be said to produce a matrix of reiterative and recursive structures, which, as we have argued, has troubled critical comprehension, and disrupted its ideological efficacy and institutional purpose. Moreover, Hardy's interlacing of countless aspects and facets that go to comprise his narratives finds its echoes in both the formal levels of the text and their archival and encrypted preservation of disparate, heterogeneous literary, cultural and historical traces. Every Hardy text, it might be said, offers a singular archaeological or archival formation, albeit one from the reading of which an origin or source cannot be traced. Seen from another perspective, Hardy's text displays repeatedly a rhizomic ingenuity, through a complex of endless interdependencies that are unavailable to any architectonic prioritization or ontological ordering. The patterns of tension and resistance to easy comprehension suggest that the more we seek a single narrative thread, the more we come to realize how each thread is interwoven into, shot through by, and generative of countless others. There is thus given us to read in Hardy's fictions a haunting surplus irreducible to the very site from which such flows are glimpsed.

The staging of excess and rupture as the arrival of historical disordering of the narrative present takes place within vision given formal coherence through mimetic representation of reality through Hardy's acts of 'disproportioning'. That matter of that other vision within vision already alluded to through reference to Hardy's journal entries is figured by the eruption of the past within the present moment of recording, as the representation of the sheep-shearing barn in *Far from the Madding Crowd* makes apparent.

The passage with which we are concerned is long and complex, but worth quoting *in extenso* before examining the detail:

> They sheared in the great barn, called for the nonce the Shearing Barn, which on ground plan resembled a church with transepts. It not only emulated the form of the neighbouring church of the parish, but vied with it in antiquity. Whether the barn had ever formed one of a group of conventual buildings nobody seemed aware: no trace of such surroundings remained. The vast porches at the sides, lofty enough to admit a waggon laden to its highest with corn in the sheaf, were spanned by heavy pointed arches of stone, broadly and boldly cut, whose very simplicity was the origin of a grandeur not apparent in erections where more ornament has been attempted. The dusky, filmed, chestnut roof, braced and tied in by huge collars, curves, and diagonals, was far nobler in design because more wealthy in material than nine-tenths of those in our modern

churches. Along each side wall was a ranging of striding buttresses, throwing deep shadows on the spaces between them, which were perforated by lancet openings combining in their proportions the precise requirements of beauty and ventilation.

One could say about this barn, what could hardly be said of either the church or the castle, its kindred in age and style, that the purpose which had dictated its original erection was the same with that to which it was still applied. Unlike and superior to either of those two typical remnants of mediaevalism, the old barn embodied practices which had suffered no mutilation at the hands of time. *Here at least the spirit of the builders then was at one with the spirit of the beholder now. Standing before this abraded pile the eye regarded its present usage, the mind dwelt upon its past history*, with a satisfied sense of functional continuity throughout, a feeling almost of gratitude, and quite of pride, at the permanence of the idea which had heaped it up. The fact that four centuries had neither proved it to be founded on a mistake, inspired any hatred of its purpose, nor given rise to any reaction that had battered it down, invested this simple grey effort of old minds with a repose if not a grandeur which a too curious reflection was apt to disturb in its ecclesiastical and military compeers. For once mediaevalism and modernism had a common stand-point. The lanceolate windows, the time-eaten arch stones and chamfers, the orientation of the axis, the misty chestnut-work of the rafters, referred to no exploded fortifying art or worn out religious creed. The defence and salvation of the body by daily bread is still a study, a religion, and a desire. (FMC 125–6; emphasis added)

Initially, of this description of the barn divided into two paragraphs by Hardy, the first paragraph is the more straightforwardly 'documentary' or representational. There is a mimetic fidelity to the paragraph. It records in detail the barn, drawing attention to particular aspects of its medieval structure, which are situated in contrasting context through reference to the similarities in design and appearance to a church. Utility and beauty are registered in equal measure, and the overall aesthetic impression given is determined by the announcement of a preference for the ageing barn over the design of the majority of 'our modern churches'. So Hardy 'draws a picture', the order of description following, responding to, the architectonics of pictorial order, observation of the spatial relations admitting of historical knowledge, and serving to contrast the medieval with the modern.

Were the passage to stop there, one might be mistaken in reading this as a continuance of that utopian, idealist and romanticized medievalist aesthetic captured in the work of Tennyson, William Morris, or the Pre-Raphaelites. However, in contradistinction to the aesthetics of those other artists, Hardy's second paragraph addresses precisely those more ostensibly abstract issues previously sketched, and so moves beyond the merely mimetic. Not only does there occur a shift from a minimally inflected but ostensibly objective observation, resulting in a largely realist representation, to one in which the mind's eye of the 'seer' (as Hardy has it) takes over. There is also an overfolding as well as an unfolding of discrete temporal moments and the indirect perception of those absent times in the experience of the subject's translative gaze as it is touched by the traces, fragments and signs of the barn's 'memory work'. The spirit of the past arrives in the present moment of observation, to exceed the empirical and realist, and to disorder the time of the modern through its resonance and revenance. This is most immediately captured in those sentences highlighted. Two spirits conjoin and communicate as an inner vision is unveiled from within the reportage of everyday function. This is of course already anticipated, if not captured, in the intimation of cyclical function, the barn being put to use in the same fashion generation after generation, and century after century regardless of the histories and ideologies for which churches and castles serve as symbolic reminders – and of which they, unlike the barn, are also ideological and temporal anachronistic remainders in the modern moment. Thus it is that the ghosts of labour, of building and shearing, return, given a material archived and archival presentation in the barn, and furthermore cited and recited, even as they haunt the actions of the present farm hands who occupy the scene.

Hardy's interpretive description is significant also, in that perspective is doubled. First, it is a question of *what* one sees. Perhaps more to the point, there is someone at least hypothetically or in the imagination *to see* that, which in the present moment, is otherwise overlooked. An invisible gaze hovering liminally at the edges of the present presentation (and implicitly the ghost of the reader to come) opens that present through the gaze to the traces of cultural memory that inform the present scene. Perspective doubles and divides itself. It stages itself as a structure or formation rather than being some essential, fixed position because narration envisions someone who could be on hand to see in this particular phantasmic manner. Narration, itself a phantom articulation, posits an imagined perspective on the constructed performative of an imagined viewer. There appears after a fashion some shadowy figure neither of the scene nor in it exactly, but capable of gazing at the barn (or landscape, or church, or cliff face). Hardy thus enacts the Fichtean condition of

Darstellung (staging, presentation, presencing) as the 'activity of consciousness that consists in representing the empirical subject as *Vorstellung* [an *a posteriori* general representation, conception or mental image]' (Helfer 1996, 67). The staging or presencing is not part of the empirical consciousness. What is represented marks the limit of the representational force in its ability to produce a mimetically controlled and controlling image. However, this is complicated because between *Darstellung* and *Vorstellung* there arrives a mental image that is between and other than either gazing consciousness and image. From this, what emerges is that it is a question of *how* one sees and, therefore, *what* one comes to see and what comes to be seen in a visionary communion with that which is of the past but irreducible to the material reality of the structure. In this act of envisioning, an act which disproportions reality, the aesthetic perception figures not only 'a transformed *encounter* with' the empirical world, but instead and more forcefully 'an epistemic *overcoming*' of that world (Seel 2005, 7). Hardy deploys an 'aesthetic attentiveness' as an articulation of the 'here and now' of being, 'as it becomes accessible only in openness to the play of appearance of a given situation' (Seel 2005, 16–17).

The 'openness' is precisely that which gives the possibility of such revenance as we witness above, in which the historicity of spirit comes to be articulated, the echoes of the past apprehended in such a singular fashion, like the shimmering of a heat haze or the glimpse of a memory at the edge of consciousness, by which one becomes suspended temporally. Hardy exploits this through the echo of details from the first of the two paragraphs in the second. In their structural return, they present the reader with an apprehension that, because of the somewhat ghostly presence of Hardy's modern 'beholder', perspective on mere architectural detail has been transformed. The *now* of the scene is translated by the persistence of the past. While it is true then that the 'synchronic and diachronic . . . intersect in Hardy's metaphor of landscape' (Bivona 1990, 96), the landscape is not the only place in which this occurs. In Hardy's writing it can take place in buildings, through the play of documents, in marks left on roads or on walls, or in the practice of rituals such as midsummer dances, mummers' plays, or the repetitious seasonal lighting of bonfires as a 'custom of the country' in *The Return of the Native*, a novel set in the 1840s, as Hardy remarks in his Preface to the 1895 edition (*RN* 429).

Having described the activity around the bonfires, through the vision of another of those hypothetical onlookers (who move like so many phantoms throughout Hardy's narratives; *RN* 18), the narration provides another markedly transtemporal vision of countless previous moments similar to, and therefore haunting, the present one being recorded. The idea of the present is haunted by the cyclical revenance of the event, and the phantoms of all those who reiterate the moment and experience its taking place. Again the 'present' moment (already displaced, in the past, sometime between 1840 and 1850 and so at a generation's remove at least from the time of Hardy's readers) is disproportioned and with it literary realism:

> It was *as if* these men and boys had suddenly dived into past ages, and fetched there from an hour and deed which had before been familiar with this spot. The ashes of the original British pyre which blazed from that summit lay fresh and undisturbed in the barrow beneath their tread. The flames from funeral piles long ago kindled there had shone down upon the lowlands as these were shining now. Festival fires to Thor and Woden had followed on the same ground and duly had their day. Indeed, it is pretty well known that such blazes as this the heathmen were now enjoying are rather the lineal descendants from jumbled Druidical rites and Saxon ceremonies than the invention of popular feeling about Gunpowder Plot. (*RN* 20; emphasis added)

That *as if* (which is an echo of the exact same phrase in the previous paragraph, and thus a material enactment of temporal iterability) introduces us into the realm of the fictional, the phantasmic. Multiple historical singularities are implied in such traces as are witnessed here. Hardy's disruption of the real is felt forcefully here not because any single past is recorded as leaving its traces in the present, but instead because the passage signals several times – of Druids and Saxons, Vikings and other pagan cultures. The pasts do not simply erupt from within, overflowing the present. The ritualistic nature of the activity suggests the fiction of time travel on the part of the heath's inhabitants, the disquieting, uncanny suggestiveness of the moment found in the suggestion that it was *as if* those involved in the ritual had travelled back in time to return to the present expressly for the purpose of bringing those 'past ages' into their own time. Is Hardy borrowing on the resources of a modern conceptual epistemology, such as phenomenology, or is this Hardy's narration of some more archaic discourse articulating the practices of folkloric magic? Modernity *and* atavism coexist and correspond across time, across cultures, within the same culture. One cannot decide on how to read the scene. One cannot gain access unequivocally to the right code. As with the scene of the barn, the 'spirit' of pagan revellers is *seen* in that visionary manner to be in communication with, as Hardy puts it, *the spirit of the beholder now*. (Which beholder, we might ask: that ghostly figure who may have seen the bonfires, had he or she been there? The narrator, so-called? Or the reader?) The scene is disturbing for other reasons also, I would aver. For not only are there multiple times, thereby informing the moment with the perception of anachrony, but, through this, knowledge is overthrown and one reads a subversion of received historical wisdom, and with that the location of the 'origin' of bonfires being linked to the Gunpowder Plot of 1605. As a result of such disruptive temporal flows emerging out of any one given location, Hardy's art can be said, with all justification, to be 'a haunted art' (Reilly 1993, 65).

Whether historical 'reality' and its representation concerns a barn, then, or a castle (as in *A Laodicean*), a family genealogy (as in *A Laodicean*, again, or in *A Pair of Blue Eyes*), or else is revealed through cyclical ritual events, here we are given to read the signs of Hardy's difference as a novelist concerned with the problem of history and representation in the nineteenth century, both from many of his English contemporaries but also, significantly, from his immediate historical and generational predecessors. Disregard for, and disproportioning within, the conventions of formal coherence has also been observed in Hardy's presentation of that hybrid and heterogeneous discourse we call the 'narrator'. If shortly before his death Dickens can still locate in the 1860s an originary place from which the fiction of the narrator 'does the police in different voices' (in his own well-known phrase concerning the description of Sloppy's reading and mimicry skills in *Our Mutual Friend*), Hardy's acts of narrative have no such easily attributable origins or essential location. The myth or fiction of the editor or narrator given particular historical form in *The Pickwick Papers* and finding its most majestic, Olympian 'voice' in *Middlemarch* has reached a certain impasse by the 1870s. There is no Boz for Hardy. His narratives are, instead, glossolalic and spectral. As Simon Gatrell remarks, 'the narrator in any Hardy novel is a complex organism . . . [it] speaks with (at least) three different accents' (Gatrell 2000, 56). Furthermore, most, if not all, of Hardy's novels function – and thereby disable or disarm easy comprehension – through 'generically mixed plots', as Suzanne Keen has it (1998, 129). Such complexity enfolds and unfolds within the heteroglossic, hetero-affective field of signs that compose Hardy's texts for the reader's perception – and occasional discomposure – of the numerous layers of narrative form, the interrelation and interactions of its characters, and, in active interanimation, the intercalation of signs, times, phenomena, events, and that network of places constituting Wessex.

Disproportioning is unending in Hardy's writing. It is an endless work that demands an endless reading of the signs of history, the past, occluded cultural memory, and the necessity to go beyond the present in an archiving process of staging witness to the past. Indeed, I would go so far as to suggest that the disproportioning of reality *is* Hardy's primary concern, his commitment to the other of history. In his introduction to *The Mayor of Casterbridge* Keith Wilson addresses patterns of doubling, 'and at times tripling and quadrupling', which structure the text and complicate the act of reading (Wilson *MC* xxviii). Wilson aptly describes such patterns as 'forming themselves into a dense web' (Wilson *MC* xxviii). In the introduction to another edition of the same novel, Norman Page also considers the structural and formal complexity: 'In the construction of the narrative, repetition and circularity are . . . prominent features' (Page *MC* 23). Furthermore, there is 'a polyphony of different, even contrasting [narrative] voices'. The two editors see this intricate patterning serving different purposes. For Wilson, the doubling and multiplying folds serve to articulate the rejection of 'absolutist notions of identity' (Wilson *MC* xxviii) and a proto-modernist exploration of the fragmentation of the self, pursued principally through the character of Henchard, but also through other characters, their 'protean relationships' which serve to relativize identity (Wilson *MC* xxviii), and the various doubles they invoke (Wilson *MC* xxxi). Page, on the other hand, relates the structural network to Hardy's 'recovery of the past [in the novel's present] both spatially and temporally' (Page *MC* xxvii). These two brief examples – concerning ontology and temporality – and, from there, those other problematic issues that suggest themselves in consequence of such considerations, identify that which, most broadly perceived, permeates all Hardy's writing, whether the novels or the poetry.

As we have seen in the examples of the bonfires of *The Return of the Native* or the barn from *Far from the Madding Crowd*, it is precisely in the affirmative resistance of Hardy's writing, exemplified by those occasions when 'archaic practices of an ancient environ erupt out of' (Keen 1998, 132) the contemporary present moment in *Mayor* and other Hardy novels, that we may also read instances of discursive insurgence arriving from within the present scene of novel-writing in the1880s to interrupt and deform accepted conventions and norms of realist fiction. Identity, meaning, and ontology are haunted by their own 'alienated image[s]'. Hardy's characters, Hardy's locations, Hardy's plots – all manifest repeatedly 'pattern[s] of self-undoing' (Eagleton 2005, 195, 197). In this, Hardy's writing has proved particularly resistant to what Eagleton terms the 'literary ideological process' (1985, 129) of recuperation and insertion into a canon formed on ideas of organic wholeness, greatness, beauty or truth. Instead, as Eagleton puts it, 'the significance of Hardy's writing lies precisely in the contradictory constitution of his linguistic practice' (1985, 128), which in turn, mediates Hardy's negotiation of social and ideological crisis, as Raymond Williams has argued (1970, 106f.).

A question of reading, or the postal principle

If you recall, it is Michael Mail who delivers the address to his contemporaries that *times have changed from the times that used to be*. This simultaneously clear *and* enigmatic statement demands a recognition of the times of reading. What is read in one generation may not be accessible to another. What is not read, and therefore not received in its initial posting or transmission, may be read at a later date, or arrive unexpectedly demanding reading, like a telegram or email delivered by some ghostly postman – Michael *Mail*? – from the dead letter office. What happens to Hardy in his critical reception comes down precisely to this problem with delivery, and therefore to a question of reading. Reading for Hardy and in Hardy often concerns the problematics of perspective, vision, and the deciphering of the invisible within the visible, the pasts within any present. Identifying this interest in Hardy, we find ourselves back at the work of Dickens in *Pickwick*. It is, we might venture, the old story, *but with a difference*. In the matter of textual misreading or misapprehension concerning what the author may be up to, there is a chance irony here. For many of Hardy's novels involve, or structure themselves around, the uncertain reception of texts, the fact that texts can go awry, can be misunderstood, or received in fact without ever being read. Texts can have effects when quite unintended by the author, beneficial or detrimental.

Hardy understands and demonstrates the strange powers of communication throughout his texts in its material forms such as letters, notes, or telegrams and their transmission. They are everywhere in Hardy. One might even say that Hardy's novels constitute a network of postal effects, and mark their epoch – the second generation, so-called, of Victorian consciousness – as one determined in its ontology by a *postal* system or relay. Much of what happens in any Hardy novel does so as a result of some mode of communication, some vehicle of transport or transmission. Moreover, in every example, characters either come up against the limits of reading, being unable to decipher or otherwise being led into misreadings, or they become, in a particular manner, the addressees of such messages. Yet again, there is a repeated emphasis on the untimeliness of delivery. Communications go awry, they are delivered at inappropriate moments causing discomfort or precipitate action, or they arrive too late. At the end of the nineteenth century, as Patricia Ingham has illustrated, apropos *The Woodlanders*, texts interior to the narrative are crucial to that narrative's development and form, and to the fortunes of its characters. Ingham comments of Hardy's 1887 novel that, by the time he came to write it, 'he had given much attention to the subject of decoding words and other phenomena' (Ingham *W* xviii). Of *The Woodlanders* again, she asserts 'The importance of the written word is enacted by the reliance of the narrative dynamic on written forms: in letters, legal documents, the marriage service and, in one instance, graffiti'. Ingham continues: 'Episodes involving documents are the characteristic events of the narrative and the triggers for many changes and crises' (Ingham *W* xix). The lives of Hardy's characters are therefore 'acted out and partly determined by reading or misreading, by using or misusing what is written' (Ingham *W* xx).

To come back to the novels of the years 1871–82, what goes for *The Woodlanders* holds particularly true of *Desperate Remedies*, *A Pair of Blue Eyes*, *Two on a Tower*, and *A Laodicean*. In each of these, but also in the other novels published in the decade or so with which we are concerned, other forms of 'text', such as paintings, telegrams, photographs, and even a tattoo structure the many acts of misreading, revelation, catastrophe, and the determination of the reading subject's subsequent identity. Structured to greater or lesser degrees by writings and the fortunes of reading (both for the reader and for the characters), Hardy's narratives, taken singly or together, are nothing less than sustained meditations on the wager of reading, and how the past demands to be read but without any surety for the reader of getting it right. One must read but one cannot govern that act. How one reads or fails to read signs depends on one's epistemological location, even while no one mode of reading can master all signs or, indeed, have access to the signs except to stand in mute witness before what seems unreadable. At the same time, the modern reading subject runs the risk of being transformed by the reception of some interpreted or translated text. This principle informs both form and content. We read and see how Hardy's characters must risk reading, wagering their futures, if not their lives on the deciphering and translation of signs.

In *Far from the Madding Crowd* for instance, Farmer Boldwood's future is destined by the receipt of a Valentine sent as a joke by Bathsheba Everdene. He becomes the recipient, the subject of the card, subject to its address, through acts of reception and misreading. Hardy goes so far as to signal the significance of writing and reading, coding and decoding, by titling the chapter in which Boldwood receives and reads that Valentine 'Effect of the letter: Sunrise' (*FMC* 87). In the same novel, Gabriel Oak and Jan Coggan take pursuit after figures they believe to be robbers. Losing the sound of their quarry, they have to resort to tracking, at Coggan's suggestion. At this juncture, Coggan stops before some tracks, of which the narrator records that 'the footprints forming this recent impression were full of information as to pace: being difficult to describe in words, they are given in the following diagram' (*FMC* 184). On the page before the reader appear two parallel, hand-drawn lines within which are shapes resembling horse's hooves. Hardy reproduces such prints several more times (*FMC* 185–6). In these pages Coggan deciphers the tracks, for both Oak, whose knowledge is scanty and of the most general kind at best, and, importantly, for the reader. Not only is the pace translated, so too is the fact that the horse being tracked is recently shod, and that it is lamed eventually. Such is what we are given to read in the 'mystic charactery' of the hoof-prints (*FMC* 186).

Hardy's depiction of a world in which reading must take place and yet can cause the reader to falter or to be 'translated' is not only a portrayal of the world of Wessex, or the world internal to his novels. It is also a representation of the 'modern' world of the 'Victorian' reader. The past is a series of signs. The past amounts to so many networks of transmissions. These webs of signals and traces, marks and flows, fluctuations and pulses, come and go either remaining to be read, or, in their arrival and reception, transforming the Victorian subject as he or she is opened to the other of history. Hardy's attention to the textual and its forces is therefore significant for the following reason: though turned repeatedly within his narratives to previous generations and focused on the rural world of the West of England over the previous seventy years, it is also an act of reading itself, one which reads the textualized subjectivity of the modern reader enmeshed within a network of knowledge, information, and communication, in the 1870s and 1880s. It is the deployment of a reading of the self, as well as being a self-reading that situates the English subject as a historical production of just such a pattern, system, or complex of intercommunications.

Every Hardy novel thus involves such moments of transmission, communication, and translation of one sort or another as we have argued, and this is always a fraught process. Not every character has the same knowledge, and so not every communication communicates in the same way, or indeed at all. In this manner, Hardy produces a world composed of signs for which there is no common access code, no 'universal translator'. If this world is figured as a web or network, it is one in which there are frequent gaps, breaches, omissions, and aporias. There are multiple, often heterogeneous and mutually exclusive epistemological levels within the structure of any given novel. But, more than this, the levels are not simply synchronous. They do not exist merely in one historical moment on a historically consonant plane. Traces from the past are also everywhere, arriving in the different 'dialects' and tongues, becoming confused, mistranslated, and sent awry to unintended destinations in their transmission.

Such modes of communicative displacement are to be read on numerous occasions, as Hardy makes it clear that the rupture of historicity is one intimately bound up with the historicity of one's being. Following the death of her father, and being left only with her brother for support and friendship, Cytherea Graye, the somewhat passive focal point of Hardy's first novel, *Desperate Remedies*, applies for a position as a 'lady's companion' by placing an advertisement. Hardy reproduces the advertisement on the page, utilizing typography typical of such advertisements of the time, and thereby reproducing the materiality of the word for the reader. The advertisement appears then materially, reiterated from its implied proper context. In this gesture, the technology of printing is employed to reproduce and so draw attention to its own material and immaterial forces. A 'modern' technology given commercial manifestation, advertising becomes the sign of the self as an other self, as the accumulation of traits and signs, available for communication and therefore open to other times. One departs from oneself, one sends oneself away from oneself. In doing so, one admits that one's modern being, infinitely reproducible, legible, available for translation, is always already haunted by one's finite temporality. Through the agency of modern communications tele-technology, the self is haunted by its own historicity.

Seeing herself, in her own words a 'YOUNG LADY' (*DR* 22), Cytherea is caused to pause and reflect on this inscribed figure that is uncannily double, both herself and not herself: 'It seemed a more material existence than her own that she saw thus delineated on the paper. "That can't be myself; how odd I look," she said, and smiled' (*DR* 23). There is a powerful sense of being's historicity in this moment of doubling and division. Staged as a cipher of herself, Cytherea is made to feel the uncanniness of modernity, and the modernity of the uncanny. More than this though, her sense of the uncanny is also a sensation of *Unheimlichkeit*, of unhomeliness, by virtue of the arrival of the 'dead' materiality of the hetero-affective trace. And this Freudian aperçu haunts Cytherea in the modernity of her condition of being, quite literally, homeless as a result of the death of her father. The second generation of Victorians is imagined here through the figure of Cytherea Graye. For hers is a self-conscious knowledge of historical subjectivity expelled from the safe home of the past, on which so many novelists of the first generation gaze. This effect appears as a result of the becoming-conscious of the self as written, inscribed in some phantasmatic manner. As John Goode puts it, 'writing is at the very root of Hardy's self-consciousness', and this is clearly seen to be so in the particular instance of the advertisement, as is the truth of Goode's remark that 'the writing age is an age of dislocation' (1988, 2). In communication, correspondence breaks. Writing, relay, deferral, and delay take over from the illusory immediacy of the mimetic form.

Tracing a path between Goode's comments, we may read both an understanding of Hardy's formal experiment with modes of self-reflexive perception and a response to the historicity of the text itself, whereby Hardy's transformative fictional process is itself understood as mediated by the age of technological reproducibility (to invoke Walter Benjamin) and the translation, difference, and loss by which being, identity, subjectivity, are all marked (Koepnick 2002, 110). While Cytherea appears not to be dismayed by the deferral and differentiation of presence through the death of the self occasioned by appearance of the self's other through the technicity of writing and its technological reproduction, the effect is disquieting, to say the least. As Maurice Blanchot has it, 'to write (of) oneself is to cease to be' (1986, 64). Hardy, we see, anticipates this uncanny condition. For what resonates even today is that for Hardy writing is more material, somehow more real, than the organic self. Cytherea writes, thereby producing herself as 'the other, a reader'. The subject only knows the self it is through a form of representation that is indirect, analogical rather than strictly or merely mimetic. That Cytherea both writes and reads her other self, that she is involved actively in the doubling and dividing of her subjectivity, and that it travels back to her as a disembodied transmission, is quite startling. Commenting further on reading and the literary, Blanchot comments:

> as a reader . . . I have present in my mind neither the words that I read and that the meaning makes disappear, nor this meaning that no defined image presents, *but only an ensemble of connections and intentions, an opening onto a complexity yet to come* . . . (Blanchot 1986, 74; emphasis added)

As we can see from her reading of the advertisement, Cytherea Graye inhabits *Desperate Remedies* as a reader of signs and as that figure of difference that acknowledges the impossibility of a full or fulfilled awareness. Hardy's texts mark the always-adventitious opening of the present from within itself, not only by the returns of past *nows* but also by figuring in the opening, the *nows* to come. Without presence as such, memory is always the articulation of the past within the present that haunts presence. The novels deploy the past-in-the-present and that which is to come or which arrives unexpectedly as a disfiguration of full presence so as to indicate the text's revelation of being's always haunted, always untimely experience of its divided modernity.

A Laodicean

The text of Thomas Hardy is readable as a constantly differentiated discourse on the self's historicity in the closing decades of the nineteenth century. Modernity in Hardy is not so much an assured if embattled ontology or identity as it is a site for the contest of differing ontological affirmations apropos selfhood. As Jim Reilly has averred, 'the tension of the age is enacted in Hardy's *A Laodicean* . . . where Paula Power . . . owns and puzzles over the style – Gothic or classical, faithfully restorative or boldy redesigning? – in which to revamp a castle so old that its origins – Saxon or Norman? – seem unrecoverable' (1993, 13). Hardy insists on the paradoxical condition of the age, and with that the contest within and as the sign of being's historicity, in the opening chapter of *A Laodicean*, Hardy's eighth novel and published in 1881, in which the narrator comments on, thereby imagining the image of, 'the spectacle of a summer traveller from London sketching mediaeval details in these neo-Pagan days' (*L* 5). Hardy's concern with the historical and the historicity of identity is orientated 'less in terms of "how [the] work reflect[s] historical trends and events" . . . than in terms of the way in which the self [and the text] is constituted by and writes itself into history' (Armstrong 2000, 2). In Hardy's case, writing the self into history occasions reflection on one's identity or ontology both as this has come to be transmitted and as it may come to be received. Hardy is aware of this somewhat uncanny apperceptive self-reading from very early on in his career. In *A Pair of Blue Eyes*, Elfride Swancourt asks Henry Knight, one of her two lovers:

> 'You are familiar of course, as everybody is, with those strange sensations we sometimes have, that our life for a moment exists in duplicate.'
> 'That we have lived through that moment before?'
> 'Or shall again.' (*PBE* 166)

In a moment of what we familiarly term for our experience of the unfamiliar introjection of a memory that is never ours, *déjà vu*, Elfride draws attention to the way in which the self is shot through by other selves, other times. Of an older generation, if not precisely that of her father's, Knight is led through his somewhat geological and archaeological understanding of the world to translate Elfride's remark purely in terms of retrospective temporal revenance. His version concedes that we only experience an intimation of the past, clutching after its memory traces. However, what dislocates and estranges is Elfride's suggestive self-consciousness concerning how the self, in writing itself into history, becomes its own supplement, transmitted into the future that it will come to haunt. Not to over-emphasize the matter, it is this question of self-inscription as a self-reading of the grounds of being that has been misperceived, if noticed at all.

A Laodicean is equally remarkable for its power to disturb the idea of the present from within. Indeed, it goes further, staging the present and modern identity as a constantly contested anachronic, and ultimately undecidable site. It is a novel that generates uncloseable aporia within any discourse concerning generations, historical locatability, provenance or authority. Hardy's eighth novel concerns principally Paula Power, daughter of a wealthy railway magnate, who buys a castle belonging originally to the De Stancy family, and George Somerset, a young architect. Somerset recalls a number of architects and professional men in Hardy's novels, suspended as it were between modes of existence and figuring a liminal location between country and city, practical and theoretical existence, the past and the present. Not least amongst these is Stephen Smith, an architect's apprentice, from *A Pair of Blue Eyes*, and the three architects of *Desperate Remedies*. The professional and personal relationship between Paula and Somerset is not the only narrative thread. Hardy complicates matters through the introduction of other figures, including various members of the De Stancy family, most especially Captain De Stancy, who seeks to win Paula's hand, and to whom Paula is attracted despite her infatuation with Somerset.

Amongst the other significant characters there is also Havill, an architect, like George, but older, and so not schooled in the theoretical aspect of architecture but instead taught through apprenticeship and practical involvement with the building and rebuilding of houses and other structures. This difference between *praxis* and *theoria* is a markedly historical, and therefore temporal, as well as cultural affair. For Somerset's education is gained in London in an office, while Havill's is acquired practically on local building sites throughout Wessex. But George Somerset is a *theorist* in another manner also. If we recall that the root of *theory* in Greek means to watch, contemplate, view and/or picture mentally, my choice of the term 'theory' to refer to Somerset as architect becomes clearer. Somerset is frequently witnessed contemplating various scenes. He observes as he sketches, he sees telegraph wires and follows them to their location, De Stancy Castle. His role is to view, he is a disinterested modern spectator, and given to mental reflection. His 'theoretical' or 'visionary' bent is captured when it is remarked that for 'Somerset there was but one scene: the imagined scene of the girl herself [who, the reader finds out is Paula Power] as she sat alone in the vestry' (*L* 15).

As the earlier sentence introducing George Somerset as the contemplative summer traveller intimates, Somerset is placed within the scene but is himself actively constituted in the reciprocal entanglement of old and new, ancient and modern, which is addressed in the phrase 'these neo-Pagan days'. Somerset forgets on occasion 'everything of the present altogether' (*L* 7), while his mind frequently undergoes 'kaleidoscopic change', which is symptomatic of a markedly 'modern malady', according to the narrator (*L* 7). One other character should also be mentioned in light of the persistence of vision and its relationship to temporal and historical inflections or mediations: William Dare, who is familiar with photographic technology and owns what he claims to be, in his words, a 'patent photographic process' (L 171). Though Dare is not a primary focus here, his interest in modern technology pairs him structurally with Paula's father, through the latter's professional involvement with railroads. Both men serve as figures for modern technology, while it is architecture itself and the genealogical longevity of the De Stancy family that serve as the indices of antiquity and other histories. The question of technology is a significant historical matter in the novel, especially in its most anonymous manifestation, that of a telegraph wire, by which George Somerset comes into contact with Paula Power.

On leaving the chapel where he first glances Paula, Somerset sets off across the fields towards the inn at which he is lodging. His attention is attracted by the humming of a telegraph wire (L 16), which initially is taken to be the hum of a night bee. In this brief moment, Hardy rudely introduces the modern in the technological form of communication and transmission. More than that, he marks what might be described as a sylvan scene with a line that, picking up figurally the shadows of trees streaking 'like a zebra' the lane with their shadows (L 16), provides the reader with an analogical graphic interruption on the field of vision signifying not nature but human intervention in the natural. For while the shadows are an inevitable 'natural' temporal mark on the scene, the telegraph wire most obviously is not. It is strung across the scene as a means to disorientate through its modernity. Following the 'lead of the wire' across the countryside (L 16), Somerset comes eventually to a spectacle standing in anachronistic contrast to the telegraph wire on the one hand, and the natural world on the other: 'there appeared against the sky the walls and towers of a castle, half ruin, half residence' (L 17). On closer inspection, the decaying erection is seen to have a 'comparatively modern wing' (L 17). Of no one time itself, and therefore having no stable or proper identity, the castle, described in the metaphors of nineteenth-century science as 'this fossil of feudalism', is found by Somerset to be 'the journey's-end of the wire' (L 18). Hardy emphasizes the anachrony of the vision for Somerset, a vision presented through the temporal but also technological and epistemological juxtaposition of cultural identities situated in the 'stolid antagonism of the interchange of ideas' as these are represented by the castle and the telegraph wire. On the one hand, the former signifies synecdochally 'hard distinctions of blood and race, of deadly distrust of one's neighbour in spite of the Church's teaching, and of a sublime unconsciousness of any other force than a brute one' (L 18). On the other hand, the wire, as metonymic trace, affirms beyond it a 'machine which beyond everything may be said to symbolize cosmopolitan views and the intellectual and moral kinship of all mankind' (*L* 18). Feudalism and modernity, past and present, isolation and communion, brute materiality and, via that tele-technology, the spectral affiliation of a disembodied modern culture: as that wire crosses into the castle, witnessed and heard in its function by Somerset, so too do the signals of profoundly different cultural identities historically riven intersect with one another to produce a perceptual contest.

The novel demonstrates this from its opening pages. The reader's attention is drawn to the 'chevroned doorway' (*L* 3) formally noted as one element in the overall composition before Somerset's vision, his *theoretical* perspective if you will, *and* in his drawing of the same building, along with the 'tall mass of antique masonry', the 'battlemented parapet', and the 'moulded stonework' (*L* 3). All such traces bring back the past, as it were, into the present, a moment which is effectively suspended by this foregrounding of the trace of the old in the new. The reader is privy to a double time in the opening chapter: the double time of Somerset sketching and of his own being sketched – for the reader. All that has 'passed into the unseen' six hundred years prior to this inaugural narrative moment returns to be illuminated, and in the fact that the material scene is itself haunted by the 'performers', as Hardy puts it, who had constructed the church originally, as well as those who, before the church had been given material manifestation, had traced the envisioned contours, sketching a design not yet come into being. A curious effect is produced here, in the final paragraph of the novel's first page. Somerset is observed in the process of 'copying the exact contour[s] of each moulding to his drawing . . . mark[ing] down the line thus fixed' (*L* 3).

Hardy shows us the observer observed, the sketcher sketched, as I have already said. What he also illustrates is another sketcher, another observer: himself. He presents a figure in the shadows, engaged in the auto-occlusive work of penumbral adumbration to be sure – but one more figure tracing the lines of that prior figure, who only comes to appear, to be observed in inverse and anachronic order. Hardy thus reveals the extent to which what we call history is always a process of reiteration, of transference, of the singular moment of following the lines in order that the unseen traces come to be seen once more. What is also unveiled in this is the relay and multiplication of gazes and the concomitant dislocation of any central or originating position or perspective, either within the scene or across time. Yet of course what is also revealed in this moment of suspension and oblique reflection – which is intended undeniably to give pause to the act of reading-as-witness in order that reading might become a moment of being 'brought to reflection' concerning 'human decline and death that [the scene] illustrates' (*L* 3) – is the belated disorder of all temporal reflection on being and the events of history and the traces of the past. As with the title of the novel, any story of to-day (as the subtitle has it) must necessarily have folded within it the traces of the past, the ruined architecture of other historical and material moments. *This* is the story of to-day. This is, in effect, Hardy's apprehension of modernity: to be modern, one traces, copies, illustrates and reflects, and so becomes aware of oneself historically, reading oneself in relation to those echoes. The unseen is invoked through the illustration of the seen, if reflective perception (seeing oneself obliquely through what one is directed to see elsewhere) is caused to take place. Hardy makes possible such reflection by the deliberate and stark juxtaposition between present and past, the living and the dead, the figure of the sketcher and the intimation of the dead hand behind the material remnants of the past.

A disquietingly hybrid novel then. *A Laodicean*'s hybridity is all the more disruptive because it admits of no origins or sources, no 'genuine' or authoritative identity out of which hybridity is formed. In the scene just discussed, neither feudalism nor modernity is sited as the locus of meaning. The groundlessness of the novel is opened to our view through moments just such as those described immediately above, and repeatedly throughout in its concern with transmission, motion, flow and flight, with intersection, intercommunication and miscommunication in the constitution of the (implicitly English) self in history. The self's constitution by and location within 'history' in this novel is central to its interests, even as the very idea of self is traced in its mutability and protean flux. This makes it all but impossible to read identity, whether of oneself or another. And this is all the more pointedly addressed in that the impossibility of choice leads to the self becoming a Laodicean: someone historically determined as vacillating, rendered inactive by an aporetic experience of the traces of history. The 'modern' subject for Hardy is a passive sufferer of his or her time, subsequently given over to a kind of cultural restlessness or febrile activity (that is captured formally in aspects of the prose), or else ennui. *A Laodicean*'s full title is *A Laodicean; or, the Castle of the De Stancys. A Story of To-day*. The word *Laodicean*, described by the *OED*

as archaic, can be employed as either an adjective or a noun. It signifies the quality of being indecisive regarding religious or political
beliefs. Someone who is a Laodicean evinces such vacillating habits of
thought ideologically or theologically.

If we extend the use of the term to the title itself, it might be said
that Hardy's title is appropriately 'laodicean' in that use of *or*, which
signals the oscillation between the former and the latter parts of the
title. It is as if Hardy could not make up his mind, or was only half-
heartedly committed to either choice for his title. The archaism seems
fitting, however, albeit unintentionally, in that the second part of the
title acknowledges as its subject a castle, specifically that belonging to
the De Stancys. This name, with its qualifying Francophone 'de', indicates another sign of the archaic. The title is or appears to be haunted
by that which is not of the present. Though arriving in the 1880s, the
very material from which the title is built is glaringly anachronistic.
And it is as if Hardy does perceive this in his further addition to the
title, when he adds a second subtitle: 'a story of to-day'. Archaic and
obscure terminology, references to medieval architectural structures
and possibly Norman families – all figure the title and in doing so
whisper suggestively of that condition of haunted modernity. If *A
Laodicean* is a story of today, it is a story inescapably haunted by the
traces of the past. 'To-day' as the title has it is always already woven
by all the 'inherited traits' that make themselves appear, and so
impress the mind of the modern subject, taking 'possession' of her (*L*
166). The 'modern' as non-synonymous supplement for 'to-day' is
received as an ontological determinant shot through with those
'hauntological' ruins, the very marks of which arrive as if to affirm
that modernity only takes place by virtue of anachrony, and by virtue
of an uncanny possession.

The experience of history

Such possession, experienced in the reading of Hardy's texts and also
as that imposed on his protagonists, is nothing other than the experience of history. This phrase, also my title for this section, is a double
genitive. On the one hand, it comments on the subject's experience
of 'being historical', of being in history, so to speak. It addresses an
awareness of one's material embeddedness within a culture, a
language, a perception of shared cultural identity. On the other hand,
the phrase may be read as *history's experience*, that which history gives

one or causes one to experience as the singular condition of one's being. Positing the problem of historicity, of modernity as the dawning of a self-reflexive perception concerning identity and materiality towards the end of the nineteenth century, it has to be stressed that experience in Hardy's world is not limited to physical experiences. That the world is as much phantasmatic and textual, that it is both phenomenological in apperception and empirical in experience, suggests both groundedness and historicity in its precise moment of encounter and articulation, or staging. Hardy's narratives present, or rather 'presence', and so stage, a world in which representation undergoes transformation from within.

In this Hardy's subjects, and I would argue we as his readers, experience an alteration in our perception. We receive the past as we might an unanticipated postal delivery, and so become implicated, inscribed in and as the provisional subjects of a postal relay, one which never arrives at a final destination because it never ceases in its being sent. In perceiving our reception, we may 'ascribe to the mind the faculty of experience . . . even though the mind does not possess any obvious equivalent to our eyes or ears for registering what is given to us' (Ankersmit 2005, 8). This faculty of experience is clearly of a different order than that which is purely physical or material. It is phantasmic in nature, and yet bears directly on material and historical realities and events. Arthur Schopenhauer, with whom Hardy was familiar, provides us with an interesting insight into this matter. 'Every incident', he writes, 'even if very insignificant, which stirs a disagreeable emotion, will leave in our mind an after-effect which, as long as it lasts, obstructs a clear and objective view of things and circumstances. In fact, it tinges all our thoughts, just as a very small object, brought close to our eyes, limits and distorts our field of vision' (Schopenhauer 1974, 592). Beginning with the material event Schopenhauer's commentary registers the effect-as-reception of what he terms the incident as it returns thereby haunting, memory, perceived as those 'after-effect[s]' which 'in our mind' produce a colouration and distortion related to the figure of sight as *in*sight, memory as *re*vision. The double moment is then redoubled, spaced temporally, and thus 'historically', and simultaneously dispersed, in that *re*vision names both the return of a vision, a phantasm, to the mind's eye, as that trace of the other, and the 'sight' by which we see what once had been invisible.

Hardy's text mediates such apprehension endlessly in the mental recollection or moments of insight endured by his characters.

Memory recalls the past encounter between self and other, as in the moment when in *Desperate Remedies* Cytherea Graye is disorientated by the 'wet shining road', which in turn, in the illumination's penetration of the eye and the mind, calls into being the oscillating phantasms of Edward Springrove and Aeneas Manston: 'The wet shining road threw the western glare into her eyes with an invidious lustre which rendered the restlessness of her mood more wearying'.

> Her thoughts flew from idea to idea without asking for the slightest link of connection . . . One moment she was full of the wild music and stirring scene with Manston – the next, Edward's image rose before her like a shadowy ghost. Then Manston's eyes seemed piercing her again . . . (*DR* 141)

Such experience is mediated by a 'movement comprising at the same time the *discovery* and *recovery* of the past' (Ankersmit 2005, 8). Subjective encounter or experience is most intimately engaged through the attempts to read the texts that are placed before one, whether these are letters, paintings, telegrams, or the forms of architecture, archaeology, the landscape, or topography. As disparate as these forms may be, in Hardy's world there is always present someone for whom these are visual forms primarily, to be decoded, to be read. Reading produces another form of vision, a visualization or envisioning beyond the merely visible, material and empirical world. Historical transmission is therefore given singular form because the juxtaposition of subject and 'historical' text involves 'complementary movements of the discovery (loss) and the recovery of the past (love) that constitute the realm of historical experience' (Ankersmit 2005, 9).

It might be observed, apropos his star-crossed lovers, that Hardy's tales are more concerned with focusing on loss, or discovery, than on love, or recovery. If there is love, then all too often love is lost. Hardy, it might be argued, transforms the writing of the novel and marks the historical moment of his productions by abandoning the 'past' conventions of much Victorian realist fiction, which is most succinctly expressed in the words of Jane Eyre: 'Reader, I married him'. Marriage as the gesture of utopian closure in the novel of the nineteenth century attempts to deny, displace, hold off history, to suspend the movement of time in effect. The figure of marriage seeks to establish an 'endless present' in its idealized unity. Rarely do Hardy's novels offer such closure or consolation, in a gesture that places the end of narrative at a remove from historical flow for all time. *Desperate Remedies*, Hardy's first novel, situates such an ending, or appears to, as will be discussed below. Generally though, Hardy repeatedly forestalls this evacuation of the material and historical conditions of experience. In this he discovers history and with that the loss that is memory and historical experience. It is this which, at the close of *A Laodicean*, authorizes Paula Power to remark to her lover, while standing before the smouldering ruins of her castle, that she wishes she still had her relic of the past intact, and that Somerset belonged to the anachronistic De Stancy family: 'I wish my castle wasn't burnt; and I wish you were a De Stancy!' (*L* 379). Knowledge, like desire, can only search after that which is impossible to attain. *A Laodicean* concludes therefore with impossibility, with the discovery of the irrecuperable past as the subjective, historical experience of the world. What cannot be recovered is precisely the past, and the memory's ability to bring back, to dis-cover what is hidden about the nature of the past – that it is only available as ruins, traces, fragments – serves merely to intensify the experience of loss as the condition of hindsight. Coming face to face with loss, absence, impossibility, the present is structured as always already haunted by the very condition of reflection and encounter that makes any present possible. The conclusion of *A Laodicean* allows not only Paula Power belated insight but the reader also. The reader is given insight into Paula's subjectivity, and perhaps subjectivity in general, not only through reflection on loss, but through the constitution of identity by loss. The mnemotechnic relay of consciousness, inscribed by a history that can never belong to it properly because the past is irrecuperable as such, projects from within itself the remembrance, if not of things past in themselves, then of that which affirms what one is.

What many if not all of Hardy's characters can be said to share in common is precisely that which escapes their knowledge even as, paradoxically, if or when it arrives it does so only belatedly, and for the reader if not for them. This knowledge is often to do with the subject's historicity, and one's material embeddedness in that, while also being written by the signs of the past. It also is a matter of position or perspective. While one person may have an empirical or epistemological advantage over an other or others, there is no transcendent location in Hardy's novels, unless it be that given to the good reader of Hardy who observes his characters observing one another but not knowing themselves to be observed. Perhaps the most hilarious image of this comes from *Desperate Remedies*, in a scene that somewhat parodically illustrates the impossibility of absolute knowledge in Hardy's world, while also introducing the significance and limit of perspectival vision and lines of sight into his text. Anne, Manston's wife, follows her husband out of the house, on an evening when 'Night herself seemed to have become a watcher' (*DR* 373). She perceives an 'other watcher' (*DR* 372). This shadowy figure follows Manston. Manston does not know he is being watched, either by Anne or the anonymous figure. The anonymous watcher is unaware that anyone is looking at him. Then, as a fourth in these comic proceedings, there is an 'unknown woman' who watches also the unknown watcher who watches Manston. It is hardly any wonder that Anne was 'impressed . . . with the sensation of people in hiding . . . [and that] Nobody was visible' (*DR* 372). So, the 'four persons proceeded across the glade, and into the park plantation, at equidistances of about seventy yards' (*DR* 373). Only the 'Night herself' witnesses the strangely comic, strangely odd parade. And there still remains some consciousness to observe and reflect on the Night, personified as a watcher but unaware that she is watched.

The person who can 'read' and have equal knowledge of the significance of bonfires, trilobites, or barns rarely inhabits the world of Hardy's fictions, if at all. Meaning is always contingent, and perspective is never universal. Either the limit or belatedness of consciousness and perception constitutes Hardy's characters not as abstractions but as 'modern', self-consciously 'historicized' subjects 'in the given' (Deleuze 1991, 87), in particular experiences, events, or historical situations. This is what the scene from *Desperate Remedies* maps. Precisely (first), because the subject is *in* the world; and (second), because the mental faculty operates, articulates, and responds to the *given* that is the world; and (third) due to the fact that the *world* is not simply the sum of what is, but is also historically stratified in terms of mental apprehension: then (finally) it is for these reasons that each of Hardy's characters embody and live out a constellated collection of experiences beyond their ken, coming to be informed by the traces of the historical in their world of which they are often only dimly aware. Hardy's writing makes available to his readers an awareness of the extent to which the mind is world, but the world is not a totality. That which Hardy understands as 'character', 'mind', or 'subject' is 'a particular set or a particular collection' of experiences, and begins from 'an animated succession of distinct perceptions' (Deleuze 1991, 87). Experience, in Hardy's world, 'is succession, or the movement of separable ideas, insofar as they are different, and different, insofar as they are separable' (Deleuze 1991, 87–8).

That differentiation and separation are called into question at least in part here by Deleuze is not to doubt their validity but to call attention to the limits of consciousness of apprehending in experience difference, singularity, and separation. The affirmation of the limit in Hardy's world is borne witness to in the fact that so many of his characters act out repeatedly similar mistakes. Mistakes are made, misapprehensions hold sway, because the limits of consciousness prohibit or at the very least make problematic for his characters the possibility of thinking '*at the right moment*, of a harmony between the unknown powers on which the given appearances depend and the transcendent principles which determine the constitution of a subject within the given' (87; emphasis added). *At the right moment* indeed, for no such moment is ever seen to arrive in Hardy's world. The 'real problem', as Deleuze puts it, in Hardy's world 'would be to think of a harmony between the powers of nature and the subject' (88). It is precisely the contingency of being-modern that makes such harmony impossible.

Hardy's narrators afford scant glimpses of such a harmony. For the novelist's creatures the problem remains even more insoluble because, in being suspended in the given, they are of course caught in mortal time. Henry Knight recognizes this when hanging from a cliff edge in *A Pair of Blue Eyes*. A novel that 'revolves entirely around secrets' (Dalziel *PBE* xvii), *A Pair of Blue Eyes* addresses the question of self-reading, identity, and knowledge in a scene that offers the Hardy reader an exemplary figure for perceiving the relationship between one's being and one's historicity. Archetypal Victorian male that Henry Knight is, heir to Lyell and Darwin and a generation of close readers and translators, he observes embedded into the cliff face a fossilized trilobite, eye to dead 'eye' with him:

> Knight was a geologist . . . his mind found time to take in, by a momentary sweep, the varied scenes that had had their day between this creature's epoch and his own. There is no place like a cleft landscape for bringing home such imaginings as these.
>
> Time closed up like a fan before him. He saw himself at one extremity of the years, face to face with the beginning and all the intermediate centuries simultaneously. (*PBE* 214)

Geology and paleontology aside, this 'face to face' with the other leads Knight into a self-reflective consideration of temporality and mortality, and the place of the self in the universe perceived historically. Here is the trauma of becoming-conscious of one's historicity up close. Knight's experience of a radical, destabilizing anachrony, with

its simultaneous phantasmagoria of past moments in which he apprehends his own instant as just one more in a temporal sequence, takes
place precisely because he is written into history at this moment. The
historicity of his being is traumatically unveiled to his consciousness,
because apprehension involves the phenomenological reflection –
and anticipation – of his moment of modernity as being imminent in
its own passing away. Despite his theoretical knowledge of geology,
he cannot anticipate the sudden apocalypse of 'sensuously accessible
phainomena' (Seel 2005, 22) that project themselves 'in the ephemerality of this . . . presence of appearing', which is the result not only of
his personal education but also as the historical result of much scientific research in the nineteenth century (Seel 2005, 20). Knight's training in geology has not prepared him for the aesthetic mode of
sensuous apprehension by which self-reading comes to takes place. In
this scene, we might suggest, is a motif or metaphor for the untimeliness of all reading, and with that the perception of one's own modernity. The world in all its times is to be read, if only we know how; but
knowing how is by no means guaranteed, and the risk is that if we
become the addressees for whom historicity's postal relay is destined,
we might come into uncomfortable knowledge concerning our identities. As is remarked in *Two on a Tower*, 'the knowledge that scarce
any other human vision was travelling within a hundred million
miles of their own gave them such as sense of the isolation of that
faculty as almost to be a sense of isolation in respect their whole
personality, causing a shudder at its absoluteness' (*TT* 57).

Hardy offers other instances of such apprehension, albeit not in
quite so stark or terrifying a manner. For example, he provides a
perspective on and for Gabriel Oak in *Far from the Madding Crowd* in
his relation to a lamb he tends, and their location in the universe
(*FMC* 12). In a different context, Aeneas Manston is offered the same
model of perspectival reflection when looking at the miniscule creatures skimming across the surface of water in a rain-butt (*DR* 221–2).
Two on a Tower offers similar perceptions, with its stark historical and
cultural juxtapositions of eighteenth-century towers built in imitation
of Tuscan classical style, ancient burial sites, the origins of which
cannot be known but which are variously speculated on as either
Saxon or Roman (*TT* 5), and the technological modernity of telescopes, telegrams and, of course, the postal system. Such devices and
images demonstrate the existence of an impossibly fraught,
anachronic world, in which the traces of cultures exist together in the
same sites, in a manner at once all too possible and yet impossible.

One is thus offered simultaneously the apprehension of, *and yet also* the impossibility of communication between worlds or any absolute understanding of one's place in modernity when touched by both the archaic and the modern. How is one to perceive one's identity in the face of the contest of signs? What does one receive in this intricate web, and how does one read? The infinitesimal breadth of the universe, its abyssal space and time opened to view through a telescope, places Swithin St Cleave, the astronomer, and Lady Constantine in a location of unbearable self-conscious awareness concerning the condition of being (*TT* 28–9).

Such moments illustrate that even the intimation of absolute knowledge in touching the subject threatens to annihilate the self, as Lady Constantine comments (*TT* 29). The 'ghastly chasm which' one bridges 'by a fragile line of sight' only forces on one the weight of one's modernity (*TT* 29). What may be available as knowledge for one is not for another. Even God's perspective is not absolute, if we pause from considering Hardy's novels to reflect on a poem from 1906. Because Hardy's characters are embedded, like the trilobite, in radically material conditions, they cannot become, nor are they given access to the possibility of becoming, transcendent figures. In one of the poems from *Time's Laughingstocks*, 'New Year's Eve', God is interrogated by the poet. The narrator asks 'what good' is creation, for what purpose and why has it taken place again. As the second stanza querulously demands in its search for the reason for existence, why is there something rather than nothing? – a query that anticipates Martin Heidegger's major work *Being and Time*. God can only reply 'My labours – logicless – /You may explain; not I:/. . . without a guess/ . . . I evolved a Consciousness/To ask for questions why' (*CP* 277–8, ll. 16–20). And God continues:

> Strange that ephemeral creatures who
> By my own ordering are,
> Should see the shortness of my view,
> Use ethic tests I never knew,
> Or made provision for!
> (*CP* 277–8, ll. 21–5)

God acts, then, not only without reason or purpose but also without either consciousness or conscience; certainly his actions take place with no foresight or apprehension as to the ramifications of his 'ordering' (suggestive both of 'arrangement' and 'commands'). Thus,

God is brought by the demand of the human to reflect in a moment of belated consciousness on the limits of his own knowledge. The exclamation used as end-stopping for the final line increases in intensity God's perplexity, his being taken unawares, and the sense, for God, that knowledge arrives as a somewhat forceful, but still perplexing *après-coup*. If Hardy's characters, his minute life forms thrown into topographical and historical relief by the landscape, its structures, and its pasts, are frequently unequal to the task of apprehending in any full or meaningful way the experience or event that they are in, then no comfort is to be found in the thought of a higher, divine power having any greater wisdom or insight. As the example of the divine limit attests, no being, no consciousness is capable or demonstrates capability of reflecting on and digesting the details or phenomena of that experience in any greater perspective.

The world is thus structured and rendered by partial, fragmented, occasionally incoherent or failed, transmission and comprehension. On occasions, such limitation of consciousness is taken to extremes in Hardy's world, as the following passage from *Tess of the D'Urbervilles* demonstrates:

> The swede field in which she and her companion were set hacking was a stretch of a hundred-odd acres, in one patch, on the highest ground of the farm, rising above stony lanchets or lynchets – the outcrop of siliceous veins in the chalk formations, composed of myriads of loose white flints in bulbous, cusped, and phallic shapes. The upper half of each swede-turnip had been eaten-off by the live-stock, and it was the business of the two women to grab out the lower or earthy half of the root with a hooked fork called a hacker, that it might be eaten also. Every leaf of the vegetable having already been consumed, the whole field was in colour a desolate drab; it was a complexion without features, as if a face, from chin to brow, should be only an expanse of skin. The sky wore, in another colour, the same likeness; a white vacuity of countenance with the lineaments gone. So these two upper and nether visages confronted each other all day long, the white face looking down on the brown face, and the brown face looking up at the white face, without anything standing between them but the two girls crawling over the surface of the former like flies. (*TD'U* 285)

In this, the human is reduced to the inhuman at both a macroscopic and microscopic level. Material conditions consume humanity, and the strange quasi-anthropomorphization of the land and sky is all the more uncanny for being so nearly human but held back from that. Human consciousness and reflection are erased from the earth. What we have here is an experience without the human, except as a condition of representation, in the choices made by the narratorial voice. This disembodied consciousness plays with the prosopopoeic, neither affirming it nor rejecting it outright, and mocking the registration of consciousness between one being and its other in those brown and white 'faces' of land and sky in a brutal and mute materialism that is almost entirely without history. The effect is primeval, atavistic, and, perhaps for some, monstrously engulfing.

I say the scene is *almost* without history advisedly. For there is in this bleak description the merest traits of human intervention, both diegetically and in the narrative framing of the scene. This is of course farmland, however poorly cultivated or maintained. Then, more subtly, there is the allusion to naming, and with that the intervention of a consciousness through language, the hooked fork being described as having been *called* a hacker. Then finally, there is the indecision over the choice of term, the 'stony lanchets or lynchets', which momentary indeterminability is resolved through recourse to the more 'scientific' and classical determination of these outcrops as 'siliceous veins in the chalk formation'. A consciousness is there, beyond and above that of the women, who, coming along after the cows, are merely perceived as insects, parasitical existences on the impoverished, and archaic world. And to a consciousness that can hesitate between dialect words (Old English in their derivation), before assuming the guise of the scientist in its discourse (inheriting the word from Davy's *Elements of Agricultural Chemistry* (1813) or Darwin's *Journal of researches into the natural history and geology of the countries visited during the voyage of the Beagle* (1845)), and can, moreover, make the distinction that something is named, rather than merely being that object, as though there were no subjective intervention, these human figures are merely lower forms of life.

That there is a choice at all between dialect words and the subsequent elevation into a disinterested classical taxonomy implies a knowledge of such distinctions, and the relation without relation by which beings are cut off from one another. Yet, that knowledge, and the consciousness that manifests it, arrives without a subject *sensu stricto*. The example thus serves economically to make the point about an architectonics of consciousness, wherein the distinguished and differentiated levels are structured in a manner analogous with the strata of land to which the passage refers. To push this point further, the passage is an analogical performative. It inscribes in the representation that which exceeds and is irreducible to representation of the landscape, or mimetic modes of representation in general. In doing so it enacts the condition of temporal sedimentation, as if the passage were the land it described. Historicity is here embedded in the contest for determination; bearing witness to the naming of traces, the historical trace itself is captured there, in the representation of the landscape, like a fossil or remnant of other civilizations. Old English or Anglicized Latin, the fragments signify the same thing but without reconciliation. The subjective consciousness registers historicity in its own articulation, an articulation aiming at representation but at a remove, disconnected, in a war-economy of difference. The field is thus the field of the historical, irrespective of local human agency or intervention. In this Hardy's narrative explores historical experience inasmuch as historical experience is registered as both an 'attribute' of the world 'and the attribute of the subject' (Ankersmit 2005, 8), however uncanny or ghostly that subject may be.

Tess, like Gabriel, is riven by her historicity through that inheritance of traces bequeathed to her by impersonal nature, impersonal historical forces, and collective memory that constitute the given phantasmically. At the same time, her tragedy is that such epistemological reflection is unavailable to her, though not to the reader necessarily. This is as sure as the imposition of the phantasmagoric trace that takes possession of Paula Power when she discerns the 'inherited traits' of the De Stancy line in the face of Captain De Stancy (L 166). Hardy's subjects, this 'collection of perceptions' that are his human figures, 'cannot call upon anything other than themselves', and though they are written by the past they are not able to read its signs in any significant fashion so as to anticipate the future (Deleuze 1991, 89). Some of Hardy's characters perceive this of course. And what is given Hardy's characters is that knowledge or consciousness of becoming historical that Hardy addresses also to his readers.

Desperate Remedies

Hardy's first novel draws our attention to the constructedness of history through the foregrounding of chronological and calendrical markers and divisions. Human temporality therefore marks the times of narrative structure, through dates and times being given as chapter titles and subdivisions. Such self-conscious artifice announces the times to which narrative draws our attention, the events in the world of the novel and the times of its characters' lives. At the same time,

the times by which narrative is divided figure as marginal nomina-
tions for the historical retrospect and overview of the reader outside
the narrative. The phantasmic world of the story and the real world of
the reader are those conjoined through a strange erasure of the boundaries between fiction and the real. The phantasmatic and the material
experience are mirrored in one another. What we take for granted
concerning narrative time is opened, split apart, and fragmented by
Hardy in the work to which he puts his titles. In foregrounding narrative temporality in its multiple, differential moments and movements,
Hardy displaces implicit assumptions and notions of stable presence,
moment, or location, in drawing attention to the iterability of the
temporal moment and the narrator's arbitrary choice of temporal
moment. Moreover, the novel begins oddly with the recuperation and
therefore the return, the posting of a memorial fragment, an uncanny
recapitulation of a prior narrative, to which the present narrative-
proper of the novel responds, and by which it is generated and
haunted. The first chapter thus traverses, as its title has it, 'the events
of thirty years' (*DR* 7), a generation according to that definition given
near the introduction of this chapter. The first chapter begins in the
years 1835–36, arguably the beginning of what by the time of the
novel's publication would have been referred to commonly as the
Victorian age. It then moves forward across the generation of Cytherea
Graye's architect father, telling his story, to arrive at 'October the
twelfth, 1863' (*DR* 11), in which Cytherea Graye, 'now about eighteen'
(*DR* 12), is introduced, in the proper chronological place as it were.
From this arrival, which is simultaneously the locus of departure for
the contemporary narrative, *Desperate Remedies* crosses almost another
four years, until in the epilogue 'we are brought on to midsummer
night, one thousand eight hundred and sixty-seven' (*DR* 401), at
which temporal and historical juncture, combining Christian calendar
and pagan ritual, linear, dated progression and cyclical, seasonal recurrence, Hardy shifts the narrative from past to present tense. Taken
back to the past, the reader is taken possession of by an ever-present
moment, but one which, by virtue of its having passed, is only ever a
phantom present, one without presence.

Reiteration and duplication take place generationally in *Desperate Remedies* in other ways, most pronouncedly in the doubling of
Cytherea. There are two Cythereas. Ambrose Graye, the architect of
the first thirty years, and the subject of the first chapter, becomes
infatuated with a young woman of 'about nineteen or twenty, and her
name was Cytherea' (*DR* 7). The two cannot marry, and, though

haunted by the memory of this first Cytherea, Ambrose Graye nonetheless marries, his wife having two children, Owen and a daughter whose Christian name was Cytherea, and, as Hardy self-referentially announces, 'it is easy to guess why' (*DR* 11). Each is therefore figured, in name at least, as the double of the other. At the same time, we may also suggest that one appears to promise to live out in some uncanny fashion the life of the other. There is also in this doubling a motion in which historically repetition is opened beyond itself as a transmission that is also a translation.

What is taking place though, with the estranging foregrounding of the temporal marked in the chapter and division titles? Coming back to these via that intrusive narrative voice that alerts us to the narrative manipulation of the represented reality, I would argue that Hardy's gesture, so simple apparently, is quite startlingly radical. For, in arriving with only the calendrical order of years, months, weeks and days, and, at the same time, the chronological order of hours and minutes as indices of progression, and in inviting the reader to note this fractured, foregrounded presentation of time, the chapters interrupt the very conventions of narrative realism that rely on the assumption of a temporal order that is coherent and unified. If we recall that the novel covers more than thirty years and doubles its heroine, one hypothesis for the opening of temporal gambits as being at the abyssal heart of narrative might be that Hardy seeks, or at least can be read as seeking, to map the time of the novel in the nineteenth century as being, in some fashion, over. He begins by staging a sketched sensational recapitulation of the past through a telegraphed, melodramatic and somewhat clichéd or hackneyed narrative. It is as if the first part of the opening chapter is an abstract for a novel yet to be written, but which is now out of time. Having arrived at a certain epochal moment, the novel turns back on itself, and must do so necessarily in a particular manner, in order to move forward from the dead ends of a fictional paradigm into which it has written itself. Hence, the radicality of a self-conscious gesture that, on the one hand, writes a narrative of the most stock, predictable kind (the 'sensation novel'), a narrative that in its populism speaks of the exhaustion of Victorian ideological modes of production, reduced as they are to a seriality of clichés and easily recognizable tropes having to do with power, gender, and other manifestations of identity. On the other hand, from within that very cul-de-sac of a genre's – and a culture's – predictability, narrative inaugurates its own dehiscent bursting forth, giving shape to a narrative in which, while there appears to be a single, authoritative narrative voice, there is, in reality, only an endless series of perspectives bearing witness to the different times of narrative process.

Desperate Remedies thus begins through the projection of a narrative trajectory that is involved with, and implicates itself in, a doubled movement, of both history and narrative of the previous generation. To proffer a strong reading of this, it can be said that we are both readers of and witness to a narrative and a history of the novel throughout the middle third of the nineteenth century, as well as to a narrative trace, a gesture of anamnesis, which is arguably the memory of 'the novel in the nineteenth century'. It is arguable that one can imagine the thwarted love of Ambrose and Cytherea (the first) being the plot of almost any novelist of the previous generation. *Desperate Remedies* is itself double. It is both fiction *and* testimony. In the moments before Cytherea's father plunges to his death towards the end of Chapter 1, there is a brief moment of temporal suspension as Cytherea is held at the threshold of her future, in order that the narrator can draw attention to her. Time is frozen as the narrator admits to the limits of realist technique apropos mimetic representation and the adequate visual projection of the subject: 'But to attempt to gain a view of her . . . from a measured category, is as difficult as to appreciate the effect of a landscape by exploring it at night with a lantern' (*DR* 13). There is description of outward appearance, but we are given to understand that description is not everything. One cannot read from the surface what is not available to either pictorial portrayal or empirical observation. And what remains to be read is the encrypted future. Narrative is then marked as both narrative of narrative and a break with, from within, and as other than narrative conventions historically given. As we read of Cytherea's 'last hour of experience she ever enjoyed with a mind entirely free from a knowledge of the labyrinth into which she stepped immediately afterwards' (*DR* 13–14), it is, for Hardy at least, also the reader's last moment before the fall into the complexities and snares of 'modern' narrative convolution and the insoluble problems of being in the present, being modern.

There is something violently symbolic to the conclusion of Hardy's opening. For Ambrose Graye, the architect, falls to his death from a church spire, as he is supervising repairs (*DR* 14–15). All the more shocking, perhaps, is that Hardy gives us a perspective on this event. He places Cytherea seated at a window, and allows the reader to watch not only the fall but also Cytherea watching the fall. In this scene, the gaze is doubled, divided. There is no single eyeline to the moment, no simple perspective on this event. With the death of the architect – and do not forget that Hardy's architectural metaphor for Cytherea's own 'fall' from innocence is the labyrinth – Hardy might not be proclaiming the death of the author exactly. However, this inaugurating gesture does mark itself as signalling a forceful and irrevocable rupture from the heightened perspectival control of realism and omniscience. Being plunged into a labyrinth proscribes one from taking a properly architectonic view of things. The subject becomes enmeshed, and so she must decipher the partial signs available to her, without having access to an overview. Such vision belongs to the past, to the 'innocence' of realist fiction in the previous generation.

Like nearly every novel of Hardy's, much of *Desperate Remedies* relies on acts of reading and writing, their transmission, and the chances of transport and communication, particularly as this concerns Cytherea's ability to navigate the mazes of the novel's prehistory. The pause in the sentence already cited acknowledges the coming to reading as the fall into knowledge for Cytherea, but the doubling of the name is also the mapping of literature's iterability and its law. For, as we have observed, the second Cytherea comes to reading through the painful traversal of and immersion in the labyrinth of narrative in a way that her elder counterpart never can. While the older Cytherea is, arguably, only ever a function of narrative convention and therefore unable to step outside the meshes that construct her, Cytherea Graye bears witness to the labyrinthine workings and relays of literature and its disordering symptoms, as the first chapter makes clear. She becomes displaced from herself, and thus is placed both within and outside the mazy structure through the historicity of self-reflection that phenomenological perception affords, and which materially marks her being, as has been illustrated already through the example of Cytherea's advertisement.

Take, as example of this, the epilogue, that ending beyond closure, of *Desperate Remedies*. In this, on Midsummer's Eve in 1867, we find ourselves in a belfry, with a group of bell ringers (*DR* 401–7). No longer outside, looking up at the church spire, we are inside the tower of the church, amongst a group of equals. We are witness to the scene of the eight bell ringers and one stranger (*DR* 401), by the illumination of a single candle. In this scene, the ancient and the modern cohabit, in the same space, for it is remarked that the bell ringing had taken place here for four hundred years (*DR* 401). In that remark, I would aver, we the readers are invited to 'hear' the sound of the bells ringing down, and resonating iteratively, throughout the centuries, where all the sound falls, to paraphrase Joyce, upon the living and the dead. Of interest is Hardy's use of the present tense, already discussed previously in this chapter. It functions to maintain an always ghostly present, a 'now' without present. For every time you read, the bells toll in the instant of reading, they are not consigned to the past of narrative history. That shift to present tense dislodges the historical record of dating and fixing in place to which the previous narrative history is now consigned. An other history is thus ghosted here in this collective, visionary moment and its experience, which, with its contrapuntal pagan revenance, figures the scene with a vigorous instance of iterable alterity.

Of course, it is impossible to hear the bells as such. They are irreducible to any but the most indirect narrative representation. If figured at all, their sound registers, perhaps, only apophatically. They may be imagined as heard, through a visual analogy in the moving, spectral image of 'ever changing shadows [that] mingle on the wall in an endless variety of kaleidoscopic forms' (*DR* 401). From the shadows, our attention is drawn to another image: 'the eyes of all the nine are religiously fixed on a diagram like a large addition sum, which is chalked on the floor' (*DR* 401). We read the following movement in this scene: from abstraction to abstraction; from spectrality to geometry; from the dissolution of the image and fixed representation to the indirect figuring of an encrypted semiotic trace that is simultaneously already translated by the bell ringers and yet to be read by the reader. That symbol on the floor is, though, as unavailable as the sound of the bells. The narrator does direct us, however, to the possibility of a reading. We are invited to 'read' that the eyes read the diagram and so 'translate' the otherwise mute marks into corporeal, rhythmic and contrapuntal movement, which in turn becomes the peal, the changes being rung. And this we will never hear of course. Everything is irreducibly phantasmatic. However, the peals are themselves significant. They are encrypted messages, to the meaning of which, unless we are campanologists, we have no access. This makes me ask, why is there no footnote for the triple-bob-major (*DR* 402), a phrase arguably the least translatable for the reader in the entire novel. Presumably, the editor feels this is not as significant as Shakespeare. Yet, why not? Is the ringing of changes not as significant to particular histories of Englishness as a given author? Arguably, as that figure of '400 years' attests, change ringing is important to the life of a community, to the survival of the spirit of community, its living on across four centuries and longer, beyond the mere life of individuals. Hardy leaves such signs, undeciphered, to be read, or to remain unread and so to be read, when they arrive at some future date, however adventitiously.

Yet, if we turn away from the bell ringing, there remains in the bell tower the odd figure of the ninth bell ringer, a stranger, 'who has appeared from nobody knows where' (*DR* 401), and who, we find out, is a reporter. To understand his presence, we should turn to the final paragraphs of the epilogue. The ringing of the changes might be read perhaps as Hardy's signal that one order or a different generation supplants its predecessor. In this acknowledgement of ritual practice, the narrative thereby signals a new direction for the novel, with the arrival of a different generation (Hardy himself). The narrative ushering in different, historically grounded epistemological models of knowledge and different modes of consciousness performs its own inescapably contratemporal condition. Its own articulation is caught up in the anachrony of witness. The peal concluded, Clerk Crickett and the stranger walk away, the journalist having to catch a train. As they walk, Crickett relates the remaining events of Cytherea's life, thereby introducing a spaced, spacing perspective on that narrative, and shaping it as a displaced, no longer central narrative presented as if it were the only version, and so embedded in Crickett's recounting of events. In the course of their walk, they pause on one side of a lake to take a view of Knapwater House, the inherited country home of Cytherea and Edward, who are now married. Hardy remarks on the fact that the two men halt.

I would suggest that in the image of the house, and stepping out in front of it 'two contrasting figures' who remain motionless, Cytherea and Edward Springrove, we are presented with the most artificial of narrative endings, a moment of closure that could only happen in novels. And this stale predictability is authorized by the instant of static, framed representation (*DR* 406), as the house is described: 'a magnificent *picture* of the English country-house'. It is as if Hardy is consigning the conventions of realist fiction to a frame, leaving it to stand as something at which to look from a distance, and on which to take a suitably disinterested perspective. Far more important, arguably, are the motion and conversation between the journalist and Crickett. In their animated image one may read Hardy's persistent interests. Clerk Crickett is the 'bowdlerized rake', he is the bearer of doxa and carrier of the oral tradition. He 'translates' legal documents into hearsay and provides plot outline and recapitulation for a sensation novel, offering self-reflexive comments such as 'And so the romance has ended well' (*DR* 405), or 'I've illustrated my story with rale live specimens' (*DR* 406). Then of course we have the reporter, a stranger, and an anonymous writer without authority, generating writing for mass production, dated writing, documentary writing, the machinic memory of communities disseminated and communicated, transmitted in newspapers. So we are given the choice, a static and illusory closure, typical of recent historical narrativization and the outmoded institutions of the previous generation's 'realism'. Or we have the ancient and modern dialogically juxtaposed. The reader is presented not with a monolithic narrative authority and voice, but the division of communication between the oral and the printed. The novel thus speaks to the necessity of an interanimation of cultural anamnesis and personal memory. It speaks of the need for preservation, recording, and archiving. These are the forms for Hardy by which being is always a becoming-conscious in its historicity. In coming to this partial perspective, we may move forward beyond the confines of realism, and beyond conventional ending also. We may communicate or transport the traces of ourselves into and as that which remains to come, what remains to be read, but also what is carried, transmitted, however precariously, from culture to culture, in all its heterogeneous traces.

That we are vouchsafed visions of midsummer days, such as the one on which the bell ringing occurs – one ends not only *Desperate Remedies*, but also *Under the Greenwood Tree* and *The Return of the Native* – and their constant return not as natural moments but as indices in a cyclical pagan calendar, suggests the importance of the gaze, of vision and sight as the place where the materiality of history imposes itself and the auratic experience related to a history older than industrial communities and marked by ritual occurrence may take place. This is an auratic vision tied to a materialist historiography on Hardy's part. It brings that which is impossibly distant into a phantasmatic proximity, *as if* past and present were conjoined in the experience, affording a glimpse of the long view historically, temporally. The angel of history moves forward, looking back. In Hardy's world, and for those who know how to read in Hardy's generation, that auratic gaze, in its admission to the phantasmic historicity of one's being, bears only the comfort of knowing that communal integration is merely the sign of one's own inevitable passage of becoming posthumous. Hardy's is an uncanny modernity, a post(humous)modernity that arrives ahead of modernism in a haunting and untimely fashion. Time and again.

Hardy: the signs of history, the historicity of signs

Texts take time to arrive, if they arrive at all, and are never on time when they do reach some destination. The time of arrival is radically disordered. If interpreted precipitately, texts miss being read and so remain to be received. Yet the reader cannot help but be precipitate, overly anxious, or laggardly, and so either miss the reading or arrive at it belatedly. Moreover, reading always involves loss in translation, impoverishment through transmission. Hardy perceived this, and gave expression to it in a commentary on the Dorset dialect poetry of William Barnes. Interpreting, explaining or annotating dialect words provided only 'a sorry substitute for the full significance the original words bear . . . without translation' (Barnes 1908, vii). From another perspective, Hardy knew that words and signs arrive with a rapidity that inevitably produces indirect, sensuous apprehension causing 'a feeling before it get᠎ defined' (Taylor 1983, 306). In this, I would wish to argue, Hardy belongs not to some realist school of narrative to which he fails to gain complete access, but instead marks himself as a novelist of, and for, future generations, for an other time. Certainly, he is the novelist of the nineteenth century who, more than any other, affirms the past, cultural memory, and the traces of historicity as the traits of other times, the times of the other. Perceiving this, we come to see that, in their transmission and critical reception Hardy's novels act on some of their readers in a manner analogous with the effect on his characters of the many missives, telegrams, signs, paintings and other modes of communication that pepper his texts to which we have already alluded.

The historicized, historicizing modes of representation that inform Hardy's writing mark and remark the time of their having taken place. They thus record both image and mental image, the world and mental reflection on or image of that world. In this, furthermore, Hardy's historicizing records are themselves memento mori, archived and archiving (re)collections of heterogeneous traces. They are researches into, remembrances of, times past, affirming the ruins of the past signalling, sending themselves into an unprogrammable future, and risking everything on reading or unreadability. Hardy shares then with the technology of photography the ability to bear the burden of memory through the inscription of the haunting trace, as Tim Armstrong makes clear. Of photography, he remarks: 'alongside its status as an index of the real, the photograph itself becomes ghostly; it comes to represent mourning, abstracting and estranging its subject-matter' (Armstong 2000, 59). Such estrangement and abstraction give one the sense of how intimately close and yet impossibly far Hardy is from our time, from the time we consider ours. To make us feel, rather than to make us see, except by that indirect vision of insight, this it might be said is Hardy's desire, his narrative and historical obsession. Hence, a complex textual weave emerges, comprising so many folds and threads, so many echoes in different registers. Once a note is sounded in Hardy, an impossible number of others resonate for the patient reader, attentive to the difference of historicity, its signs and traits.

Note

1. The use of 'generation' as a fixed pole for the purpose of making comparative historical statements is a precarious gesture. The boundaries implied by the fixity suggested in 'generation' are porous, or perhaps 'leaky' might be a better word. I use the word here, however, in order to sketch only the roughest cultural frame. However, of interest perhaps are the shifts within identity that the provisional notion of 'generation' might illuminate, as part of a rhetorical gambit for challenging implicitly static conventional notions of Victorian identity.

Selective Chronology
1832–84

Births and deaths	Publications	Cultural and scientific events; music and visual arts	Political and historical events
1832 Gustave Doré b. (d.1883); Lewis Carroll b. (d.1898); Leslie Stephen b. (d.1904); Jeremy Bentham d. (b.1748); George Crabbe d. (b.1754); Walter Scott d. (b.1771)	Harriet Martineau, *Illustrations of Political Economy* (–1834); Charles Babbage, *On the Economy of Machinery and Manufactures*; Byron (posth.), *The Works of Lord Byron*, 17 vols (–1834); Walter Scott, *Tales of My Landlord*; Alfred, Lord Tennyson, *Poems*; P. B. Shelley, *The Mask of Anarchy*; Benjamin Disraeli, *Contrarini Fleming*; Douglas Jerrold, *The Factory Girl*; William Wordsworth, *The Poetical Works*; Edward Bulwer-Lytton, *Eugene Aram*; Frances Trollope, *Domestic Manners of the Americans*	Charles Dickens becomes parliamentary reporter; cholera epidemic in London; Durham University founded; *Tait's Edinburgh Magazine* founded; *Penny Magazine* founded; Morse invents telegraph; John Constable, *Waterloo Bridge from Whitehall Stairs*	First Reform Act; slave insurrection in West Indies; Greece recognized as independent kingdom under Treaty of London; Irish Reform Bill
1833 Edward Burne-Jones b. (d.1898);	Dickens's first published story, 'A Dinner at Poplar'	The Oxford Movement begins (–1841); Charles	Factory Reform Act; abolition of slavery;

Births and deaths	Publications	Cultural and scientific events; music and visual arts	Political and historical events
Edmund Kean d. (b.1787); Richard Trevithick d. (b.1771)	Walk', in *Monthly Magazine*; E. B. Browning, trans. *Prometheus Bound*; Caroline Bowles, *Tales of the Factories*; Felicia Hemans, *Hymns on the Works of Nature for the Use of Children*; Charles Lamb, *The Last Essays of Elia*; John Henry Newman, *Tracts for the Times* begins; Bulwer-Lytton, *England and the English*	Babbage describes analytical engine	Britain invades Falkland Islands
1834 William Morris b. (d.1896); James McNeill Whistler b. (d.1903); James Thomson b. (d.1882) Samuel Taylor Coleridge d. (b.1772); Thomas Malthus d. (b.1766); Charles Lamb d. (b.1775)	Thomas Carlyle, *Sartor Resartus*; Maria Edgeworth, *Helen*; William Harrison Ainsworth, *Brookwood*; Bulwer-Lytton, *The Last Days of Pompeii*; Thomas de Quincey, *Recollections of the Lakes*	Hansom cabs in London; fire damages Houses of Parliament; Tolpuddle Martyrs transported for 7 years; Christmas becomes national holiday; London Statistical Society founded; William Wilkins begins building National Gallery	Poor Law Amendment Act; Viscount Melbourne (Whig) PM; Sir Robert Peel (Tory) PM (–1835); Robert Owen organizes Grand National Consolidated Trades Union (Jan.–Oct.)
1835 Alfred Austin b. (d.1913); Samuel Butler b. (d.1902); Mary Elizabeth Braddon b. (d.1915); John	R. Browning, *Paracelsus*; Bulwer-Lytton, *Rienzi*; John Clare, *The Rural Muse*; Wordsworth, *Yarrow Revisited & Other Poems*	Brunel's Great Western Railway between London and Bristol opened; Charles Darwin arrives at Galapagos Islands;	Melbourne PM (–1841); Highway Act; Municipal Corporations Act

Births and deaths	Publications	Cultural and scientific events; music and visual arts	Political and historical events
Nash d. (b.1752); William Cobbett d. (b.1763); James Hogg d. (b.1770); Felicia Hemens d. (b.1793)		Constable, *The Valley Farm*	

1836

Births and deaths	Publications	Cultural and scientific events; music and visual arts	Political and historical events
Walter Besant b. (d.1910); Isabella Beeton b. (d.1865); W.S. Gilbert b. (d.1911); Lawrence Alma-Tadema b. (d.1912); William Godwin d. (b.1756)	Charles Dickens, *Sketches by Boz*; Felicia Hemens (posth.), *Collected Works*; Joanna Baillie, *Dramas*, 3 vols; Disraeli, *Henrietta Temple*; Walter Savage Landor, *Pericles and Aspasia*; Frederick Marryat, *Mister Midshipman Easy*; Augustus Welby Northmore Pugin, *Contrasts*	Newspaper tax reduced from 4 pence to 1 penny; Royal Charter extended to University of London; London Working Men's Society founded	Factory Act; Irish Constabulary Act

1837

Births and deaths	Publications	Cultural and scientific events; music and visual arts	Political and historical events
William IV d. (b.1765); Algernon Charles Swinburne b. (d.1909); Augusta Webster b. (d.1894); Mary Elizabeth Braddon b. (d.1915); John Field d. (b.1782); John Constable d.	Carlyle, *The French Revolution*; Dickens, *The Pickwick Papers*; Disraeli, *Venetia*; Landor, *The Pentameron & Pentalogia*; Marryat, *The Dog Fiend, or Snarleyow*; Martineau, *Society in America*; Frances Trollope, *The Vicar of Wrexhill*	Official birth registration introduced; Pitman invents shorthand; smallpox epidemic; Euston Station (first London railway station) opens; East London Democratic Assoc. founded; J. M. W. Turner, *The Parting of Hero & Leander*	Victoria succeeds to throne (first monarch to live at Buckingham Palace); Disraeli gives maiden speech in House of Commons; abolition of pillory; state registration of births introduced

Births and deaths	Publications	Cultural and scientific events; music and visual arts	Political and historical events
(b.1776); John Soane d. (b.1753)			

1838

Edwin Abbott b. (d.1926); Octavia Hill, housing reformer, b. (d.1912)	E. B. Browning, *The Seraphim and Other Poems*; Dickens, *Oliver Twist*; R. S. Surtees, *Jorrocks' Jaunts & Jollities*; Thackeray, *Yellowplush*; Frances Trollope, *The Widow Barnaby*; Charles Lyell, *Elements of Geology*; Wordsworth, *Sonnets*	National Gallery opens; Brunel's Great Western steamer crosses Atlantic; Public Record Office est.	First Anglo–Afghan War (–1842); Abolition Act; public house licensing hours regulated; Anti-Corn Law League est.; People's Charter issued – Chartist Movement founded (–1849)

1839

Walter Pater b. (d.1894); Ouida (Marie Louise de la Ramée) b. (d.1908); George Cadbury b. (d.1922)	Dickens, *Nicholas Nickleby*; Darwin, *Zoology of the Voyage of H.M.S. Beagle* (5 vols., –1843); Sarah Stickney Ellis, *The Women of England*; Michael Faraday, *Experimental Researches in Electricity* (–1855); Carlyle, *Chartism*; Ainsworth, *Jack Sheppard*; Bulwer-Lytton, *Cardinal Richelieu*; Laetitia Landon, *The Zenana & Minor Poems*; P. B. Shelley, *Poetical Works*, ed. Mary Shelley; Martineau, *Deerbrook*	First Grand National; invention of daguerrotype; Theodor Schwann proposes that living organisms are composed of individual cells; first Henley Royal Regatta; Kirkpatrick Macmillan constructs first bicycle	First Anglo-Chinese Opium War; Custody of Infants Act; Treaty of London est. Belgium as Kingdom; Postal Duties Act; Royal Commission on Police meets; first Factory Inspectors' Report

Births and deaths	Publications	Cultural and scientific events; music and visual arts	Political and historical events
1840			
Rhoda Broughton b. (d.1920); Thomas Hardy b. (d.1928); John Addington Symons b. (d.1893); Rhoda Broughton b. (d.1920); Fanny Burney d. (b.1752); Beau Brummell d. (b.1778)	Frances Trollope, *Michael Armstrong, Factory Boy*; R. Browning, 'Sordello'; Shelley, *A Defence of Poetry*; Thackeray, *Catherine*; Ainsworth, *The Tower of London*; Eliza Cook, *Melaia & Other Poems*; Dickens, *Master Humphrey's Clock* begins serial publication; Leigh Hunt, *A Legend of Old Florence*; Catherine Napier, *Women's Rights and Duties*; Joanna Baillie, *Fugitive Verses*	Victoria marries Albert of Saxe-Coburg-Gotha; Botanical Gardens at Kew open to public; Fox Talbot invents collotype photography; British colonists reach New Zealand; Penny Post: Penny Black (first postage stamp) issued; Stockport viaduct completed; Pugin and Barry begin building new Palace of Westminster (–1852); Nelson's Column erected	New Zealand annexed; transportation of criminals to New South Wales ended
1841			
Edward VII b. (d.1910); David Wilkie d. (b.1785)	R. Browning, 'Pippa Passes'; *Punch* begins publication; Dickens, *The Old Curiosity Shop*, *Barnaby Rudge*; Carlyle, *On Heroes, Hero Worship, & the Heroic in History*; Macaulay, *Warren Hastings*; Thackeray, *Samuel Titmarsh & the Great Hoggarty Diamond*	First issue of Bradshaw's Railway Guide; London Library opens; Thomas Cook arranges first travel excursion; Fox Talbot awarded photographic process patent; Chemical Society founded	Peel PM (–1846); British sovereignty proclaimed over Hong Kong; New Zealand becomes British colony
1842			
Arthur Sullivan b. (d.1900); Thomas Arnold d.	Tennyson, *Poems*, 2 vols; R. Browning, *Dramatic Lyrics*; Chadwick, *Report on the Sanitary Condition*	Victoria takes first rail journey; Mudie's Circulating Library opens; Pentonville Prison	Treaty of Nanking ends Opium War; riots and strikes in industrial areas of north of England;

Births and deaths	Publications	Cultural and scientific events; music and visual arts	Political and historical events
(b.1795); John Cotman d. (b.1782)	of the Labouring Population; Dickens, American Notes; Bulwer-Lytton, Last of the Barons; Macaulay, Lays of Ancient Rome	opened; London–Manchester railway; Illustrated News begins publication	Poor Law renewed; Copyright Act; Income Tax Act
1843 Henry James b. (d.1916); Robert Southey d. (b.1774)	Dickens, A Christmas Carol; Hood, 'Song of the Shirt'; Tennyson, 'Morte D'Arthur', 'Locksley Hall'; Carlyle, Past & Present; Ruskin, Modern Painters Vol. I (–1860); John Stuart Mill, 'Logic'; E. B. Browning, The Cry of the Children; R. Browning, Return of the Druses; Macaulay, Essays; Ainsworth, Windsor Castle	The Economist begins publication; Wordsworth made Poet Laureate; British Archaeological Association and Royal Archaeological Institute of Great Britain and Ireland founded; Thames Tunnel built between Rotherhithe and Wapping; first Christmas cards; M. W. Balfe, The Bohemian Girl	Theatre Regulation Act; Factories Act; Natal, South Africa, becomes colony
1844 Gerard Manley Hopkins b. (d.1889); Friedrich Nietzsche b. (d.1900); Robert Bridges b. (d.1930); Luke Fildes b. (d.1900); William Beckford d. (b.1759)	Disraeli, Coningsby; Thackeray, Barry Lyndon; Dickens, Martin Chuzzlewit; E. B. Browning, Poems; Coventry Patmore, Poems; Dickens, The Chimes	YMCA founded; J. M. W. Turner, Rain, Steam and Speed – the Great Western Railway; first public telegraph line; Hood's Magazine founded; New British Review begins publication; first public baths; Rochdale Society of Equitable Pioneers founded	Fleet Prison for debtors abolished; Metropolitan Improvements Committee (–1851)

Births and deaths	Publications	Cultural and scientific events; music and visual arts	Political and historical events
1845 Thomas Hood d. (b.1799)	Engels, *The Condition of the Working Class in England*; Disraeli, *Sybil, or the Two Nations*; Dickens, *The Cricket on the Hearth*; Geraldine Jewsbury, *Zoe*; Wordsworth, *Collected Edition*; R. Browning, *Dramatic Romances*; Newman, *Essay on Development*; Carlyle, *Oliver Cromwell's Letters & Speeches*; De Quincey, *Suspiria De Profundis*	First submarine cable laid across English Channel; Newman converts to Catholicism; invention of rubber band; Oxford–Cambridge boat race staged at Putney for first time	Irish Potato Famine (–1850); Lunacy Act makes provision for county asylums
1846	George Eliot (Mary Ann Evans), translation of Strauss, *Das Leben Jesu*; Dickens, *The Battle of Life*; G. W. M. Reynolds, *The Mysteries of London*; Hood (posth.), *Poems*; Edward Lear, *Book of Nonsense*, C., E. & A. Brontë, *Poems by Currer, Ellis, & Acton Bell*; Dickens, *Pictures from Italy*	Dickens and Angela Burdett Coutts establish Home for Homeless Women; Elizabeth Barrett marries Robert Browning; planet Neptune discovered; protoplasm discovered; G. F. Watts, *Paolo & Francesca*; J. M. W. Turner, *Angel Standing in the Sun*	Lord John Russell (later Earl) (Liberal) PM (–1852); Repeal of Corn Laws; first medical officer of health appointed
1847 Bram Stoker b. (d.1912); George Grossmith b. (d.1912); Flora Annie Steel b. (d.1929);	Charlotte Brontë, *Jane Eyre*; Emily Brontë, *Wuthering Heights*; serialization of Thackeray's *Vanity Fair* begins (–1848); Thackeray, *Snobs of England*; Tennyson,	Chloroform used as anaesthetic	'10 hour' Factories Act; First Communist Congress, London

Births and deaths	Publications	Cultural and scientific events; music and visual arts	Political and historical events
Annie Besant b. (d.1933)	*The Princess*; Marryat, *The Children of the New Forest*; James Esdaile, *Mesmerism in India*; Landor, *Hellenics*; Disraeli, *Tancred*; Anthony Trollope, *The Macdermots of Ballycloran*; Rymer, *Varney the Vampire*		
1848			
Richard Jefferies b. (d.1887); Ellen Terry b. (d.1928); W. G. Grace b. (d.1915); Hubert Parry b. (d.1918); Frederick Marryat d. (b.1792); Emily Brontë d. (b.1818)	Dickens, *Dombey & Son*; Anne Brontë, *The Tenant of Wildfell Hall*; Gaskell, *Mary Barton*; Marx and Engels, *The Communist Manifesto*; Thomas Babbington Macaulay, *History of England* (–1861); Mill, *Principles of Political Economy*; John Henry Newman, *Loss & Gain*; Trollope, *The Kellys & the O'Kellys*; Jewsbury, *The Half Sisters*	Pre-Raphaelite Brotherhood founded (D. G. Rossetti, Holman Hunt, Millais); cholera epidemic (–1850); Cambridge University Fitzwilliam Museum completed; Millais, *Ophelia*	First Public Health Act; revolutions throughout Europe; higher education for governesses opened at Oxford University; Second Sikh War; Irish Confederation founded; Communist League founded
1849			
Edmund Gosse b. (d.1903); Grant Allen b. (d.1899); Anne Brontë d. (b.1820); Maria Edgeworth d. (b.1767); Pierce Egan d. (b.1772)	C. Brontë, *Shirley*; Henry Mayhew, *London Labour & the London Poor*; Ruskin, *The Seven Lamps of Architecture*; Bulwer-Lytton, *The Caxtons*; Matthew Arnold, *Strayed Reveller & Other Poems*; Baillie, *Ahalya Baee: A Poem*; Holman Hunt, *Rienzi*;	Bedford College for Women founded; Karl Marx moves to London; Millais, *Lorenzo & Isabella*	British annex Punjab; Navigation Laws repealed

Births and deaths	Publications	Cultural and scientific events; music and visual arts	Political and historical events
	Macaulay, *History of England* (–1861)		
1850 Robert Louis Stevenson b. (d.1894); Lafcadio Hearn b. (d.1904); William Wordsworth d. (b.1770)	Charles Kingsley, *Alton Locke*; Tennyson, *In Memoriam A.H.H.*; Dickens, *David Copperfield*; E. B. Browning, *Sonnets from the Portuguese*; C. Brontë, *Shirley*; Thackeray, *Pendennis*, *Rebecca & Rowena*; R. Browning, *Christmas-Eve & Christmas-Day*; Wilkie Collins, *Antonina, or the Fall of Rome*; Trollope, *La Vendée*	Bunsen burner invented; Tennyson named Poet Laureate; Dickens founds *Household Words*; Pre-Raphaelites found *The Germ*; Dover and Calais connected by telegraph; Royal Meteorological Society founded; School of Mines, London (later College of Science and Technology) est.; Millais, *Christ in the House of His Parents*	Public Libraries Act for England and Wales
1851 Mrs Humphrey (Mary Augusta) Ward b. (d.1920); J. M. W. Turner d. (b.1775); Joanna Baillie d. (b.1762); Mary Shelley d. (b.1797)	Ruskin, *The King of the Golden River*; *The Stones of Venice*; E. B. Browning, *Casa Guidi Windows*; Joanna Baillie, *The Dramatic & Poetical Works of Joanna Baillie*; Meredith, *Poems*; Carlyle, *Life of John Sterling*; Le Fanu, *Ghost Stories and Tales of Mystery*; Harriet Taylor Mill, 'The Enfranchisement of Women' published in *Westminster*	George Eliot assistant editor of *Westminster Review*; Great Exhibition, Crystal Palace; William Thomson publishes first and second laws of thermodynamics; first chess competition in London; first double-decker bus; Liverpool Children's Hospital est.; Cambridge University Natural Sciences Tripos est.;	Repeal of Window Tax

Births and deaths	Publications	Cultural and scientific events; music and visual arts	Political and historical events
	Review; Jewsbury, Marian Withers	King's Cross Station constructed	
1852 George Moore b. (d. 1933); Charles Villiers Stanford b. (d.1924); Arthur Wellesley, Duke of Wellington d. (b.1769)	Wilkie Collins, Mr Wray's Cash Box; Charles Reade, Masks & Faces	Houses of Parliament reopened; first women's public toilets opened in London; Great Ormond Street Hospital opened; Convocation of Church of England revived; Holman Hunt, The Light of the World; formation of United All-English Cricket Eleven	Earl of Derby (Con.) PM; Earl of Aberdeen (Tory) PM (–1855); UK recognizes independence of Transvaal
1853	Gaskell, Cranford; C. Brontë, Villette; Dickens, Bleak House; Arnold, Poems; Charlotte Yonge, The Heir of Redcliffe	Cholera epidemic; Operative Cotton Spinners union formed; Charles Dickens gives first public readings; Victoria allows use of chloroform to be administered during birth of her seventh child; vaccination against smallpox made compulsory	
1854 Oscar Wilde b. (d.1900)	Dickens, Hard Times; Eliot, translation of Feuerbach, The Essence of Christianity; Tennyson, 'The Charge of the Light	London Underground begins construction; William Frith, Ramsgate Sands; Working Men's College founded	Crimean War (–1856)

Births and deaths	Publications	Cultural and scientific events; music and visual arts	Political and historical events
	Brigade'; Patmore, *The Angel in the House*; Wilkie Collins, *Hide & Seek*		
1855 Marie Corelli b. (d.1924); Arthur Wing Pinero b. (d.1934); Charlotte Brontë d. (b.1816); Soren Kierkegaard d. (b.1813)	R. Browning, *Men and Women*; Gaskell, *North & South*; *Lizzie Leigh & Other Tales*; Trollope, *The Warden*; Jewsbury, *Constance Herbert*; Tennyson, *Maud & Other Poems*	*Daily Telegraph* est.; London Board of Works est. to oversee sewer construction; last Bartholomew Fair, London, held; stamp duty removed from newspapers	Viscount Palmerston (Liberal) PM (–1858)
1856 Sigmund Freud b. (d.1939); H. Rider Haggard b. (d.1925); Vernon Lee (Violet Paget) b. (d.1935); George Bernard Shaw b. (d.1950)	Dinah Craik, *John Halifax, Gentleman*; Wilkie Collins, *After Dark*; Eliot, 'The Natural History of German Life', 'Silly Novels by Lady Novelists'; Jewsbury, *The Sorrows of Gentility*; Reade, *It is Never Too Late to Mend*	National Portrait Gallery opened; Victoria institutes Victoria Cross	Second Anglo-Chinese Opium War; County and Borough Police Act; Britain grants self-government to Tasmania
1857 George Gissing b. (d.1903); Joseph Conrad b. (d.1924); Edward Elgar b. (d.1934); Robert Baden-Powell b. (d.1941); Douglas	Eliot, *Scenes of Clerical Life*; Dickens, *Little Dorrit*; Thomas Hughes, *Tom Brown's School Days*; Anthony Trollope, *Barchester Towers*; David Livingstone, *Missionary Travels and Researches in South Africa*; E. B. Browning, *Aurora*	Laying of Atlantic telegraph begun; Sheffield F.C. world's first football club; Charles Hallé founds Hallé Concerts in Manchester; Science Museum, South Kensington, founded	Indian Mutiny; Matrimonial Causes Act makes divorce possible

Births and deaths	Publications	Cultural and scientific events; music and visual arts	Political and historical events
Jerrold d. (b.1803)	*Leigh*; Wilkie Collins, *The Dead Secret*; Gaskell, *The Life of Charlotte Brontë*; Borrow, *Romany Rye*; Thackeray, *The Virginians*		
1858 John Meade Falkner b. (d.1932); Edith Nesbit b. (d.1924); Robert Owen d. (b.1771)	Robert Ballantyne, *Coral Island*; Trollope, *The Three Clerks, Doctor Thorne*	*English Woman's Journal* begins publication; William Frith, *Derby Day*	Victoria claims permanent British rule over India; Earl of Derby PM (–1859); Medical Act
1859 Kenneth Grahame b. (d.1932); Alfred Housman b. (d.1936); Henry Havelock Ellis b. (d.1939); Edmund Husserl b. (d.1938); Arthur Conan Doyle b. (d.1930); Henri Bergson b. (d.1941); Isambard Kingdom Brunel d. (b.1806); Thomas Babbington Macaulay d. (b.1800); Thomas De	Darwin, *On the Origin of Species*; Tennyson, *Idylls of the King*; Eliot, *Adam Bede*; Dickens, *A Tale of Two Cities*; Mill, *On Liberty*; Samuel Smiles, *Self-Help*; Eliot, *The Lifted Veil*; Wilkie Collins, *The Queen of Hearts*; Trollope, *The Bertrams*; Jewsbury, *Right or Wrong*	Suez Canal begins construction; Dickens founds *All the Year Round*; Big Ben first used; first observation of solar flares by Richard Carrington; Whistler, *At the Piano*	Viscount Palmerston PM (–1865)

Births and deaths	Publications	Cultural and scientific events; music and visual arts	Political and historical events
Quincey d. (b.1785); Sidney Owenson (Lady Morgan) d. (b.1780); James Henry Leigh Hunt d. (b.1784)			
1860			
J. M. Barrie b. (d.1937); George Egerton b. (d.1945); Philip Wilson Steer b. (d.1942)	Eliot, *The Mill on the Floss*; Wilkie Collins, *The Woman in White*; Ruskin, *Unto this Last*; E. B. Browning, *Poems before Congress*; Trollope, *Castle Richmond*; Braddon, *Three Times Dead*	Bare-knuckle boxing outlawed; *Cornhill Magazine* started; Dion Boucicault, *The Colleen Bawn*; English Church Union founded; Holman Hunt, *Finding the Saviour in the Temple*	Italian unification; Maori Wars, New Zealand
1861			
Amy Levy b. (d.1889); Prince Albert d. (b.1819); Elizabeth Barrett Browning d. (b.1801); Arthur Hugh Clough d. (b.1819)	Ellen Wood, *East Lynne*; Isabella Beeton, *Book of Household Management*; Dickens, *Great Expectations*, *The Uncommercial Traveller*; Palgrave, *Golden Treasury*; Trollope, *Framley Parsonage*; Braddon, *Trail of the Serpent*; Eliot, *Silas Marner*; Reade, *The Cloister & the Hearth*	First English cricket series in Australia; Dickens gives further public readings (–1863); Royal Academy of Music founded	
1862			
Frederick Delius b. (d.1934)	Braddon, *Lady Audley's Secret*; Christina Rossetti,	Albert Memorial designed by Gilbert Scott	'Cotton famine' and implementation of poor relief as a

Births and deaths	Publications	Cultural and scientific events; music and visual arts	Political and historical events
	Goblin Market; Wilkie Collins, No Name; E. B. Browning, Last Poems; Trollope, Orley Farm, The Struggles of Brown, Jones, and Robinson		result of embargo imposed by American Civil War (1861–65)
1863 Arthur Quiller-Couch b. (d.1944); Arthur Morrison b. (d.1945); Arthur Machen b. (d.1947); William Makepeace Thackeray d. (b.1811)	Charles Lyell, Antiquity of Man; Reade, Hard Cash; Kingsley, The Water Babies; Thackeray, The Roundabout Papers; Eliot, Romola; Gaskell, Sylvia's Lovers; Trollope, Rachel Ray; Braddon, Aurora Floyd, Eleanor's Victory, John Marchmont's Legacy; Mill, Utilitarianism	D. G. Rossetti, Beata Beatrix; Whistler, Little White Girl	
1864 Israel Zangwill b. (d.1926); R. S. Surtees d. (b.1805); J. Walter Savage Landor d. (b.1864); Adelaide Proctor d. (b.1825); John Clare d. (b.1793)	Newman, Apologia Pro Vita Sua; Tennyson, Idylls of the Hearth; Trollope, The Small House at Allington; Herbert Spencer, Principles of Biology (–1867); Gaskell, Wives & Daughters (unfinished); Braddon, The Doctor's Wife	Red Cross founded; first edition of Wisden Cricketers' Almanack published	Contagious Diseases Act
1865 W. B. Yeats b. (d.1939); Rudyard Kipling b. (d.1936);	Dickens, Our Mutual Friend; Lewis Carroll, Alice's Adventures in Wonderland; Arnold, Essays in Criticism;	Barbara Bodichon founds women's suffrage movement; Reform League est.; Joseph Lister begins	Earl Russell PM (–1866)

Births and deaths	Publications	Cultural and scientific events; music and visual arts	Political and historical events
Arthur Symons b. (d.1945); Elizabeth Gaskell d. (b.1810); Isabella Beeton d. (b.1836)	Claude Bernard, *An Introduction to the Study of Experimental Medicine*; Trollope, *Miss Mackenzie, Can you Forgive Her?*; Swinburne, 'Atalanta in Calydon'	use of antiseptic in surgery; London Metropolitan Fire Service est.	
1866 Beatrix Potter b. (d.1943); H. G. Wells b. (d.1946); Thomas Love Peacock d. (b.1785)	Eliot, *Felix Holt*; Swinburne, *Poems and Ballads*; Ruskin, *Crown of Wild Olive*; Wilkie Collins, *Armadale*; Trollope, *The Belton Estate*; Braddon, *The Lady's Mile*	Cholera epidemic; Royal Aeronautical Society founded; Mary Elizabeth Braddon begins editing *Belgravia* (–1876); Dickens undertakes further reading tour; Dr T. J. Barnardo opens first home for destitute children in Stepney, East London	Earl of Derby PM (–1868)
1867 John Galsworthy b. (d.1933); Arnold Bennett b. (d.1931); Michael Faraday d. (b.1791)	Ouida, *Under Two Flags*; Arnold, 'Dover Beach'; Joseph Lister, 'Illustrations of the Antiseptic System'; Hesba Stretton, *Jessica's First Prayer*; Marx, *Das Kapital*; Walter Bagehot, *The English Constitution*; Wilkie Collins, with Dickens, *No Thoroughfare*; Trollope, *Nina Balatka, The Claverings, The Last Chronicle of Barset*	First public readings in USA by Dickens; Millais, *Boyhood of Raleigh*; Sullivan, *Cox & Box*; John Graham Chambers devises Queensbury Rules	Second Reform Act; Canada granted dominion status

Births and deaths	Publications	Cultural and scientific events; music and visual arts	Political and historical events
1868 Granville Bantock b. (d.1946)	Wilkie Collins, *The Moonstone*; Eliza Linn Linton, *The Girl of the Period*; R. Browning, *The Ring and the Book* (–1869); Trollope, *Linda Tressel*; Eliot, *The Spanish Gypsy*	Last public hanging	Benjamin Disraeli (Con.) PM; William Gladstone (Liberal) PM (–1874); Trades Union Congress founded in Manchester
1869 Edwin Lutyens b. (d.1944)	Arnold, *Culture and Anarchy*; Mill, *On the Subjection of Women*; R. D. Blackmore, *Lorna Doone*; Trollope, *Phineas Finn, the Irish Member, He Knew He Was Right*	Girton College, Cambridge, admits women; Suez Canal opens; Anglican Church of Ireland disestablished	Debtors' Act
1870 Charles Dickens d. (b.1812)	Dickens, *The Mystery of Edwin Drood* (unfinished); Herbert Spencer, *Principles of Psychology*; Henry Maudsley, *Body & Mind*; Wilkie Collins, *Man & Wife*; Trollope, *The Vicar of Bullhampton*; Disraeli, *Lothair*	Dickens's farewell readings in London; Keble College, Oxford, founded	Education Act makes elementary education for all children compulsory; Franco-Prussian War (–1871); Home Government Association founded in Ireland; Forfeiture Act abolishes hanging, drawing, and quartering
1871	Darwin, *Descent of Man*; Carroll, *Through the Looking-Glass*; James Maxwell Clark, *Theory of Heat*; Trollope, *Sir Harry Hotspur of Humblethwaite, Ralph*	FA Cup est.; Rossetti, *The Dream of Dante*; Albert Hall opened; bank holidays introduced	Legalization of trade unions; Paris Commune

Births and deaths	Publications	Cultural and scientific events; music and visual arts	Political and historical events
	the Heir; Hardy, Desperate Remedies; James, Watch & Ward; Ruskin, Fors Clavigera (–1887)		
1872 Aubrey Beardsley b. (d.1898); Max Beerbohm b. (d.1956)	Hardy, Under the Greenwood Tree; Eliot, Middlemarch; Darwin, The Expression of Emotions in Man; Samuel Butler, Erewhon; Wilkie Collins, Poor Miss Finch; Trollope, The Golden Lion of Granpere	Thomas Cook world travel packages est.; London Metropolitan Police strike; Whistler, The Artist's Mother	Voting by secret ballot est.; Union of Agricultural Labourers est.
1873 John Stuart Mill d. (b.1806); Joseph Sheridan Le Fanu d. (b.1814); Edward Bulwer-Lytton d. (b.1803)	Pater, Studies in the Renaissance; Mill, Autobiography; Hardy, A Pair of Blue Eyes; Wilkie Collins, The New Magdalen; Trollope, The Eustace Diamonds	Dissolution of East India Company (founded 1600)	Ashanti War
1874 G. K. Chesterton b. (d.1936); Gustav Holst b. (d.1934)	Hardy, Far from the Madding Crowd; James Thomson, The City of Dreadful Night; William B. Carpenter, Principles of Mental Physiology; Trollope, Phineas Redux, Lady Anna, Harry Heathcote of Gangoil; Eliot, The Legend of Jubal and Other Poems	Women's Trade Union League est.	Disraeli PM (–1880); Factory Act

Births and deaths	Publications	Cultural and scientific events; music and visual arts	Political and historical events
1875 John Buchan b. (d.1940); Charles Kingsley d. (b.1819); Charles Lyell d. (b.1797)	Trollope, *The Way We Live Now*; Hopkins, *The Wreck of the Deutschland*; Wilkie Collins, *The Law & the Lady*; James, *Roderick Hudson*	Midland Railway abolishes second-class fares, leaving only first and third; Gilbert & Sullivan, *Trial by Jury*; London Medical School for Women founded; London sewerage system completed	Picketing legalized; age of consent raised to 16
1876 Harriet Martineau d. (b.1802)	Eliot, *Daniel Deronda*; Cesare Lombroso, *The Criminal Man*; Wilkie Collins, *The Two Destinies*; Trollope, *The Prime Minister*; Hardy, *The Hand of Ethelberta*; Braddon, *Joshua Haggard's Daughter*	Alexander Graham Bell invents and patents telephone	Victoria proclaimed Empress of India
1877 Harley Granville-Barker b. (d.1946); Walter Bagehot d. (b.1826)	Anna Sewell, *Black Beauty*; Harriet Martineau, *Autobiography*; George Henry Lewes, *The Physical Basis of Mind*; Trollope, *The American Senator*; James, *The American*	Thomas Edison develops phonograph; All England Lawn Tennis Championships first played at Wimbledon	Annexation of Transvaal by British Empire
1878 John Masefield b. (d.1967)	Hardy, *The Return of the Native*; Wilkie Collins, *The Haunted Hotel, My Lady's Money*; Trollope, *Is He Popenjoy?*; James, 'Daisy Miller'; *The Europeans*;	Salvation Army est.; University of London admits women to degrees; Oxford University permits women to attend lectures; invention of light	Zulu War; Matrimonial Causes Act; CID, New Scotland Yard, est.

Births and deaths	Publications	Cultural and scientific events; music and visual arts	Political and historical events
	Swinburne, *Poems & Ballads*; William Morris, *The Decorative Arts*	bulb; *Whistler* v. *Ruskin* libel trial; Gilbert & Sullivan, *H.M.S. Pinafore*; Cleopatra's Needle removed from Egypt and erected in London; electric street lighting introduced in London	
1879 E. M. Forster b. (d.1970)	George Meredith, *The Egoist*; Henrik Ibsen, *A Doll's House*; *Boy's Own Paper* published; R. Browning, *Dramatic Idylls*; Wilkie Collins, *The Fallen Leaves*; Trollope, *An Eye for an Eye, John Caldigate, Cousin Henry*; Braddon, *Vixen*; Eliot, *The Impressions of Theophrastus Such*; James, *Confidence*; Stevenson, *Travels with a Donkey*	Gilbert & Sullivan, *Pirates of Penzance*; Irish National Land League founded by Charles Stuart Parnell; Edison patents light bulb	Legal recognition of suicide
1880 Giles Lytton Strachey b. (d.1932); Christabel Pankhurst b. (d.1958); George Eliot d. (b.1819); Geraldine Jewsbury d. (b.1812)	Butler, *Unconscious Memory*; Thomas Henry Huxley, *Science & Culture*; Wilkie Collins, *Jezebel's Daughter*; Trollope, *The Duke's Children*; Hardy, *The Trumpet-Major*; James, *Washington Square*		Gladstone PM (–1885); elementary education compulsory for all children aged 7–10

Births and deaths	Publications	Cultural and scientific events; music and visual arts	Political and historical events
1881 P. G. Wodehouse b. (d.1975); Alexander Fleming b. (d.1955); Benjamin Disraeli d. (b.1804); Charles Babbage d. (b.1791); Thomas Carlyle d. (b.1795); George Borrow d. (b.1803)	James, *The Portrait of a Lady*; R. L. Stevenson, *Treasure Island*; Mark Rutherford, *Autobiography of Mark Rutherford*; Wilkie Collins, *The Black Robe*; Trollope, *Dr Wortle's School*, *Ayala's Angel*; Hardy, *A Laodicean*	*Evening News*, London, begins publication; flogging abolished in British Army and Navy	Irish Land Acts; first Anglo-Boer War
1882 Virginia Woolf b. (d. 1941); D. G. Rossetti d. (b.1828); William Harrison Ainsworth d. (b.1805); James Thomson d. (b.1834); Anthony Trollope d. (b.1815); Charles Darwin d. (b.1809)	Arnold, 'Literature & Science'; Hardy, *Two on a Tower*; Trollope, *Kept in the Dark*, *Marion Fay*, *The Fixed Period*	British Chartered Institute of Patent Agents founded; Gilbert & Sullivan, *Iolanthe*	Married Women's Property Act; Egyptian War, British Protectorate est.; Mahdi uprising against British in Sudan
1883 Gustave Doré d. (b.1832) Compton Mackenzie b. (d.1972)	Olive Schreiner, *Story of an African Farm*; Wilkie Collins, *Heart & Science*	Royal College of Music founded	

Births and deaths	Publications	Cultural and scientific events; music and visual arts	Political and historical events
1884 Charles Reade d. (b.1814)	First volumes of *Oxford English Dictionary* published; Wilkie Collins, *I Say No*; Braddon, *Ishmael*	Prime Meridian conference; Greenwich Mean Time est.	Third Reform Act; Fabian Society founded

Annotated Bibliography

The following bibliography is a suggested first 'port of call' for significant critical works on aspects of nineteenth-century literature, culture and history. Some, though not all, are cited in the main body of the text. To avoid repetition these are not included in the main Bibliography, which is restricted to those works cited.

Armstrong, Isabel. *Victorian Poetry: Poetry, Poetics, and Politics*. London: Routledge, 1993.

A theoretically and historically sensitive volume, *Victorian Poetry* is a sophisticated, innovative assessment of the full breadth and complexity of Victorian poetry. Armstrong provides the most compelling and comprehensive single-volume critique of the aesthetics and ideological interests of the canonical works of the age.

Armstrong, Nancy. *Fiction in the Age of Photography: The Legacy of British Realism*. Cambridge, Mass.: Harvard University Press, 1999.

Armstrong's study examines how fiction of the nineteenth century enters into a relationship with photography and its pictorial transformation of understanding of the world, its people and places. Moreover, she explores how key novelists and poets changed the language of mimetic realism to incorporate a discourse of visual convention drawn from photography.

Armstrong, Tim. *Haunted Hardy: Poetry, History, Memory*. Basingstoke: Palgrave Macmillan, 2000.

In its articulation of the invisible relations between poetics, history and memory, Armstrong's study of Hardy presents an exemplary model of criticism addressing the location and production of the self in relation to the material world, ideology, religion, biological inheritance, language, literary influence, and other key concerns.

Collins, Thomas J. and Vivienne J. Rundle, eds. *The Broadview Anthology of Victorian Poetry and Poetic Theory*. Peterborough, Ontario: Broadview Press, 1999.

The anthology gathers together approximately 600 poems, as well as almost 300 pages of essays addressing poetics, aesthetics, and related topics. There is no discernible effort to direct the reader towards any particular assumptions concerning Victorian poetry, except to indicate, through a comprehensive collection, a sense of the inexhaustible breadth and depth of the material in question.

Feltes, N. N. *Modes of Production of Victorian Novels*. Chicago: University of Chicago Press, 1986.

Feltes' materialist analysis of internal and external modes of production extends earlier Marxist modes of critical intervention, in a dialectical analysis of the determining influences on nineteenth-century publishing practices. This volume places the production of the novel firmly in historical and cultural contexts concerned with the English book market.

Francis, Mark and John Murrow. *A History of English Political Thought in the 19th Century*. London: Duckworth, 1994.

Moving from decisive ideological and epistemic breaks effected at the beginning of the nineteenth century with the demise of political philosophy, this volume charts the transformations of political life, organization and language, from literary radicals, while assessing the internal debates giving shape to Whig and democratic liberalism, through the varieties of Toryism, and the role of evolution theory on political discourse, before concluding with the return to political theory and the rise of socialism.

Hall, Catherine, Keith McClelland and Jane Rendall. *Defining the Victorian Nation: Class, Race, Gender and the Reform Act of 1867*. Cambridge: Cambridge University Press, 2000.

Starting from the Reform Act of 1867, and moving to a consideration of the complex discursive, ideological, and material relations in mid-nineteenth-century society and the ideologies that society fostered, embraced and mediated, the authors offer a striking example of historical scholarship. Hall and her co-authors analyse what leads up to, and results from, the Act; they also give consideration, in the process, to discourses and projections of gender, class, and culture, and to questions of colonialism and the nation particularly with regard to Jamaica and Ireland.

Homans, Margaret. *Royal Representations: Queen Victoria and British Culture, 1837–1876*. Chicago: University of Chicago Press, 1986.

Homans positions Victoria as a privileged agent of her own culture, also examining the ways in which the Queen served in the production of cultural meanings, images, and identities. In addition to considering a range of writers who produce versions of Victoria in their publications, Homans also engages with the photography of Julia Margaret Cameron, as well as offering analyses of paintings and architectural memorials. In doing so, she moves from questions of representation in literature to the fraught problems of political self-representation.

Jones, Jason B. *Lost Causes: Historical Consciousness in Victorian Literature.* Columbus: Ohio State University Press, 2006.

A series of closely concatenated readings, *Lost Causes* challenges the commonplaces of historicist approaches to nineteenth-century literature, its perceptions of historicity, and its own historicizing acts, through interpretation, informed by psychoanalysis, of the epistemological and ontological charge of 'history'. Jones presents readings that address a historicized sense of being in the world for Victorian subjects that is subtle, sophisticated, and often counterintuitive in its inventiveness.

Keen, Suzanne. *Victorian Renovations of the Novel: Narrative Annexes and the Boundaries of Representation.* Cambridge: Cambridge University Press, 1998.

Keen's is an invaluable, innovative approach to the reading of different genres and modes of representation, including social fictions, fictional autobiographies, condition-of-England fiction, the *Bildungsroman*, romances and realism. Taking the overarching project of Victorian writing to be the 'renovation' of fictional form, Keen examines 'narrative annexes', which interrupt the principal contours of fictive form, allowing for the introduction of subjects, characters and events that might otherwise not find a place in fiction, and which, in turn, transform fiction from within.

Mighall, Robert. *A Geography of Victorian Gothic Fiction: Mapping History's Nightmares.* Oxford: Oxford University Press, 1999.

A comprehensive critical assessment of the tropes and narrative forms of the Gothic as they persist to haunt nineteenth-century literature, culture, and identity. Examining urbanism, the intermixing of Darwinian discourse with the Gothic, and the complex overencodings of the vampire with anxieties concerning sexuality, Mighall provides a telling account of the historicity of Gothic and its mythologizing force.

Miller, J. Hillis. *The Disappearance of God: Five Nineteenth-Century Writers.* Urbana: University of Illinois Press, 2000.

In a series of exemplary close readings informed by astute philosophical, linguistic, and epistemological insight, Miller confronts the Victorian consciousness of God's absence and the undecidability of the import of this perception.

Otis, Laura, ed. *Literature and Science in the Nineteenth Century.* Oxford: Oxford University Press, 2002.

A comprehensive anthology, *Literature and Science in the Nineteenth Century* offers an impressively balanced selection for the reader new to Victorian scientific discourse and its place in the various contexts of nineteenth-century cultural and literary life. Otis places extracts from important documents in the sciences of the Victorian era next to skilfully edited passages from key literary works.

Reitz, Caroline. *Detecting the Nation: Fictions of Detection and the Imperial Venture.* Columbus: Ohio State University Press, 2004.

Reitz considers the ways in which detective fiction, one of the major 'inventions' of the nineteenth century, was essential in the cultural acceptance of new police organization in early Victorian Britain and in educating the reading public in the venture of the British Empire. In doing so, Reitz moves detective fiction out of its genre-ghetto to reconfigure the significance of detective fiction as central to the concerns, anxieties, and modes of representation at the heart of English identity in the period.

Smith, Alison. *The Victorian Nude: Sexuality, Morality and Art.* Manchester: Manchester University Press, 1996.

Smith examines the centrality of the nude in Victorian art and the debates it provoked concerning morality and the legitimacy of forms of representation in relation to questions concerning the regulation of sexual activity.

Sutherland, J. A. *Victorian Novelists and Publishers.* Chicago: Chicago University Press, 1976.

Sutherland traces the tensions between writerly innovation, experiment and novelty, and the commercial pressures imposed by publishing houses in the mid-nineteenth century. Drawing on matters of legality, the joint profit system and the language of contracts, Sutherland's volume presents a complex historical picture of the dialectic between author and publisher.

Taylor, Joshua C., ed. *Nineteenth-Century Theories of Art.* Berkeley: University of California Press, 1987.

An invaluable collection of extracts from polemical and philosophical reflections on art, Taylor's volume brings together discussions from not only British writers but also European and North American critics and artists, indicating in the process that, while ideas may undergo translation from nation to nation, culture to culture, there are nonetheless ways to understand that one cannot think the literature of a particular nation or culture in isolation from others.

Wahrman, Dror. *Imagining the Middle Class: The Political Representation of Class in Britain, c. 1780–1840.* Cambridge: Cambridge University Press, 1995.

Wahrman's volume is a successful account of the historical transition of the middle classes in Britain in their hegemonic ascendancy. *Imagining the Middle*

Class looks at the foundational ways in which modern British identity emerges, and examines key historical texts in the moulding of self-representation.

Wheeler, Michael. *Heaven, Hell, and the Victorians*. Originally published as *Death and the Future Life in Victorian Literature and Theology* (1990). Cambridge: Cambridge University Press, 1994.

Wheeler presents a wide-ranging reading of the implications for literary modes of representation in the Victorian period of the nineteenth-century fascination with theology, eschatology, and the material manifestations and cultures of bereavement, death, and funeral rituals. Examining the various theological and intellectual positions of writers from the age, Wheeler's volume is an impressive analysis of the discourses of faith, doubt, and the role of death in Victorian identity.

Bibliography

Ackroyd, Peter. *Dickens*. London: Sinclair Stevenson, 1990.

Ackroyd, Peter. *Notes for a New Culture*, rev. edn. London: Alkin Books, 1993.

Anger, Suzy (ed.). *Knowing the Past: Victorian Literature and Culture*. Ithaca: Cornell University Press, 2001.

Ankersmit, F. R. *Sublime Historical Experience*. Stanford: Stanford University Press, 2005.

Anonymous. Review of Thomas Hardy, *The Return of the Native*. *The Athenaeum*. 23 November 1878. (No page numbers.)

Anonymous. Review of Thomas Hardy, *The Return of the Native*. *The Times*. 5 December 1878. (No page numbers.)

Anonymous. Review of Thomas Hardy, *A Laodicean*. *World*. 11 January 1882, p. 18.

Arnold, Matthew. *Arnold: The Complete Poems*, 2nd edn. Ed. Kenneth and Miriam Allott. London: Longman, 1979.

Augé, Marc. *Oblivion*. Trans. Marjolijn de Jager. Foreword James E. Young. Minneapolis: University of Minnesota Press, 2004.

Bagehot, Walter. *The English Constitution*. Ed. and Intro. Miles Taylor. Oxford: Oxford University Press, 2001.

Barker, Francis. *The Tremulous Private Body: Essays on Subjection*. London: Methuen, 1984.

Barnes, William. *Selected Poems*. Ed. Thomas Hardy. London: Henry Frowde, 1908.

Beer, Gillian. *Darwin's Plots: Evolutionary Narrative in Darwin, George Eliot and Nineteenth-Century Fiction*. London: Ark, 1985.

Beer, Gillian. *Arguing with The Past: Essays in Narrative from Woolf to Sidney*. London: Routledge, 1989.

Benjamin, Walter. 'The Signatures of the Age'. In *Selected Writings Volume 3: 1935–1938*. Trans. Edmund Jephcott and others. Ed. Howard Eiland and Michael W. Jennings. Cambridge, Mass.: The Belknap Press, 2002a, pp. 139–40.

Benjamin, Walter. 'Theory of Distraction'. In *Selected Writings Volume 3: 1935–1938*. Trans. Edmund Jephcott and others. Ed. Howard Eiland and Michael W. Jennings. Cambridge, Mass.: The Belknap Press, 2002b, pp. 142–3.

Benjamin, Walter. 'On the Concept of History'. (1940) In *Selected Writings Volume 4: 1938–1940*. Trans. Edmund Jephcott and others. Ed. Howard Eiland

and Michael W. Jennings. Cambridge, Mass.: The Belknap Press, 2003, pp. 380–400.

Bergson, Henri. *Matter and Memory*. Trans. N. M. Paul and W. S. Palmer. New York: Zone Books, 1999.

Bivona, Daniel. *Desire and Contradiction: Imperial Visions and Domestic Debates in Victorian Literature*. Manchester: Manchester University Press, 1990.

Blanchot, Maurice. *The Writing of the Disaster*. Trans. Ann Smock. Lincoln: University of Nebraska Press, 1986.

Bodenheimer, Rosemary. 'Knowing and Telling in Dickens's Retrospects'. In Suzy Anger, ed. *Knowing the Past: Victorian Literature and Culture*. Ithaca: Cornell University Press, 2001, pp. 215–33.

Bowen, John. *Other Dickens: Pickwick to Chuzzlewit*. Oxford: Oxford University Press, 2000.

Brewer, John. *The Pleasures of the Imagination: English Culture in the Eighteenth Century*. London: HarperCollins, 1997.

Brown, Laura. *Fables of Modernity: Literature and Culture in the English Eighteenth Century*. Ithaca: Cornell University Press, 2001.

Byerly, Alison. *Realism, Representation, and the Arts in Nineteenth-Century Literature*. Cambridge: Cambridge University Press, 1997.

Carlyle, Thomas. *Sartor Resartus*. Ed. Kerry McSweeney and Peter Sabor. Oxford: Oxford University Press, 1991.

Childers, Joseph W. *Novel Possibilities: Fiction and the Formation of Early Victorian Culture*. Philadelphia: University of Pennsylvania Press, 1995.

Chittick, Kathryn. '*Pickwick Papers* and the *Sun*'. *Nineteenth-Century Fiction*. 39, 3 (December 1984), 328–35.

Christ, Carol T. and John O. Jordan (eds). *Victorian Literature and the Victorian Visual Imagination*. Berkeley: University of California Press, 1995.

Clark, Timothy. *The Poetics of Singularity: The Counter-Culturalist Turn in Heidegger, Derrida, Blanchot and the Later Gadamer*. Edinburgh: Edinburgh University Press, 2005.

Colley, Linda. *Britons: Forging the Nation 1707–1837*. London: Pimlico, 1992.

Conrad, Joseph. *Heart of Darkness*. Foreword A. N. Wilson. London: Hesperus Press, 2002.

Costa Lima, Luiz. *Control of the Imaginary: Reason and Imagination in Modern Times*. Trans. Ronald W. Sousa. Afterword Jochen Schulte-Sasse. Minneapolis: University of Minnesota Press, 1988.

Cottom, Daniel. *Social Figures: George Eliot, Social History, and Literary Representation*. Minneapolis: University of Minnesota Press, 1987.

Crary, Jonathan. 'Modernizing Vision'. In Hal Foster, ed. *Vision and Visuality*, Vol. 2. Seattle: Bay Press, 1988.

Crary, Jonathan. *Techniques of the Observer: On Vision and Modernity in the Nineteenth Century*. Cambridge, Mass.: MIT Press, 1990.

Crosby, Christina. *The Ends of History: Victorians and 'the Woman Question'*. London: Routledge, 1991.

Dart, Geoffrey. 'The Cockney Moment (The Character of the "Cockney" in Dickens's *Pickwick Papers* and *Sketches by Boz*)'. *Cambridge Quarterly*. 32, 3 (2003), 203–23.

Davidson, Donald. 'The Traditional Basis of Thomas Hardy's Fiction'. *Southern Review*. 6 (Summer 1940), 163–78.

Davie, Donald. *With the Grain: Essays on Thomas Hardy and Modern British Poetry*. Ed. and Intro. Clive Wilmer. Manchester: Carcanet, 1998.

Davy, Sir Humphry. *The Collected Works of Sir Humphry Davy*, Vol. IV. Ed. John Davy. London: Smith, Elder & Co., 1839.

de Bolla, Peter. *The Discourse of the Sublime: Readings in History, Aesthetics, and the Subject*. Oxford: Blackwell, 1989.

Defoe, Daniel. *Robinson Crusoe*. Ed. J. Donald Crowley. Oxford: Oxford University Press, 1983.

Deleuze, Gilles. *Empiricism and Subjectivity: An Essay on Hume's Theory of Human Nature*. Trans. and Intro. Constantin V. Boundas. New York: Columbia University Press, 1991.

Derrida, Jacques. 'Positions: Interview with Jean-Louis Houdebine and Guy Scarpetta'. *Positions*. Trans. Alan Bass. Chicago: University of Chicago Press, 1981, pp. 37–96.

Derrida, Jacques. *Acts of Literature*. Ed. Derek Attridge. New York: Routledge, 1992.

Derrida, Jacques. *Archive Fever: A Freudian Impression*. Trans. Eric Prenowitz. Chicago: University of Chicago Press, 1996a.

Derrida, Jacques. '"As If I Were Dead": An Interview with Jacques Derrida'. *Applying: To Derrida*. Ed. John Brannigan, Ruth Robbins and Julian Wolfreys. Basingstoke: Macmillan, 1996b, pp. 211–26.

Derrida, Jacques. 'Economimesis'. *The Derrida Reader: Writing Performances*. Ed. Julian Wolfreys. Edinburgh: Edinburgh University Press, 1998, pp. 264–93.

Derrida, Jacques. 'Telepathy'. Trans. Nicholas Royle. *Deconstruction: A Reader*. Ed. Martin McQuillan. Edinburgh: Edinburgh University Press, 2000, pp. 496–527.

Derrida, Jacques. *The Work of Mourning*. Ed. Pascale-Anne Brault and Michael Naas. Chicago: University of Chicago Press, 2001.

Derrida, Jacques. '"Le parjure," Perhaps: Storytelling and Lying ("Abrupt Breaches of Syntax")'. Trans. Peggy Kamuf. *Acts of Narrative*. Ed. Carol Jacobs and Henry Sussman. Stanford: Stanford University Press, 2003, pp. 195–234.

Derrida, Jacques. 'The Principle of Reason: The University in the Eyes of its Pupils'. Trans. Catherine Porter and Edward P. Morris. In *Eyes of the University: Right to Philosophy 2*. Trans. Jan Plug *et al*. Stanford: Stanford University Press, 2004a, pp. 129–55.

Derrida, Jacques. '"Je suis en guerre contre moi-même": entretien avec Jean Birnbaum'. *Le Monde*. 18572 (12 October 2004b), pp. 6–7.

Derrida, Jacques. *On Touching – Jean-Luc Nancy*. Trans. Christine Irizarry. Stanford: Stanford University Press, 2005.

Dickens, Charles. *The Dent Uniform Edition of Dickens' Journalism, Volume I: Sketches by Boz and Other Early Papers 1833–39*. Ed. Michael Slater. London: J. M. Dent, 1994.

Dickens, Charles. *The Personal History of David Copperfield*. Ed. and Intro. Jeremy Tambling. London: Penguin, 1996, pp. 11.

Eagleton, Terry. *Marxism and Literary Criticism*. Berkeley: University of California Press, 1976.

Eagleton, Terry. *Criticism and Ideology: A Study in Marxist Literary Theory*. London: Verso, 1978.

Eagleton, Terry. *Walter Benjamin or, Towards A Revolutionary Criticism*. London: Verso, 1985.

Eagleton, Terry. *The Ideology of the Aesthetic*. Oxford: Blackwell, 1990.

Eagleton, Terry. *The English Novel: An Introduction*. Oxford: Blackwell, 2005.

Easson, Angus. 'Don Pickwick: Dickens and the Transformation of Cervantes'. In Alice Jenkins and Juliet Johns, eds. *Rereading Victorian Fiction*. Foreword John Sutherland. Basingstoke: Palgrave Macmillan, 2002, pp. 173–88.

Ebbatson, Roger. 'Hardy and Class'. In Phillip Mallett, ed. *Thomas Hardy Studies*. Basingstoke: Palgrave Macmillan, 2004, pp. 111–34.

Eliot, George. *Daniel Deronda*. Ed. Barbara Hardy. Harmondsworth: Penguin, 1986.

Eliot, George. *Selected Essays, Poems and Other Writings*. Intro. A. S. Byatt. Ed. A. S. Byatt and Nicholas Warren. London: Penguin, 1990.

Eliot, T. S. *Four Quartets. Collected Poems 1909–1962*. London: Faber & Faber, 1963, pp. 187–223.

Engel, Eliot and Margaret F. King. *The Victorian Novel before Victoria: British Fiction during the Reign of William IV, 1830–37*. London: Macmillan, 1984.

Ermath, Elizabeth Deeds. *The English Novel in History 1840–1895*. London: Routledge, 1997.

Fenves, Peter. *'Chatter': Language and History in Kierkegaard*. Stanford: Stanford University Press, 1993.

Fohrmann, Jürgen and Helmut J. Schneider (eds). *1848 und das Versprechen der Moderne*. Würzburg: Königshausen & Neumann, 2003.

Foucault, Michel. *The Order of Things: An Archaeology of the Human Sciences*. London: Routledge, 1989.

Fynsk, Christopher. *Language & Relation: . . . that there is language*. Stanford: Stanford University Press, 1996.

Gale, Steven H. 'Cervantes' Influence on Dickens, with Comparative Emphasis on *Don Quijote* and *Pickwick Papers*'. *Anales Cervantinos*. 12 (1973), 135–56.

Gallagher, Catherine. *The Industrial Reformation of English Fiction: Social Discourse and Narrative Form 1832–1867*. Chicago: University of Chicago Press, 1985.

Gasché, Rodolphe. *Of Minimal Things: Studies on the Notion of Relation*. Stanford: Stanford University Press, 1999.

Gash, Norman. *The Age of Peel*. New York: St Martin's Press, 1968.

Gatrell, Simon. 'The Mayor of Casterbridge: The Fate of Henchard's Character'. The Mayor of Casterbridge: New Casebook. Ed. Julian Wolfreys. Basingstoke: Palgrave Macmillan, 2000, pp. 48–79.

Givner, Jessie. 'Industrial History, Preindustrial Literature: George Eliot's Middlemarch'. ELH. 69 (2002), 223–44.

Goode, John. Thomas Hardy: The Offensive Truth. Oxford: Blackwell, 1988.

Goodman, Kevis. Georgic Modernity and British Romanticism: Poetry and the Mediation of History. Cambridge: Cambridge University Press, 2004.

Grossman, Jonathan H. 'Representing Pickwick: The Novel and the Law Courts'. Nineteenth-Century Literature. 52, 2 (September 1997), 171–97.

Hall, Catherine and Leonore Davidoff. Family Fortunes: Men and Women of the English Middle Class, 1780–1850. Chicago: University of Chicago Press, 1987.

Hall, Catherine. White, Male and Middle Class: Explorations in Feminism and History. Cambridge: Polity Press, 1992.

Hardy, Thomas. 'An Indiscretion in the Life of an Heiress'. In Pamela Dalziel, ed. An Indiscretion in the Life of an Heiress and Other Stories. Oxford: Oxford University Press, 1994, pp. 43–113.

Hardy, Thomas and Florence Henniker. 'The Spectre of the Real'. In Pamela Dalziel, ed. An Indiscretion in the Life of an Heiress and Other Stories. Oxford: Oxford University Press, 1994, pp. 184–211.

Harvie, Christopher. The Centre of Things: Political Fiction in Britain from Disraeli to the Present. London: Unwin Hyman, 1991.

Helfer, Martha B. The Retreat of Representation: The Concept of Darstellung in German Critical Discourse. Albany: State University of New York Press, 1996.

Henley, W. E. Review of The Return of the Native. The Saturday Review. 4 January 1879. (No page numbers.)

Hobsbawm, Eric. The Age of Revolution 1789–1848. New York: Vintage, 1996.

Homans, Margaret and Adrienne Munich, eds. Remaking Queen Victoria. Cambridge: Cambridge University Press, 1997.

Hoppen, K. Theodore. The Mid-Victorian Generation. Oxford: Oxford University Press, 1998.

Horton, Susan R. 'Were They Having Fun Yet? Victorian Optical Gadgetry, Modernist Selves'. Victorian Literature and the Victorian Visual Imagination. Berkeley: University of California Press, 1995, pp. 1–26.

Husserl, Edmund. The Phenomenology of Time-Consciousness. Trans. James S. Churchill. Bloomington: Indiana University Press, 1964.

Johnston, Adrian. Time Driven: Metapsychology and the Splitting of the Drive. Foreword Slavoj Zizek. Evanston: Northwestern University Press, 2005.

Kincaid, James R. Annoying the Victorians. London: Routledge, 1995.

Kittler, Friedrich A. Discourse Networks 1800/1900. Trans. Michael Metteer. Stanford: Stanford University Press, 1992.

Knezevic, Borislav. 'An Ethnography of the Provincial: The Social Geography of Gentility in Elizabeth Gaskell's Cranford'. Victorian Studies. 41, 3 (Spring 1998), 405–26.

Koepnick, Lutz. 'Aura Reconsidered: Benjamin and Contemporary Visual Culture'. In Gerhard Richter, ed. *Benjamin's Ghosts: Interventions in Contemporary Literary and Cultural Theory*. Stanford: Stanford University Press, 2002, pp. 95–120.

Koselleck, Reinhart. *The Practice of Conceptual History: Timing History, Spacing Concepts*. Foreword Hayden White. Trans. Todd Samuel Presner *et al*. Stanford: Stanford University Press, 2002.

Krauss, Rosalind. 'The Im/Pulse to See'. In Hal Foster, ed. *Vision and Visuality*. Seattle: Bay Press, 1988.

Krueger, Christine L. 'The Female Paternalist as Historian: Elizabeth Gaskell's *My Lady Ludlow*'. In Linda M. Shires, ed. *Rewriting the Victorians: Theory, History, and the Politics of Gender*. London: Routledge, 1992, pp. 166–83.

Langland, Elizabeth. *Nobody's Angels: Middle-Class Women and Domestic Ideology in Victorian Culture*. Ithaca, NY: Cornell University Press, 1995.

Levinas, Emmanuel. *Is it Righteous To Be? Interviews with Emmanuel Levinas*. Ed. Jill Robbins. Stanford: Stanford University Press, 2001.

Liu, Alan. *Wordsworth: The Sense of History*. Stanford: Stanford University Press, 1989.

Lucas, John. *England and Englishness: Ideas of Nationhood in English Poetry 1688–1900*. London: The Hogarth Press, 1990.

Lukács, Georg. *History and Class Consciousness: Studies in Marxist Dialectics*. Trans. Rodney Livingstone. Cambridge, Mass.: MIT Press, 1972.

Macaulay, Thomas Babington, Lord. *The History of England*. Ed. and abridged Hugh Trevor-Roper. Harmondsworth: Penguin, 1986.

Marion, Jean-Luc. *The Crossing of the Visible*. Trans. K. A. Smith. Stanford: Stanford University Press, 2004.

Marlow, James E. 'Pickwick's Writing: Propriety and Language'. *ELH*. 52, 4 (Winter 1985), 939–63.

McMaster, Juliet. 'Visual Design in *Pickwick Papers*'. *Studies in English Literature 1500–1900*. 23, 4 (1983), 595–614.

Meckier, Jerome. *Hidden Rivalries in Victorian Fiction*. Lexington: University of Kentucky Press, 1987.

Merleau-Ponty, Maurice. *The Visible and the Invisible*. Trans. Alphonso Lingis. Ed. Claude Lefort. Evanston: Northwestern University Press, 1968.

Miller, Andrew H. *Novels Behind Glass: Commodity Culture and Victorian Narrative*. Cambridge: Cambridge University Press, 1995.

Miller, J. Hillis. *Charles Dickens: The World of His Novels*. Cambridge, Mass.: Harvard University Press, 1958.

Miller, J. Hillis. 'Optic and Semiotic in *Middlemarch*'. In Jerome H. Buckley, ed. *The Worlds of Victorian Fiction*. Cambridge, Mass.: Harvard University Press, 1975, pp. 125–45.

Miller, J. Hillis. *The Ethics of Reading: Kant, de Man, Eliot, Trollope, James, and Benjamin*. New York: Columbia University Press, 1987.

Miller, J. Hillis. *Theory Now and Then*. Hemel Hempstead: Harvester Wheatsheaf, 1991.

Miller, J. Hillis. 'History, Narrative, and Responsibility: Speech Acts in "The Aspern Papers"'. In Gert Buelens, ed. *Enacting History in Henry James: Narrative, Power, and Ethics*. Cambridge: Cambridge University Press, 1997, pp. 193–210.

Miller, J. Hillis. 'Thomas Hardy, Jacques Derrida, and the "Dislocation of Souls"'. In Julian Wolfreys, ed. *Literary Theories: A Reader and Guide*. Edinburgh: Edinburgh University Press, 1999, pp. 288–97.

Musselwhite, David E. *Partings Welded Together: Politics and Desire in the Nineteenth-Century English Novel*. London: Methuen, 1987.

Musselwhite, David. *Social Transformations in Hardy's Tragic Novels: Megamachines and Phantasms*. Basingstoke: Palgrave Macmillan, 2003.

Palmer, William J. *Dickens and the New Historicism*. New York: St Martin's Press, 1997.

Payne, David. *The Reenchantment of Nineteenth-Century Fiction: Dickens, Thackeray, George Eliot and Serialization*. Basingstoke: Palgrave Macmillan, 2005.

Pisters, Patricia. *The Matrix of Visual Culture: Working with Deleuze in Film Theory*. Stanford: Stanford University Press, 2003.

Pite, Ralph. *Hardy's Geography: Wessex and the Regional Novel*. Basingstoke: Palgrave Macmillan, 2002.

Potau, Mercedes. 'Notes on Parallels between *The Pickwick Papers* and *Don Quixote*'. *Dickens Quarterly*. 10, 2 (June 1993), 105–10.

Price, Richard. *British Society 1680–1880*. Cambridge: Cambridge University Press, 1999.

Rainsford, Dominic. *Authorship, Ethics and the Reader: Blake, Dickens, Joyce*. London: Macmillan, 1997.

Reilly, Jim. *Shadowtime: History and Representation in Hardy, Conrad and George Eliot*. London: Routledge, 1993.

Ricciardi, Alessia. *The Ends of Mourning: Psychoanalysis, Literature, Film*. Stanford: Stanford University Press, 2003.

Ricoeur, Paul. *Memory, History, Forgetting*. Trans. Kathleen Blamey and David Pellauer. Chicago: University of Chicago Press, 2004.

Rigney, Ann. *Imperfect Histories: The Elusive Past and the Legacy of Romantic Historicism*. Ithaca: Cornell University Press, 2001.

Robbins, Ruth. *Pater to Foster, 1873–1924*. Basingstoke: Palgrave Macmillan, 2003.

Rogers, Shannon L. 'Medievalism in the Last Novels of Thomas Hardy: New Wine in Old Bottles'. *English Literature in Transition 1880–1920*. 42, 3 (1999), 298–316.

Rosenblum, Joseph. '*The Pickwick Papers* and *Paradise Lost*'. *Dickens Quarterly*. 3 (1986), 47–54.

Ruskin, John. *The Works of John Ruskin*. Ed. E. T. Cook and Alexander Wedderburn. 39 vols. London: Allen, 1903–12.

Schmitt, Cannon. *Alien Nation: Nineteenth-Century Gothic Fictions and English Identity*. Philadelphia: University of Pennsylvania Press, 1997.

Schopenhauer, Arthur. *Parerga and Paralipomena*, Vol. 2. Trans. E. F. J. Payne. Oxford: Clarendon Press, 1974.

Schor, Hilary M. 'Affairs of the Alphabet: Reading, Writing and Narrating in *Cranford'. Novel: A Forum on Fiction.* 22, 3 (Spring, 1989), 288–304.

Seel, Martin. *Aesthetics of Appearing.* Trans. John Farrell. Stanford: Stanford University Press, 2005.

Shuttleworth, Sally. *George Eliot and Nineteenth-Century Science: The Make-Believe of a Beginning.* Cambridge: Cambridge University Press, 1986.

Simpson, Jacqueline. 'Urban Legends in *The Pickwick Papers.' Journal of American Folklore.* 96:382 (1983): 462–70.

Smith, Lindsay. *Victorian Photography, Painting and Poetry: The Enigma of Visibility in Ruskin, Morris and the Pre-Raphaelites.* Cambridge: Cambridge University Press, 1995.

Staten, Henry. 'Is *Middlemarch* Ahistorical?' *PMLA.* 115, 5 (October 2000), 991–1005.

Stockton, Kathryn Bond. *God Between Their Lips: Desire Between Women in Irigaray, Brontë, and Eliot.* Stanford: Stanford University Press, 1994.

Stoddart, Judith. 'Tracking the Sentimental Eye'. In Suzy Anger, ed. *Knowing the Past: Victorian Literature and Culture.* Ithaca: Cornell University Press, 2001, pp. 192–211.

Stone, Harry. *The Night Side of Dickens: Cannibalism, Passion, Necessity.* Columbus: Ohio State University Press, 1994.

Taylor, D. *Literary Language and Victorian Philology.* Oxford: Clarendon Press, 1983.

Taylor, Jenny Bourne. *In the Secret Theatre of Home: Wilkie Collins, Sensation Narrative, and Nineteenth-Century Psychology.* London: Routledge, 1988.

Tiffany, Daniel. *Radio Corpse: Imagism and the Cryptaesthetic of Ezra Pound.* Cambridge, Mass.: Harvard University Press, 1995.

Trotter, David. 'Dickens's Idle Men'. In John Schad, ed. *Dickens Refigured: Bodies, Desires, and Other Histories.* Manchester: Manchester University Press, 1996, pp. 200–18.

Tucker, John L. 'George Eliot's Reflexive Text: Three Tonalities in the Narrative Voice of *Middlemarch'. SEL.* 31 (1991), 773–91.

Waters, Sarah. 'Introduction'. In Mary Elizabeth Braddon. *The Trail of the Serpent.* Ed. Chris Wallis. New York: Modern Library, 2003, pp. xv–xxiv.

Welsh, Alexander. 'Waverly, Pickwick, and Don Quixote'. *Nineteenth-Century Fiction.* 22 (1967–68), 19–20.

Widdowson, Peter. *Hardy in History: A Study in Literary Sociology.* London: Routledge, 1989.

Widdowson, Peter. 'Hardy and Critical Theory'. *The Cambridge Companion to Thomas Hardy.* Cambridge: Cambridge University Press, 1999, pp. 73–92.

Williams, Raymond. *The English Novel from Dickens to Lawrence.* London: Hogarth Press, 1970.

Williams, Raymond. *Marxism and Literature.* Oxford: Oxford University Press, 1977.

Williams, Raymond. *Politics and Letters: Interviews with the New Left Review.* London: Verso, 1981.

Williams, Raymond. *Writing in Society.* London: Verso, 1983.

Woolf, Virginia. *The Common Reader.* London: Hogarth Press, 1919.

Young, Kay. '*Middlemarch* and the Problem of Other Minds Heard'. *Literature Interpretation Theory.* 14 (2003), 233–41.

Index of Names

Index of Subjects